Transfers in an Urbanized Economy

Theories and Effects of the Grants Economy

Edited by

Kenneth E. Boulding
University of Colorado

Martin Pfaff
Wayne State University
and University of Augsburg

Anita Pfaff
Wayne State University
and University of Augsburg

Wadsworth Publishing Company, Inc.
Belmont, California

ISBN: 0-534-00196-3

L. C. Cat. Card No.:   72-86729

Printed in the United States of America

1 2 3 4 5 6 7 8 9 10---77 76 75 74 73

This book has been printed on recycled paper.

Introduction to the Series on Grants Economics

This series of volumes might almost be described as radical economics by regular economists. Most of the contributors are members of the Association for the Study of the Grants Economy, and some may indeed be members of the Union for Radical Political Economy too, although most of them are not, we are sure. Nevertheless, the significance of grants economics may well be that it contains the most important clues to the questions the radicals are asking but, alas, are not often answering.

The central idea of grants economics is that exchange economics is not enough. From the days of Adam Smith economics has been dominated on the whole by the analysis of how society is organized by exchange. This is a necessary, but not sufficient, idea on which to base an understanding of the economic system. Exchange, that is, two-way transfer (*A* gives something to *B* and *B* gives something to *A*), is a powerful organizer of economic life, but it is not the *only* organizer. The *grant*, or one-way transfer (*A* gives something exchangeable to *B*, *B* gives nothing exchangeable to *A*), is becoming an increasingly common instrument of economic and political organization. Grants economics contends that grants must not be regarded as something exotic, outside the economic system proper, but must be integrated into both the theory and the empirical study of the economy.

The failure to do this has, in part at least, produced radical economics. Pure exchange economics cannot come to grips with some of the most important problems of our day – for instance, those involving the distribution of power, income, and wealth, which exchange economics takes for granted. The dissatisfaction with exchange economics is one of the most important sources of radical dissent. However, radical economists often destroy their own case by throwing exchange economics out the window altogether, thereby "turning off" the "straight" economists to the point where no communication takes place. Grants economics insists that *both* grants and exchange are necessary to the organization of a modern economic system and that any intelligent reform must be based on an integrated view of the system, which includes both grants and exchange as interacting mechanisms.

These volumes are addressed to serious students of economics and the social sciences. We believe that they will fill a crucially important gap in the present state of knowledge and that their influence will be felt far beyond the particular problems to which they are addressed.

Kenneth E. Boulding and Martin Pfaff
Series Editors

Contents

Urbanization and the Grants Economy: An Introduction 1

Urbanization and the Grants Economy: An Introduction

This is the second volume of papers concerned with problems of nonmarket redistribution – that is, redistribution through the grants economy – within the United States. Most of the papers were presented at the meetings held jointly by the Association for the Study of the Grants Economy and the American Economic Association, the American Association for the Advancement of Science, or the Public Choice Society in December 1969 and 1970.

This volume focuses on the spatial, or geographic, patterns of tax incidence and the public and private redistribution that characterize the urbanized American economy. This view entails not only an examination of the patterns of redistribution between the different component parts of the metropolis, such as suburban versus central city or central city versus specific ghetto areas, nor is the main concern with the problems associated with urbanization per se, although the papers are grouped around such problem areas. Rather, the primary concern is the means we use collectively or individually to finance public goods or to bring about reform and to solve problems. The main issue, therefore, is the role that exchange, or the market mechanism, can play in solving relevant contemporary problems as compared with nonmarket means, which we call the private or public grants economy. In this sense, *transfers* are instruments used to finance the supply of goods through the grants economy.

In the simplest conception, a grant or a transfer involves a one-way economic relationship whereby party A conveys an exchangeable to party B without receiving in return an exchangeable of equal market value. This definition focuses on changes in net worth of the grantor and the grantee. Under exchange the net worth of two parties is unchanged, whereas under a grant the net worth of the grantor is diminished and the net worth of the grantee is increased. This is clearly an economic definition, which neglects cultural, social, political, or, more generally, psychic benefits that accrue to the grantor in a particular granting situation. Furthermore, the grants economy is the predominant vehicle of financing nonprivate—or public— goods through provision or transfer of economic goods or services; thus it often effects an income redistribution. Public goods are, by definition, goods that are not financed through the private exchange or market economy because they are characterized by large externalities and the exclusion principle does not apply to them. However, the dichotomization into private exchange and public nonexchange (or grant) is by no means unambiguous. Rather, an examination of many types of goods traditionally classified as private and public goods in the literature of public finance reveals that both contain exchange and grant components.[1] For example, public financing of education provides both benefits to the individual, because it increases his potential income, and benefits to society at large, because educated individuals are of benefit to others through their contribution to the output of the total socio-economy. Furthermore, within the private sector a stunning amount of nonexchange transactions occur. In 1970, U.S. intrahousehold transfers alone were estimated at $313 billion.[2]

This apparatus provides insights into the social nature of many private phenomena not generally considered part of public finances. Private transfers between family members within the household, between families, and from corporations, grants from foundations, and transfers in cash or in kind from the vast network of institutions constituting the sprawling "nonprofit" sector of the economy have not generally been considered part of the public economy, yet they convey sizable external benefits to others or to the system at large.

On the other hand, many economic processes in the public sector that show up in public budgets are based on the exchange calculus: beneficiaries pay for these services, just as if they were being supplied by a private corporation. This situation calls for a conceptual scheme that does greater justice to this new reality, and which, in our view, justifies the intellectual effort invested in developing the language, the analytical apparatus, and the empirical analysis of grants economics. The aim is not to replace but to complement the literature on the public economy and public finance, by providing a particular point of view. By thus setting as the cornerstone of our inquiry the distributive consequences of economic acts, we emphasize that equity, together with efficiency, stability, and growth, should provide the normative criteria for grants allocations. Grants economics goes beyond even this widened normative frame and places the norm of social integration and the maintenance of a viable socioeconomic system as an explicit norm on the firmament of the policy maker. Thus grants economics may be viewed as an approach to the political economics of nonmarket phenomena.

1. See M. Pfaff and A. Pfaff, "Grants Economics: An Evaluation of Government Policies" (Congress of the International Institute of Public Finance, Leningrad, September 1970), *Public Finance*, September 1971; M. Pfaff and A. Pfaff, with an introduction by K. E. Boulding, *The Grants Economy* (Belmont, Calif.: Wadsworth Publishing Co., forthcoming); and K. E. Boulding and M. Pfaff, eds., *Redistribution to the Rich and the Poor* (Belmont, Calif.: Wadsworth Publishing Co., 1972).

2. James Morgan and Nancy Baerwaldt, "Changing Patterns of Intra-Family Transfers." Paper presented at the joint session of the American Economic Association for the Study of the Grants Economy, New Orleans, La., December 1971.

Thus, although we are concerned with both private and public transfers in general, public transfers occupy our major interest in this volume, largely because they are much more sizable in the present economic system than private transfers between individuals and between families. These public transfers are themselves a phenomenon of the past three decades. This is not to imply that public giving had not previously been a characteristic feature of governmental social welfare policy but that the magnitude and the range of public transfers has increased, particularly in the last three or four decades, so as to make public giving a major force in economic life.

The growth, both relative and absolute, in magnitude and significance of public transfers is intimately connected with urbanization, which has drastically transformed most Western societies during the past century and a half. Urbanization has led to a relative deemphasis of the role of private transfers for the purposes of promoting health, education, and welfare, largely due to the break up of the extended family and the decline of the small, geographically based community. On the other hand, the decline of the emphasis on private transfers could also be viewed as a compensatory reaction to the increased dominance of the market as a social mechanism for the attainment of human needs. The rise of the market has been closely tied in with specialization, or more generally, with industrialization. When we talk of the urbanized economy then, we refer to this whole complex of economic or industrial processes as well as their social, political, and cultural consequences and antecedents. The study of the role of transfers in an urbanized economy thus entails an examination of the role of transfers in remedying problems associated with an urbanized and industrialized society. More specifically, we are interested in relating specific problem areas of an urbanized economy to the public policy measures that have been adopted to combat them. This process generally involves a study of the flow of benefits and costs associated with a particular policy, say the provision of higher education within a geographic entity such as a municipality, or a state. However, among these various geographic, or spatial, entities, the main interest centers on larger aggregates of individuals or urban clusters associated with the metropolis.

Apart from the empirical investigation of various types of transfers, the volume is concerned with explanations of the role that transfers can or should play in the urbanized economy. A major point of departure is the *theory of market failure*, which presumes that markets cannot achieve certain types of economic ends, and hence nonmarket means – transfers – are needed to achieve these ends. In the literature of public finance, market failures are generally associated with the presence of monopoly elements in the economy; with the prevalence of increasing returns to scale, within which the competitive calculus cannot operate; with indivisibilities in production or consumption, where the marginal logic is not applicable; and with externalities on both the production and consumption sides. The last of these aspects of market failure will occupy our special attention. In various contexts we shall explore the effects that external benefits and costs have on various aspects of public policy. Just as we note market failures in the areas of urban education, housing, and so on, we may also speak of *failures of the grants economy* in these areas. Far from acting as an effective remedy to market failures, the grants economy often is characterized by "perverse" effects; instead of attaining goals not attainable within the market, the grants economy often leads to results opposite from those intended by the policy makers. From the various papers we learn that many of the problems in an urbanized economy are the result of this perversity of allocative mechanisms, whether they are caused by the market or by the grants economy. One of our objectives is to point out these perverse effects, as reflected in the inequity of the distributive results of public policy or in the inappropriate choice of instruments for taxation.

The central message of this volume is thus by no means cheering. Although we point out that grants may be an instrument for the solution of urban problems, we also note that sophistication in their use leaves much to be desired at the present. We therefore call for a social technology to combat urban problems that would include a more skillful use of transfers on both the taxation and the expenditure side of public budgets.

We are concerned not only with explicit transfers, which are characterized by cash flows between grantors and grantees, but also with implicit grants, which are not reflected in such obvious flows. An example of an implicit public grant is the economic benefit conveyed to the owner by rezoning of land from farm to commercial use. Such implicit grants often arise through the legislative, administrative, or judicial activities of the government in its interface with economic or market forces. Furthermore, we are interested in mixed transactions, which involve both exchange and non-exchange flows. These transactions generally can be broken down into their grant equivalent and exchange equivalent or if they deal with nonmarket or public flows, into their tax equivalent or grant equivalent.[3]

The papers are arranged in the following order. In part 1 patterns of redistribution within the metropolis are examined by means of two specific case studies. In the first case the problem of equity involving relations between suburban communities and central cities is examined. William Neenan asks whether suburban communities do compensate the central city adequately for expenses that it undertakes on their behalf. His empirical base is derived from a study of the Detroit area. This case is followed by Earl Mellor's study of the cost and benefits of public goods and expenditures in a Washington, D.C., ghetto area. He is specifically concerned with the question of whether a low-income neighborhood is self-sufficient with regard to its immediate needs, such as providing for safety, education, and welfare.

---

3. Tax equivalent denotes the net cost borne by a particular individual over and above the value of a public service received by him; grant equivalent refers to the net benefits received after his payments in the form of taxes have been considered.

It appears that these two questions are central to the relationship between the inner city and its suburban environment. Many problems of financing programs for education, transportation, and so on result from the perception of equity and legitimacy.

In part 2 the impact of voluntary and involuntary transfers through charity and the tax system is examined with special reference to the inner-city poverty areas. Harold Hochman and James Rodgers explain urban income transfers through "utility interdependence." Daniel Fusfeld studies the relationship between the public welfare payment and the ghetto economy for the United States in general, and Anita Pfaff examines empirically the distributive and poverty-reducing effects of social welfare payments to large metropolitan poverty areas. Finally, Irving Leveson explores alternative strategies for remedying urban poverty. Part 2 thus relates to a specific aspect of urbanization – namely, poverty and urban concentrations of poverty areas.

The next few sections look at some of the problems that are or might be associated with the increase in public grants and with the opportunity for a better allocation of the public grant system. In part 3, one of the main effects of transfers on the market for labor is examined, specifically the effect transfers have on participation in the labor force by grants recipients. Two papers report on empirical work carried out in the past and present to measure the work-disincentive effect of public transfer payments. This topic is of special concern because many people believe that public welfare payments make it possible for able-bodied individuals to live without working and that it in fact encourages laziness and the willingness to live on handouts. Christopher Green and Alfred Tella look at the effect of nonemployment income and wage rates on the work incentives of the poor. David Elesh, Jack Ladinsky, Myron Lefcowitz, and Seymour Spilerman based their study on the ongoing New Jersey–Pennsylvania experiment, which is designed to assess the effect of public transfers on work behavior.

As participation in the labor force or in the market economy provides one remedy for the problems of the ghetto and of urban poverty, education may be viewed as the second major key to individual advancement and, by implication, to the alleviation of urban poverty and of urban problems in general. In part 4 the role of taxes and transfers as instruments of financing educational policies is explored in both theoretical and empirical veins. Byron Brown poses some basic questions on the potential of state grants for promoting equality of opportunity in education; Thomas Muller estimates the impact that recent state education grant proposals are likely to have on local tax burdens and thus on the distribution pattern of the public grants economy; Charles Waldauer analyzes the fiscal interdependence among various government levels and the implication of the external effects of school aid; and Donald Phares studies implicit public grants resulting from the exportation or importation of taxes between different states and regions and their implications for educational policy. While the case for federal action is thus strengthened, David Porter and David Warner point out some of the problems of current federally supported education programs that result from information and control aspects.

Part 2 thus looks at short-term remedies to urban poverty conveyed by transfer payments, whereas parts 3 and 4 focus on long-run mechanisms that could remedy the impact of human ecology on the status of the urban poor through participation in the labor force and through educational advancement. Part 5 examines the more general problem of the physical ecology, specifically of pollution, which tends to make the plight of the poor who live in concentrated urban areas even more difficult. Part 5 is thus concerned with remedies to some of the basic problems of an industrial society, which tend to affect not only urban areas in general but particularly persons who already have the greatest problems – namely, the poor. The focus again is on the limitations and strengths of the market economy versus the grants economy in solving problems of pollution and environment. On the whole, part 5 employs a theoretical approach to these basic questions. Myrick Freeman sets the stage by looking at the implications of grants as instruments and products of pollution-control policies in general. He focuses specifically on the relationship between exchange and grants processes in solving these problems. Thomas Havrilesky singles out technology from other forces as a major variable of concern; he points out that pollution is an area in which the market exchange mechanism simply breaks down. Allan Schmid examines the foundations of the market and relates it to the concept of private property and its uses and abuses in causing environmental crises. The concluding two papers by George Daly and Fred Giertz and by Robert Strotz and Colin Wright place these issues in the more formal framework of welfare economics.

The picture is drawn on a very broad canvas. A variety of elements that account for urban problems and for approaches to their solution are discussed. The deeper a person enters into these issues the more he sees that the supply of public funds, although it is a necessary condition, is by no means sufficient for the remedy of many of these problems. The economist is perhaps most adept in handling this instrument, although as the papers indicate, our level of knowledge in the use of these instruments is rudimentary at best. But this situation may be seen as an indication of the need for a high priority of effort on the part of economists in an area which is so intimately related to some of the greatest contemporary problems.

1

Exploitative Transfers in the Metropolis

The political and legal boundaries drawn between the city and the suburban environment often reflect rather arbitrary differences; generally the city and suburbia are part of an overall system which has its cultural, social, political, and economic dynamics and interrelationships. The boundaries assume an even greater importance at a time of social crisis because they raise questions of equity and legitimacy and thus cut at the very heart of human community.

Equity is one of the main norms by which individuals as members of groups evaluate the socioeconomic system: from the point of view of equity, the central question is whether the different components pay their own way in the system or whether they in fact constitute a burden to the rest of the system. If these components, or subgroups, are characterized by differences in income, status, and power, it can be questioned whether there is exploitation of one by the other, of the many by the few, or of the few by the many. In a very specific manifestation, we can question whether there is exploitation of the city by the suburban communities, which use the public facilities of the city perhaps without adequately compensating the city for those benefits. An alternative view focuses on the poverty area itself; the inverse of the former thesis, whether the poverty areas pay their way in terms of the public goods and services they require for their operation, has been posed frequently. The negation of this question would imply de facto "exploitation" of the city and suburbia by the inner-city poverty area, which is the recipient of social goods paid for, presumably involuntarily, by others. This exploitation is a matter of degree; often it involves the redistributive transfers voted voluntarily by the majority for the minority poverty group. Nonetheless, these two questions aim at the problem of *public* redistribution between the components of the urban conglomerate. The main focus, therefore, is not on exploitation through the operations of monopoly or other market forces but on deviations from some social equity norms engendered by the use of public funds and resources and by competing groups endowed with different degrees of power.

The papers of part 1 do not provide conclusive answers to all these basic questions. However, some general insight based on two case studies if applicable in a specific case and may also be generalized, with varying degrees of confidence, to other metropolitan areas.

Based on a study of the relationship between the city of Detroit and its suburban areas, William Neenan concludes that "if benefits are measured by willingness to pay, suburban municipalities, in varying degrees, do receive a welfare gain at the expense of Detroit." His views of the willingness to pay principle can be viewed both as an efficiency criterion and as an equity criterion for determining the tax contribution of residents and non-residents of urban areas. By contrasting net public sector benefit flows (as measured by willingness to pay) with the revenue flows, Neenan is able to show that "in all instances the revenue flows to Detroit fail to compensate fully for the public sector benefits flowing from Detroit to the . . . public sector, ranging from $1.73 per capita for Highland Park to $12.58 per capita for Birmingham."[1] He concludes: "For a family of four this welfare gain is estimated to range from nearly $7.00 to over $50.00 a year. These figures are averages for the suburban communities. For some families there may well be no gain; for others, with more frequent contact with Detroit, the welfare gain is undoubtedly much larger. Thus the one obvious conclusion that emerges from this analysis is that the tax contribution of suburban residents to the central city can be markedly increased without offsetting the welfare gain they are currently enjoying from the central city public sector."

Earl Mellor studies the low-income neighborhood of the Shaw-Cardozo area in Washington, D.C., in order to find out whether it is "self-sufficient with regard to its most immediate needs, such as providing for neighborhood safety, education, and welfare." He points out that his paper neither proves nor disproves any assertion of the implicit subsidy being conveyed by this area to the city at large, "because either a net inflow or a net outflow can be 'proven,' depending on what items are considered necessary and/or desired public functions and on the assumptions made with regard to the incidence of various tax burdens." Nonetheless, he estimates the benefits for education conveyed by public schools and the benefits for public safety imparted by police protection, corporation council, the courts, the Department of Corrections, fire protection, and other measures. He also looks at welfare benefits that arise from hospitals, vocational rehabilitation, highways and traffic, sanitation, urban renewal, city overhead, and social insurance.

Mellor then compares the outflows in the form of contributions for social insurance, federal income tax, District of Columbia income tax, property taxes, and so on with the benefits, or inflows. "The result (using feasible taxation) is a net outflow from the area amounting to $10.1 million using the minimum benefit estimate and a small net outflow of $8 million using the feasibly possible estimate. The wide range of net benefits indicates

---

1. The former is a moderate-income municipality encircled by Detroit's central city area; the latter is a traditionally affluent suburb.

that with present data the case of net inflows or net outflows with regard to the Shaw-Cardozo area is not settled. It can be stated that the area is reasonably paying its way – perhaps more than paying its way – and that its residents are capable of providing a reasonable level of public functions."

The first two papers thus look at exploitative transfers – that is, transfers which generally are not paid voluntarily on the part of the transferors. Part 2 is concerned both with private voluntary transfers made for charitable and other purposes and with partly involuntary transfers made through the tax system; parts 3, 4, and 5 address themselves mainly to public transfers, which may be construed to have elements of voluntariness and coercion, depending upon the degree of interdependence or identification between the individual and the community at large.

1

William B. Neenan:
Suburban-Central City Exploitation
Thesis: One City's Tale

A metropolitan area, both central city and suburbs, is a natural economic and social unit. We are learning that Henry Ford's prescription, "we shall solve the City Problem by leaving the City," does not work. Problems, just as easily as people, can tumble over artificially constructed boundaries. Even though interdependency within metropolitan areas is subscribed to in the abstract, there is still, however, no commonly accepted response to the basic question: Do suburban communities compensate the central city adequately for expenses it undertakes in their behalf? Much political heat, heightened by traditional American antipathy toward city life as well as class and racial biases, has been generated over the exploitation thesis: suburbanites stoutly maintain there should be no taxation without representation; central citians are resentful of what they consider freeloading, claiming that every tub should stand on its own bottom.

Despite widespread recognition of the importance of this question and some empirical research, the exploitation question is largely unresolved. Recently in this *Journal* a leading student of urban finance commented: ". . . it is important to remember that we do not yet have a satisfactory and systematic benefit-cost study on the question of whether the suburbanite subsidizes or is being subsidized by the central city."[1] In this article the dimensions of the exploitation thesis in the Detroit SMSA [standard metropolitan statistical area] will be explored. Benefit and revenue flows between Detroit and six other municipalities in the Detroit SMSA will be estimated. Central to this examination of the exploitation thesis will be a willingness to pay model proposed for evaluating public services. The primary conclusion of this article is that if benefits are measured by willingness to pay, suburban municipalities, in varying degrees, do receive a welfare gain at the expense of Detroit.

From *National Tax Journal*, Vol. XXIII, No. 2, June 1970. Reprinted by permission of the publisher and author. Mr. Neenan is Assistant Professor of Economics, The University of Michigan. He is grateful for the helpful criticisms from many: from Robin Barlow, Harvey Brazer, Gunter Schramm, and Sidney Winter; from members of the public finance seminar, especially Larry Dildine, Irv Garfinkel, Gary Fields, and Steven Gold; and from students in the graduate course in government expenditures at The University of Michigan. Sandra J. Rice collected most of the data which appear here. She has been a helpful critic and most generous at all times. The Institute of Public Policy Studies of The University of Michigan provided financial support for the study.

1. David Davies, "Fiscal Effort, A Comment," *National Tax Journal*, XXII September, 1969), p. 423.

The specific agenda of this article is: (1) a brief review of previous research concerning exploitation; (2) specification of a model for citizen welfare maximization in the public sector; (3) review of voter and survey data to test this model; (4) public sector benefit flows between Detroit and six suburban municipalities; (5) revenue flows between Detroit and these municipalities; and (6) a concluding remark.

I. Previous Research

There have been a few scattered empirical explorations of the hypothesis that central cities are exploited by their suburban ring, in the sense that they bear costs for services which are enjoyed by the whole metropolitan area. There is evidence, for example, that the central city bears a disproportionate share of the metropolitan costs of poverty. Moreover, there have been several attempts to determine the impact a suburban population has on the level of expenditures for all municipal functions. Hawley found that, in 1940, per capita public expenditures of 76 central cities with 100,000 or more population were positively correlated with the percentage of the SMSA population residing outside the central city. Thus he concluded that residents of the central city

> . . . are carrying the financial burden of an elaborate and costly service installation, i.e., the central city, which is used daily by a noncontributing population in some instances more than twice the size of the contributing population.[2]

Margolis reports similar results from an examination of 1957 per capita payments for government payrolls for all local governments which overlay the central city in the 36 largest SMSAs.[3] However, Margolis does not accept these findings as necessarily confirmatory of the exploitation thesis. He feels that these larger expenditures of the central city may well be offset by the fact that central cities have a larger industrial and commercial tax base, and that retail sales to, and the employment of nonresidents may generate increased property tax revenues which more than offset the higher government expenditures. For Margolis, "The argument that central cities are exploited by the noncentral cities is not well established. If anything, central cities may be relatively better off."[4]

---

2. Amos H. Hawley, "Metropolitan Population and Municipal Government Expenditures in Central Cities," *Journal of Social Issues*, VII (1951), p. 107.

3. Julius Margolis, "Metropolitan Finance Problems: Territories, Functions, and Growth," in James M. Buchanan (ed.), *Public Finances: Needs, Sources and Utilization* (Princeton: Princeton University Press, 1961), p. 256.

4. *Ibid.*, p. 259.

Brazer found that 1953 per capita expenditures of the overlying governments of the 40 cities with over 250,000 population were negatively correlated with the ratio of the central city population to the SMSA population. Even though these results are an additional indication that suburban communities have a positive impact on central city government expenditures, Brazer likewise is not willing to conclude with certainty that the suburbs exploit the central city. Higher expenditures are not sufficient of themselves to establish exploitation. "Conceivably the suburbanite, through his contacts with the city, contributed as much or more to the latter's tax bases as is required to finance the additional expenditures he imposes upon it."[5]

There have been several attempts to measure the flow of benefits and tax revenue within one metropolitan area. Typical of these attempts is the study Banovetz has done for the Minneapolis-St. Paul metropolitan area.[6] He implicitly examines the exploitation thesis to see whether either Minneapolis, St. Paul, or the suburban area is exploited by one of the others. He assumes that "benefits," measured by cost of service, accrue to an area on the basis of the number of direct program recipients residing in the area. He further assumes that the incidence of the local property tax and the state income tax, the funding sources of these programs, is the situs of collection.

The "benefits" allocated to each area on this basis are paired with the area's total tax liability, estimated by the incidence assumptions just described. If its "benefits" exceed its tax liability, an area is assumed to be subsidized by the other areas. On the basis of such an analysis, Banovetz reports ". . . that no conclusive evidence can be found to support charges that either the core cities of Minneapolis and St. Paul or their suburbs in Hennepin or Ramsey Counties, respectively, are subsidizing the other to any appreciable extent."[7]

This and similar studies leave unresolved many questions raised by the exploitation thesis. First of all, benefits, from several functional categories, such as highways, police and fire protection, libraries and cultural facilities, and utility services, are not estimated in the Banovetz study. Secondly, no attempt is made to account for the indirect subsidies provided by the tax exemption enjoyed by various public and private facilities. The omission of these two points underestimates the benefits provided by the core cities to the surrounding population. Thirdly, costs of poverty are assumed to be "benefits" only for the jurisdiction in which direct program recipients reside. This assumption means that Minneapolis and St. Paul, with their

---

5. Harvey E. Brazer, *City Expenditures in the United States* (New York: National Bureau of Economic Research, 1959), p. 58.

6. James M. Banovetz, "Governmental Cost Burdens and Service Benefits in the Twin Cities Metropolitan Area" (Minneapolis: Public Administration Center, University of Minnesota, 1965).

7. Banovetz, *op. cit.*, p. 29.

relatively large dependent population, are allocated a relatively heavier burden of the poverty costs of the whole metropolitan area. Finally, the suburban areas are treated as if they were homogeneous, when in reality there is a mixture of industrial and residential suburbs, with a wide range of income levels. Residential suburbs and industrial enclaves have substantially different relationships with the central city.

II. Citizen Welfare Maximization Model

The benefits stemming from any government expenditure can, in the last analysis, be measured only by the beneficiaries themselves. Neither government agency, social critic, priest, pope, nor party chairman can judge with infallibility when a course of action benefits any citizen. He alone judges that. Thus it is theoretically invalid and in practice misleading to assume that city parks, for example, generate benefits equally for all residents of a municipality.[8]

The private market provides remarkably well for consumer idiosyncrasies. Personal tastes, social attitudes, education, and income, all are reflected in an individual's consumption pattern. Combined with market supply conditions, they determine the relative price structure or the relative evaluation of all goods privately produced. Jack Sprat can luxuriate over his lean meat while his wife relishes her suet pudding, with this constraint: the J. Sprats must pay a higher price for their nourishment since they are more numerous, just as affluent, and since beef cattle all have just so much lean meat and so much suet.

Thus in the private sector, people vote with their dollars, and given a minimum number of others with similar tastes and constrained by the resources at their command, they effectively maximize their welfare. In the

---

8. In his small classic on the personal income tax, Simons illustrates a similar problem of welfare evaluation arising when income in kind is imputed to an individual. "We are asked to measure the relative incomes of an ordinary officer serving with his troops and a Fluegel-adjutant to the sovereign. Both receive the same nominal pay; but the latter receives quarters in the palace, food at the royal table, servants, and horses for sport. He accompanies the prince to the theater and opera, and, in general, lives royally at no expense to himself and is able to save generously from his salary. But suppose, as one possible complication, that the Fluegel-adjutant detests opera and hunting." Henry C. Simons, *Personal Income Taxation* (Chicago: University of Chicago Press, 1938), p. 53. Thus, in the context of metropolitan services, a municipal opera company which is financed by general tax revenue generates greater net benefits for opera buffs than for the area's Fluegel-adjutants.

That tastes vary, has also been pointed out in the comic strip "Peanuts" by Charles Schultz. Lucy is castigating Snoopy, who listens dutifully. "You think you're so smart," chides Lucy. "You know what you'll never be able to do? You'll never be able to hold a furry kitten in your arms, and stroke it and listen to it purr." As Lucy stalks off, Snoopy, unimpressed, muses, "I'll try to survive."

public sector, however, signals cannot be transmitted so clearly and so it is difficult to judge whether individuals are as effective in maximizing their welfare. Benefits of public services can be measured by effective demand, or the willingness to pay criterion, only darkly, by peering through the screen of the political process.

The few studies which have allocated benefits of public services to individuals have notably avoided any attempt to measure benefits by effective demand.[9] Instead, benefits have typically been measured by the cost of providing the service, with these costs ("benefits") then allocated to the immediate beneficiaries of the programs to determine the benefit incidence of government expenditures. In the case of a collective consumption good, for example, national defense, total expenditures have been allocated by some arbitrary criterion, such as equality of benefits per capita.[10] Although measuring benefits by their cost has not been defended on theoretical grounds, it has been tolerated apparently under the belief that benefit measurement is a task eminently in need of doing and no other basis seems feasible. In this article the willingness to pay index of government benefits is proposed as a feasible alternative.

In recent years an economic theory of political decision making, purporting to explain how citizen attitudes are translated into budgetary actions, has received considerable attention.[11] In such a model, officeholders seek to maximize the number of votes they will receive by implementing programs which provide a surplus of perceived benefits over perceived costs for a majority of voters. If this is so, the political winnowing process gives some assurance that citizen attitudes are reflected with considerable faithfulness in actual budgetary decisions. Thus if voters are assumed to be maximizers, an examination of voting data should offer insights into the pattern of perceived benefits and costs of various expenditure and tax decisions and suggest normative guidelines for metropolitan public finance. Voting patterns in local elections more closely reflect attitudes toward local expenditure and tax policy than is true on the national level where elections are more often charged with questions of war, peace, and dominant personalities. Survey data can serve as a valuable complement and check on election results, since the latter may reflect merely the attitudes of the actual voters rather than all citizens.

Before examining certain voting and survey data for insights into the nature of effective demand in the metropolitan public sector, we will first

---

9. See for example, W. Irwin Gillespie, "Effect of Public Expenditures on the Distribution of Income," in R. A. Musgrave (ed.), *Essays in Fiscal Federalism* (Washington: The Brookings Institution, 1965), pp. 122–186. For other studies, see *ibid.*, p. 123.

10. *Ibid.*

11. Two leading contributions to this development are Anthony Downs, *An Economic Theory of Democracy* (New York: Harper and Row, 1957), 310 pp.; James M. Buchanan and Gordon Tullock, *The Calculus of Consent* (Ann Arbor: University of Michigan Press, 1965), 361 pp.

establish one testable hypothesis concerning willingness to pay for public services. The model to be used is that of the traditional theory of individual consumer welfare maximization in the private sector. With appropriate modifications it will be extended to citizen welfare maximization in the public sector.

Consumer theory provides the following description of welfare maximization: If we assume independent utility functions for individuals, determinate price ratios, and an initial distribution of income and wealth, there exists one package of expenditures which maximizes any consumer's welfare. In notational form, the consumer's utility function is

$$U' = U' (e_1 , \ldots e_m)$$ (1)

subject to the constraint

$$Y - \sum_{i=1}^{m} p_i \, e_i = 0$$ (2)

where e_i = consumer goods and services
Y = income of consumer
p_i = price for the ith consumer good or service.

The voluntary exchange model has been the instrument for extending consumer welfare maximization analysis to the public sector.[12] However, this can be done only with several crucial modifications of the analysis. It has been clearly demonstrated that citizen welfare maximization can be *defined* but not automatically attained, as is the case in the private market, under the usual assumptions. Due to its inability to elicit revealed preference for collectively consumed goods, the voluntary exchange approach is not an operational model. Samuelson has stated this fact succinctly:

> One could imagine every person in the community being indoctrinated to behave like a "parametric decentralized bureaucrat" who *reveals* his preferences by signalling in response to price parameters or Lagrangian multipliers, to questionnaires, or to other devices. But there is still this fundamental technical difference going to the heart of the whole problem of *social* economy: by departing from his indoctrinated rules, any one person can hope to snatch some selfish benefit in a way not possible under the self-policing competitive pricing of private goods. . . .[13]

However, even though the maximization of citizen welfare cannot be attained along the path of laissez-faire as in the private market exchange

---

12. I am referring here to the work most notably associated with Erik Lindahl, Howard Bowen, Richard Musgrave, and Leif Johansen.

13. Paul A. Samuelson, "The Pure Theory of Public Expenditure," *The Review of Economics and Statistics*, XXXVI (1954), p. 389.

model, the voluntary exchange model does define a welfare maximization situation which has normative value.[14] Furthermore, insofar as the citizens perceive that the political process produces fiscal results which deviate from this norm, they will be discontent.[15]

Therefore we can say that the citizen derives utility from the consumption of both private and public goods:

$$U'' = U'' (e_1, \ldots e_m; g_1, \ldots g_n) \tag{3}$$

subject to the constraint

$$Y - \sum_{i=1}^{m} p_i e_i - \sum_{i=1}^{n} t_j g_j = 0 \tag{4}$$

where Y = income of citizen

g_j = public sector goods and services

t_j = tax-price for the jth public sector good or service

and it is assumed there is no savings.

Every budgetary action produces a perceived benefit whose welfare implications may be described in terms of the kth citizen's utility function:

$$\frac{\delta U''^k}{\delta g_j} = \begin{array}{l} \text{perceived marginal benefit to the } k^{th} \text{ citizen} \\ \text{from a marginal alteration in public program } g_j. \end{array} \tag{5}$$

But in addition to increasing citizen k's welfare, a budgetary action also imposes a perceived tax-price, t_j^k. The perceived tax-price of public service j for citizen k is

$$t_j^k = a Y^k \tag{6}$$

where

$$a = f(C,S,K) \tag{7}$$

where C = tax contribution of others

S = the tax structure as it applies to the kth citizen

K = cost conditions pertaining to the supply of public sector goods and services.

with $\qquad \dfrac{\delta a}{\delta C} < 0, \quad \dfrac{\delta a}{\delta S} < 0, \quad \dfrac{\delta a}{\delta K} > 0.$

---

14. For a discussion of this point in connection with the Lindahl voluntary exchange decision model, see Martin C. McGuire and Henry Aaron, "Efficiency and Equity in the Optimal Supply of a Public Good," *The Review of Economics and Statistics*, LI (February, 1969), pp. 31–39. Reprinted in K. E. Boulding and M. Pfaff, eds., *Redistribution to the Rich and Poor* (Belmont, Calif.: Wadsworth Publishing Co., 1972), pp. 41–56.

15. For a discussion of this point, see Albert Breton, "A Theory of the Demand for Public Goods," *Canadian Journal of Economics and Political Science*, XXIII (1966), pp. 455–467.

If the citizen maximizes his utility subject to the income constraint we have

$$\frac{\delta U''^k}{\delta e_i} = \lambda p_i = \frac{\delta U''^k}{\delta g_j} = \lambda t_j^k \quad \text{for all } i\text{'s and } j\text{'s} \tag{8}$$

where λ = a Langrangian multiplier.

λp_i = the disutility of the market price for consumer good i.

λt_j^k = the disutility for citizen k of the tax-price for public service j.

The concept of "fiscal residuum" is useful at this point in understanding the dynamics of citizen effective demand for public services.[16] The difference, expressed in welfare terms, between a person's perceived benefits and perceived tax liability of any budgetary adjustment is his fiscal residuum. If he judges that the sum of all the additional benefits he perceives flowing from a program adjustment (namely, the investment, consumer, and redistributive benefits[17]) are greater than the perceived tax liability, he enjoys a positive marginal fiscal residuum. In notational form[18] a positive marginal fiscal residuum exists when

$$\frac{\delta U''^k}{\delta g_j} > \lambda t_j^k \tag{9}$$

In this model, we have assumed welfare-maximizing motivation for the citizen. In other words, we assume he will favor program extensions only if the benefits he perceives are at least as large as the disutility he anticipates from tax adjustments. Similarly, he will oppose all programs for which the

---

16. Buchanan has used the term "fiscal residuum" to describe any citizen's difference between total taxes and total benefits in a federal system of government. In his analysis, different fiscal residua for citizens with the same income but residing in different states is a justification for equalizing grants from the federal government to low income states. In addition to this different use of the concept, Buchanan also defines "benefits" in terms of cost-of-service, rather than the willingness-to-pay index employed here. See James M. Buchanan, "Federalism and Fiscal Equity," *American Economic Review*, 40 (1950), pp. 583–599.

17. For some analyses it is useful to distinguish benefits in this threefold fashion: (1) An *investment* benefit is any increase in the capitalized net worth of an individual. (2) A *consumption* benefit is the nonpecuniary satisfaction one receives from some good or service. (3) A *redistributive* benefit is the value one receives from the maintenance of a program, even though he himself is neither currently served nor anticipates being served by the program, nor expects to receive some indirect monetary benefit from the program. The principal determinant of the effective demand for any welfare economy program, such as public assistance, veterans' subsidies, and farm support programs, is this redistributive benefit perceived by citizens other than the clientele group of the program. An indication of the existence of such benefits is given in this summary of a survey of citizen attitudes toward government expenditures: "Many people favor expenditures (for example, on education, city improvement, or help for needy people) from which they themselves will not derive any direct advantage." Eva Mueller, "Public Attitudes Toward Fiscal Programs," *Quarterly Journal of Economics*, LXVII (1963), p. 235.

18. Constant marginal utility of money is assumed by this notation.

perceived tax liability is greater than benefits and the citizen surplus is consequently negative.

One hypothesis concerning the effective demand for public services in metropolitan areas can be tested in terms of this model.[19] This hypothesis is that, given most local tax systems, perceived benefits of budgetary actions rise more rapidly than do their perceived tax liability as one moves up the income scale. Higher income citizens thus are expected to experience larger positive citizen surplus from increased public services and to be more favorable towards these services than are low income citizens. If low income citizens do evaluate public services less favorably than high income persons a municipal tax structure which does not assign them a tax liability commensurate with this attitude will produce negative citizen surplus among them. It is expected that local tax structures, which are typically regressive, impose a pattern of tax liability which generates negative citizen surplus among lower income citizens, and hence often political opposition to the expansion of local services.

If this model[20] offers a fruitful frame of reference for explaining and predicting such attitudes, we will possess some guidelines for deriving both a qualitative measure of the effective demand for public services and general parameters for the relation between the willingness to pay for public services

---

19. A second testable hypothesis is that a citizen with a given income residing in a high income community, other things equal, is expected to be more favorable toward increasing public services than are his peers residing in low income communities. Similarly, we expect citizens of higher income communities to oppose any proposals for financing services through a metropolitan jurisdiction which embraces a taxing area with a lower mean income than their own residence. These expectations follow from the fact that the higher the mean income in any municipality, the lower is the cost of increasing the level of public service to a resident with a specific income level, given most local tax systems. Thus the perceived tax liability of a given budgetary increase typically is smaller and the fiscal surplus consequently larger in higher income communities.

An analogous phenomenon is seen in municipalities with a large industrial or commercial property tax base. To the extent the tax on these properties is exported to nonresidents, the price of public services to residents is reduced. Thus due to this favorable price effect, residents of such municipalities would be expected to be more positively disposed toward budgetary increases than are citizens with the same income, residing in cities with a smaller industrial and commercial tax base.

20. This model does not consider the question of why certain programs are popular and others are not. There is a considerable political science and sociology literature dealing with factors which affect the level of support for any program. This model, however, assuming the level of support for any program in a community, purports to explain the continuum of attitudes from completely opposed to strongly in favor by means of economic variables.

In adducing evidence in support of this hypothesis, we do not intend to disregard the importance of such variables as education, political leadership, family and ethnic background, occupational grouping, and individual psychological factors in the formation of voting attitudes. Furthermore, some elections, especially at the national level, often turn on issues which cannot be readily cast in terms of the citizen surplus model.

For an illuminating survey of attitudes toward federal government programs, see Eva Mueller, *op. cit.* She concludes that "the data show that it is *not* true, as is sometimes supposed, that upper income groups are less favorably disposed toward extension of government programs than lower income groups" (pp. 228–229).

and family income. More specifically, we will have at hand a willingness to pay index for the public services supplied across municipal boundaries in the Detroit metropolitan area and so be able to suggest guidelines for intergovernmental fiscal exchanges that allow all groups in the metropolitan area to maximize their total citizen surplus without unwillingly subsidizing others.[21]

Willingness to pay is first of all an efficiency criterion for judging the appropriateness of the level and mix of public services as well as the incidence of their financing. Furthermore, since many public services are collectively consumed, the marginal cost of making them available to nonresidents is often close to zero. Hence there is the problem of allocating the costs of a service which is supplied by one jurisdiction but then enjoyed by others. In these instances the willingness to pay index can serve also as an equity criterion for determining the appropriate tax contribution of residents and nonresidents. It is assumed here that the welfare positions of residents in the metropolitan area should not be relatively altered merely because of legal residence in one or another jurisdiction. If the tax liability in support of these services is assessed according to willingness to pay, this initial, hypothetical welfare distribution over the metropolitan area is maintained.

III. Citizen Attitudes

Three studies of voter attitudes in a metropolitan context can be adduced in support of the hypothesis. Baskoff and Zeigler conducted a survey of voter attitudes immediately following a $22,900,000 bond referendum in 1961 in DeKalb County, Georgia, in which all nine items passed with comfortable margins.[22] The respondents to the survey were grouped in four income classes: under $5,000; $5,000 to $10,000; $10,000 to $15,000; and over $15,000. Support for each of the expenditure items on the referendum was positively related to income, with a strong tendency for support to increase with each succeeding income class.[23] Only 8.4 percent of those with income over $10,000 supported none or only one of the referendum items, whereas 66 percent supported all the issues. However, 33 percent of those

---

21. Admittedly, even with a general functional relationship established between willingness to pay for public services and family income, there remain cases such as the rose fever sufferer who must hold his peace while his tax money goes for more and larger rose gardens. But if we can safely assume that rose fever and similarly eccentric likes and dislikes are scattered rather thinly throughout the population of the metropolitan area, we can be satisfied that our norms are reasonably equitable.

22. Alvin Baskoff and Harmon Zeigler, *Voting Patterns in a Local Election* (Philadelphia: J. B. Lippincott Co., 1964), 195 pp. DeKalb County, contiguous to Atlanta, is increasingly becoming a suburban area, with a rural fringe and an older urban area in Decatur.

23. *Ibid.*, p. 45.

with income under $10,000 supported none or only one item, whereas 47 percent supported all items.[24]

Similar results emerge from a survey study of middle income residents of an urban renewal project and low income residents of a contiguous unrenewed neighborhood in Kansas City, Missouri.[25] Twenty-three percent of those interviewed who lived in the renewal project and none who resided in the contiguous neighborhood had incomes over $10,000. Of the project residents, only 3 percent thought city taxes were too high and should be cut and 47 percent were willing to pay higher taxes. However, 28 percent of the low income families thought taxes were too high and should be cut and only 19 percent were willing to pay higher taxes for "more policemen, firemen, city parks, and libraries."[26] Thus in both the DeKalb County and Kansas City studies, higher income citizens indicate a greater willingness to pay for increased public services, given their local tax structure.

In another recent study, Wilson and Banfield tested the following hypothesis:

> The voter tries to maximize his family income or (the same thing) self-interest narrowly conceived. We assume that the voter estimates in dollars both the benefits that will accrue to him and his family if the proposed public expenditure is made and the amount of the tax that will fall on him in consequence of the expenditure; if the estimated benefit is more than the estimated cost, he votes for the expenditure, if it is less, he votes against it.[27]

In other words, their hypothesis is that voters in municipal referenda seek to maximize a fiscal residuum. The difference between this fiscal residuum and the citizen surplus concept discussed above is that, for Wilson-Banfield, benefits are measured by cost of service, whereas in the citizen surplus analysis benefits are determined by effective demand. If homeowner status is controlled for,[28] these conclusions emerge from the Wilson and

---

24. *Ibid.*, p. 105.

25. Richard A. Watson, *The Politics of Urban Change* (Kansas City: Community Studies Inc., 1963), 81 pp.

26. *Ibid.*, p. 53.

27. James Q. Wilson and Edward C. Banfield, "Voting Behavior on Municipal Public Expenditures: A Study in Rationality and Self-Interest," in Julius Margolis (ed.), *The Public Economy of Urban Communities* (Washington: Resources for the Future, 1965), p. 74.

28. Wilson-Banfield's results also indicate the influence of a price effect and/or tax illusion operative in voting patterns of low income renters. Renters systematically show a greater taste for public expenditures to be financed by the property tax than do homeowners of the same income class. Apparently they perceive less disutility from increased property tax than do homeowners. Whether such attitudes are based on "objective" tax incidence is arguable, especially if allowance is made for the fact that homeowners can itemize property tax payments for federal income tax purposes.

Banfield study of thirty-five referenda concerning expenditure proposals in seven cities between 1957 and 1963:

1. Very low income wards and precincts (i.e., $3,000 or less family income) overwhelmingly support proposals, typically with the per-cent-yes votes ranging from 75 to over 90.
2. The percent-yes votes drops markedly across the lower middle income range.
3. The highest income districts (i.e., $10,000 or more family income), however, support proposals, including the funding of welfare pro-grams, by majorities close to that found among the very poor.[29]

On the basis of these results, Wilson and Banfield rejected the hypothe-sis they were testing. The low and middle income voting behavior indeed supported their hypothesis. Thus low income voters could have perceived they would receive services without a proportionate increase in their tax liability and so supported the proposals overwhelmingly. Middle income voters could well have anticipated a relatively higher tax burden which exceeded the benefits they anticipated from the services directed to them and so were markedly cooler toward the programs. However, according to this logic, high income classes, facing even higher tax liabilities to finance programs which often do not affect them directly, would be expected to reject the proposals massively. But since the high income voters supported measures that "would give them only trivial benefits while imposing sub-stantial costs upon them",[30] the authors rejected the hypothesis that voters seek to maximize family income.

The finding that higher income groups have a consistent tendency to be more favorable toward public expenditures replicated the results of the DeKalb County and Kansas City surveys. The only notable difference in the results of these three studies is that for DeKalb County and Kansas City attitudes become more favorable over all income classes while Wilson-Banfield indicate a consistently more favorable attitude only above the very low income class. This discrepancy can be explained by the fact that only the Wilson-Banfield study distinguishes the largely propertyless, very low income class from the slightly higher income class in which property ownership is more common.

The Wilson and Banfield findings do not support their formulation of an income maximization hypothesis. However, they are thoroughly consis-tent with the citizen surplus model of welfare maximization. The supporting

---

29. *Ibid.*, pp. 78 and 81.

30. *Ibid.*, p. 79. They found that in referenda in Cuyahoga County, Ohio, ethnic influences had a strong explanatory power. For a more lengthy discussion of these ethnic influences on voting patterns, see James Q. Wilson and Edward C. Banfield, "Public-Regardingness as a Value Premise in Voting Behavior," *American Political Science Review* (December, 1964), pp. 882–887.

evidence from Wilson and Banfield can be summarized in terms of our model as follows:

1. Very low income voters perceive positive benefits with a negligible anticipated tax liability from proposed budgetary actions. Thus their perceived citizen surplus is positive and they favor the proposals.
2. Middle income voters may indeed perceive benefits from proposed budgetary action but above a certain threshold their anticipated dis-utility from increased taxes is likewise significant. Often, therefore, this group faces negative citizen surplus from proposed actions and hence has negative attitudes toward them.
3. Higher income voters have a more favorable attitude toward in-creased expenditures because they evaluate benefits, especially redistributive benefits, more favorably than do middle income families. This disposition coupled with the regressive incidence of most local tax structures tends to generate positive citizen surplus for high income groups.

The results of the three studies can be generalized in terms of the functions shown in Figure 1. For three different hypothetical expenditure proposals, A, B, C, the percent-yes vote is a U-shaped function of family income. The total-yes vote, however, may vary considerably from one proposal to another, proposal A receiving the largest number of yes-votes in our example. Thus family income is not of itself sufficient information to enable us to predict whether any particular proposal will receive majority approval. Even millionaires are not willing to purchase every expensive bauble available in the private market. The same is to be expected of behavior in the public sector. However, willingness to pay for any given public service will typically be a rising function of income, above a minimum threshold level, designated approximately ON in Figure 1.

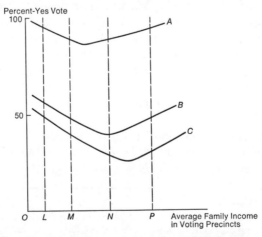

Figure 1. Relationship between Percent-Yes Vote and Average Family Income in Voting Precincts

The percent-yes vote as a function of family income is not of itself sufficient to define a willingness to pay parameter. Very low income citizens, for example, vote heavily in favor of expenditure proposals apparently because they anticipate little or no tax liability if the proposal is adopted, not because they are willing to pay for the service. In nearly all the expenditure proposals analyzed above, the increased level of spending was to be funded by a property tax levy. Consequently the percent-yes vote as a rising function of income reflects not merely attitudes toward public services, but also anticipated tax liability under the property tax. If the incidence of the property tax were proportional with respect to income and the percent-yes vote were constant over all income classes, we could conclude that willingness to pay for public services is a proportional function of income. Most property tax incidence studies, however, indicate that the impact of the property tax is regressive.[31] Consequently, the fact that the percent-yes vote is a rising function of income above a threshold does not necessarily mean that willingness to pay, or the perceived benefits of government programs, are also a rising function of income. For example, if a proportional or progressive tax structure were substituted for the currently regressive structure, and disregarding any tax illusion, we would expect the percent-yes vote in referenda generally to shift upward across lower income classes and fall in the higher income classes. Thus the effect of the regressive tax structure and the rising percent-yes phenomenon tend to offset each other. Until more precise measures of voter attitudes are available, we cannot hope to resolve this problem more definitively. For our purposes, however, we will assume that these two factors by and large neutralize each other and that willingness to pay for public services rises proportionately with income.[32]

---

31. For a summary of such incidence studies, see Dick Netzer, *Economics of the Property Tax* (Washington: The Brookings Institution, 1966), pp. 32–66.

32. Although there has been no definitive research dealing precisely with the question of citizen willingness to pay for local services in relation to family income, some studies provide a few indications of this relationship. For a multivariate analysis of voter data on public expenditure referenda in New York State, see William C. Birdsall, "A Study of the Demand for Public Goods," in Richard A. Musgrave (ed.), *Essays in Fiscal Federalism* (Washington: The Brookings Institution, 1965), pp. 235–294. Insights can be gathered also from cross sectional studies of the determinants of local government expenditures. Fabricant found that in 1942 the elasticity of state and local government expenditures with respect to per capita income was .90, controlling for urbanization and population density. [Solomon Fabricant, *The Trend of Government Activity in the United States Since 1900.* (New York: National Bureau of Economic Research, Inc., 1952), p. 125]. Brazer found that expenditures in 1951 for 452 cities on various functions had an elasticity with respect to median family income ranging between .30 and .56, controlling for population variables, commuter influence, and intergovernmental fiscal assistance. [Harvey E. Brazer, *City Expenditures in the United States* (New York: National Bureau of Economic Research, 1959), p. 27]. Gensemer, likewise using multivariate analysis, found that in 55 Michigan school districts local taxes exhibited a 1.3 elasticity with respect to income in the district. [Bruce L. Gensemer, *Determinants of the Fiscal Policy Decisions of Local Government in Urban Areas: Public Safety and Public Education* (unpublished Doctoral Dissertation, University of Michigan, 1966, p. 133). However, since these studies employ aggregate income concepts, the derived income elasticities represent the percentage change in government expenditure

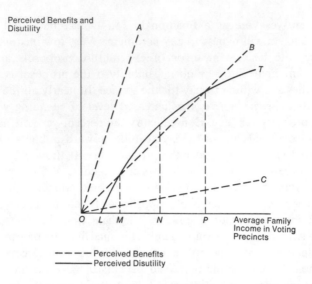

Figure 2. Relationship between Perceived Benefits and Disutility of Budgetary Actions in Relation to Family Income

The relationship between perceived benefits of expenditures and the perceived disutility of taxes can be seen with the aid of Figure 2. The hypothetical benefit functions OA, OB, and OC (corresponding to programs A, B, and C in Figure 1) and the tax function LT are drawn in Figure 2 to indicate that local government budgetary actions will generate widespread support among low income citizens. Given the level of perceived disutility from the perceived tax liability function, LT, all three programs generate positive citizen surplus for very low income citizens. The shape of LT differs from the profile derived from most tax incidence studies which purport to measure the "objective" incidence of taxes for all income classes. Such studies assume that the property tax on rental housing is shifted to occupants and thus falls relatively more heavily on low income families who typically rent their lodgings. From the voting data we have examined, however, it seems that such families do not imagine they are paying the property tax, and so do not perceive disutility from funding programs through increases in the property tax. The shape of LT above low income levels is assumed to be of the general form reported by tax incidence studies.

Although OA, OB, and OC may well represent perceived benefit functions for three local government programs ranging from the very popular to totally unpopular, the benefit function OB together with the tax disutility

---

associated with a 1 percent increase in the *average* level of income in the political jurisdictions. Therefore, an extension of these findings to a cross-sectional income elasticity of demand for services by individuals can be made only with caution. Furthermore, multivariate analysis of the determinants of variations in government spending levels is not designed to measure the attitudes of individual taxpayers. There may be extraneous factors, such as constitutional debt limitations, malapportioned legislatures, or a large business property tax base, which influence the *de facto* expenditure pattern in a city. These influences make it difficult to derive other than a general indication of taxpayer attitudes toward government expenditures from multivariate analysis.

Table 1. Willingness to Pay Multipliers
for Detroit SMSA Municipalities

Municipality	Willingness to Pay Multiplier
Allen Park	1.48
Birmingham	2.02
Dearborn	1.34
Detroit	1.00
Grosse Point Park	2.09
Highland Park	0.89
Roseville	1.24

Source of Income Data: Detroit Regional Transportation and Land Use Study

function LT best explain the voting and survey data we have examined. For the class with income below OM, citizen surplus is positive, becoming negative for families with incomes between OM and OP, and positive again for incomes above OP. There is, of course, in actuality some variance around these functions, which purport merely to indicate central tendencies of citizen attitudes rather than to specify exactly the attitudes of all voters.

On the basis of these observations we can formulate a willingness to pay multiplier for adjusting benefits which were initially measured by cost of service. If the perceived benefits of local government services rise proportionately with income, and a citizen with $6,000 annual income will pay $5.00 for a particular service, a citizen with $12,000 annual income will pay $10.00 rather than do without it. Willingness to pay multipliers, constructed on this basis, for Detroit and six suburban municipalities are shown in Table 1.[33] In the next two sections we will (1) estimate the benefit flows

33. Since our analysis has been concerned with marginal evaluation, we must assume either (a) the public services are evaluated at the margin or (b) average and marginal evaluations are the same. We have also assumed that the Detroit median family income is the base and the willingness to pay index has been calculated in reference to it. Thus if

$$\frac{\frac{\Delta P}{P}}{\frac{\Delta Y}{Y}} = 1$$

where P = willingness to pay for public services and Y = median family incomes, and median family income is $6,350 for Detroit and $8,500 for Dearborn in 1965, then for Dearborn,

$$\frac{\frac{\Delta P}{P}}{\frac{2.150}{6.350}} = 1 \text{ and } \frac{\Delta P}{P} = .34$$

Thus, willingness to pay for the same public services is 34 percent higher in Dearborn than in Detroit. The multipliers in Table 1 for adjusting the cost of service benefits to a willingness to pay basis for the various municipalities are all computed in this manner.

between Detroit and these six municipalities on a cost of service basis, (2) adjust them by the multipliers in Table 1 and (3) estimate the revenue flows between Detroit and the six municipalities. By comparing the benefits thus adjusted and the revenue flows we will be able to evaluate the validity of the exploitation thesis in the Detroit SMSA.

IV. Detroit SMSA Benefit Flows

There are three major classifications of benefits enjoyed by citizens because they reside in a metropolitan area: (1) collective benefits resulting from population concentration, (2) gains from economic exchange, and (3) benefits conferred by the local public sectors.

Certain benefits accrue to all residents of a metropolitan area from the mere fact of a heavy population concentration. Many external economies as well as cultural amenities are possible only if a threshold critical population mass is reached. For example, the diverse employment possibilities present in a large city reduce the danger of widespread unemployment. Specialized labor skills as well as specialty manufacturers and printers are available only in a large market. Similarly, subcontracting becomes an alternative for firms that may find it unprofitable to tool up to supply merely occasional needs.

A theater district, museums, fine restaurants, and other cultural and recreational facilities need a potential clientele of considerable size before they become feasible. A British scholar, Florence, has stated this somewhat archly: "My own experience is that apart from the special habitat of intellectuals, Oxford or Cambridge, a city of a million is required to give me, say, the twenty or thirty congenial friends I require."[34] Benefits such as these follow from high population density and do not necessarily have social costs connected with them.

Secondly, benefits in the form of increased income and property values are generated by interaction between residents of a metropolitan area. As we have seen, several perceptive students of metropolitan problems suggest that such increased values may fully compensate the central city for services it provides to suburbanites. However, the mutuality, or the gains from trade, present in most economic transactions are especially difficult to isolate and quantify in the case of metropolitan exchange. Some relevant dimensions of this problem are suggested if we imagine that there is at first only one municipality, A, encompassing the whole metropolitan area. In this case a particular pattern of property values and residential family income levels would emerge from economic activity.

If we assume that a second municipality, B, were then separated from the former municipality, A, and the flow of economic activity in the whole

---

34. Quoted in Jane Jacobs, *The Death and Life of Great American Cities* (New York: Random House, 1961), p. 118.

area remained the same (as we might expect in the short run) property values and income distributional patterns would not change. Presumably residents of both municipalities would continue to gain from their economic exchanges, but neither more nor less than before their political separation. If we assume the impact of the public sector on all residents of the metropolitan area is the same both before and after separation, their relative welfare positions are not affected. The principal welfare question which does arise with separation, however, is precisely whether and to what extent residents of the two municipalities actually do compensate each other for public services supplied to nonresidents and thus whether welfare positions are affected. If we assume that community B is a bedroom suburb and community A a business center, for example, then there arises the problem of providing a mechanism for equitably financing the public services provided by A to commuters. If after political separation, all such services are financed by A, then clearly A's relative welfare position has deteriorated.

Thirdly, benefits supplied through local public sectors typically include services to commuters and other nonresidents. In this section the principal benefits supplied to nonresidents through local public sectors in the Detroit SMSA will be identified and measured. No attempt, however, will be made to quantify either the collective benefits or the gains from economic exchange accruing to the various municipalities in the metropolitan area on the grounds that these are not decisively relevant to the exploitation question.

In addition to Detroit, six suburban communities in the Detroit metropolitan area have been chosen so that many of the characteristic relationships of metropolitan municipalities may be exemplified. Certain demographic and economic characteristics of the municipalities are shown in Table 2. In addition to Detroit, the municipalities chosen may be characterized briefly as follows:

1. Low income, industrial suburb (Highland Park)
2. Modest income, residential suburb (Roseville)
3. Middle income, industrial suburb (Dearborn)
4. Middle income, residential suburb (Allen Park)
5. High income, residential and commercial suburb (Birmingham)
6. High income, residential suburb (Grosse Pointe Park)

The inter-jurisdictional public sector benefit flows measured first by cost of services and then adjusted by a willingness to pay multiplier will be estimated for the following categories:[35]

---

35. Where possible expenditures will refer to fiscal year 1966, July, 1, 1965 to June 30, 1966.

Any tax liability exported outside the municipalities cannot be construed as a burden on residents. Thus to the extent services supplied to nonresidents are financed by exported taxes, they cannot be considered a benefit supplied to nonresidents by residents. Consequently, adjustments will be made for the fact that a considerable portion of the property tax on industrial and commercial property and, in the case of Detroit, the corporate income tax and the nonresident individual income tax is not a burden for residents. Furthermore, consideration is given to the fact that the deductibility of all local taxes under

1. Benefits provided directly by public sector to users:
    a. Library
    b. Art Museum
    c. Zoo
    d. Recreation and parks
    e. Streets and traffic control
2. Costs of poverty in the metropolitan area
3. Benefits provided indirectly by public sector subsidies:
    a. Water Department subsidy
    b. Tax exemption for hospitals, universities, and limited access highways.

A summary of the net benefits supplied to residents of the six suburban municipalities from five direct services is shown in Table 3. In all instances benefits are estimated by allocating to each municipality a fraction of the total expenditures for the service equal to the ratio of that municipality's use of the facility to total use.[36] Even though there are no publicly supported suburban art museums or zoos, and Detroit residents do not frequent suburban library or park systems to an appreciable extent, they do travel on

---

the Internal Revenue Code permits shifting part of all local tax liability to the federal treasury.

Assumptions that are made regarding the incidence of local taxes are:
1. *The property tax on:*
    a. residential property: all borne by residents
    b. industrial property: none borne by residents; except for Detroit and the Counties: 15 per cent borne by residents
    c. commercial property: one-half borne by residents.
2. *The local income tax on:*
    a. Residents: all borne by residents
    b. Nonresidents: none borne by residents
    c. Corporate income: 15 percent borne by residents.
3. Deductibility under federal income tax: It is assumed that for 1966, 50 percent of the property tax and income tax is paid by federal itemizers with a typical marginal rate of 20 percent. Thus 10 percent of property and income tax liability is assumed shifted to the federal treasury. Under these assumptions, the percentages of tax liability borne by residents of jurisdictions in the Detroit area are:

Allen Park	76 percent
Birmingham	68
Dearborn	28
Detroit	55
Grosse Pointe Park	81
Highland Park	35
Roseville	69
Macomb County	51
Oakland County	51
Wayne County	51

36. For example, .76 percent of the users of the Detroit Main Library in 1966 were residents of Allen Park. On this basis, and assuming that Detroit residents bear 55 percent of the ultimate incidence for Detroit taxes, Allen Park received through the Detroit Library System a per capita benefit from Detroit valued at $.32, as shown in Table 3, column 1. In a similar manner user data have been combined with Detroit expenditures to estimate the benefits measured by cost of service enjoyed by suburban residents from the Detroit Art Museum, Zoological Park, public parks, and street facilities. A more detailed statement of the methodology employed is available from the author.

Table 2. Characteristics of Seven Metropolitan Detroit Municipalities

Municipality	County	Population[1]	Per Capita Property Values[2]	Residential Property as Percent of Total Property
Allen Park	Wayne	38,336	$2,943	79
Birmingham	Oakland	24,684	4,077	57
Dearborn	Wayne	112,571	6,438	23
Detroit	Wayne	1,538,487	3,085	38
Grosse Pointe Park	Wayne	15,030	4,103	80
Highland Park	Wayne	36,666	4,525	25
Roseville	Macomb	56,780	2,378	66

Municipality	Commercial and Industrial Property as Percent of Total Property[3]	Median Family Income[4]	Percent of Families with Income under $5,000[4]	Percent of Families with Income $15,000 and over[4]
Allen Park	10	$ 9,420	7.9	9.4
Birmingham	34	12,850	8.4	38.2
Dearborn	77	8,500	20.2	10.1
Detroit	57	6,350	35.0	4.6
Grosse Pointe Park	20	13,250	12.9	42.1
Highland Park	71	5,620	33.2	3.3
Roseville	31	7,870	17.5	5.1

Sources: [1] Population estimates for August, 1965 to February, 1966, Detroit Regional Transportation and Land Use Study.
[2] 1966 State Equalized Value which is by law 50 percent of market value. *1967 Michigan Municipal Financial Abstract.*
[3] *1967 Michigan Municipal Financial Abstract.*
[4] 1965 family income estimates from Detroit Regional Transportation and Land Use Study.

Table 3. A Summary of the Per Capita[1] Benefits (Cost of Service)
Supplied Directly to Municipalities by Detroit,[2] 1966

Municipality	Library System[3]	Art Museum[4]	Zoo[5]	Recreation and Parks[6]	Streets and Traffic Control[7]	Total
	(1)	(2)	(3)	(4)	(5)	(6)
Allen Park	$.32	$.11	$.04	$.04	$2.10	$2.61
Birmingham	.97	.11	.04	.05	1.78	2.95
Dearborn	.31	.11	.04	.07	1.99	2.52
Grosse Pointe Park	.72	.12	.04	.19	2.93	4.00
Highland Park	.53	.11	.04	.19	3.80	4.67
Roseville	.22	.06	.04	.03	2.30	2.65

[1] Per capita refers to suburban municipal population.

[2] Under assumptions of tax incidence shown on pages 27-28, footnote 35.

[3] Computed from data from Detroit Metropolitan Library Project and *City of Detroit Budget, 1965–66.*

[4] Computed from data supplied by Detroit Regional Transportation and Land Use Study, and *City of Detroit Budget, 1965–66.*

[5] Computed from data in Laurence A. Schenk, "An Analysis of Visitors to the Detroit Zoological Park," (East Lansing: Unpublished Master's Thesis, Michigan State University, 1967); and *City of Detroit Budget, 1965–66.*

[6] Computed from 1959 Huron-Clinton Metropolitan Authority Park User Survey and data supplied by City of Detroit, Parks and Recreation Department.

[7] Computed from data supplied by Detroit Regional Transportation and Land Use Study and *City of Detroit Budget, 1965–66.* This figure includes expenditures for street cleaning and repair, traffic control, and police.

suburban streets. The cost of service value of this facility which is provided to Detroit, estimated from user data and assuming tax incidence listed on pages 27–28, footnote 35, is shown in Table 4. This benefit flow, measured in terms of per capita of the suburban municipality ranges from $.04 for Birmingham to $.85 for Dearborn.

The incidence of poverty is not evenly distributed throughout the Detroit metropolitan area. The poor are heavily concentrated in the central city and certain suburbs. Due to the political fragmentation which fiscally isolates these municipalities with high poverty incidence, the costs associated with poverty are not evenly distributed throughout the metropolitan area. The poverty expenditures funded by Detroit general revenue sources in 1966 are shown in Table 5 to be over $15,000,000. Of this amount, $8,426,000 were costs borne by Detroit residents under the tax incidence assumptions described above. The poverty expenditures of the other six municipalities and the three county governments in the Detroit SMSA calculated on a similar basis, are also shown in Table 5.

A horizontal equity criterion, compatible with the cost of service measure of benefits, is that the price of a collective good should be the same for all residents of the benefit area. On this basis, the burden of supporting

Table 4. Benefits to Detroit from Six Municipal Street Systems,[1] 1966

Municipality	Total Benefits	Per Capita Benefits[2]	Per Capita Benefits[3] Financed by Municipality
	(1)	(2)	(3)
Allen Park	$ 2,713	$ .06	$.05
Birmingham	1,156	.05	.04
Dearborn	341,712	3.04	.85
Grosse Pointe Park	854	.06	.05
Highland Park	42,140	1.15	.40
Roseville	15,361	.27	.19

[1] Includes expenditures for street cleaning and repair, traffic control, and police.
[2] Per capita refers to suburban municipal population.
[3] Under assumptions listed on pages 27-28, footnote 35.
Sources: Various municipal budgets and Detroit Regional Transportation and Land Use Study.

poverty expenditures should fall with equal intensity on all residents of the metropolitan area. If the price to residents of one area is above the average, they are in effect subsidizing residents of other metropolitan jurisdictions for whom the price is less than the average. A first-approximation implementation of this equity criterion would be the allocation of the poverty costs on a per capita basis throughout the SMSA. However, even adopting this allocation does not standardize the price to all. The municipalities with relatively large poverty programs would still face a relatively higher price for the poverty programs. This results from the fact that relatively more poor families reside in these municipalities and poor families, qua recipients

Table 5. Poverty Expenditures of Municipalities and Counties, 1966

Municipality	Total Poverty Expenditures	Total Financed by Municipality or County[1]
Allen Park	$ 11,300	$ 8,600
Birmingham	6,000	4,100
Dearborn	182,100	51,000
Detroit	15,320,000	8,426,000
Grosse Pointe Park	3,100	2,500
Highland Park	149,000	52,150
Roseville	9,800	6,800
County		
Macomb	2,660,000	1,336,000
Oakland	5,170,000	2,636,700
Wayne	16,600,000	8,466,000
Total : :	$40,141,300	$21,049,850

[1] Under assumption listed on page 28, footnote 35.
Sources: The various city and county budgets.

of poverty services, are presumably not intended to be contributors to the support of these programs. To assume they are contributors, in allocating the costs of the program, penalizes the nonpoor residents of municipalities with many low income families.

To correct for this bias in measuring the extent to which intercity subsidies do exist, the costs of the poverty programs of the Detroit metropolitan area borne by Detroit residents are here allocated on a per capita basis to the *nonpoverty* population of the various municipalities.[37] The total poverty expenditures of Detroit, the six suburban municipalities, and the three counties, borne by residents in 1966 were about $21,000,000. (See Table 5.) If we disregard the poverty expenditures of the other municipalities in the Detroit SMSA, we can say that total poverty expenditures in the SMSA were $7.00 per capita for the nonpoverty population. The per capita contribution of Detroit's nonpoverty population was $10.69. Since Detroit is the only municipality whose contribution is larger than $7.00 per capita, the difference between $7.00 and the per capita contribution to poverty costs of each municipality is a measure of the benefit enjoyed by that municipality from Detroit. The per capita contributions to poverty expenditures of the six municipalities together with their subsidy from Detroit, measured on this basis, are shown in Table 6.

Four subsidies to the suburbs indirectly financed by Detroit are shown in Table 7. The subsidy through the Detroit Department of Water Services (DWS) is due to less than full-cost pricing procedures.[38] The other three

---

37. The "poverty population" for the Detroit metropolitan area is assumed to be all those living in families with less than $5,000 family income.

38. The Detroit Department of Water Services (DWS) is the only major supplier of water in the metropolitan area, with the exception of Highland Park. Its total budget in 1966 was $25,514,520 (City of Detroit, *1965–66 Budget*), financed almost entirely by sale of water. DWS retails water to residents of Detroit as well as being a wholesale supplier to suburban communities. The suburban communities in turn, retail water to their own residents with a markup from the wholesale price. The profits on this transaction are typically added to the municipalities' general funds. If water is evaluated by effective demand, the simple fact that suburbs realize a profit on their water sales indicates DWS's wholesale price is less than its value to suburban residents and thus constitutes a welfare gain for them from the Detroit public sector.

A recent examination of DWS pricing practices concluded that the water sold by DWS to suburban communities is underpriced. (Benjamin C. Stanczyk, "A Study of the Department of Water Supply," (Unpublished Paper, Ann Arbor, Michigan, 1969). In his analysis Stanczyk relies on data in an unpublished report of Black and Veatch on water rates.) According to this study, the revenue derived from sale of water to the suburbs does not equal the full cost of supplying the water. It is estimated that the extent of such underpricing is 4.3 per cent. Since revenue from total DWS sales just covers full cost, Detroit water users are subsidizing suburban users. If 4.3 per cent is accepted as the cost of service measure of the underpricing then the per capital subsidy through the DWS to each of the six municipalities ranges from $.19 per capita for Roseville residents, to $.49 per capita for Dearborn residents, as shown in Table 7, column 1.

Table 6. Resident Tax Contributions to Poverty Expenditures and
Benefits from Detroit, Nonpoverty Per Capita,[1] 1966

Municipality	Per Capita Tax Contributions of Nonpoverty Population	Nonpoverty Per Capita Benefits Financed by Detroit[2]
	(1)	(2)
Allen Park	$2.86	$4.14
Birmingham	1.28	4.72
Dearborn	2.97	4.03
Grosse Pointe Park	5.37	1.63
Highland Park	6.41	.59
Roseville	.53	6.47

[1] "Per Capita" in this Table means "nonpoverty" per capita and so is not comparable with "per capita" figures in other tables.

[2] Under assumptions listed on page 27, footnote 35.

Sources: See Table 3 and Detroit Regional Transportation and Land Use Study.

Table 7. A Summary of Certain Net Per Capita Benefits[1] (Cost of Service) Supplied Indirectly to Municipalities by Detroit, 1966

Municipality	Department of Water Services[2]	Tax-Exempt Hospital Facilities[3]	Tax-Exempt University Property[4]	Tax-Exempt Limited Access Urban Highways[5]	Total
	(1)	(2)	(3)	(4)	(5)
Allen Park	$.26	$ (.65)	$.03	$ .32	$(.04)
Birmingham	.21	.16	.10	.92	1.39
Dearborn	.49	(.03)	.03	.71	1.20
Grosse Pointe Park	.26	.53	.03	1.51	2.33
Highland Park	—	(2.45)	.03	2.01	(.41)
Roseville	.19	.35	.08	1.01	1.63

[1] Per capita refers to suburban municipal population.

[2] Computed from DWS Sales data. Highland Park has its own water source.

[3] Computed from hospital user data and property values supplied by Hospital Association of Detroit. Figures in parentheses indicate a subsidy to Detroit.

[4] Computed from Wayne State University attendance data and City of Detroit property values.

[5] Use of freeways by nonresidents is assumed to be the same as nonresident use of all city streets. (See Tables 3 and 4.) Total value of exemption is assumed to equal: (acres occupied by limited access highways) (State Equalized Value of average acre in each municipality) (mileage rate in each municipality).

subsidies are provided through tax exemption of properties used by non-residents.[39]

The major intrametropolitan public sector flows in the Detroit SMSA estimated on a cost of service basis, are summarized in Table 8, column 1. However, to be expressed in terms of a welfare measure, these costs of service benefits must be adjusted by the willingness to pay index, shown in Table 1. The results of this translation are shown in Table 8, column 2. The total direct, indirect, and poverty benefits, measured in terms of willingness to pay, and financed by Detroit in favor of the other six municipalities range from $3.96 per capita for Highland Park to $18.22 per capita for Birmingham.

Table 8. Summary of Public Sector Benefit Flows Between Detroit and Six Municipalities, Per Capita, 1966

From Detroit to:	Benefits Measured by Cost of Service[1]	Benefits Adjusted for Willingness to Pay[2]
	(1)	(2)
Allen Park	$ 6.66	$ 9.86
Birmingham	9.02	18.22
Dearborn	6.90	9.25
Grosse Pointe Park	7.91	16.53
Highland Park	4.45	3.96
Roseville	10.56	13.09

[1] Tables 3, 4, 6, and 7. The poverty figures from Table 6 have been adjusted to a per capita basis comparable with the other data.

[2] Column 1 adjusted by multipliers in Table 1.

39. The exemption of certain classes of property from the property tax provides an indirect subsidy to its users. The principal beneficiaries of such a subsidy in the Detroit metropolitan area are those who use hospitals, colleges and universities, and limited access urban highways. Although all streets in the metropolitan area can be construed as a source of such a subsidy, the construction of limited access highways in recent years involves the current elimination of previously taxable property from the tax base. Thus to the extent users of such highways are nonresidents they enjoy an indirect tax subsidy.

Allen Park, Dearborn, Detroit, and Highland Park all have hospitals which serve citizens of the metropolitan area and beyond. From hospital user surveys and the estimated value of hospital property, a cost of service value of the net benefit flow from Detroit to the various municipalities is estimated and shown in Table 7, column 2. Allen Park, Dearborn, and Highland Park provide a net subsidy to Detroit ranging from $.03 per capita from Dearborn to $2.45 per capita from Highland Park. Although not shown in Table 7, these three suburbs also minimally subsidize the other three municipalities.

There are several colleges and universities in the Detroit metropolitan area. The largest is Wayne State University in Detroit. If it is assumed that the value of the tax exempt University property is equal to other property in Detroit with the same land area, then this tax exemption cost Detroit $245,000 in 1966. If this subsidy is allocated to students enrolled in Wayne State University on the basis of their home residence, the per capita subsidy to the six municipalities ranges from $.03 to $.10 as seen in Table 7, column 3.

The *net* value in 1966 of the subsidy to the six municipalities from Detroit through the exclusion of property from the tax rolls for limited-access urban highways ranged from $.32 per capita to $2.01, if allowance is made for Detroiters' use of suburban facilities.

V. Detroit SMSA Revenue Flows

The welfare gains for the six municipalities from the benefit flows estimated in the last section are considerable. However, two principal mechanisms exist through which the municipalities conceivably compensate Detroit for these benefit flows: (1) state revenue sharing with the municipalities[40] and (2) the Detroit tax on income earned by nonresidents.

In Michigan in 1966 there were three principal programs under which funds were distributed to municipalities from state revenue sources.[41] (1) One-eighth of total state sales tax collections are distributed to cities, villages and townships by a per capita formula based on the latest decennial census. (2) $9.5 million of the revenue derived under the state Intangibles Tax Act is distributed to cities, villages, and townships in the same manner as the sales tax remittance. (3) In 1966, 18 percent of the revenue derived from the state tax on gasoline and diesel fuel and the motor vehicle license tax was distributed to cities and villages according to a complex formula.

The estimated per capita contributions of the six municipalities to Detroit in 1966 through these state revenue sharing mechanisms are shown in Table 9. These estimates allow for the exporting of tax liability both directly to non Michigan taxpayers and to the federal level through itemized deductions for the federal corporate and individual income taxes. Total per capita contributions to Detroit through state revenue sharing ranges from nothing from Highland Park (which is itself a beneficiary of such grants) to $1.93 from Grosse Pointe Park.

The net contributions of residents of the six municipalities to Detroit through the Detroit tax levied on income earned in Detroit by nonresidents is seen in Table 10.[42] The per capita contribution of suburban municipalities

---

40. The distributional pattern of state-financed public services is not considered here on the basis that we are attempting to estimate the welfare effects of public sector flows between jurisdictions in a metropolitan area and that the provision of services through the state government is a separate issue. Although it is to a certain extent arbitrary, the various mechanisms of state revenue sharing have been included in the analysis on the grounds they are properly considered offsets to locally generated externalities.

It is, of course, likely that some welfare distribution in the metropolitan area is had through the state provision of public services, state aid to elementary education, and federally financed services.

For an attempt to deal with the distributional impact of federal expenditures at the state level, see National Industrial Conference Board, *The Federal Budget* (New York, 1969) pp. 38–43; and U.S. Congress, House Committee on Government Operations, *Federal Revenue and Expenditure Estimates for States and Regions, Fiscal Years, 1965–67*, (Washington: U.S. Government Printing Office, 1968), 44 pp.

41. In 1967 a state income tax was adopted and 17 percent of the net revenue from the personal income tax is allocated one half to counties and one half to cities, villages, and townships on a per capita basis.

42. The Michigan Uniform City Income Tax Statute prescribes the following provisions for all city income taxes in Michigan: the taxable base (in general, federal adjusted gross income, but with no nonbusiness deductions allowed); the exemptions ($600 personal exemptions); and the rates (2 percent on residents of Detroit, 1 percent on residents in all other cities, and $\frac{1}{2}$ percent on all nonresidents).

Table 9. Contributions of Six Municipalities to Detroit through Sales Tax, Intangibles Tax, and Motor Fuel and Vehicle Registration Tax Payments, Per Capita, 1966

Municipality	Sales Tax[1]	Intangibles Tax[2]	Motor Fuel and Vehicle Registration Tax[3]	Total
	(1)	(2)	(3)	(4)
Allen Park	$ .01	$.09	$.81	$ .91
Birmingham	.73	.28	.77	1.73
Dearborn	.18	.08	.00	.26
Grosse Pointe Park	1.37	.28	.28	1.93
Highland Park	.00	.00	.00	.00
Roseville	.63	.14	.65	1.42

[1] These figures are one-eighth of estimated per capita sales tax payments based on assumptions regarding the relation between family income and purchase of taxable goods and services. They have been adjusted to allow for deductibility of the sales tax for those who itemize on their federal income tax returns and an estimated payment of 5 percent of sales tax by nonresidents of Michigan.

It has been assumed that the following percentages of sales tax payments are exported through the federal offset:

Allen Park	10 percent
Birmingham	15
Dearborn	10
Detroit	5
Grosse Pointe Park	15
Highland Park	5
Roseville	10
Local Units Outside the Detroit SMSA	5
Michigan	7

[2] These figures are calculated by allocating $9.5 million of the intangibles tax revenue to the various jurisdictions, making certain assumptions regarding the holding of taxable wealth by residents of the various communities. The figures have been adjusted to allow for deductibility of the intangibles tax liability by those individuals and institutions that itemize on the federal income tax returns. Nearly sixty percent of intangibles tax payments in fiscal 1967 were by institutions. It has been assumed that the following percentages of intangibles tax payment is exported through the federal offset:

Allen Park	40 percent
Birmingham	45
Dearborn	40
Detroit	35
Grosse Pointe Park	45
Highland Park	35
Roseville	40
Local Units Outside the Detroit SMSA	35
Michigan	35

[3] These figures are 18 percent of the total gasoline and diesel fuel taxes, and the vehicle license tax. They have been adjusted (1) to allow for deductibility of the fuel tax by those who itemize on their federal income tax returns: (It is assumed that the same federal offset applies here as for sales tax payments.) (2) to allow for the payment of an estimated 25 percent of the fuel tax by nonresidents. Estimates of fuel consumption and vehicle tax payments for the various jurisdictions are based on data supplied by the Detroit Regional Transportation and Land Use Study concerning the number of daily trips by household and the number of cars per family.

Sources: Computed from data supplied by Michigan Department of State Highways; Michigan Department of Treasury; Detroit Regional Transportation and Land Use Study; and County Treasurers of Macomb, Oakland, and Wayne Counties.

Table 10. Net Contributions of Municipalities to Detroit
through Local Income Tax, 1966

	Total	Per Capita[1]
Allen Park	$ 93,420	$2.43
Birmingham	95,412	3.86
Dearborn	255,852	2.27
Grosse Pointe Park	117,578	7.82
Highland Park	81,950	2.23
Roseville	108,040	1.90

[1] Per capita suburban municipality population.

Source: Estimated from income and journey-to-work data
supplied by the Detroit Regional Transportation and Land Use Study.
Allowance has been made for the deductibility of local income
tax liability for those who itemize for federal income tax purposes.
The value of the federal offset assumed here is the same as for the
sales tax shown in Table 9, footnote 1.

ranges from $2.27 for Dearborn to $7.82 for Grosse Pointe Park. The
relatively large contribution of Grosse Pointe Park is due to the fact that
not only is it a high income community but also a significant percentage of
its residents earn income in Detroit.

In Table 11 are shown summaries of the Detroit SMSA net public
sector benefit flows measured by willingness to pay (column 1) as well as
revenue flows (column 2). The difference between these two for each municipality is shown in column 3. In all instances the revenue flows to Detroit
fail to compensate fully for the public sector benefits flowing from Detroit
to the municipalities. Consequently, all the municipalities enjoy a welfare

Table 11. Summary of Public Sector Benefit and Revenue Flows Between
Detroit and Six Municipalities, Per Capita, 1966

Between Detroit and:	Benefits[1]	less	Revenue[2]	equals	Net Subsidy from Detroit
	(1)		(2)		(3)
Allen Park	$ 9.86		$3.34		$ 6.52
Birmingham	18.22		5.64		12.58
Dearborn	9.25		2.53		6.72
Grosse Pointe Park	16.53		9.75		6.78
Highland Park	3.96		2.23		1.73
Roseville	13.09		3.32		9.77

[1] Table 8, column 2.
[2] Tables 9 and 10.

gain from Detroit through the public sector, ranging from $1.73 per capita for Highland Park to $12.58 per capita for Birmingham.[43]

VI. Final Remark

The analysis of this article indicates that six suburban communities in the Detroit SMSA enjoy a considerable welfare gain through the public sector from Detroit. For a family of four this welfare gain is estimated to range from nearly $7.00 to over $50.00 a year. These figures are averages for the suburban communities. For some families there may well be no gain; for others, with more frequent contact with Detroit, the welfare gain is undoubtedly much larger. Thus the one obvious conclusion that emerges from this analysis is that the tax contribution of suburban residents to the central city can be markedly increased without offsetting the welfare gain they are currently enjoying from the central city public sector.

---

2   Earl F. Mellor: A Case Study:
Costs and Benefits of Public Goods
and Expenditures for a Ghetto

Daniel P. Moynihan, President Nixon's urban affairs advisor . . . suggested that we start thinking in terms of "sub-city governments." . . . "It must be real government," he said, "not pretend government." . . . The sub-cities would have taxing power, Moynihan said. When newsmen pointed out there was not much to tax in most ghettos, he suggested they could receive funds on a transfer basis from other levels of government.
Washington *Post*, June 1, 1969

A topic of current concern is whether a low-income neighborhood is capable of providing the public services it desires if it were severed from the larger community and from the nation as a whole – that is, is it self-sufficient with regard to its most immediate needs, such as providing for neighborhood safety, education, and welfare? The assertion that the low-income neighborhood could be self-sufficient has been made by many who advocate de-

---

43. The case of Grosse Pointe Park is peculiar. It receives services from Detroit which it values at $16.53 and pays Detroit $9.75. However, these services cost Detroit only $7.91. Thus both Grosse Pointe Park and Detroit currently enjoy a welfare gain from their public sector relationships. Thus caution must be observed in using the figures in Table 2, column 3 as an index of "exploitation".

Presented at the Tenth Institute for Policy Studies, Washington, D.C., Reprinted by permission of the author. Mr. Mellor is from the University of Maryland.

centralized government, claiming that the poor neighborhood is subsidizing the city and the rest of the country. Other decentralists charge that the other neighborhoods and the nation pour more resources into poverty areas than is coming out in tax revenues (for example, residents of a middle-income area seeking to become independent of Gary, Indiana), placing what is considered an unfair burden on more affluent areas. Centralists argue both ways, citing moral and social goals to justify a net inflow or citing economies of scale to justify a net outflow. Then there are the advocates of laissez-faire, who believe that the free market will provide the goods and services people desire, and anarchists, who oppose government functions on a variety of grounds, usually individual freedom.

This paper does not prove or disprove any of these assertions, because either a net inflow or a net outflow can be "proven," depending on what items are considered necessary and/or desired public functions and on the assumptions made with regard to the incidence of various tax burdens. Still another consideration is what type of tax, income, political, and legal structure would arise in the event of a hypothetical political or functional decentralization. Also, some tax outflows would be embodied in any goods and services purchased from areas outside the separated territory unless one would go so far as to disavow imports, and such a scheme would negate the desirability of specialization and large-scale economies in the private sector as well. The issue will be no more resolved at the conclusion of this study; however, attempts will be made to raise concrete and speculative questions regarding the costs and benefits of public services.

Some attempts have been made to estimate costs and benefits within a particular income range, but a given neighborhood is subject to a wide dispersion of incomes, regardless of its median income level, which indicates an area of poverty or affluence. This dispersion is more likely in the core of a central city than in a suburban or rural location of equal area. The neighborhood chosen for this study is the Shaw-Cardozo area of Washington, D.C., for the fiscal year 1967. The area, which had an estimated population of 83,700 in 1966, contains 78,900 nonwhite residents and has an estimated median annual family income of $5,600.[1] Part of the area constitutes a large portion of the Washington Model Cities program, now in the planning stage. Population and income characteristics are extrapolated from 1960 census data, supplemented by data from the city's Demographic Analysis Unit.[2]

---

1. Beginning at the southeast corner and proceeding clockwise, the boundaries of the area are as follows: Massachusetts Avenue, Eleventh Street, S Street, Sixteenth Street, Harvard Street, Michigan Avenue, First Street, Bryant Street, Second Street, Florida Avenue, and North Capitol Street, all northwest Washington (Census tracts 34, 35, 36, 37, 43, 44, 46, 47, 48, and 49).

2. The total population, estimated by the Demographic Analysis Unit, is 83,700, which is 31 percent above the official 1960 census. This figure is 9.8 percent of the total city population. Based on the 31 percent increase and 1960 census data are the following characteristics: 16,640 heads of primary families, 10,220 primary individuals, 2.9 persons per family household, 24,500 persons under eighteen (10.2 percent of the city's under eighteen population), 6,810 persons 65 or older (7.6 percent of the city's elderly population), 13,760 persons enrolled in public schools (9.6 percent of the city's public school enrollment), and 5,240 persons living in group quarters, mainly Howard University students.

Estimation of Income and Tax Payments

In order to estimate tax outflows to the public sector, it is necessary to obtain income information. Census data contain income groupings for 1959. Assuming that incomes in the Shaw-Cardozo area rose by the same proportion as for the city as a whole (40 percent), that income distribution remained the same, and that income changes did not result in population shifts, the estimated family income distribution is as follows:[3]

Median 1959 Income	Midpoint 1959	Midpoint January 1967	Estimated No. of Families	Total Personal Income (in million $)
Below $1,000	$ 750	$ 1,050	1,350	1.42
$ 1,000 – 1,999	1,500	2,100	1,950	4.10
2,000 – 2,999	2,500	3,500	2,860	10.01
3,000 – 3,999	3,500	4,900	2,790	13.67
4,000 – 4,999	4,500	6,300	2,360	14.87
5,000 – 5,999	5,500	7,700	1,650	12.71
6,000 – 6,999	6,500	9,100	1,320	12.01
7,000 – 7,999	7,500	10,500	850	8.93
8,000 – 8,999	8,500	11,900	690	8.21
9,000 – 9,999	9,500	13,300	420	5.59
10,000 – 14,999	12,500	17,500	860	14.88
15,000 – 24,999	20,000	28,000	170	4.76
More than 25,000	27,500	38,500	13	0.50

Data for primary individuals are not given, but judging by the degree to which median income for families and individuals combined is lower than for families alone in each census tract, the following rough estimates may be appropriate:

Midpoint January 1967	Estimated No. of Individuals	Total Personal Income (in million $)
$ 750	1,020	0.77
1,500	2,040	3.06
2,500	2,040	5.10
3,500	2,040	7.14
4,500	1,530	6.89
5,500	760	4.18
6,500	500	3.25
7,500	270	2.03

3. Total personal income for the area is estimated at $144,080,000 or 4·5 percent of the total personal income of city residents. This figure does not include income of nonresidents earned in the area.

These figures relate to personal income only. In order to arrive at a basic taxable income, we must consider transfer payments to families and individuals as well as contributions for social insurance made by the employee.

Transfer Payments

Veterans' benefits are attributed to this area on the basis that it contains 15.6 percent of the city's families in poverty, although also unrelated individuals receive payments. Payments are for retirement, compensation for partial and total disability, to survivors, and other benefits. Cash payments to city residents are estimated at $23.5 million, or $3.43 million for the area. See Table 1 for distribution of benefits among families and individuals in the various income classes. The percent of poor families seemed a justifiable criterion of imputing payments to the area since surviving families and

Table 1. Personal Income, Cash Transfer Payments, Contributions for Social Insurance, and Income Tax Payments: Taxable Income and Disposable Income, Shaw-Cardozo Area of Washington, D.C. Fiscal Year 1967

Midpoint 1959 P.I.	Mid-1966–67 P.I.	Number of Households	Total P.I. (in million $)	Veterans' Benefits (in million $)	OASDHI Benefits (in million $)	Unemployment Benefits (in million $)	Welfare Benefits (in million $)
Families							
$ 750	$ 1,050	1,350	1.42	0.35	0.20	0.05	1.00
1,500	2,100	1,950	4.10	0.52	0.80	0.10	1.50
2,500	3,500	2,860	10.01	0.78	1.00	0.20	1.50
3,500	4,900	2,790	13.67	0.75	1.00	0.20	1.30
4,500	6,300	2,360	14.87	—	0.20	0.20	—
5,500	7,700	1,650	12.71	—	—	0.10	—
6,500	9,100	1,320	12.01	—	—	—	—
7,500	10,500	850	8.93	—	—	—	—
8,500	11,900	690	8.21	—	—	—	—
9,500	13,300	420	5.59	—	—	—	—
12,500	17,500	860	14.88	—	—	—	—
20,000	28,000	170	4.76	—	—	—	—
27,500	38,500	13	0.50	—	—	—	—
Primary Individual							
	750	1,020	0.77	0.20	0.30	0.05	—
	1,500	2,040	3.06	0.40	0.60	0.10	—
	2,500	2,040	5.10	0.40	0.60	0.10	—
	3,500	2,040	7.14	—	—	0.10	—
	4,500	1,530	6.89	—	—	0.10	—
	5,500	760	4.18	—	—	0.03	—
	6,500	500	3.25	—	—	—	—
	7,500	270	2.03	—	—	—	—
Total			144.08	3.40	4.70	1.33	5.30

Table 1 continued on p. 42

Table 1—*continued*

P.I. Less Transfers (in million $)	Earned Y Subject to OASDHI (in million $)	OASDHI Base (10)/.957 (in million $)	Earned Y not subject to OASDHI (in million $)	Total Taxable Income (in million $)	Tax Y/ House-hold	Federal Tax Exemptions	Federal Tax Deductions
			Families				
0.0	0	—	—	—	—	1,800	—
1.18	1.18	—	—	1.23	$ 630	1,800	60
6.53	6.53	6.82	—	6.82	2,380	1,860	240
10.42	10.42	10.89	—	10.89	3,900	1,860	390
14.47	14.16	14.80	0.31	15.11	6,400	1,860	640
12.61	9.90	10.34	2.71	13.05	7,910	1,860	790
12.01	7.92	8.28	4.09	12.37	9,370	1,860	940
8.93	5.10	5.33	3.83	9.16	10,780	1,860	1,080
8.21	4.14	4.33	4.07	8.40	12,170	1,860	1,220
5.59	2.52	2.63	3.07	5.70	13,570	1,860	1,360
4.88	5.16	5.39	9.72	15.11	17,570	1,860	1,760
4.76	1.02	1.07	3.74	4.81	28,290	1,860	2,830
0.50	0.08	0.08	0.42	0.50	38,460	1,860	3,850
			Primary Individual				
0.22	0.22	0.23	—	0.23	230	660	20
1.96	1.96	2.05	—	2.05	1,000	660	100
4.00	4.00	4.18	—	4.18	2,050	660	210
7.04	7.04	7.36	—	7.36	3,610	660	360
6.79	6.79	7.10	—	7.10	4,640	660	460
4.15	4.15	4.34	—	4.34	5,710	660	570
3.25	3.00	3.13	0.25	3.38	6,760	660	680
2.03	1.62	1.69	0.41	2.10	7,780	660	780
129.53	96.91	101.27	32.62	133.89			

Federal Tax Base	Federal Tax/ Household	Federal Tax × Number of Households (in million $)	D.C. Tax Exemptions	D.C. Tax Deductions	D.C. Tax Base	D.C. Tax/ Household	D.C. Tax × Number of Households (in million $)
			Families				
—	—	—	2,600	—	—	—	—
—	—	—	2,600	60	—	—	—
280	40	0.11	2,600	240	—	—	—
1,650	240	0.67	2,600	390	910	30	0.08
3,900	600	1.42	2,600	640	3,160	90	0.21
5,260	860	1.42	2,600	790	4,520	140	0.23
6,570	1,110	1.47	2,600	940	5,830	200	0.26
7,840	1,350	1.15	2,600	1,080	7,100	270	0.23
9,090	1,820	1.26	2,600	1,220	8,350	330	0.23
10,350	1,900	0.80	2,600	1,360	9,610	390	0.16
13,950	2,750	2.37	2,600	1,760	13,210	600	0.52
23,600	5,330	0.91	2,600	2,830	22,860	1,180	0.20
32,750	8,980	0.12	2,600	3,850	32,010	1,730	0.02
			Primary Individual				
—	—	—	1,100	20	—	—	—
240	30	0.06	1,100	100	—	—	—
1,180	170	0.35	1,100	210	740	20	0.04
2,590	380	0.78	1,100	360	2,150	51	0.10
3,520	540	0.83	1,100	460	3,080	80	0.12
4,480	710	0.54	1,100	570	4,040	120	0.09
5,420	890	0.45	1,100	680	4,980	160	0.08
6,340	1,060	0.29	1,100	780	5,900	210	0.06
		14.95					2.65

Disposable personal income = 126.48

persons receiving compensations and pensions would tend to be associated with poverty. If the allocation should be by some other (lower) percentage (such as population), taxable income would be higher and would yield greater tax payments than those estimated here.

Public welfare is also attributed to the area by the poverty allocator of 15.6 percent of the city's cash payments made by the public welfare department. Cash payments are approximately 80 percent of the total welfare budget. A small portion of the payments are for old age assistance and aid to the blind, but the poverty allocator is probably the best indication of payments to the area—a total of $5.23 million.

Unemployment compensation is attributed according to the fact that the area had 11.0 percent of the city's unemployed in 1960 and probably had the same percentage in 1966–67, unless the area had become worse off relative to other parts of the city as far as unemployment is concerned. Although one would expect that in this area the duration of benefits would be greater than the city average, this fact probably would be counterbalanced by the scheduling of benefits according to income earned before becoming unemployed. The estimated benefits for the Shaw-Cardozo area are $1.33 million for the fiscal year 1967. OASDHI payments made by the Social Security Administration for old age, survivors, and disability were $62.08 million for the entire city. Allocating benefits according to the percentage of the city's elderly population residing in the area in 1960 results in cash benefits of $4.72 million. The fact that benefits are based on previously earned income should compensate for the fact that one would expect a greater percentage of the elderly in this area to be beneath any cutoff income level to qualify for these Social Security benefits.

Contributions for Social Insurance

Once cash transfers are subtracted from personal income, we arrive at a transitional figure at each income level (see table 1), which is not yet the tax base because the resulting number is gross taxable income less the employee's contribution for social insurance. Although the first $6,600 of income is subject to the OASDHI tax, the base is assumed to stop at $6,000 in order to allow for those who earn higher incomes and who may not be subject to social insurance contribution. The tax rate for the employee and for the employer is 4.3 percent (4.2 percent during the second half of 1966, 4.4 percent during the first half of 1967). The estimated tax paid by employees was $4.35 million during the year. (The employer contributes an estimated $5.37 million, which includes an average 1.0 percent District of Columbia unemployment tax.)

Following these adjustments the gross taxable income is $133.89 million. This figure represents possibly an understatement to the extent of allocating transfers at each income level to the income class rather than to specific earning units (that is, income classes shown in table 1 appear to pay no taxes but only some of these families may be living entirely off transfer payments, whereas others may be living entirely off earned income and paying taxes), in addition to whatever income is not reported.

By allowing as exemptions $1,850 for each family unit (each nonprimary individual household has an average of 2.9 members, plus additional exemptions for elderly population) and $650 for each primary individual for the federal income tax, and $2,600 per family unit and $1,100 per primary individual for the District of Columbia income tax, plus 10 percent of gross income after exemptions for deductions (assuming no large loopholes, which would not be generally available to the levels of income involved here), a true net base for computing income taxes for each income group is reached. Using the tax schedules for 1967 (same as 1966), it is estimated that the federal income tax burden is $14.95 million, and the District income tax burden is $2.65 million (see table 1).

It is to be assumed that the full burden of both employees' and employers' contributions for social insurance represents taxes leaving the neighborhood. The latter's share could have various estimates, assuming part of the tax is shifted onto the employer himself and part onto the consumer of the employer's products. Both shares, without such shifting, would total $9.72 million. As already mentioned, consideration has been given to income not subject to this tax. Instances of underreporting taxable income, of course, are not considered here, but to the extent that such unreported income is consumed, additional taxes would leave the area indirectly.

Federal and city income taxes leave a disposable personal income equal to $126.48 million. It would be reasonable to estimate that 95 percent of disposable income is consumed, or $120.15 million. If 50 percent of consumer expenditures are for items subject to the 3 percent District of Columbia sales tax and 25 percent of expenditures for items subject to the 1 percent sales tax rate, the burden of the sales tax would be $2.10 million. The other 25 percent of consumer expenditures are assumed to be tax exempt – items such as a large part of gross rent, medical and personal services, as well as any purchases of illegal goods and services.

Property taxes for the area amounted to $2.95 million according to District tax rolls for the fiscal year 1967. About two-thirds of property in the area (in terms of taxable assessed valuation) is residential, of which one-third is estimated to be on owner-occupied property. Estimated tax collections on rented property – property for which residents pay an estimated $16 million in rent (net rent, which excludes utilities and any furnishings) – is just under $1.5 million. Property tax as a proportion of rent appears low; for most metropolitan areas this tax is one-fourth of net rent. Unless other costs are relatively high, the rental business in this area is quite lucrative.[4]

The area's burden of the corporate and proprietor's income taxes and

---

4. The official tax rate during the fiscal year 1967 was $2.70 per $100.00 assessed valuation, which would be approximately $1.30 per $100.00 market value, according to official financial reports.

various nonincome taxes in the production process of consumer goods before they arrive in the district depends on estimates of embodied taxes and the degree of shifting the burden on the consumer. If these taxes for all stages of production were 10 percent of sale price and the forward shifting were two-thirds, the burden on the area would be $7.71 million. Studies on shifting cite burdens from one-third (or $3.85 million for the area) to 100 percent. A 50 percent shifting forward would amount to $5.78 million.

Labor department consumer studies indicate that approximately 3 percent of income is spent on alcohol and tobacco products subject to federal and District excise taxes. We would need specific data on consumption of the various types of these products to arrive at a precise tax base, but if one-half the purchase price represents these excises, there is an additional outflow of $1.73 million. The tax for hard liquor is well above 50 percent, whereas for beer and wine it would be well below.

If one-half the households have telephones, with an annual charge of $72, the 10 percent federal telephone excise would total $93,000. If additional consideration is given for extensions and toll calls producing an average yearly charge of $84, and 70 percent of households with phone service, the yield would be $152,000.

If automobile ownership for the area increased proportionately to population, approximately 8,000 cars would be owned by residents, each paying a registration fee of $22.50 per year for a total of $180,000. Operator's licenses for an estimated one-half of the population between the ages of eighteen and sixty-four would add another $26,000. If each auto burned five gallons of gasoline per week, the $.04 a gallon of federal tax and the $.07 of District tax adds another $2.2 million. If 2,000 of these autos were newly purchased during the year, bearing a 7 percent federal excise tax on manufacturer's sales, the automobile tax bite is increased by $250,000 (assuming a federal excise tax of $126 per car).[5] Tax on automobile tires would add another $8 per car, or $16,000 for the area. Generally the consumer bears the full burden of these automobile excise taxes, just as he does with the telephone tax.

Estimation of Benefits

Estimates of taxable income and tax burdens could easily vary by as much as 10 percent in either direction, but the subject of calculating benefits is even hazier, even in the case of cash benefits, as one could discern from the discussion in the previous section. There are at least two reasons for this situation: (1) the reluctance of public officials to publish taxation or disbursement figures by census tract, perhaps to convince the public of the

---

5. Assumes car value leaving manufacturer is $1,800.

confidentiality of the census itself, and (2) the fact that by definition, the value of "public" goods cannot be allocated to specific areas or individuals. Thus the allocations of benefits to follow are only estimates – wide-ranging estimates – none of which is necessarily a sound measure.

If the provision of these various government goods and services were within the arena of a free, competitive market, perhaps the construction of demand and supply curves (a task in itself) would provide us with the best possible estimates, but these benefits are "public" goods, and thus it is unlikely that a free competitive market situation could ever exist for them. There is also that fact of life outside the public sector: there is neither a free nor a purely competitive market for any good or service in the gross national product.

One item which will not be considered is national defense, the largest single item provided by a government in the U.S. The defense budget is more than twice the amount allocated for any specific item in the budget of any country in the world. How could this be allocated? Should we allocate the benefits of defense to the Shaw-Cardozo area on the basis of its population? Its income? Its wealth? Its share of property income for the nation? The degree of anti-Communist sentiment in the area? Or by the value the residents would be willing to pay for national defense? Maybe even zero, since by many social indicators as health, education, employment (and for much of the population, income, as well as domestic tranquility), this neighborhood is worse off than the population of many of those nations against which we are defending. Perhaps a negative number since area residents are summoned forth to give time and life to the national military. Other specific items which won't be considered are such expenditures as the space program, foreign aid, State Department activities, the CIA, and the FBI. Agricultural subsidies, to the extent that government purchases farm surplus to support prices, are of negative benefit to residents each time they pay the higher price at the corner grocery stores or the few supermarkets in this part of the city. Likewise the Post Office Department deficit subsidized by the taxpayer does not help area residents. Their small amount of business ownership hardly allows them to benefit from third-class mailing privileges, which cause the postal deficit; these people paid six cents per ounce to send their letters, and probably need to pay six cents per day to discard the third-class advertisements they receive, only to add to the costs of the sanitation department. First-class mail operates at a profit for the post office.

Many federal government expenditures – chiefly health, education, welfare, various antipoverty programs – and unemployment disbursements do benefit the area and can roughly be estimated because they are received by individuals as well as by the District of Columbia government as grants-in-aid.[6] Expenditures by the Veterans' Administration do benefit area residents, but these are in return for military service rendered to the government

---

6. See the Washington *Post*, May 29, 1969, front page.

at below market wages. If these were to be included as direct benefits, the other side of the coin would have to be included with the tax outflow estimates.

Basically the analyses to follow are of those aspects of public activity most people would consider of immediate day-to-day interest, such as police and fire protection, education, health, welfare, street maintenance, garbage collection, and some recreation facilities. Water and sewer services are not enumerated because they are paid for by a user charge. Items stated involving the District of Columbia budget include not only current expenditures but also capital expenditures and federal grants-in-aid. (See table 2.)

Education

Public Schools   This is probably the simplest item to handle. The most logical allocation of benefits is according to the area's percentage of total public school children in the city. In 1960 the Shaw-Cardozo area contained 9.6 percent of the District's public school children, or $12.66 million of total school expenditures. Other estimates could be made if there is evidence that expenditures per student vary from neighborhood to neighborhood. Charges of such variations have been made (and will continue to be made), depending on such items as racial and income differences within the city. Variations in educational quality could also alter the estimate, but for our purposes the assumption of equality will be made.

Libraries   Allocating by population, the area's benefit from the library system would be $502,000, by school children, $492,000. Use of facilities depends on proximity as well as on educational levels. The main library lies on the southern boundary line for the area; the level of education is low in this area relative to the city as a whole; and residents of suburban areas use the library as well. Probably $400,000 is a reasonable estimate.

Public Safety

Second to a school budget of more than $130 million is a public safety budget of $90 million for the fiscal year 1967. Like other municipal functions, data are nonexistent with regard to expenditures in a particular neighborhood. Public safety includes the police and fire departments, the Corporation Counsel, civil defense, the entire court system, the Department of Corrections, the Department of Licenses and Inspections, and the District of Columbia National Guard.

Police Protection   Expenditures for the police department were almost $44 million. If an allocation is made by the neighborhood's share of .

the District's estimated 854,000 residents, the benefit to Shaw-Cardozo would be about $4.27 million. If allocated by a share of the District's day-time and nighttime population (including suburban workers, tourists, traveling businessmen) the figure would be roughly $3.52 million. On the basis of the area's share of the city's total personal income, the allocation would be $2.02 million. If residents hold 2 percent of total city wealth, a wealth allocation for police protection would result in a figure of $900,000. Wealth or income might be considered reasonable proxies for stealable and damageable goods. If income-earning property owned by residents were used for an estimator, the police allocation would be even lower. These bases for computing the allocation do not include the value of human life and safety, but people generally fall victim to crime for what they have, not what they are.

The value assigned to police protection is always a sensitive matter, and in a given neighborhood, whether it is in a central-city slum or an affluent suburban subdivision, some people will value it highly and others will cite low or zero figures. If police are allocated in accordance with crime rates, the area may warrant an estimate of $10 million; others would say that it is a low crime rate, not a high one, that measures the value of police protection. Others might argue that policing would be less necessary if the residents of a neighborhood were given the freedom to make and enforce their own laws as long as they did not infringe upon the rights of others. An example is the argument of those who say that District crime would be reduced by one-third to one-half if heroin were legal in order that its price could fall. This situation would eliminate the "need" of addicts to commit robberies, larcenies, and burglaries to support a high-priced habit. Conversely, an efficient police force may eliminate the drug entirely, ending addiction and habit-supporting crimes. Some people would see police protection differently – as an occupying army from the suburbs strictly enforcing pedestrian violations at Fourteenth and U streets while suburban motorists may be free to travel down Sixth Street at twice the speed limit in order to catch every light green between Rhode Island and Massachusetts avenues. The local newspapers illustrate the multitude of ways in which groups in the city value police.

The incalculable value of human life can be used to warrant almost any estimate. (FBI crime statistics indicate that a large proportion of the three most serious crimes – murder, rape, and aggravated assault – is committed by relatives and acquaintances of the victim, often in the home in the case of murder. If home is truly where the murder is, an expensive police force would be of little deterrent.) But by avoiding such delicate matters as harassment, brutality, and double standards, one-half the per capita estimate is probably reasonable. This figure – a feasibly probable allocation of $2.14 million – allows for suburbanites working in the city, the 16 million annual tourists, the 500,000 annual business visitors, and nonresident-owned property.

Corporation Counsel and the Courts   Perhaps the Corporation Counsel should be included in the broad category city overhead, but because it is connected with public safety functions it is placed here. The Corporation Counsel "furnishes legal advice to the commissioner, the District of Columbia Council, and the several, departments of the District. Legal opinions rendered by the Corporation Counsel, in the absence of specific action by the commissioner to the contrary or until overruled by controlling court decisions, are the guiding statements of law, to be followed by all District officers and employees in the performance of their official duties."[7] Insofar as the counsel can be associated with the judiciary function, discussion of the Corporation Counsel and the courts will be combined. The total fiscal 1967 expenditures for both were $11.14 million. Allocated on the basis of population, the neighborhood under study would be receiving $1.09 million in benefits. Allocating on an income basis, the sum would be $.5 million, and on an estimated wealth basis, $.22 million. But how does the neighborhood value these services? Because residents own little property it is possible that the lower estimates are more feasible. How much these functions provide for the safety of the community must be considered too, and much of this valuation might lie with the valuation placed on the correctional system. A feasible estimate might be the mean of the above three estimates, or $.60 million, or one-half the population as the population allocator (as done with police), or $.56 million.

Department of Corrections   Estimates for corrections range from $1.12 million allocated by population to $.51 million allocated by income and $.23 million allocated by estimated wealth. Regardless of the political institutions of any segment of the city, were it to be separate, certain criminal elements must be isolated from everyday society. Ideally this would be solely for the protection of others and the rehabilitation of the criminal so that he could be a productive asset to his family, community, and nation on his release. Any prison system provides the first function in the short run (provided it is escape proof), but failing to provide the rehabilitation function defeats the first function in the long run. Recent evidence of most correctional systems in the nation is hardly complimentary. If our prisons merely amount to training grounds for more hardened antisocial behavior, then its long-run value may be zero, because the benefits derived from having the criminal off the streets are repaid at compound interest on his release. This is not to mention the psychological damage to the individual resulting from guard brutality and rapes by fellow inmates, among other things. A feasible estimate is probably the mean of the four possible numbers previously cited ($.47 million). This figure is not far from what would be obtained from using the same allocation as was done for police.

---

7. *Budget Estimates of the District of Columbia*, 1970, p. C–10–1.

Fire Protection   Allocated on a population basis, the value of the services rendered by the District of Columbia Fire Department to this area would be $2.03 million by income and estimated wealth, $.93 and $.41 million respectively. If the feasible estimate attempts to allow for nonresident business property, suburban workers, and visitors to the city, the figure is $1.02 million. This does not consider the likelihood of fires in a particular area resulting from disorders or the poor construction of housing units. Obviously the likelihood of a renter-occupied dwelling unit becoming the victim of a blaze depends in part on the service rendered by the Bureau of Licenses and Inspections in enforcing housing laws and in part on the teaching of fire prevention in public schools.

Other Public Safety   The three remaining items are civil defense, the National Guard, and the Bureau of Licenses and Inspections. Civil defense benefits would be allocated as $34,000, $16,000, and $7,000 by population, income, and wealth, respectively. The National Guard would be $22,000, $10,000, and $4,000 by the same measures. The Bureau of Licenses and Inspections would be estimated at $410,000, $188,000, and $84,000. Estimates done in the manner considered feasibly probable for other public safety functions would be $17,000 for civil defense, $11,000 for the National Guard, and $205,000 for the Bureau of Licenses and Inspections. One must keep in mind, however, that area residents may not feel a need for civil defense (because fallout shelters from a ground zero thermonuclear attack are useless), that area residents contribute manpower to the guard, and that charges of laxness in enforcing building codes on rented housing have often been made.

Welfare Department

Payments and services handled by the public welfare system in the District are estimated at $5.14 million on the basis of population and $8.19 million on the basis of the area's share of poverty. The higher estimate is obviously more feasible, and it includes the cash payments that make up 80 percent of the welfare budget. An allocation might be made by the percentage of the city's population having some income above the generally cited $3,300 poverty level, due to the fact that large households with higher incomes may qualify for aid to families with dependent children. Because part (a small part) of the budget is aid to the elderly and the blind, the $8.19 million figure might be reduced, but this assistance is small compared to AFDC, in addition to the fact that old age and blindness tend to be correlated with poverty.

Health and Hospitals

These items are estimated by the percent of District of Columbia families residing in the area having less than a $5,000 income in 1959. By

1967 these incomes would be considerably higher, but it is unlikely that the proportion changed greatly unless there were large demographic shifts. People of all income groups receive some benefits, but lower-income people in particular receive the largest proportion of these services. Non-District residents also benefit from these expenditures. Using the above estimator, the area in question would receive $8.15 million in benefits from such public services as preventive services, mental health and retardation services, hospitals, medical care, environmental health services, and from planning, research, and administration. Using the 15.6 percent poverty allocator, the value would be $10.17 million; a population distribution would allot $6.39 million.

Vocational Rehabilitation

Vocational rehabilitation had an estimated budget of $2.54 million, which allocated by population would yield $249,000 in benefits to the area. These services include the following in addition to administration and general rehabilitation services: services to the mentally ill and retarded, services to adolescents, services to the visually impaired, plus special projects and disability determinations.

Parks and Recreation

The crowded conditions of any large city make the provision of parks and recreation facilities for enjoyment as well as for physical and mental health a vital necessity. The best allocator for the District of Columbia Recreation Department is probably the area's share of school-age children, or $898,000, because the park facilities used by suburban residents and visitors to the nation's capital are not in the Recreation Department's jurisdiction. In the case of the National Park Service and the zoo, one must realize that Washington, D.C., serves as a center for people who reside far beyond the boundaries of the standard metropolitan statistical area. Allocating by the neighborhood's share of SMSA population alone, benefits are estimated at $158,000 for the National Park Service and $65,000 for the zoo. The reverse situation of ghetto residents making use of suburban park areas is highly unlikely. There is the additional fact that park police help to control nonresidents using the Baltimore-Washington Parkway and the Potomac and Rock Creek Parkway as commuter routes.

Highways and Traffic

Automobile ownership in the Shaw-Cardozo area is low. The 1960 census indicates that residents own fewer than 3.9 percent of the cars in the city and only 1.1 percent of the cars in the metropolitan area. Most residents use public transportation to travel to work. The neighborhood is crossed by fine routes used by a large number of suburban dwellers who work in the city. These include New York Avenue, Rhode Island Avenue, and such boundary thoroughfares as Sixteenth Street, North Capitol Street, and the Michigan Avenue-Harvard Street commuter route. It could be argued that many of these streets are of little direct benefit to the area and that these benefits may be nullified by the fact that they create a safety hazard and interrupt the pedestrian at each intersection. Throughout, traffic light timing and other control devices favor the commuter rather than local users when the two conflict. Huge expenditures on freeways benefit the suburban areas except for local residents who use the automobile to travel to suburban jobs. Present freeway construction in the Shaw area also displaced people from their homes. Other than street repairs and displaced residents, the only tangible project involving this area is the four-year-old widening of New York Avenue (the main commuter and tourist route into the city), which will provide only three lanes in rush direction, the same as it did in 1965. A population allocation for streets and roads would be $5.37 million; allocating by automobile ownership in the city, the estimate would be $2.14 million; and an allocation by SMSA car ownership would give an estimate of $603,000. This lowest figure is feasible because a still lower one would arise from considering visitors to the city.

Sanitation

Most of the functions of the Department of Sanitary Engineering are paid for by the user. Trash and garbage collection is not; thus this function, as well as part of overhead costs, must be allocated. If we assume that the total city cost for this service is $11 million and is allocated by population, the area's benefit would be $1 million. If one-half this figure involves services to nonresident-owned business establishments, the benefit estimate would be $500,000. Another consideration is that allegations have been made that service in Shaw-Cardozo does not compare with the sanitation service west of Rock Creek and in the central business district.

Urban Renewal

Allocations for urban renewal approached the $6 million level in the fiscal year 1967 for such items as land acquisition, relocation, and construction of public housing. Part of the area discussed here is currently being renewed (the area to the southwest of Capitol and M streets, NW). The benefits can be considered questionable, however, because urban renewal displaces people from their homes (increasing economic and social instability), crowds more people into other parts of the city, and pays landowners (few are residents) the "fair market value" for real estate. The "fair value" is often an expensive proposition as a result of past and present speculation and high returns from slum property. If present Shaw-Cardozo residents, especially those who formerly lived in the Southwest Urban Renewal Area, were to allocate benefits to the neighborhood, very likely the benefits would be negative. Most urban renewal represents expenditures for a public *purpose* but private *use*,[8] while public housing would be considered public use. During the fiscal year 1967 Sibley Plaza (with its no loitering signs in the lobby) was yet to be constructed. A fair estimate would be to take the difference between "fair market values" of rent and actual rent paid to the city's housing agency and to multiply by the number of occupants who had lived in Shaw-Cardozo during 1967, data which are not easy to come by. This figure would probably be counteracted by the various inconveniences caused by the renewal program. If an allocation were made by population, it would be $579,000; by poverty it would be $922,000.

City Overhead

This category includes such items as the executive office, general administration, most of the regulatory and miscellaneous agencies, Occupations and Professions, Buildings and Grounds, as well as Personal Services, wage board employees, settlement of claims and suits, loans and interest, and federal obligations. Additional costs for conventions and funds allocated for the nonexistent, congressionally stalled rapid rail system are excluded. If rapid rail becomes a reality the data can be revised. The total overhead would amount to $3.1 million if allocated by population, $1.4 million if allocated by income, $0.6 million if allocated by wealth, and $1.5 million if allocated by one-half the population estimate to allow for nonresidents in the city and their property. It is possible that some of these overhead expenses are costs of bureaucracy for its own sake in the large city; dispersion of power might reduce costs, or if there are presently economics of large-scale government, decentralization might raise overhead costs. Many of these costs are the result of the fact that Washington, D.C., is a center whose tributary areas extend far beyond the limits of the SMSA; this should be the case particularly with the regulatory agencies and Occupations and Professions.

Residents of Shaw-Cardozo are likely to receive direct benefit from the functions of wage, safety, and hour law administration, the school transit

---

8. See M. Anderson, "The Sophistry that Made Urban Renewal Possible," in J. Bellush and M. Hausknecht, eds., *Urban Renewal: People, Politics and Planning* (Garden City, N.Y.: Doubleday & Co., 1967), p. 52.

subsidy, the Commissioner's Youth Council, the Council on Human Relations, and the Board of Elections. These benefits total $55,000 allocated by employment, school children, the population under eighteen, the total population, and the total population, respectively. Another means to allocate is by benefits received from all functions, excluding overhead as a proportion of total city budget (including grants) less overhead items. This figure would vary, with many possible combinations because of the several alternative estimates for each of the services discussed above.

Social Insurance

The District government administers disbursement of unemployment compensation, estimated on pages 41 to 43 at $1.33 million for the area. The Social Security Administration administers benefits for old age, survivors, disability, and health insurance, the last item unapplicable to fiscal year 1967. These have already been estimated at $4.72 million on page 43.

Net Inflows and Outflows

Below is a chart showing estimated outflows to government bodies and various estimates for benefits going into the area. The text above lists several estimates for many of the items, whereas this chart lists three types of estimates: minimum probable, feasibly probable, and maximum probable.

Outflows
(In Millions of Dollars)

	(1)	(2)	(3)
a. Contributions for social insurance		9.72	
b. Federal income tax		14.95	
c. D.C. income tax		2.65	
d. Property taxes		2.95	
e. D.C. sales tax		2.10	
f. Burden of business income taxes	3.85	7.71	11.56
g. Tobacco and alcohol excise		1.73	
h. Telephone excise	0.10	0.15	
i. Auto and gasoline		2.67	
Totals	40.0	44.63	50.0

Note: With regard to taxation minimums and maximums not itemized except for two cases, the total could deviate by 10 percent in either direction. Item f above is a very crude estimate.

Benefits
(In Millions of Dollars)

	Minimum	Feasible	Maximum
a. Education (incl. library)	13.06	13.06	13.16
b. Police	0.90	2.14	10.00
c. Courts and corp. counsel	0.22	0.56	1.09
d. Corrections	0.00	0.47	2.12
e. Fire	0.41	1.02	2.03
f. Other public safety	0.10	0.23	0.47
g. Welfare department	5.14	8.19	8.19
h. Health and hospitals	6.39	8.15	10.17
i. Vocational rehabilitation	0.25	0.25	0.25
j. Recreation department	0.90	0.90	0.90
k. National Park Service and zoo	0.22	0.22	0.22
l. Highways and traffic	0.50	0.60	5.37
m. Sanitation	0.50	0.50	1.00
n. Urban renewal	negative	0.00	0.92
o. Overhead	0.06	1.50	3.10
p. Unemployment compensation	1.33	1.33	1.33
q. OASDHI	4.50	4.72	5.00
Totals	Below 34.48	43.84	64.32

The result (using feasible taxation) is a net outflow from the area amounting to $10.1 million using the minimum benefit estimate and a small net outflow of $0.8 million using the feasibly possible estimate.

The wide range of net benefits indicates that with present data the case of net inflows or net outflows with regard to the Shaw-Cardozo area is not settled. It can be stated that the area is reasonably paying its way – perhaps more than paying its way – and that its residents are capable of providing a reasonable level of public functions. However, this is not to say the area could separate from the city (or even the nation) and still be able to provide these functions. We offer several reasons (and there are probably others) such a conclusion cannot be made: (1) there would continue to be tax outflows to outside governments embodied in production costs, excise, and other indirect taxes; (2) migration into and/or from the area may change the income structure of the population favorably or unfavorably; (3) there may be economies of scale involved either to the area's advantage or disadvantage; (4) the area may have to provide for its common defense against an outside enemy; (5) the area could become either more or less cohesive, thus altering the structure of costs of and benefits from neighborhood public functions.

Table 2. District of Columbia Budget (in thousand $)

Item	Operating	Capital	Grants	Total
Executive office	613.0		22.1	635.1
General administration	10,860.1		234.3	11,094.4
Regulatory and miscellaneous				
Alcoholic beverages	288.3			288.3
Adm. parole laws	424.3			424.3
Death investigations	227.9			277.9
Adm. of insurance laws	302.6			302.6
Adm. wage, safety, hour laws	260.4		1.9	262.3
Filing and rec'g prop. & corp. papers	536.5			536.5
Public service commission	334.1		3.1	337.2
Planning and zoning	124.9		2.2	127.1
Metropolitan area transit commission	85.0			85.0
School transit subsidy	32.0			32.0
Boards of appeals and review	40.3			40.3
Commissioner's Youth Council	150.3		45.7	196.0
Office of urban renewal	149.8		5,759.9	5,909.7
Council on human relations	63.7		3.0	66.7
Metropolitan council of governments	76.3			76.3
Metropolitan area transit authority	257.3			257.3
Board of Elections	1.0			1.0
Occupations and professions	543.8			543.8
Public library	4,461.1	347.0	315.8	5,123.9
Veterans' affairs	118.1			118.1
Building and grounds	3,381.5	551.0	3,932.4	7,869.9
Surveyor	306.4		1.9	308.3
Public safety				
Corporation Counsel	1,394.1			1,394.1
Metropolitan police	42,235.0	125.0	1,177.4	53,537.4
Fire department	19,779.7	852.7	15.9	20,648.3
Civil defense	153.7		193.2	346.9
Courts	9,690.4		51.6	9,742.0
Corrections	10,803.4	502.0	95.8	11,401.2
Licenses and Inspections	4,019.2	150.0	18.5	4,187.7
National Guard	222.3			222.3
Public Schools	86,491.5	27,213.1	18,150.1	131,854.7
Recreation department	6,400.9	1,252.9	1,699.5	9,353.3
National park service	4,931.0			4,931.0
Zoo	2,028.1			2,028.1
Vocational rehabilitation	805.5		1,731.4	2,536.9
Public health	57,514.8	1,203.0	6,455.3	65,173.1
Welfare (incl. unemployment compensation)	32,563.8	1,368.8	18,563.5*	52,496.1
Highways and traffic	15,350.0	15,455.0	23,983.6	54,788.6
Sanitation Engineering	24,708.5	12,747.0	1,329.6	38,785.1
(sanitation dept. only, excl. water and sewer about 10 million)				
Personal Service, wageboard	706.0			706.0
American Legion convention	233.0			233.0
Settlement of claims and suits	42.1			42.1
Loans and interest	—	6,077.6		6,077.6
Federal obligations	—	1,350.0		1,350.0
Rapid rail transit	—	4,527.5		4,527.5

    *41,871.6 is total less unemployment compensation

Sources: House of Representatives D.C. Budget Hearings for Fiscal Year 1968 and Senate Hearings for Fiscal Year 1969. Due to scattered nature of the data, there may be small amounts of double counting. It is unfortunate that operating, capital and grants were not presented in one table.

References

Advisory Commission on Intergovernmental Relations. *State and Local Finances: Significant Features 1966 to 1969*. Washington, D.C.: U.S. Government Printing Office, 1968.

Bellush, J., and Hausknecht, M. eds., *Urban Renewal: People, Politics and Planning*. Garden City, N.Y.: Doubleday & Co. 1967.

Daedalus 97, no. 4 (1968).

District of Columbia Government. *Budget Estimates of the District of Columbia, Fiscal Year 1970*. Washington, D.C., 1969.

Musgrave, R., ed. *Essays in Fiscal Federalism*. Washington, D.C.: The Brookings Institution, 1965.

U.S. Bureau of the Census. *Statistical Abstract of the United States: 1968*. Washington, D.C.: U.S. Government Printing Office, 1968.

U.S. House of Representatives, Subcommittee on District of Columbia Appropriations. *District of Columbia Appropriations, 1968*. Washington, D.C.: U.S. Government Printing Office, 1967.

U.S. Senate, Committee on Appropriations. *Hearings: District of Columbia Appropriations for Fiscal Year 1969*. Washington, D.C.: U.S. Government Printing Office, 1968.

2

Voluntary and Involuntary Transfers through Charity and the Tax System: Their Effects on Urban Poverty

The phenomenon of public transfers can only be understood if we recognize the changing role of private voluntary redistribution. Throughout history, the family, the clan, or the tribe, if not a larger entity, acted as an instrument for meeting the health, education, and welfare needs of its members. The role of private and voluntary redistribution is dramatically illustrated by the household economy, which is generally not organized along exchange lines. To examine urbanization in the context of private transfers, therefore, would warrant a theory that explains why private transfers do occur, even at a time when public means of redistribution exist. Such a theory is provided by the recognition of the systemic nature of man, which is reflected in utility interdependence at the level of the individual: it denotes that an individual's welfare is not a function solely of the stock of goods he may consume but also of his perception of the welfare of others. His utility function does contain an interdependence component reflecting his degree of identification with others.[1]

In the first paper in this part, Harold Hochman and James Rodgers describe the main features of a theory of income transfers based on utility interdependence. They test their theoretical model by means of data on private transfers that take place in urban areas. The model implies that the propensity to contribute to charity within a community should vary directly with the average income of community members and the dispersion of the

---

1. For an evolution of the concepts of utility interdependence as an explanator of income transfers, see (in historical order): K. E. Boulding, "Notes on a Theory of Philanthropy," in *Philanthropy and Public Policy*, ed. F. G. Dickinson (New York: National Bureau of Economic Research, 1962), pp. 57–71; M. Pfaff and A. Pfaff, "The Relationship between the Transfer and Exchange Sectors of the Economy," *Proceedings of the Business and Economic Statistics Section of the American Statistical Association* (August 1969), pp. 532–70; H. M. Hochman and J. D. Rodgers, "Pareto-Optimal Redistribution," *American Economic Review* 59 (September 1969): 542–47; and M. Pfaff and A. Pfaff, "Interdependence, Regulation, Distribution: Some Functions of the Grants Economy" (Paper read at the meeting of the Association for the Study of the Grants Economy and the American Economic Association, December 1969); M. Pfaff and A. Pfaff, with an introduction by K. E. Boulding, *The Grants Economy* (Belmont, Calif.: Wadsworth Publishing Co., forthcoming). Several more recent papers are referenced therein.

distribution of income among them. They test this hypothesis specifically by looking at variations of average charitable contributions between cities. They add as a third variable the number of persons in the community, to recognize that urbanization, by increasing the size of the cluster of individuals, produces what is generally termed "free-rider" behavior in the theory of collective goods. The social pressure to contribute is relatively small, and the recognition that one's own contribution is relatively unimportant may lead individuals not to give voluntarily – that is, to get a "free ride" because of the systemic concern of others. "This line of reasoning is the heart of Friedman's contention that urbanization, by increasing the size of the group over which interdependence extends, reduces social pressure and makes it necessary to collectivize charity." They note, however, that if donors are motivated to give by factors other than interdependence, then "paradoxically, altruism is more likely than egoism to result in a suboptimal level of charitable giving."

The authors recognize that community size may not always be reflected adequately by population size and that other locational breakdowns may be better explanators of interdependence relations. Based on a set of regression equations, they conclude that private contributions do not have a significant negative association with population size. However, they note that highly significant positive associations between charitable giving and income on the one hand and dispersion in the distribution of income on the other hand could be established. The authors point out that "it may be possible to use what we know about redistribution through charity . . . to resolve the social question of how much redistribution ought to be brought about under public auspices to achieve a Pareto optimum."

Whether urbanization indeed brought about the necessity for the collectivization of charity or whether urbanization itself was the result of changes in the interdependence or community structure of society may be a moot point at this stage. It is a fact, however, that public transfers increased under the impetus of urbanization and that their main means of financing is the tax system. The purpose of the remaining papers of part 2 is to assess generally and specifically the effect on urban poverty of public transfers made through the welfare system.

Daniel Fusfeld notes the historic rise of the magnitude of public transfers during the past twenty-five years. Nonetheless, he concludes that when comparing the amount of these transfers with the poverty-level income, these payments are rather inadequate: "The unmet needs of welfare recipients in 1968 . . . have been about $1.27 billion based on the Orshansky poverty line and about $3.60 billion based on the BLS [Bureau of Labor Statistics] poverty line." He quotes Daniel Moynihan, who argues that the system "maintains the poverty groups in society in a position of impotent fury. Impotent because the system destroys the potential of individuals and families to improve themselves. Fury because it claims to be otherwise." He then proceeds to note that "the level of welfare payments is such that it keeps the recipients in poverty. Their poverty, in turn, tends to reinforce itself because of the social and psychological impact of poverty on the poor. ... The ghetto economy differs markedly from the rest of the economic system. ... It is permanently depressed, with unemployment rates normally at the high levels that are characteristic of depressions when they occur in the national economy. It is backward and underdeveloped, lacking the dynamic, progressive changes that bring advancement to the rest of the economy. ... Physical capital flows out of the ghetto largely through failure to replace depreciation of housing and public facilities. The ghetto landlord takes a large portion of his gains in the form of capital withdrawals that come from failure to maintain his property. ... Public facilities are subject to the same outward flow through failure to maintain schools, streets, sidewalks, parks, and other public facilities in ghetto areas. Manpower also leaves when it can." His conclusion on the effect of public transfers is: "This is the fundamental dilemma faced by public policies that seek to ameliorate the condition of ghetto residents: although they may succeed in improving conditions of life for the recipients, they also result in preservation of the ghetto as a whole. ... The function of welfare payments in the social system as a whole is to preserve the urban ghetto as a residual subsystem and as a source of low-wage workers."

In her study of the distributive and poverty-reducing effects of social welfare payments Anita Pfaff looks at the twelve large standard metropolitan statistical areas (SMSAs) and their central-city poverty areas. She concludes that: (1) Of the seemingly massive amount of social welfare payments, only 7.44 percent are disbursed to central-city poverty areas. (2) Although average social welfare payments to blacks are higher than to whites, no substantial reduction in the income disparity is achieved by these public grants. (3) Whereas Social Security mainly benefits those with some other income, public assistance benefits the poor predominantly; however, in most instances benefits do not suffice to remove recipients from poverty. (4) Families with female heads tend to have a lower income before and after transfers despite their higher average transfers; a much larger proportion of such families can be found among residents of central-city poverty areas than of large SMSAs in general. (5) Public transfers go primarily to families whose head did not work at all; a sizable share of transfers, however, go to full-time workers. (6) In large SMSAs only 52 percent and in central-city poverty areas only 74.1 percent of all transfers go to poor families. (7) Social welfare payments succeed in reducing the poverty gap by only one-third of their amount, leaving a poverty gap of $2.4 billion in large SMSAs. (8) Public assistance removes not only absolutely but also relatively far fewer families from poverty than Social Security, which cannot be considered a poverty-reduction program either, however.

Irving Leveson is concerned with the development of strategies for the amelioration of urban poverty. Rather than rely on supplementing income as a measure of well-being, he suggests the use, for analytical purposes, of a social index that is a weighted combination of social indicators reflecting health, comfort, safety, and other considerations that enter more directly into the utility function. In terms of Lancaster's formulation, these indicators are characteristics derived from activities in a technology of consumption; and activities in turn are produced with goods. There may be many underlying causal mechanisms, each operating through several variables, and any one policy may influence a number of social indicators. Policy decisions therefore should be based on a consideration of the effect of the policy variable on an overall social index, taking into account the effects of the variable that came about through all causal mechanisms. This approach is based on an econometric model of determinants of a Social Index and is conjecturally applied to an examination of major alternatives.

The efficiency of an income-maintenance strategy and a strategy of providing additional services to the poor is discussed. Leveson suggests that redistribution of income may be inefficient because the poor have to rely on the same inadequate services and may not stress those with high social benefits. The author argues that there is a conflict between the efficiency conditions for producing services and those for producing improvements in social indicators. Improving the well-being of the poor through restructuring of service production and delivery patterns appears to have some promise over the long run. This route offers no easy or immediate solution and requires a concerted effort at expansion and adaptation of knowledge. It is an emphasis on innovation as an evolutionary process operating across the board rather than on particular programs. Efforts to improve equality of opportunity should be coordinated and combined with efforts at urban innovation.

Concentrations of poverty and race are likely to persist and even to increase for a long time. Support in the form of both income and services will be necessary for those whose conditions derive from past neglect. Development of an urban innovation strategy can both facilitate moving out of poverty and result in more effective support for those who suffer from past disadvantages. At the same time we can begin to develop a national population policy to reduce harmful concentrations of poverty, to improve the matching of workers with jobs, and to reduce costs of housing.

3

Harold M. Hochman and
James D. Rodgers:
Utility Interdependence and
Income Transfers through Charity

Introduction

Recent years have witnessed a heightened concern with the problem of poverty, as evidenced by a growing literature in the social sciences,[1] culminating in the proposed Family Assistance Program and the work of the President's Commission on Income Maintenance, particularly its negative income tax proposal.[2] This literature has focused on specific proposals for adjusting the size distribution of income. Accordingly, the lion's share of the attention has been devoted to measuring the incidence of poverty, analyzing the incentive effects of various transfer schemes, and estimating the number of families that would be raised above the "poverty line" by changes in existing income maintenance programs.

Still, some of the most important issues, positive *and* normative, associated with income transfers have received little attention. At the conceptual level little has been done to rationalize the increased interest in income transfers and welfare programs save, conventionally, by reference to overt value judgments that equate reductions in income inequality with "social justice." Distribution has been interpreted as a matter of equity and has been divorced from the Paretian criterion of economic efficiency, in terms of which economists judge the allocation of resources.[3] Although this is due to

---

Printed by permission of the authors. All rights reserved.

1. A sample of useful recent works dealing with poverty and income maintenance includes O. Eckstein, ed., *The Economics of Income Maintenance Programs* (Washington, D.C.: The Brookings Institution, 1967); C. Green, *Negative Taxes and the Poverty Problem* (Washington, D.C.: The Brookings Institution, 1967); and C. Wilcox, *Toward Social Welfare* (Homewood, Ill.: Richard D. Irwin, 1969).

2. The President's Commission on Income Maintenance Programs, *Poverty Amid Plenty: The American Paradox* (Washington, D.C.: U.S. Government Printing Office, 1969).

3. A typical example of the prevailing view is that "judgment on questions of income redistribution lies beyond the purview of economic analysis. By wide acceptance, economic theory plays a subordinate role in matters of this kind: one is confined to questions of ways and means and to pointing out unintended effects of a proposed measure." (D. Berry, "Modern Welfare Analysis and the Form of Income Redistribution," in *Income Redistribution and Social Policy*, ed. A. T. Peacock [Oxford: Alden Press, 1954], p. 41.)

economists' agnosticism with respect to questions of distribution, it can be shown that this, in part at least, derives from an inadequate model of individual choice and an incomplete conception of what constitutes rational behavior.

The fact is that our profession lacks a theory that can cope with distributional issues, at either the normative or the positive level. It has neither a normative theory that can be used in guiding policy, indicating *how much redistribution ought to be brought about* through income transfer programs, nor a positive theory explaining *why the observed amount of redistribution does in fact occur*. Further, we have only recently begun to develop effective methods of determining empirically how much redistribution actually does occur through fiscal activities,[4] and no good estimates of the redistributive effects of private interpersonal transfers are even available.

This paper, by relaxing a common assumption, will fill part of this lacuna. Instead of viewing distributional questions in the traditional formulation of rational behavior, in which individuals relate to each other *only* through market transactions, we assume "benevolent and Pareto-relevant interdependence"[5] among their utility functions, so that economic efficiency requires income transfers.[6]

As an initial attempt to verify this model, which we developed in our earlier paper, we try to ascertain whether private gifts and contributions are correlated with the dispersion of the community's income distribution and other socioeconomic variables, as they should if they are motivated by utility interdependence. At the positive level this approach can improve our understanding of the logic of income transfers. At the normative level, it is, to use Harvey Leibenstein's phrasing, a step toward "the establishment of

---

4. See W. I. Gillespie, "Effect of Public Expenditure on the Distribution of Income," *Essays in Fiscal Federalism* (Washington, D.C.: The Brookings Institution, 1965), pp. 122–86; and *Tax Burdens and Benefits of Government Expenditures by Income Class, 1961 and 1965* (New York: Tax Foundation, 1967). For a criticism of these studies see H. Aaron and M. C. McGuire, "Benefits and Burdens of Government Expenditures," *Econometrica* (in press).

5. "Benevolent interdependence" simply refers to the situation in which one person receives satisfaction from increments in the welfare or income of other persons. Whether this results from altruism, from a distaste for the manifestations of poverty, or from fear of antisocial behavior of the poor makes no difference in our analysis of transfers. See our earlier paper, "Pareto-Optimal Redistribution," *American Economic Review 59* (September 1969): 542–47. Another, more rigorous treatment of this subject is G. Becker, "A Theory of Social Interactions" (Chicago, September 1969).

6. Milton Friedman, who put forward the basis elements of this argument in *Capitalism and Freedom* (Chicago: University of Chicago Press, 1962), argued that transfers occur because of altruistic interdependence among individual utility functions. However, Friedman did not develop this point, and neither its welfare implications nor the possibility of explaining actual transfers in terms of interdependence had been explored before the recent efforts we have mentioned.

welfare economics on an empirical basis."[7] Appropriately extended, our analysis of utility interdependence may well suggest some norms or guidelines for policy in the distributional area.[8]

Interdependent Preferences and Consumer Choice

The thrust of our argument is that charity, as a vehicle for income transfers, indicates utility interdependence, which gives rise to individual dissatisfaction with the initial size distribution of income. The notion that every individual may find *some* income distributions, including the initial or pretransfer distribution to be unacceptable is intriguing, for it opens the way to use of the Pareto criterion in discussing distributional questions, and it therefore challenges the neoclassic doctrine.[9]

In our paper "Pareto-Optimal Redistribution"[10] we examined the normative implications of benevolent utility interdependence, first in a two-person model and then for the N-person case. Its analysis assumed that an individual's desire to make an income transfer (in the two-person case) is a matter of his preferences and the initial difference between his market-determined income and the other person's. It also assumed that preferred or Pareto-optimal transfers reduce income inequality – that is, that no individual wishes to make a transfer to someone with a higher initial income. Construing the N-person case as a simple aggregation of pairwise outcomes, an individual's "propensity to transfer" or "rate of benevolence" (with respect to own-income) in this model turns out to be a matter of his income or transfer elasticity[11] and his position in the distribution of income (which determines how many individuals he will make transfers to and how many

---

7. H. Leibenstein, "Long-Run Welfare Criteria," in *The Public Economy of Urban Communities*, ed. Julius Margolis (Washington, D.C.: Resources for the Future, 1965), p. 41.

8. However, a word of caution is in order. Although our model may suggest that utility interdependence makes some distributions inefficient, there remains a residual set of income distributions, all of which are Pareto optimal among which a society cannot choose without stronger ethical judgments than those implicit in the Pareto criterion.

9. For a clear statement of the traditional view, which sharply separates allocation (efficiency) and distribution (equity) questions, see R. A. Musgrave, *The Theory of Public Finance* (New York: McGraw-Hill Book Co., 1959), chap. 1.

10. Hochman and Rodgers, "Pareto-Optimal Redistribution." The simplifying assumptions of our model of Pareto-optimal redistribution are spelled out in this paper and clarified further in Hochman and Rodgers, "Pareto-Optimal Redistribution: A Reply," *American Economic Review* 60 (December 1970): 997–1002.

11. "Transfer elasticity" is analogous to *income elasticity* but differs because our model of Pareto-optimal redistribution treats the initial income differential as the critical independent variable in the two-person case. See Hochman and Rodgers, "Pareto-Optimal Redistribution," p. 547.

he will receive transfers from in the N-person situation). This in turn implies, for reasons to be expanded later, that the total volume of Pareto-optimal transfers in any community should vary with its mean income and the dispersion of its income distribution.

In "Pareto-Optimal Redistribution," we assumed that the fiscal structure should be the mechanism of redistribution, which we measured as net fiscal incidence, defined in terms of fiscal residuals.[12] The existence of nonzero fiscal residuals can be interpreted as necessary (though not sufficient) evidence of utility interdependence. However, this procedure has one major defect. It assumes that fiscal outcomes, which are generated through coercive means, accurately reflect individual preferences – in this instance, individual tastes for the consumption of others, at the cost of own-consumption and own-accumulation. Although one would predict some rough correspondence between tastes and government activities, redistribution effected by government is the outcome of a complex set of influences, originating in the past as well as in the present. This paper, which tries to test the empirical validity of our utility interdependence model, focuses on individual charity, which, though by no means completely free of coercion (in terms of social pressure to contribute) more closely approximates voluntary behavior.[13] The virtue of considering income transfers through charity, for present purposes, is that they are *not* channeled through the fiscal process and are therefore relatively more suitable for testing the implications of our utility interdependence model.[14]

Let us now consider momentarily the relevance and the deficiencies of a "charitable contributions" variable in indicating and measuring the extent to which private behavior reveals Pareto-relevant utility interdependence. Although all income transfers by definition produce income redistribution, not all the redistributive effects reduce income inequality. Similarly, not all charitable contributions result in income transfers. Some expenditures, nominally contributions, are simply private purchases of collective services. This may be true, for example, of many, perhaps most, religious contributions; "indulgences," to cite an extreme example, involved the purchase of

---

12. The fiscal residual for any income level is the difference between benefits and tax burdens imputed to the average individual with that income.

13. Note that the household itself is a logical place to look in studying utility interdependence, because in its internal behavior it is to a considerable extent a transfer economy. Although we do not develop this point, it does suggest the economist's need for useful sociological data.

14. There is another reason why it is preferable to focus on voluntary transfers. If one's ultimate concern is with devising norms for distribution policy based on individual preferences, it may be methodologically invalid to use observed fiscal incidence to infer norms for establishing the desired pattern of fiscal incidence. This point ought not to be stretched too far, however. Methodologically it may be quite acceptable to use preferences revealed in the fiscal structures of one jurisdictional level or unit of government in deciding on the distribution policy or incidence pattern that is appropriate for another unit or level of government.

a private good, "salvation." However, all charitable contributions, whether or not income transfers are the intended effect and whether or not they are equalizing, result in an improvement in the contributor's welfare. If this were not so, such contributions would not occur, because in a legal sense they are voluntary.

In the model we discussed the income transfers required by utility interdependence are equalizing. Moreover, they can be brought about, in principle if not in fact, through either private or public action. If the model is at all accurate in its representation of individual preferences, the amount of distribution-equalizing income transfers in any political community varies directly with the generosity of its members in contributing to charity – even though charity is surely an imperfect measure of such transfers. Thus, for the initial test of the utility interdependence formulation, to be described here, we shall simply postulate that charitable contributions, a variable for which measurements are available, are a satisfactory proxy for private equalizing income transfers.

This is not to imply that a charity variable is free from ambiguity. Voluntarism, except in such special cases as the purchase of CARE packages, is not absolute. Although failure to contribute does not invoke legal sanctions, "social pressure" is present and it can result in other, equally real sanctions: noncontributors can be ostracized.[15] Moreover, given the deductibility of charitable contributions for purposes of income tax computations, charity is not independent of the existing fiscal structure; the community at large shares as a partner in all itemized contributions, which have both price and income effects on consumer choice.[16]

The division of income transfers between public and private modes hinges in the first instance on the size of the group of individuals experiencing distributional externalities and on whether this group coincides with the dominant coalition of voters in the political community. Given existing political boundaries, transfers tend to be carried out by government. The problem is left for private charity when this condition is not met, either because the externalities are narrower than any existing political unit or because they cut across such units within which they cannot command effective majorities.[17]

---

15. For an analysis of the effect of social pressure on incentives to contribute to charity, see D. B. Johnson, "The Fundamental Economics of the Charity Market" (Ph.D. diss., University of Virginia, 1968), chap. 7.

16. The implications of deductibility are discussed in M. K. Taussig, "Economic Aspects of the Personal Income Tax Treatment of Charitable Contributions,"*National Tax Journal 20* (March 1967): 1–19.

17. The division is, of course, not so clear cut as these statements might imply, because tradition is also a significant factor, and adjustments to new political boundaries and social values take time. Still, it seems the best conceptual basis for distinguishing between situations in which private and public transfer mechanisms are operative.

An Empirical Test of the Utility Interdependence Explanation of Charitable Giving

This section reports on our initial effort to estimate a "propensity-to-transfer" function by determining whether intercity variation in charitable giving can be explained by the independent variables suggested by our model. In constructing our empirical test, let us explain first why the utility interdependence model suggests that contributions vary directly with income (the community mean income) and its dispersion. The basic reason (returning to the two-person model) is that the benefactor's desired transfer varies directly with his income if such transfers are a normal good. Increases in the higher-income individual's income may increase his desired transfer or lead individuals who had not been making transfers before to make them, because evaluated at lower own-incomes, marginal utility of own-consumption had exceeded the marginal utility of increments in the donee's income. When the benefactor's income increases, such latent utility interdependence becomes marginally relevant.

Similarly, there is ample reason to expect the level of transfers to vary with the dispersion or degree of inequality in the community's income distribution. So long as individuals' marginal propensities to transfer (vis-à-vis initial income differentials) are positive, the levels of their preferred transfers increase when pairwise income differentials become larger, which is what happens, *ceteris paribus*, when dispersion increases.[18] In the present analysis the implications of the initial income differential for the Pareto-optimal level of transfers enters through the dispersion variable – the more divergence there is among relative levels of well-being, as indicated by income, the higher we can expect the level of contributions to be.[19]

A third variable that might be relevant (on *a priori* grounds) is the number of persons in the political community. The theory of public goods distinguishes between cases in which a large number of persons benefit from provision of a collective good and cases in which the number of beneficiaries is small. Large groups are characterized by anonymity, and the benefits an individual receives from the transfer process depend almost

---

18. Although there are also other reasons why desired transfers might vary with income, they are not relevant here inasmuch as the income variable we consider is a community average. If, as in the first instance, the initial demand is marginally relevant, an increase in income alters the desired transfer because it improves the benefactor's rank in the income distribution, thus confronting him with more potential beneficiaries. If the desired transfers vary more than proportionally with the initial income differential, the Pareto-optimal transfer increases even more because the increase in the benefactor's income widens the initial differentials between his income and the incomes of potential recipients.

19. A similar prior argument for a positive association between income inequality and charitable transfers is made in R. A. Schwartz, "Private Philanthropic Contributions – An Economic Analysis" (Ph.D. diss., Columbia University, 1966), p. 31.

entirely on what others contribute and only slightly on his own contribution. Hence, "free-rider" behavior is likely to prevail. Conversely, individuals in a small group cannot vary their contributions without affecting the behavior of other contributors, so social pressure and the recognition that one's own contribution may be relatively important can be expected to reduce "free riding."

Because noncontributors can still benefit, assuming the benefits of charity are a public good, there is reason to expect the level of private charity to be suboptimal. The amount by which giving falls short of its optimum might well be less, however, in a small community. Charity, reflecting private provision of collective wants, should be more prevalent in smaller communities, implying higher levels of per capita contributions, and *ceteris paribus*, lower per capita government budgets.

Such reasoning is the heart of Friedman's contention that urbanization, by increasing the size of the group over which interdependence extends, reduces social pressure and necessitates the collectivization of charity.[20] Friedman's argument implicitly assumes that charity is motivated by expected improvements in the welfare of its beneficiaries. The argument holds equally well for the case in which contributors desire to eliminate the more noxious manifestations of poverty – for example, shabbiness of dress and high incidence of violence in slum areas. Either of these motivations implies that an individual can benefit from charity whether or not he contributes himself, so long as the income or other characteristics of the recipients (which charity alters) enter his utility function. However, if the simple joy of giving or the publicity contributions attract is what motivates donors, the free-rider problem disappears; charity becomes a private good, or, at least, donors think of it as such, and the attainment of its benefits requires a personal contribution. Thus, paradoxically, altruism is more likely than egoism to result in a suboptimal level of charitable giving.

As an initial, though very rough, test of the hypothesis that free-rider behavior is less prevalent in small groups than in large, we include population in one set of our estimates of a propensity-to-transfer function. However, it is an imperfect measure of community size, in the sense required. It may be more appropriate to use other locational breakdowns, and ethnic background or racial characteristics may be more important than geographic boundaries in demarcating the community within which utility interdependence is found.[21] Still, it is plausible to assume that the community of individuals who have marginally relevant interdependent preferences is larger, the larger the population of the political community in which they reside. Hence, assuming that the benefits of contributions are in fact collective,

---

20. See M. Friedman, *Capitalism and Freedom*, p. 191.

21. With reference to this point, see the discussion of public and private regardingness in J. Q. Wilson and E. Banfield, "Public-Regardingness as a Value Premise in Voting Behavior," *American Political Science Review 58* (December 1964): 876–87.

free-rider behavior should increase with population, and per capita contributions may be expected to vary inversely with city size.

If the population variable were statistically significant, the results would confirm the importance of social pressure in small groups as a stimulus to charity and would support the view that most people regard its benefits as a public good. Failure of this hypothesis, however, must be interpreted more cautiously, because it might either be attributed to a failure of social pressure to diminish as a group size increases or to the fact that the benefits of charity are not a public good. Because social pressure is irrelevant if charity *is not* a public good, either of these mutually exclusive explanations could in itself account for a poor showing of the population variable.

The Data and the Regression Equations

Translated into operational form, suitable for explaining intercommunity differences in charitable giving, our model, which attributes transfers through charity to utility interdependence, reduces to the propensity-to-transfer function:

$$T_k = g(\overline{Y}_k, D_k, N_k). \tag{1}$$

In (1) T_k is the average transfer through charity (level of charitable contributions) made by individuals in a community; this is a function of $\overline{Y}_k$, which is per capita income in the kth community; D_k, which is a measure of the dispersion of its distribution of income; and N_k, which is its population. Our test of the utility interdependence formulation is then a cross-section analysis of intercity differences in contributions. While there is no assurance that the relationship specified, if significant, is inconsistent with other models as well, significance can at least tell us whether the data are consistent with our model.

Appropriate empirical counterparts of the variables in (1) are reported for a sample of thirty-two United States metropolitan areas in the *Survey of Consumer Expenditures* (SCE), taken during the period 1959–61 by the Bureau of Labor Statistics.[22] The SCE examines household income allocations, and the figures it reports, which are sample averages for various expenditure categories, include the variables we require for preliminary tests of our propensity-to-transfer function. The SCE expenditure breakdown includes an item entitled "gifts and cash contributions," defined as "cash contributions to persons outside the family and to welfare-religious, educational, and other organizations; and the cost of goods and services purchased in the survey year and given to persons outside the family."[23]

22. U.S. Department of Labor, Bureau of Labor Statistics, *The Survey of Consumer Expenditures* (Washington, D.C.: U.S. Government Printing Office).

23. *Ibid.* See report for any of the cities covered; for example, for San Francisco, see BLS Report No. 237–52, April 1964 (Second Advance Report).

The SCE also reports average after-tax income and the distribution of after-tax income in each city's sample. The reported figure for average gifts and cash contributions is taken as the empirical counterpart of R_k, and average after-tax income is the empirical counterpart of $\overline{Y}_k$.[24]

The income variable, per capita after-tax income, is the appropriate measure of per capita income – what the average individual would have had if he had not given to charity, plus the tax saving. Our distribution variable – measuring income dispersion or inequality – was calculated from the distribution of after-tax income among families sampled in each city. It was defined arbitrarily as the sum of the percentage of sample families with incomes less than 50 percent of the recorded mean and the percentage with incomes more than 50 percent above this level.[25] Conceptually, D_k thus calculated is independent of the value of $\overline{Y}_k$ itself.

N_k, which is supposed to measure community size, cannot be determined empirically, as we have pointed out. Thus population is used as a rough and perhaps inadequate proxy. The population figures used were obtained from the 1960 census.[26]

In addition to these measurable variables we also experimented with dummy variables for four geographic regions of the country (broadly defined, the West, the South, the Midwest, and the Northeast). These dummy variables were supposed to provide a rough test of whether the propensity to transfer through contributions differs among regions. In theory, interregional differences could result, because perceptions of utility interdependence vary in strength among the subcultures in the society at large, or alternatively, because the fiscal structure is a more adequate mechanism for internalizing such externalities in some sections of the country than in others.

Conventional multiple-regression procedures were used to estimate the propensity-to-transfer function. Both linear and logarithmic (or elasticity) specifications of (1) were estimated. In the logarithmic form the independent variables have a multiplicative effect on contributions. Within this frame of reference we experimented (see table 1) with formulations, including and omitting the regional dummy variables and specifications, which forced the

---

24. $\overline{Y}_k$, as used here, reflects only the increasing "marginal relevance" of utility interdependence, the first of the factors cited in our earlier discussion. However, if our estimation procedure had used cross-section observations for individual spending units or for different income classes in a single community rather than averages, $\overline{Y}_k$ would also reflect distributional changes (see footnote 19). This suggests that it might be worthwhile to look at pooled observations broken down by communities *and* income classes. (This will be done in a later paper.)

25. This measure of dispersion is easy to compute and is probably as useful for our purposes as the Gini coefficient, given the crudity of the data and the small samples involved.

26. Population figures are taken from U.S. Bureau of the Census, *U.S. Census of Population: 1960, Vol. I, Characteristics of the Population*, Part I, "United States Summary" (Washington, D.C.: U.S. Government Printing Office, 1964). Population in the thirty-two sample cities ranged from 13,311 for Fairbanks, Alaska, to 3,550,404 for Chicago, Illinois. Note that even 13,311 may be above the size range in which social pressure and free-rider behavior, which the population variable is intended to reflect, vary significantly.

equation through the origin. All of the equations (1a–1f) were estimated twice, once with the population included, as in the estimates summarized in table 2(a) and once with the population variable excluded, as in table 2(b).

The Regression Results

The regression results, as reported in tables 2(a) and 2(b) are generally consistent with the hypothesis that utility interdependence is a reasonable explanation of charitable giving:

1. All equations show a significant association between contributions and the independent variables. The F values for all of the regressions indicate significance at the 1 percent level.

2. The coefficients of after-tax income ($\overline{Y}_k$) and the dispersion in the distribution of after-tax income (D_k) are positive, as predicted, and in each regression are significant at the 1 percent level.

3. The population coefficient, our improvised measure of "community size," *never* differs significantly from zero. Although its sign is negative in most cases, conforming to the *a priori* expectation, its absolute effect is miniscule. In view of our reservations this is not surprising, and further, more formal investigation of the socioeconomic and demographic factors associated with utility interdependence is warranted.[27] It should also be

Table 1. Regression Equations

(1a) $C_k = B_1\overline{Y}_k + B_2 D_k + B_3 N_k + B_4 X_{1k} + B_5 X_{2k} + B_6 X_{3k} + B_7 X_{4k} + e_k$

(1b) $C_k = B_0 + B_1\overline{Y}_k + B_2 D_k + B_3 N_k + B_4 X_{1k} + B_5 X_{3k} + B_6 X_{4k} + e_k$

(1c) $C_k = B_1\overline{Y}_k + B_2 D_k + B_3 N_k + e_k$

(1d) $C_k = B_0 + B_1\overline{Y}_k + B_2 D_k + B_3 N_k + e_k$

(1e) $\text{Log } C_k = B_0 + B_1 \text{ Log } \overline{Y}_k + B_2 \text{ Log } D_k + B_3 \text{ Log } N_k + B_4 X_{1k} + B_5 X_{3k} + B_6 X_{4k} + e_k$

(1f) $\text{Log } C_k = B_0 + B_k \text{ Log } \overline{Y}_k + B_2 \text{ Log } D_k + B_3 \text{ Log } N_k + \text{Log } e_k$

Variables:

C_k = Average reported charitable giving in the ith city.

$\overline{Y}_k$ = Average after-tax income in the ith city.

D_k = Dispersion of after-tax income in the ith city.

N_k = Population of the ith city.

X_{1k} = Dummy variable for the western cities.
  $X_1 = 1$ if i is a western city.
  $X_1 = 0$ if i is not a western city.

X_{2k} = Dummy variable for southern cities.

X_{3k} = Dummy variable for midwestern cities.

X_{4k} = Dummy variable for northeastern cities.

e_k = Error term.

27. What is needed, of course, is experimentation with other proxies for group size and social identification – for example, measures of ethnic and racial homogeneity. See, for example, Wilson and Banfield, "Public-Regardingness."

noted that because of the insignificance of the population variable, the question of whether the charitable expenditures employed as data here are a collective good remains undecided.

4. In the linear regressions the coefficients of the geographic dummy variables either did not differ significantly from zero at any level of confidence or were significant only at the relatively low levels of 10 or 15 percent. In the logarithmic form the coefficient of X_3, the dummy for midwestern cities, is significant at the 5 percent level. This coefficient was consistently *negative* and was larger than any of the other dummy coefficients.

These results are open to opposing interpretations. The dummy coefficients might be interpreted as indicating that the public sector is more adequate in satisfying redistributive collective wants in the Midwest than elsewhere, in particular in the South. On the other hand, it might be inferred that midwesterners are slightly less generous than city dwellers in other geographical areas and that southerners are the most generous geographical group, once the influence of income and its distribution on giving has been removed.

5. The logarithmic or elasticity form [(2e) and (2f)] gives a slightly better fit than the linear regressions, as indicated by its higher R^2. This improvement in "goodness of fit" indicates that the relationship between contributions and the independent variables $\bar{Y}$ and D may be multiplicative rather than linear. However, because the improvement is small, we cannot place a great deal of confidence in this conclusion.

The Measurement of "Benevolence": Pitfalls and Prospects

Our income transfer model, which reflects a set of explicit assumptions about utility interdependence, seems capable of explaining a substantial amount of the variation in private giving. With this in mind, let us turn to the question of how useful the model is, not just in measuring utility interdependence or benevolence but in devising norms for distributional policy that are grounded in individual preferences.

In our earlier paper, "Pareto-Optimal Redistribution," we demonstrated that "altruistic" or "benevolent" utility interdependence may require a society to engage in redistribution if it is to attain Pareto optimality.[28] Individuals, in addition to engaging in voluntary redistribution through

---

28. See Hochman and Rodgers, "Pareto-Optimal Redistribution." With interdependence, the utility-possibility locus is no longer uniformly downward sloping. (For external economies this is true for as few as two persons; for external diseconomies upward-sloping portions require three or more persons.) Its upward-sloping portions, for obvious reasons, are inefficient, provided that malevolence is ruled out; in the minds of all nonmalevolent members of the society, any point on them is dominated by some point or points along the downward-sloping portion.

Table 2. Estimates of a Propensity-to-Transfer Function:
(a) Population Included as an Independent Variable

Equation	Intercept	Y	D	N	X_1	X_2	X_3	X_4	$\hat{R}^2$	F	SEE	N	K
1a	*	0.517[a] (0.093)	203.5[a] (81.1)	-0.004 (0.010)	-83.4[d] (76.8)	-75.0[d] (68.2)	-91.7[c] (70.1)	-70.1[d] (71.7)	0.644	7.5[a]	41.2	32	7
1b	-75.0	0.516[a] (0.093)	203.5[a] (81.1)	-0.004 (0.010)	-8.3 (26.6)	—	-16.7 (21.7)	4.1 (30.8)	0.644	7.5[a]	41.2	32	7
1c	*	0.425[a] (0.029)	136.6[a] (51.6)	-0.007 (0.009)	—	—	—	—	0.611	22.7[a]	40.0	32	3
1d	-76.2	0.508[a] (0.074)	202.5[a] (74.2)	-0.007 (0.009)	—	—	—	—	0.631	15.9[a]	39.6	32	4
1e	-1.48	1.161[a] (0.191)	0.184[a] (0.074)	0.000 (0.017)	-0.061 (0.082)	—	-0.093[b] (0.067)	-0.024 (0.094)	0.676	8.7	0.127	32	7
1f	-1.1	1.093[a] (0.154)	0.191[a] (0.071)	-0.006 (0.016)	—	—	—	—	0.646	17.2	0.125	32	4

Estimates of a Propensity-to-Transfer Function:
(b) Population Excluded

Equation	Intercept	Y	D	P	X_1	X_2	X_3	X_4	R^2	F	SEE	N	K
1a'	*	0.515a (0.092)	202.5a (79.8)	—	-83.8d (75.6)	-93.7d (67.1)	-71.0c (68.8)	-71.0d (70.1)	0.641	9.3a	40.6	32	6
1b'	-74.9	0.515a (0.092)	202.5a (79.8)	—	-8.9 (26.2)	—	-18.8 (20.7)	3.9 (30.3)	0.641	9.3a	40.6	32	6
1c'	*	0.427a (0.031)	139.1a (52.6)	—	—	—	—	—	0.601	45.1	39.4	32	2
1d'	-77.8	0.506a (0.073)	200.8a (73.6)	—	—	—	—	—	0.624	24.0	39.3	32	3
1e'	-1.487	1.161a (0.187)	0.183a (0.069)	—	-0.061 (0.081)	—	-0.093 (0.064)	-0.024 (0.092)	0.676	10.8a	0.125	32	6
1f'	-1.138	1.098 (0.151)	0.182 (0.066)	—	—	—	—	—	0.646	26.5	0.124	32	3

*=Intercept is suppressed.
SEE=Standard Error of Estimate.
N=Number of observations.
K=Number of independent variables

a Significant at the 1 percent level.
b Significant at the 5 percent level.
c Significant at the 10 percent level.
d Significant at the 15 percent level.

charity, may coerce themselves through the fiscal process into implementing additional distributional adjustments. The reason for this, of course, is market failure. Private transfers, if not augmented by fiscal activities, may produce "too little" income redistribution. Potential Pareto-optimal transfers that can make everyone better off remain.

Thus distribution policy must face up to the same problem encountered in deciding how much of a conventional public good to provide. This preference-revelation problem, itself inherent in market failure, makes the information required to determine and to achieve an optimum level of provision difficult to obtain. To obtain this information one must, in Paul Samuelson's words, know "the shapes of the marginal-utility curve of the public good to each man." Hence there is no question that the problem of determining "rates of benevolence" is difficult.[29]

We accept this readily enough, but the issue that concerns us here is not whether the problem is difficult but whether it is tractable. The implication of this paper is that it may well be. Our contention is that it may be possible to use what we know about redistribution through charity – albeit in an inefficient amount – in resolving the social question of how much redistribution ought to be brought about under public auspices to achieve a Pareto optimum.[30]

Two problems that inevitably confront any attempt to implement this line of reasoning must be mentioned again. First, in the short run charity is itself affected by the fiscal structure by virtue of the price and income effects of its deductibility. Nonetheless, it seems reasonable to think of the fiscal structure in this context as parametric, so that patterns of charitable giving remain valid evidence of the incremental distributional adjustments that individuals wish to implement.[31] Second, some charitable contributions may

---

29. P. A. Samuelson, "Pitfalls in the Analysis of Public Goods," *Journal of Law and Economics* 10 (October 1967): 199–204.

30. A similar argument, suggesting that "discussion of a theory of charity might be appropriate in the study of local government fiscal behavior," can be found in a paper by C. M. Tiebout and D. B. Houston, "Metropolitan Finance Reconsidered: Budget Functions and Multi-Level Governments," *Review of Economics and Statistics* 44 (November 1962): 412–17 (quotation from p. 416).

31. We are, as the analytic portion of this paper has suggested, in argument with Boulding's statement:

> The almost complete neglect by economists of the concepts of malevolence and benevolence cannot be explained by their inability to handle these concepts with their usual tools. There are no mathematical or conceptual difficulties in interrelating utility functions provided that we note that it is the perceptions that matter. The familiar tools of our trade, the indifference map, the Edgeworth box, and so on, can easily be expanded to include benevolence or malevolence, and indeed, without this expansion many phenomena, such as one-way transfers cannot be explained.

The appendix to Boulding's paper in the NBER volume on philanthropy, "Altruism and Utility," demonstrates how "benevolent" utility interdependence can be taken into account within the Edgeworth box construction. See K. E. Boulding, "Economics as a Moral Science"; and K. E. Boulding, "Altruism and Utility," in *Philanthropy and Public Policy*, ed. F. G. Dickinson (New York: Columbia University Press, 1962).

not be motivated by interdependence at all; some contributors may benefit only from the act of giving per se, not from the gifts of others. In such cases the market does not fail, and charity does not tell us anything about the distributional adjustments required by the Pareto criterion. The fact does remain, however, that the major share of all private transfers *are likely to be* of the collective good type, affecting the welfare of individuals other than their immediate donors and recipients. Thus on the basis of the evidence discussed, we remain hopeful that further development of the line of reasoning on which this paper is based will be of some help in deriving norms for distributional judgments that are consistent with the Pareto criterion of efficiency and in delimiting the extent to which this "weak" welfare norm can be used in evaluating distributional questions. Conceptual hazards notwithstanding, additional research on utility interdependence, both theoretical and empirical, seems to be warranted – for its own sake, to enrich our understanding of individual preferences, and for the sake of its implications for distributional policy. This opens up several intermediate lines of inquiry.

First, to ascertain both the motivating factors underlying charity and the effects of charity, private transfers must be disaggregated. It is important for these purposes to identify contributors to various types of charity in terms of income and other demographic and ethnic characteristics. This suggests the need to *uncover and utilize* knowledge that is usually thought to be more sociological than economic.

Examination of incidence outcomes in areas of mixed private and public activity, like the production of medical care and research and the provision of education, is also an essential part of research on utility interdependence. Cost and benefit imputations for these areas can be interpreted in light of *a priori* hypotheses about the externalities that justify public action to determine whether the methods of financing now in use are consistent with the Pareto criterion. Fiscal outcomes should also be examined to ascertain whether the utility interdependence explanation of income transfers is superior to alternative explanations of redistribution through the public sector. The interdependence explanation must be viewed within models of the collective decision-making process, and the manner in which this process channels individual preferences into government programs and political actions must be studied.

Just how useful this exercise will be is difficult to assess. However, if it is determined that observed patterns of redistribution, either through charity or public finance, can be explained in terms of utility interdependence, it may be possible to use such knowledge, particularly at lower levels of government, in designing fiscal structures that accord – more closely than fiscal structures now do – with the Pareto norm.

4

Daniel R. Fusfeld: Transfer
Payments and the Ghetto Economy

Thanksgiving Day 1969 – the festival of the bountiful board. In Louisville, Kentucky, a ten-year old boy died of starvation. The next day the newspapers carried stories asking how such a thing could happen in the middle of a big city in modern America. The answer was not hard to find, although neither of the newspapers was able to identify it. The boy was one of a family group of seven persons receiving welfare payments of $179 per month, which averages out to about 86¢ per day per person for food, clothing, shelter, and all other expenses.

An eighth person was also a member of the family group, the father of several of the children. He earned $4 to $10 per day, he said, repairing small electrical equipment. Even if he averaged $7 per day for six days a week this would bring the income per person per day up to only $1.06.

Perhaps it is possible to survive on these amounts, but in this case one child starved to death and all of the other children suffered from malnutrition. At the very best this family was surviving at the lowest level of poverty, the development of the children was severely hampered, and their poverty was being preserved not only for the present generation but for the future as well.

The Inadequacy of Welfare Payments

Although individual cases like the one described are well known to welfare personnel and the general inadequacy of welfare payments is acknowledged, estimates of how far welfare payments fall below acceptable standards have seldom been made. Yet such estimates are relatively easy to make.

The most widely accepted standard for adequacy of family income is the so-called poverty line established by the Social Security Administration and calculated by Mollie Orshansky. It is based on the cost of the economy food plan devised by the U.S. Department of Agriculture. This cost is multiplied by three, using the ratio of food to total expenditures that prevailed in low-income budgets in 1958. The resulting poverty benchmark for

Presented at the Symposium on the Grants Economy held between the Association for the Study of the Grants Economy and the American Association for the Advancement of Science, Boston, Mass., December, 1969. Reprinted by permission of the author. Mr. Fusfeld is professor of economics at the University of Michigan.

a nonfarm family of four was $3,335 per year in 1966. On a monthly basis it was $277.90.[1]

Many doubts about this poverty line can be raised. The USDA economy food plan may not be fully adequate, and it requires a sophisticated knowledge of both diets and buying that the poor usually do not have. In addition, budget patterns have changed since 1958. Among low-income families the proportion of income spent on food is now closer to one-quarter than to one-third, largely because of increases in the prices of other budget items relative to the price of food. A budget based on a 3 to 1 ratio of total expenditures to food may well leave serious inadequacies in the total. Although the "Orshansky line" is widely used, its meagerness is recognized by its originator and by most of those who use it as a standard.

A second estimate of the poverty line is available. The Bureau of Labor Statistics (BLS) developed a low-cost budget described as the amount needed to provide an urban family of four with a minimally adequate standard of nutrition, medical care, and housing. The cost of that budget for 1967 was $4,862, or $405.17 per month. Yet even this level was qualified by the statement that "although [it is] possible to achieve nutritional adequacy from the low-cost plan ... only one-fourth of those spending this amount do obtain adequate diets."[2] According to this second estimate, which is admittedly minimal, it takes 46 percent more money than the generally accepted "Orshansky line" for an urban family of four to escape poverty.

Both of these estimates will be used to measure the adequacy of payments under the program of Aid to Families with Dependent Children (AFDC). The average size of the AFDC family unit will be taken as four because the ratio of total AFDC recipients to the number of AFDC families is 3.997.[3] This ratio is fairly constant for individual states as well, so it is appropriate to use the poverty lines that have been computed for a family of four.

The estimates have been made in the following fashion: (1) We started with the average monthly AFDC payment per family for December 1968. (2) Average family income per month from other sources was added to the monthly AFDC payment. The most recent available data was for 1961, and it had to be updated. This was done by increasing the 1961 amounts by 50 percent, which is approximately equal to the increase in personal income

---

1. M. Orshansky, "Shape of Poverty in 1966," *Social Security Bulletin*, March 1968, pp. 5–6.

2. *Three Standards of Living for an Urban Family of Four Persons*, Bulletin No. 15705, U.S. Department of Labor, Bureau of Labor Statistics (Washington, D.C.: U.S. Government Printing Office, 1967).

3. "Program and Operating Statistics," *Welfare in Review* (U.S. Department of Health, Education, and Welfare, Social and Rehabilitation Service) 7, no. 3 (May–June 1969): 38.

per capita for the United States between 1961 and 1968. This figure is probably a good estimate. The 50 percent increase is somewhat high for Michigan but low for Illinois in 1968, according to preliminary data from the 1968 Survey of Welfare Recipients. In any case, the error will be small because income from sources other than AFDC payments is usually a small portion of the total.[4] (3) The total monthly income from AFDC plus other sources was subtracted from the poverty-line incomes, first the Orshansky line of $277.90 per month and then the BLS line of $405.17 per month. This figure was the unmet need per month per family. (4) This figure was multiplied by the number of families receiving AFDC payments in December 1968 to obtain the total unmet need per month. This was multiplied by twelve to obtain the annual unmet need for a twelve-month period.

The results are shown in table 1, which shows the unmet needs of welfare recipients in 1968 to have been about $1.27 billion based on the Orshansky poverty line and about $3.60 billion based on the BLS poverty line. It might be argued that these results obscure the differences between states, and indeed they do. But if the same calculations are made for the individual states and then summed, the totals fall within 1 percent of the calculations made in table 1.

Only four states provided AFDC payments large enough to bring total income for AFDC families above the Orshansky poverty line. These four were Massachusetts, Connecticut, New York, and New Jersey. Together they accounted for 355,000 AFDC families, or 23 percent of the total. No

Table 1. Estimated Unmet Income Needs of Welfare (AFDC)
Recipients, 1968

Average monthly AFDC payment per family, U.S.[1]	$167.80
Average monthly income from other sources[2] × 1.5	$40.25
Average total income per AFDC family	$208.05
Monthly unmet need per family based on	
Orshansky line ($277.90 per month)	$69.85
BLS line ($405.17 per month)	$197.12
Number of recipient families[1]	1,521,000
Annual (1968) unmet need for all recipient families based on	
Orshansky line ($3,335)	$1,274,000,000
BLS line ($4,862)	$3,597,000,000

Sources:
[1] "Program and Operating Statistics," p. 38.

[2] Department of Health, Education, and Welfare, *Characteristics of Families Receiving AFDC*. April 1963, table 48.

4. In 1961 only 19.1 percent of all support for AFDC recipients came from sources other than welfare. U.S. Department of Health, Education, and Welfare, Welfare Administration, Bureau of Family Services, Division of Program Statistics and Analysis, *Characteristics of Families Receiving AFDC*, April 1963, table 39. This percent includes OASDI payments as well as other sources of income.

state provided a level of AFDC support high enough to bring the average AFDC family up to the BLS poverty line. The data for individual states is given in Appendix 1.

Many studies of the welfare system link the low level of AFDC payments to the perpetuation of dependency and poverty. One study links payments that provide barely adequate amounts for food and shelter to conditions of "anxiety, isolation, and hopelessness."[5] An evaluation of AFDC in Chicago points out that payments are not sufficient for "reasonable subsistence compatible with health and well-being." This deprivation "sets the AFDC child apart and handicaps his ability to grow up like the other children in the community." The budget standard "is so low that it interferes with efforts to help families achieve personal and economic independence."[6] Another study argues that welfare recipients are handicapped in taking advantage of betterment programs: "When people are sick and hungry and live under demoralizing, degrading conditions, they cannot make use of opportunities or services that might ultimately lift them out of their poverty."[7]

Studies by Greenleigh Associates in New York State, Detroit, and the state of Washington all point to the perpetuation of dependency and poverty through welfare payments. In New York the welfare system "shows little regard for them [recipients] as human beings, defeats their attempts to regain self-esteem and self-direction, and tends to prolong the duration of dependency." Moving to the Midwest, the welfare program in Detroit "tends to perpetuate dependency by inadequate grants and confusing, inefficient organization." On the Pacific Coast, in Washington, "present standards of assistance tend to pauperize public assistance recipients; . . . families tend to deteriorate; . . . [the standards] may have debilitating effects on the recipients."[8]

The National Advisory Commission on Civil Disorders has charged the welfare system with contributing to tension and social disorder, encouraging dependency, alienating the recipient, and undermining self-respect.[9] The Citizens Board of Inquiry into Hunger and Malnutrition concludes that "welfare is at best irrational. At its worst – as is most often the case – it is

---

5. G. Bonem and P. Reno, "By Bread Alone, and Little Bread: Life on ADC," *Social Work* 13, no. 4: 5–11.

6. Welfare Council of Metropolitan Chicago, *ADC: Facts, Fallacies, Future: Summary of a Study of the ADC Program in Cook County* (Chicago, 1962), pp. 18–20.

7. B. Madison, "The Response of Public Welfare to the Challenge of Social and Economic Opportunity," *Public Welfare* 24, no. 4 (October 1966): 306–19.

8. Greenleigh Associates, Inc., *Report to the Moorland Commission on Welfare of the Findings of the Study of the Public Assistance Programs and Operations of the State of New York* (1964), p. 3; *Study of Services to Deal with Poverty in Detroit, Michigan* (1965), pp. 37–47; *Poverty-Prevention or Perpetration: A Study of the State Department of Public Assistance of the State of Washington, Summary Report* (1964), pp. 6, 20, 23.

9. *Report of the National Advisory Commission on Civil Disorders* (New York: Bantam Books, 1968), pp. 457–567.

an unrelenting assault on family integrity and stability."[10] Daniel Moynihan argues that the system "maintains the poverty groups in society in a position of impotent fury. Impotent because the system destroys the potential of individuals and families to improve themselves. Fury because it claims to be otherwise."[11]

Several students of the welfare system point out that it has the effect of institutionalizing poverty and dependence. Although any one family may receive welfare payments for a relatively short period of time, the system as a whole continues indefinitely, sustaining a group of welfare recipients whose membership may be in flux but which persists as a group. "Our present policy of dealing with poverty is designed not to eliminate but to institutionalize it," according to Robert Hess, who argues that "we are in the process of creating a permanent 'welfare class' . . . within a publicly financed bureaucratic structure."[12] The system is "analogous to colonialism," according to Glenn Jacobs, creating "a state of unilateral dependence, labeling and maintaining the individual in the socially defined category of the poor."[13]

We need not belabor the point any further. The level of welfare payments is such that it keeps the recipients in poverty. Their poverty in turn tends to reinforce itself because of the social and psychological impact of poverty on the poor.

Expansion of the Welfare System

A steady upswing in the size of the U.S. public assistance system began during the latter part of World War II. Just as economic growth has brought a higher GNP, increased output of goods and services, and rising prices, it has also brought an increased number of persons receiving public assistance and increased spending for that purpose. As the economy has progressed poverty has become more heavily institutionalized.

In 1945 four public assistance programs were in operation: old-age assistance, aid to the blind, AFDC, and general assistance. The first three were federal programs and the last primarily local. In that year total expenditures for the four programs was $990 million, and some 3,085,000 persons were served. The breakdown of recipients and expenditures by program is shown in table 2.

---

10. Citizens Board of Inquiry into Hunger and Malnutrition in the U.S., *Hunger, U.S.A.* (Washington, D.C.: New Community Press, 1968).

11. D. Moynihan, "The Crisis in Welfare," *The Public Interest*, no. 10 (Winter 1968): 3–29.

12. R. D. Hess, "Educability and Rehabilitation: The Future of the Welfare Class," *Journal of Marriage and the Family* 26, no. 4 (November 1964): 422–29.

13. G. Jacobs, "The Reification of the Notion of Subculture in Public Welfare," *Social Casework* 49, no. 9 (November 1968): 527–34.

Almost a quarter of a century later, in 1968, the number of public assistance programs had doubled. Aid to the permanently and totally disabled began in 1950, medical assistance for the aged in 1960, medical assistance for the poor in 1966, and emergency assistance in 1968. There has also been a startling increase in both recipients and payments. The situation in 1968 is shown in table 3.

Comparison of the public assistance programs in 1945 and 1968 shows almost no change in the number of persons receiving old-age assistance, aid to the blind, and general assistance, although the total payments have followed the cost of living upward and a little more. The largest increases among persons served were in AFDC – up from 701,000 to over 6,000,000 – and aid to the disabled – from no program to over 700,000 recipients. The largest increases in cost were in AFDC – from about $150 million to close

Table 2. Public Assistance Programs, 1945

	Recipients (Thousands)	Total Payments (Millions of $)
Old age assistance	2,056	726.6
Aid to the blind	71	26.6
AFDC	701[a]	149.7
General assistance	257	86.9
Total	3,085	989.8

[a] Includes only children.

Table 3. Public Assistance Programs, 1968

	Recipients (Thousands)	Total Payments (Millions of $)
Old-age assistance	2,028	1,778
Medical assistance for the aged	50[a]	66
Medical assistance	n.a.	3,783[b]
Aid to the blind	81	91
Aid to the disabled	703	692
Intermediate care facilities and emergency assistance	n.a.	11
AFDC	6,080[c]	2,851
General assistance	391	496
Total	9,333[d]	9,768

[a] 1967 figure, 1968 not available.

[b] Data incomplete.

[c] May include one or both parents or one caretaker relative among recipients, in addition to children.

[d] Does not include recipients of medical assistance and emergency assistance.

to $3 billion – and in Medicare's more than $3.75 billion, much of which has gone to the group receiving AFDC.

But Medicare does not provide continuing family support, and AFDC does. It supports over 6 million persons in poverty and provides close to $3 billion in income for that purpose. Furthermore, the number of persons supported by AFDC has marched steadily upward to present levels, with substantial acceleration in the growth trend in recent years. This growth is shown in chart 1.

Why has the number of recipients increased, particularly in the last few years? The usual explanation is that benefits have risen, drawing more persons onto the welfare rolls because welfare becomes more attractive than working as benefits go up. For example, the average monthly benefit payment per AFDC family was $105 in 1960 and $168 in 1968. In some states, such as New York, benefits are at considerably higher levels, reaching $249 per month per family in 1968.

Nevertheless, this simple explanation is probably inadequate. Only in New York did the increase in payment levels between 1960 and 1968 exceed the increase in wages for unskilled factory workers. In three other states, Pennsylvania, Michigan, and New Jersey, the increase in benefits just about equaled the increase in unskilled factory wages. In all other states welfare payments rose more slowly than the wages of unskilled factory labor. Yet the increase in persons and families receiving welfare payments has been nationwide. Second, both New York and California have seen dramatic increases in welfare recipients. But in New York welfare benefits, corrected for changes in the price level, rose by 50 percent between 1960 and 1968, whereas they did not rise at all in California.

There is obviously more behind the rise in the number of welfare recipients than the economic effects of the relationship between benefits and the other sources of income. A better explanation is the explosive growth of

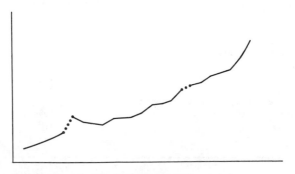

Note: Includes only children before October 1950.
      May include one parent or caretaker relative between
        October 1950 and October 1962.
      May include both parents or one caretaker relative
        after October 1962.

Chart 1. Number of AFDC Recipients, 1945–68

the urban ghettos themselves, which began in the early 1950s and culminated in the rebellions of 1967–68. I have described this phenomenon elsewhere:

> . . . A great migration of over one million blacks from southern agriculture to northern cities in 1949–55. . . . The subsequent population explosion in the black ghettos, with the attendant disintegration of the fabric of urban life. . . . The lack of adequate economic opportunities in the northern cities and the consequent increase in unemployment rates and poverty.[14]

The result was an explosive spread of the urban ghettos of central cities, which brought urban difficulties to crisis proportions.

It was inevitable that the welfare caseload should rise. The poverty, unemployment, and disintegration of family life characteristic of the urban ghetto could lead to nothing else. The riots of 1967–68 led to an acceleration of the increase, partly because of increased black militancy, partly as a result of efforts to alleviate tensions and reduce discontent, and partly because of an increased awareness of the great need. But the basic reason for the upsurge in welfare recipients is to be found not in the desire of poor people to get a free ride but in the expansion and growth of ghetto life itself.[15]

The Dynamics of the Ghetto Economy

The ghetto economy differs markedly from the rest of the economic system. It is the home of the bulk of urban poverty. It is permanently depressed, with unemployment rates normally at the high levels that are characteristic of depressions when they occur in the national economy. It is backward and underdeveloped, lacking the dynamic, progressive changes that bring advancement to the rest of the economy. Its manpower is employed in the low-wage sector of the economy primarily and provides a pool of low-skilled labor for an economy in which this resource is needed less and less. Within the ghetto an irregular economy, partly legal and partly illegal, provides many of the services needed by the low-income ghetto

---

14. "The Basic Economics of the Urban and Racial Crisis," *Conference Papers of the Union for Radical Political Economics*, December 1968, pp. 55–84, esp. pp. 60–66. An expanded version of this paper appeared in *The Michigan Academician* 2, no. 3 (Winter 1970).

15. A similar conclusion is reached by D. M. Gordon, "Income and Welfare in New York City," *The Public Interest*, no. 16 (Summer 1969): 64–88: "One can easily argue that the cause of the welfare 'crisis' is simply the widespread poverty in the city – not chiseling or welfare rights organizations or liberal administrative practices" (p. 87).

residents, which they cannot afford to pay for in the normal channels of commerce or which the regular economy does not provide at all.[16]

When we look at the relationships between the ghetto and the progressive sector of the economy, two phenomena quickly become evident. First, there is a continuous drain of income and other resources out of the ghetto. Second, there is a continuing accretion of people into it – people who are cast off as unusable by the progressive sector – which wholly or partially counterbalances those who are able to climb out.

The drain of resources includes savings, income, physical capital, and human resources. The savings of ghetto residents, small though they may be, are deposited in financial institutions whose loans are made to business firms or mortgage borrowers outside the ghetto, with a much smaller flow of capital into the ghetto for these purposes, leaving a net outflow. The size of the net outflow is unknown, but its presence is acknowledged by those who are familiar with the financial institutions that serve the ghetto.

Income is drained out in more easily observed ways. Products sold in the ghetto and to ghetto residents are produced outside the ghetto. The owners of the retail stores that sell these products and gain the profits live largely outside the ghetto. The same is true of the wholesale and shipping firms, advertising media, and other elements of the economy that service retail establishments. A large portion of the employees of ghetto retail firms live outside the ghetto, although this is less true since the 1967–68 riots than before.

Physical capital flows out of the ghetto largely through failure to replace depreciation of housing and public facilities. The ghetto landlord takes a large portion of his gains in the form of capital withdrawals that come from failure to maintain his property. This drain is large. Typically, 70 to 80 percent of ghetto residents rent their housing (as compared with 22 percent in the nation as a whole), and rent takes 35 to 60 percent of family income (as compared with 25 to 30 percent in the economy as a whole). A large portion of those rental payments represent a drain of capital out of housing. Public facilities are subject to the same outward flow through failure to maintain schools, streets, sidewalks, parks, and other public facilities in ghetto areas.

Manpower also leaves when it can. Many persons move out of the urban ghetto through education, skill, initiative, and luck. They move out primarily through jobs in the high-wage sector of the economy, and they take with them a large part of the entrepreneurship and skill that any substantial population group generates.

The net result of the drain of income and resources from the urban ghetto is the poor, backward, undeveloped slum that continues to exist in the midst of a growing, progressive society. It is drained of all resources

---

16. For a more detailed description of the ghetto economy see my paper "The Economy of the Urban Ghetto," in *Financing the Metropolis, Urban Affairs Annual Review*, vol. IV, ed. J. P. Crecine and L. H. Masotti (Beverly Hills, Calif.: Sage Publications, 1970).

that might form the base for economic development. When this situation is compounded by a weak community structure, inadequate public services, and relatively few professional skills, it is not hard to understand why the urban ghetto has been such an intractable problem.

It is legitimate to ask why the ghetto will not disappear as the progressive sector of the economy grows and draws on the manpower of the ghetto until it shrinks to nothing. Indeed, the standard liberal answer is that high rates of economic growth and full employment will indeed have that effect, and that in the future poverty in the United States will gradually and ultimately disappear, assisted by short-run programs of assistance of various sorts in education, housing, income maintenance, and so forth.

But the problem is not that simple. First, racial attitudes hold many in the ghettos who would otherwise be able to move up and out. Moving up is restricted by discrimination in employment; moving out is restricted by segregation in housing, zoning practices in the suburbs, and white attitudes toward blacks.

Second, ghetto life itself creates ways of thinking, acting, and working that are dysfunctional outside the ghetto. The habits of work characteristic of the irregular economy are not those of the usual factory or office. Attitudes towards authority, including that of the boss, are quite different. The same is true of the low-wage industries, but to a lesser extent. The same generalization applies to patterns of family life and personal relationships: ghetto patterns are different from those of the middle-class world outside the ghetto. Attitudes and behavior patterns necessary for survival in the ghetto inhibit movement out.

Finally – and perhaps more important – the urban ghetto is a place where society collects its rejects. People in the social system who for one reason or another become residuals are found in the urban ghetto. Like prisons and mental hospitals, the urban ghetto is a residual subsystem in which the human rejects from the economy and society find a place.[17] One example is the migration of the early 1950s: unskilled and poorly educated black agricultural workers, displaced from the lowest level of the economic system by mechanization of the cotton harvest and corn farming in a rural society unwilling to provide them with any other place, gravitated to the urban ghettos. There they found an even lower subsystem of the social order in which they were acceptable and in which they were able to survive. Although that example is a particularly large and visible one, the same process functions continuously on a smaller scale to provide new manpower for the ghetto.

When the process of rejection from the larger economy takes place on a larger scale and at a faster pace than the movement up and out of the ghetto, the urban ghettos expand and grow, and conditions deteriorate, which is

---

17. The concept of the urban ghetto as a residual subsystem is developed further in "The Economy of the Urban Ghetto."

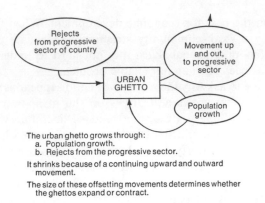

The urban ghetto grows through:
a. Population growth.
b. Rejects from the progressive sector.
It shrinks because of a continuing upward and outward movement.
The size of these offsetting movements determines whether the ghettos expand or contract.

Chart 2. Dynamics of the Urban Ghetto: Expansion and Contraction

what happened in the 1950s and 1960s. The two movements are perhaps balanced at the present time, and there are some indications that in several large cities the ghettos may be shrinking, but there is no reason to believe that either continued growth or gradual shrinkage of the ghettos is an inevitable trend. The process is diagramed in simple fashion in chart 2.

Examination of the characteristics of ghetto residents tells us the chief factors that cause rejection from the progressive sector of the economy: (1) race – blacks, Puerto Ricans, Mexican-Americans, and other minority groups; (2) recent arrival – migrants from the rural South, Southwest, and Puerto Rico; (3) cultural differences – persons with a cultural background different from the white middle-class culture; (4) low productivity – low earning power resulting from lack of skills, poor education, bad health, old age, and related factors; and (5) low income – inability to live in the style of the white middle class because of inadequate financial resources.

These factors appear to be the major reasons for rejection from the progressive sector of the economy; they are the chief barriers to movement up and out, and one tends to reinforce another. Furthermore, the fact that the ghetto is a quasi enclave, separated in a number of important ways from the rest of the economy and society, tends to reinforce and strengthen the cultural differences that make outward movement difficult. At the same time, the ghetto's poverty and permanent depression keep incomes low and reinforce the low earning power that tends to keep ghetto residents where they are.

The Role of Welfare Payments

Welfare payments perform some significant functions in the ghetto economy, the most important of which is the preservation of the ghetto economy itself. The drain of income and resources from the urban ghetto would normally be expected to set in motion a downward spiral of incomes and economic activity until the whole economic subsystem of the ghetto stabilized itself at a low level. This "normal" equilibrium, so to speak, could be sustained by the inflow of incomes to the ghetto by way of employment in the low-wage industries and other inflows of earned income and transfer payments. But at this lower equilibrium level we would expect the ghetto economy as a whole to be able to support a smaller irregular economy, the pool of low-wage labor would be larger, and higher rates of unemployment would prevail.

Welfare payments enable the economic equilibrium of the urban ghetto to be sustained at a somewhat higher level. The income transfers from the progressive sector of the economy, which welfare payments represent, increase the total income of the ghetto, support a larger irregular economy, and enable the ghetto subsystem to function at a somewhat higher level than its "normal" equilibrium. For example, welfare payments enable a larger number of family units to subsist at the poverty level, and these family units add to the demand for slum housing from the housing industry.[18] The net result is a larger ghetto area and a larger outflow of physical capital into the hands of slumlords. By contrast, if there were no welfare payments the families now receiving them would either perish or double up with related persons into even larger family units. The demand for slum housing would be smaller and the ghettos themselves would be reduced in size. But population densities would be greater, incomes would be lower (per person), and the conditions of poverty would be intensified.

It is important to note, however, that although welfare payments are able to raise the incomes of the recipient families and thereby reduce the intensity of poverty within the ghetto as a whole, they do not alter the drain of resources and income out of the ghetto. That drain continues, and property owners and businessmen who make profits out of the ghetto are expanded in number and their receipts are enlarged. This is the fundamental dilemma faced by public policies that seek to ameliorate the condition of ghetto residents: although they may succeed in improving conditions of life for the recipients, they also result in preservation of the ghetto as a whole.

This point is so important that it bears repeating: as long as welfare payments remain so low that they keep recipients mired in poverty, any given level of payments will serve to stabilize the urban ghettos at a particular level of existence. Lower welfare payments will mean a greater degree of poverty there, whereas higher payments will mean poverty of less intensity. But whatever the level, *the function of welfare payments in the social system as a whole is to preserve the urban ghetto as a residual subsystem and as a source of low-wage workers.*

---

18. See R. F. Muth, *Cities and Housing: The Spatial Pattern of Urban Residential Land Use* (Chicago: University of Chicago Press, 1969), pp. 14, 115–35, and 241–83. Public subsidy to slums through AFDC payments is also suggested in A. R. McCabe, "Forty Forgotten Families," *Public Welfare* 24, no. 2 (April 1966): 159–71, esp. p. 164.

Appendix

Estimated Unmet Income Needs of Welfare (AFDC) Recipients, 1968, by State and Region

	(1) Average Monthly AFDC Payment Per Family	(2) Average Income from Other Sources ×1.5	(3) Average Total Income Per AFDC Family	(4) Orshansky Line ($277.90 Per Month)	(5) BLS Line ($405.17 Per Month)	(6) Number of Recipient Families	(7) Total Unmet Need (000 dollars), Based on Orshansky Line	(8) BLS Line
New England states								10,857
Massachusetts	$243.70	$50.53a	294.23	+16.33	110.94	45.0	185	4,995
Maine	110.45	79.50	189.95	87.95	215.12	6.8	+735	1,462
New Hampshire	180.65	53.00	233.65	44.25	171.52	1.7	595	292
Vermont	180.35	66.50	246.86	31.05	158.32	2.9	75	459
Rhode Island	173.75	26.25	200.00	77.90	205.17	8.5	660	1,744
Connecticut	259.85	43.50	303.35	+26.45	100.82	18.9	+500	1,905
Middle Atlantic states							942	46,998
New York	248.65	51.75	301.40	+23.50	103.77	248.0	+5,820	25,742
New Jersey	236.10	47.50	271.20	+6.70	120.57	42.9	+288	4,174
Pennsylvania	158.60	29.75	187.45	89.55	216.82	78.8	7,050	17,084
East north central states							11,846	39,453
Ohio	154.10	30.75	184.85	93.05	220.32	59.5	5,540	13,108
Indiana	133.75	70.50	204.25	73.65	200.92	13.4	986	2,692
Illinois	207.55	31.00	238.55	39.35	166.62	75.0	2,960	12,495
Michigan	189.35	50.00	239.35	38.55	165.82	49.6	1,920	8,224
Wisconsin	214.95	41.00	255.95	21.95	149.22	19.6	430	2,924
West north central states							5,299	14,016
Minnesota	200.35	42.50	242.85	35.05	162.32	17.6	618	2,856
Iowa	192.25	50.25	242.50	35.40	162.67	14.2	503	2,310

Missouri	109.80	69.75	179.55	98.35	225.62	29.2	2,860	4,568
North Dakota	187.15	43.50	230.65	47.25	164.52	2.5	118	411
South Dakota	162.00	28.25	290.25	87.65	214.92	3.8	334	817
Nebraska	147.45	71.50	218.45	66.95	194.22	6.4	428	1,244
Kansas	188.5	49.25	237.40	40.50	167.57	10.8	438	1,810
South Atlantic states							22,321	45,759
Delaware	129.35	68.25	197.60	80.30	207.57	4.5	361	934
Maryland	156.50	41.75	198.25	79.65	206.92	29.2	2,320	5,041
District of Columbia	178.90	36.60	215.50	52.40	179.67	6.7	350	1,204
Virginia	131.35	53.25	184.60	93.30	220.57	15.6	1,450	3,441
West Virginia	114.75	12.75	127.50	150.40	277.67	19.6	2,980	5,443
North Carolina	112.20	53.00	165.20	112.70	239.97	26.9	3,020	6,456
South Carolina	72.00	36.50	108.50	169.40	296.67	9.2	1,560	2,740
Georgia	96.00	28.00	124.00	153.90	281.17	36.1	5,540	10,151
Florida	87.10	83.00	170.10	107.90	235.17	44.0	4,740	10,349
East south central states							17,190	30,757
Kentucky	112.35	33.50	145.85	132.05	259.32	29.8	3,950	7,727
Tennessee	102.40	35.00	137.40	140.50	267.77	27.5	3,850	7,364
Alabama	64.10	40.25	104.35	173.55	300.82	24.3	4,220	7,309
Mississippi	34.15	42.00	76.15	201.75	329.02	25.4	5,170	8,357
West south central states							14,640	28,031
Arkansas	78.05	30.50	108.55	169.36	296.63	9.8	1,660	2,907
Louisiana	103.25	41.00	144.25	133.66	260.93	37.1	4,950	9,679
Oklahoma	129.75	24.75	154.50	123.41	250.68	23.3	2,880	5,841
Texas	86.25	44.50	130.75	147.16	274.43	35.0	5,150	9,604
Mountain states							5,813	12,580
Montana	138.90	35.00	173.90	104.00	231.27	2.8	292	447
Idaho	176.35	37.00	213.35	66.55	193.82	3.3	220	970
Wyoming	141.85	47.00	188.85	89.05	216.32	1.2	107	262
Colorado	149.50	22.50	172.00	105.90	233.17	14.8	1,567	3,450
New Mexico	122.25	25.00	147.25	130.65	257.92	11.1	1,520	2,863
Arizona	118.90	36.75	157.65	122.25	244.52	10.3	1,260	2,518
Utah	153.95	43.25	197.15	80.70	207.97	7.3	588	1,518
Nevada	117.35	47.75	165.10	112.80	240.07	2.3	259	552

Continued on p. 92

Appendix—*continued*

	(1) Average Monthly AFDC Payment Per Family	(2) Average Income from Other Sources × 1.5	(3) Average Total Income Per AFDC Family	(4) Orshansky Line (277.90 Per Month)	(5) BLS Line ($405.17 Per Month)	(6) Number of Recipient Families	(7) Orshansky Line	(8) BLSLine
				Monthly unmet need per family: poverty line monthly income minus average total income per AFDC family			Total Unmet Need (000 dollars), Based on	
Pacific states								
Washington	178.15	48.50	226.65	51.35	178.62	20.1	14,846	49,995
California	185.10	40.00	225.10	52.80	180.07	236.0	1,030	3,590
Alaska	167.55	71.00	238.55	39.35	167.62	1.8	12,400	42,504
Hawaii	192.95	45.50	238.45	39.45	166.72	5.1	71	302
Oregon	145.25	41.75[a]	187.00	90.90	218.17	12.6	200	850
United States	167.80	40.25	208.05	69.85	197.12	1521.0	1,145	2,749
							106,442	299,789

Sources: See table I.

[a] Data not available, figure for the region used instead.

5

Anita B. Pfaff: Transfer Payments
to Large Metropolitan Poverty
Areas: Their Distributive and
Poverty-Reducing Effects

Introduction

The continuing existence of urban poverty introduces a jarring note into the self-image of a society that prides itself on its economic attainment and social progress. At a time of increasing prosperity and involvement in the economic development of other less developed and largely agricultural countries, the United States has come to "discover" pockets of backwardness in the heart of its industrial conglomerations in the sprawling cities. Just as less developed countries are occasionally characterized by a dual economy – islands of development and relative affluence surrounded by a sea of traditional and less affluent areas – we may view the U.S. economy in terms of its dual nature, only with the signs reversed – pockets of urban (and rural) poverty are surrounded by areas of advancement. Furthermore, if it is the industrial enclave in the developing country that produces the economic and social dynamics for the entire nation, it is the urban ghetto that is both the most dramatic symbol and the cause of the social crisis of minority groups struggling for a place in the sun.

Urban poverty goes hand in hand with a lack of skills, discrimination, and the inability to partake in the industrial process. Thus an alienated "urban proletariat" of about 4.7 million families lives in our large standard metropolitan statistical areas (SMSAs) at a level of attainment that must be classified as "poor before transfers."

The objective of this paper is to probe into the effects that social welfare legislation has had on alleviating urban poverty in large SMSAs in general and in urban poverty areas in particular. When we consider that during the fiscal year 1969 a total of $127 billion was spent on social welfare expenditures by federal, state, and local governments[1] – a figure greater than the

Printed by permission. All rights reserved. The author is assistant professor of quantitative methods at Wayne State University and Wissenschaftlichen Rat and professor at the University of Augsburg. She wishes to acknowledge the assistance and advice of Mr. David Johnstone, Wayne State University, who performed the many arduous computational tasks. She has benefited greatly from discussions with Benjamin Okner of The Brookings Institution.

1. A. Skolnik and S. R. Dales, "Social Welfare Expenditures 1968–1969," *Social Security Bulletin* 32 (December 1969).

gross national product (GNP) of a large number of less developed countries – then we raise the persistent question of what impact such a seemingly massive infusion of funds, constituting about 14 percent of GNP, has had on urban poverty.[2] Although these disbursements involve transfers or grants in cash and in kind, the subsequent analysis will be restricted to cash transfers under various programs.

What are the spatial redistributive patterns of these massive disbursements? Table 1 provides an overview of total expenditures and cash benefits of selected social welfare programs for 1966.[3] Of the total of nearly $39 billion in expenditures for the United States (shown in column 1), about $22.4 billion went for Social Security, $2.7 billion for unemployment insurance, $2 billion for workmen's compensation, $7.2 billion for public assistance, and $4.5 billion for veterans' pensions. Social Security and public assistance, the two major programs, will keep our attention in the subsequent analysis. Column 2 shows the corresponding distribution of cash benefits: Of the $20 billion in Social Security cash benefits, $7.7 billion (or 38 percent) went to large SMSAs; of that, $4 billion (or 20 percent of the total) went to central cities within these SMSAs and $3.6 billion (or 18 percent of the total) to the fringe (or suburban) areas within the large SMSAs. Within the central cities only about $1 billion (or 5.43 percent) went to the poor areas, whereas $3 billion (or 14.86 percent) was disbursed to nonpoor areas. Social Security thus is clearly not a program designed to combat urban poverty.

Of the remaining programs shown in table 1, public assistance may be examined in a similar vein. Of the $4.3 billion disbursed in the form of cash benefits, $1.8 billion (or 42.68 percent) went to large SMSAs; of that, $1.4 billion (or about 32 percent of the total) was disbursed to central cities and $807.8 million (or 18.7 percent of the total) to fringe areas. Within the central cities, poor areas received about $876 million (or 20.35 percent of the total), whereas nonpoor areas obtained about $500 million (or 11.61 percent of the total). Although it may come as a surprise to some that less than one-third of public assistance goes to large SMSAs, it may be even more surprising to note that only one-fifth goes to poor areas within these large SMSAs. However, public assistance benefits the poor areas more than the nonpoor areas in contra-distinction to Social Security.

Turning to the other programs reported in table 1, we note that urban

2. For a description and history of the various social welfare programs, see I. C. Merriam and A. N. Skolnik, *Social Welfare Expenditures Under Public Programs in the United States, 1929–1966*, U.S. Department of Health, Education, and Welfare, Social Security Administration, Office of Research and Statistics, Research Report No. 257 (Washington, D.C.: U.S. Government Printing Office, 1968).

3. This and the subsequent tables were tabulated by the author from the Office of Economic Opportunity's Survey of Economic Opportunity (SEO) file. While this study parallels the works of Benjamin Okner and Robert Lampman in many ways, figures are not fully compatible, because in this study transfer payments were weighted to program totals based on a uniform distribution of rate of error in reporting, which was not done by Okner and Lampman.

Table 1. Total Expenditures and Cash Benefits of Selected Social Welfare Programs, 1966 (In Millions of Dollars)

	Total Expenditures	Cash Benefits											
		USA		Large SMSAs									
				Total		Central City						Fringe Areas	
						Total		Poor Areas		Nonpoor Areas			
	Amount (Million $)	Amount (Million $)	%	Amount (Million $)	%	Amount (Million $)	%	Amount (Million $)	%	Amount (Million $)	%	Amount (Million $)	%
Social Security	22,438.1a	20,048.3b	100	7,674.5f	38.28	4,069.6f	20.30	1,089.5f	5.43	2,980.0f	14.86	3,605.1f	17.98
Unemployment Insurance and Services	2,707.1a	1,891.5c	100	959.1f	50.71	480.7f	25.41	175.0f	9.25	305.7f	16.16	478.4f	25.29
Workmen's Compensation	2,076.5a	1,293.0b	100	620.9f	48.02	229.8f	17.77	58.1f	4.49	171.7f	13.28	391.1f	30.25
Public Assistance	7,180.8a	4,303.8d	100	1,836.7f	42.68	1,375.5f	31.96	875.8f	20.35	499.7f	11.61	807.8f	18.77
Veterans' Pensions	4,467a	4,432.5e	100	1,463.5f	33.02	655.7f	14.79	191.6f	4.32	464.1f	10.47	461.2f	10.40
Total	38,870.2	32,108.2	100	12,554.7	39.10	6,811.3	21.21	2,390.0	7.44	4,421.2	13.77	5,743.6	17.89
No. of families (in thousands)		61,696.0f	100	24,835.8f	40.26	11,890.4f	19.27	3,651.0f	5.92	8,240.7f	13.36	12,945.6f	20.98

Source:

a *Social Security Bulletin: Annual Statistical Supplement, 1967*, p. 14, table 3, Annual Average of Fiscal Years 1965–67.

b Ibid., p. 18, table 9.

c Ibid., p. 18, table 9; includes payments by states or agents of federal government and other programs, as well as railroad unemployment.

d Ibid., p. 124, table 128.

e Ibid., p. 18, table 9; the amount somewhat overstates cash benefits due to veterans' pensions, including other veterans programs as well.

f Inferred from SEO file.

poverty areas in large SMSAs receive 9.25 percent of unemployment insurance, 4.49 percent of workmen's compensation, and 4.32 percent of veterans' pensions, for a total of 7.44 percent of all social welfare grants programs. These figures indicate that of the impressive sum of about $32 billion disbursed as cash payments, only $2.4 billion went to urban poverty areas within the large SMSAs. This may be contrasted with the not uncommon belief that public assistance and other welfare measures go largely to the poor in a few major urban ghettos. As the subsequent analysis will show, many other images of the recipients of welfare benefits are not supportable by economic facts.

The Distributive Effect of Transfer Payments

The Effect of Transfers on the Distribution of Income

An estimated 24.8 million families live in the twelve large standard metropolitan statistical areas of the United States.[4] An estimated 3.6 million families among these live in areas classified as central-city poverty areas.[5,6] Tables 2 through 6 show the distributive effects of social welfare payments on income by five socioeconomic classifiers: (1) race, (2) income, (3) family type, (4) education of family head, and (5) work experience of family head. Each table shows the distributions for the large SMSAs in general and for the central-city poverty areas of those large SMSAs in particular.

1. Table 2 exhibits the distribution of income minus social welfare payments, of social welfare payments, and income after social welfare payments, respectively, *by race of family*. It indicates that 87 percent of all families residing in large SMSAs are white, 12.1 percent are black, and the remaining 0.9 percent are members of other races. The discussion will confine itself to a comparison between whites and blacks because the third

---

4. The large standard metropolitan statistical areas are Baltimore, Chicago, Cleveland, Detroit, Houston, Los Angeles, New York, Philadelphia, Pittsburgh, St. Louis, San Francisco, and Washington, D.C.

5. Estimates of the distributive and poverty-reducing effects of public transfers to central-city poverty areas, although based on a rather small subsample of the Survey of Economic Opportunity, may be considered reasonably reliable because the sample is heavily weighted on poor respondents and black people.

6. "A poverty area is defined as (1) any area having five or more contiguous 'poor' tracts regardless of number of poor families; (2) any group of one to four contiguous 'poor' tracts containing an aggregate of 4,000 or more families; (3) any area of one or two contiguous tracts not ranked in the lowest quartile but completely surrounded by such 'poor' tracts. In some cases areas of three or four contiguous tracts not themselves 'poor' were surrounded by 'poor' tracts and were included in the neighborhood after analysis of their individual characteristics" (1967 Survey of Economic Opportunity Codebook). This definition of poverty area was updated for urban renewal.

Table 2. The Effect of Social Welfare Payments on Income Distribution by Race of Recipient

Large SMSAs

	Income before Transfers			Transfers			Income after Transfers			No. of Families	
	Amount		Mean	Amount		Mean	Amount		Mean		
White	182301.125	91.7%	8441.17	10704.973	85.3%	495.67	192998.063	91.3%	8936.47	21596.652	87.0%
Black	15051.602	7.6%	5002.00	1783.957	14.2%	592.85	16834.699	8.0%	5594.56	3009.116	12.1%
Other	1550.907	0.8%	7145.94	62.836	0.5%	289.52	1613.741	0.8%	7435.45	217.033	0.9%
Total	198903.563	100.0%	8012.94	12551.762	100.0%	505.65	211446.438	100.0%	8518.23	24822.781	100.0%

Central-City Poverty Areas

	Income before Transfers			Transfers			Income after Transfers			No. of Families	
	Amount		Mean	Amount		Mean	Amount		Mean		
White	9294.609	58.7%	4663.57	1301.259	54.4%	652.90	10595.688	58.2%	5316.38	1993.023	54.6%
Black	6258.770	39.6%	3944.29	1067.400	44.7%	672.67	7325.430	40.2%	4616.50	1586.791	43.5%
Other	268.742	1.7%	3809.58	21.200	0.9%	300.52	289.942	1.6%	4110.10	70.544	1.9%
Total	15822.117	100.0%	4334.40	2389.860	100.0%	654.69	18211.055	100.0%	4988.84	3650.357	100.0%

"Amount" in millions of dollars.
"No. of Families" in thousands.

group is very small and racially rather heterogeneous. The average income minus transfers of white families exceeds that of black families by more than $3,000. Social welfare payments are slightly redistributive to blacks. The average amount of social welfare payments received by black families is approximately $100 higher than that received by white families. However, even this redistribution of income does not significantly reduce the disparity between the income levels. (These figures are somewhat higher than corresponding amounts for the total USA, which are not shown in this paper.) The inequality in income distribution between white and black is also illustrated by the percentage amounts of income received by given percentages of the population. The percentages indicate how very slight the redistributive effect is. Whereas before transfers 12.1 percent of the population, who are black, receive 7.6 percent of total income, they receive 8 percent of total income after transfers.

The racial composition of central-city poverty areas (lower half of table 2) differs considerably from that of total large SMSAs; 54.6 percent of families living in central-city poverty areas are white, 43.5 percent are black, and 1.9 percent are members of other races. The 54.6 percent white families receive 58.7 percent of total income minus social welfare payments[7] accruing to families living in poverty areas of central cities; black families receive 39.6 percent. This indicates that white families receive higher incomes than black families. Whereas white families have a mean income of over $4,600, the mean income for black families lies below $4,000. Black residents receive slightly higher social welfare benefits on the average; the white population receives a share of social welfare payments almost proportionate to its size. The average social welfare payment to residents of central-city poverty areas is somewhat higher than the average payment to residents of total large SMSAs.[8] The pattern of the relative shares of income including transfers received by black and white families is very similar to that of income before transfers: the white population has a slightly (0.5 percent) lower share of income after transfers than of income before, whereas the black population's share is increased by 0.6 percent. This would indicate that social welfare payments favor black people in urban areas very slightly; however, no marked redistribution through public transfer payments is involved.

2. Table 3 shows the distribution of total income before transfers, the sum of the social welfare payments under consideration, and total income

---

7. Subsequently the terms *social welfare payments* and *transfers* refer to the five types included in this analysis.

8. The figures shown seem low in comparison to published data; this is explained by the fact that means are computed for the total population, including nonrecipients of the welfare payment. The average welfare payment for the population of recipients in large SMSAs is approximately $1,500 and that in central-city poverty areas $1,570. These figures are consistent with published program averages.

Table 3. The Effect of Social Welfare Payments on Income Distribution by Income after Social Welfare Payments

Large SMSAs

	Income before Transfers			Transfers			Income after Transfers			No. of Families	
	Amount		Mean	Amount		Mean	Amount		Mean		
Negative income	−53.144	−0.0%	−2450.75	0.822	0.0%	37.90	−52.322	−0.0%	−2412.84	21.685	0.1%
Zero income	0.0	0.0%	0.0	0.0	0.0%	0.0	0.0	0.0%	0.0	139.002	0.6%
$1 thru $599	48.053	0.0%	159.07	39.332	0.3%	130.20	87.385	0.0%	289.27	302.083	1.2%
$600 thru $999	156.807	0.1%	392.90	161.994	1.3%	405.90	318.796	0.2%	798.80	399.092	1.6%
$1,000 thru $1,499	396.941	0.2%	519.23	563.372	4.5%	736.94	960.301	0.5%	1256.16	764.471	3.1%
$1,500 thru $1,999	649.203	0.3%	793.90	784.070	6.2%	958.83	1433.280	0.7%	1752.74	817.737	3.3%
$2,000 thru $2,499	980.844	0.5%	1174.40	884.620	7.0%	1059.18	1865.474	0.9%	2233.60	835.187	3.4%
$2,500 thru $2,999	1154.738	0.6%	1542.64	884.938	7.0%	1182.21	2039.685	1.0%	2724.87	748.543	3.0%
$3,000 thru $4,999	10090.258	5.1%	3048.14	2954.142	23.5%	892.41	13044.020	6.2%	3940.44	3310.293	13.3%
$5,000 thru $9,999	65615.625	33.0%	6953.96	3345.146	30.6%	407.51	69459.188	32.8%	7361.30	9435.715	38.0%
$10,000 thru $24,999	101828.125	51.2%	13463.91	2342.934	18.7%	309.78	104170.188	49.2%	13773.59	7536.035	30.5%
$25,000 and above	18142.148	9.1%	36361.21	93.168	0.7%	186.73	18235.328	8.6%	36547.97	498.942	2.0%
Total	199009.563	100.0%	8013.02	12554.527	100.0%	505.50	211561.313	100.0%	8518.41	24835.758	100.0%

Central-City Poverty Areas

	Income before Transfers			Transfers			Income after Transfers			No. of Families	
	Amount		Mean	Amount		Mean	Amount		Mean		
Negative income	−3.141	−0.0%	−2565.60	0.484	0.0%	395.30	−2.657	−0.0%	−2170.30	1.224	0.0%
Zero income	0.0	0.0%	0.0	0.0	0.0%	0.0	0.0	0.0%	0.0	57.897	1.6%
$1 thru $599	30.597	0.2%	246.54	11.486	0.5%	92.54	42.082	0.2%	339.08	124.105	3.4%
$600 thru $999	61.344	0.4%	424.09	59.790	2.5%	413.35	121.134	0.7%	837.44	144.647	4.0%
$1,000 thru $1,499	107.767	0.7%	428.32	206.393	8.6%	820.31	314.156	1.7%	1248.62	251.602	6.9%
$1,500 thru $1,999	160.506	1.0%	751.51	207.151	8.7%	969.90	367.646	2.0%	1721.36	213.578	5.8%
$2,000 thru $2,499	334.552	2.1%	1216.83	275.323	11.5%	1001.41	609.864	3.3%	2218.20	274.936	7.5%
$2,500 thru $2,999	332.373	2.1%	1592.70	233.403	9.8%	1118.44	565.761	3.1%	2711.08	208.684	5.7%
$3,000 thru $4,999	2567.072	16.2%	3098.95	659.609	27.6%	796.27	3226.695	17.7%	3895.25	828.366	22.7%
$5,000 thru $9,999	7629.988	48.2%	6426.99	592.050	24.8%	498.70	8221.969	45.1%	6925.63	1187.179	32.5%
$10,000 thru $24,999	4338.883	27.4%	12389.02	143.542	6.0%	409.86	4482.426	24.6%	12798.89	350.220	9.6%
$25,000 and above	263.732	1.7%	30834.88	0.750	0.0%	87.64	264.481	1.5%	30922.52	8.553	0.2%
Total	15823.672	100.0%	4334.07	2389.981	100.0%	654.61	18213.559	100.0%	4988.66	3650.991	100.0%

"Amount" in millions of dollars. "No. of Families" in thousands.

after transfers, by *class of total income after transfers*. The upper half of the table represents the data for all large SMSAs together. More than two-thirds of the population of large SMSAs receive an income after transfers between $5,000 and $25,000. The 16.3 percent of the population with income after transfers under $3,000 receive only 0.6 percent of total income before transfers. The mean income levels of families with an annual income between $600 and $3,000 indicate that a large number of families in these groups are lifted to a different income class by transfer payments. Comparison of the percentage of families in different income classes and the transfer payments they receive indicates that on the average, families in the income classes between $600 and $5,000 receive a more than proportionate share of transfers. The mean amount of transfer payments for these income classes is relatively higher than in other income classes. Overall the effect on the distribution of income is rather small however. The income share of families under $3,000 of income after transfers is increased from 1.7 percent to 3.3 percent.

In central-city poverty areas, as may be expected, the concentration of middle-income families is not as high as in the large SMSAs. In central-city poverty areas 32.5 percent of all families have an annual income between $5,000 and $10,000; the concentration between $10,000 and $25,000 is not as high. However, a large number of families (22.7 percent) receive income between $3,000 and $5,000. Of course, a high percentage of families with very low income can be found in these areas. The overall income in poverty areas is considerably lower than in the total large SMSAs; the average difference is almost $3,700.

The average amount of public transfers per family in poverty areas is approximately $150 higher than the average amount of transfers to families in all areas of the large SMSAs. In poverty areas and total large SMSAs relatively high transfers are received by families with an income after transfers between $2,000 and $10,000. Income groups below and above this range receive less. The difference in mean income after transfers between large SMSAs and in central-city poverty areas only is still more than $3,500. In poverty areas of central cities the relative share of total income after transfers for income groups over $10,000 is decreased by 1 percent as compared to income before transfers.[9] The income share of families under $3,000 annual income after transfers is raised from 6.5 percent to 11 percent by social welfare payments.

3. A variety of socioeconomic indicators influences the level of income and the eligibility to receive welfare payments. The type of family and the public's desire to support the family outside the market – that is, through

---

9. Estimates for low-income groups based on the Survey of Economic Opportunity file are likely to be better than those for higher-income groups because the sample is more heavily weighted on the low-income and black population.

Table 4. The Effect of Social Welfare Payments on Income Distribution by Type of Family

Large SMSAs

	Income before Transfers			Transfers			Income after Transfers			No. of Families	
	Amount		Mean	Amount		Mean	Amount		Mean		
Male head and spouse	165201.375	83.1%	9967.75	6542.152	52.1%	394.73	171739.313	81.2%	10362.23	16573.574	66.7%
Male head no spouse	3762.529	1.9%	8373.56	445.184	3.5%	990.76	4207.715	2.0%	9364.34	449.334	1.8%
Female head	10211.770	5.1%	4424.32	2713.953	21.6%	1175.84	12925.195	6.1%	5599.94	2308.095	9.3%
Primary individual	16432.879	8.3%	3628.66	2621.307	20.9%	578.83	19053.430	9.0%	4207.32	4528.633	18.2%
Secondary individual	3293.116	1.7%	3376.71	230.595	1.8%	236.44	3523.703	1.7%	3613.15	975.243	3.9%
Total	198901.438	100.0%	8003.97	12553.184	100.0%	505.46	211449.188	100.0%	8514.21	24834.828	100.0%

Central-City Poverty Areas

	Income before Transfers			Transfers			Income after Transfers			No. of Families	
	Amount		Mean	Amount		Mean	Amount		Mean		
Male head and spouse	10139.141	64.1%	6330.60	851.271	35.6%	531.51	10990.270	60.3%	6862.02	1601.608	43.9%
Male head no spouse	542.796	3.4%	5872.04	100.539	4.2%	1087.65	643.333	3.5%	6959.67	92.437	2.5%
Female head	1553.005	9.8%	2672.05	688.553	28.8%	1184.70	2241.577	12.3%	3856.78	581.204	15.9%
Primary individual	2884.496	18.2%	2662.79	639.108	26.7%	589.98	3523.604	19.3%	3252.78	1083.259	29.7%
Secondary individual	703.360	4.4%	2406.59	110.438	4.6%	377.86	813.791	4.5%	2784.43	292.264	8.0%
Total	15822.789	100.0%	4334.09	2389.908	100.0%	654.63	18212.566	100.0%	4988.68	3650.771	100.0%

"Amount" in millions of dollars.

"No. of Families" in thousands.

transfers – have an impact on the family's ability to earn income. Table 4 shows the distributive pattern of income before public transfers, public transfers, and income after public transfers by *type of family*. Five different family types are analyzed. The first group involves families with a male head whose wife is present. In large SMSAs 66.7 percent – that is, about two-thirds of the population – had this particular structure. By comparison only 43.9 percent of the families living in central-city poverty areas have male heads with spouses present. The second group is families with a male head without a wife present. This group constitutes only a small proportion of the population, both in central-city poverty areas and in large SMSAs; however, in central-city poverty areas the percentage is slightly larger. The third type of families considered is the family headed by a female. Of families in large SMSAs 9.3 percent have a female head of family; 15.9 percent of families in central-city poverty areas belong to this group. The last two types are not families, strictly speaking, but individuals – that is, persons living without relatives. A primary individual is a person who lives either alone or with other single individuals. A secondary individual is a single person who lives with another family to whom he is not related; an example would be either a roomer or a housekeeper. Secondary individuals constitute only a small fraction of the population, particularly in large SMSAs; in central-city poverty areas approximately 8 percent of the "families" are classified as secondary individuals. A sizable number of "families" are primary individuals; in central-city poverty areas almost one-third of the population falls into this group.

A relatively larger share of income before and after transfers accrues to families with a male head whose spouse is present. This is also reflected in the high mean income level of families of this type. In large SMSAs their mean income level is near $10,000. Families with a male head and no spouse present have the next highest mean income. The mean income level of families with a female head is considerably lower than that of families with male heads; the mean income of families with male heads and spouses present is $9,967.75, whereas the mean income of families with female heads is only $4,424.33. The mean income of primary and secondary individuals is even lower. Transfers exhibit a redistributive pattern: among families with more than one individual, families with female heads on the average receive the lowest income, but they have the highest average transfer receipts ($1,175.84). On the other hand, families with a male head whose spouse is present have a relatively low average receipt of transfers.[10]

---

10. The high variability in these averages can be explained by the fact that the number of families receiving social welfare payments differs in different groups. If averages are taken for recipients only, the variability is reduced considerably: the average for a family with a female head would be $1,929.62, whereas the average transfer payment to families with male heads and spouses present would be $1,481.02.

Although a little more than one-quarter of families with male heads and spouses present receive social welfare payments, considerably more than one-half of all families with female heads of family receive social welfare payments. The amounts of total income after public transfers accruing to different family types show that public transfers have a slight income-equalizing effect. However, they fall far short of achieving anything near equality between different family types. Central-city poverty areas (lower half of table 4) exhibit a similar pattern, in terms of the mean levels of income, except that mean income levels are scaled down considerably to the lower mean income in central-city poverty areas. However, income levels of families with female heads of households and of individuals are very close in central-city poverty areas; they differ much more in total large SMSAs. Patterns of transfers in central-city poverty areas differ somewhat from those in large SMSAs: the largest relative share of transfer payments in large SMSAs goes to families with female heads, whereas in central-city poverty areas a larger relative share is received by families with male heads without spouses. Although social welfare payments have a slightly moderating or income-equalizing effect between different types of families, it is evident that social welfare payments by no means achieve a *sizable* redistribution between families of different structures.

4. It has been argued that receipt of transfer payments serves as a disincentive to *participation in the labor force*.[11] In a time series study of this phenomenon no conclusive support of this hypothesis could be found. The opposite could not be proved either, although a positive association seems indicated for males and a negative association for females.[12] The general relationship between participation in the labor force and receipt of transfer payments is very involved. The receipt of some social welfare payments depends strictly on prior participation in the work force (Social Security and unemployment benefits, for example). Therefore, it may be that transfer payments have a disincentive effect on participation in the labor force for one time period and an incentive effect for another time period. The latter could reflect the motive of providing possible safeguards against income fluctuations or other mishaps, or an appreciation of the things higher income can buy.

In this paper the distributive pattern of income and public transfers will be analyzed without inferring any casual relationships between public transfers and work experience. Because all data in table 5 are based on

---

11. C. Green and A. Tella, "The Effect of Nonemployment Income and Wage Rates on the Work Incentives of the Poor," *Review of Economics and Statistics*, November 1969 (reprinted in this volume).

12. W. Carter, J. Eichenholtz, E. Maycock, A. B. Pfaff, and M. Pfaff, "Public Transfers and Labor Force Participation" (Washington, D.C.: Institute for Creative Studies, 1969).

Table 5. The Effect of Social Welfare Payments on Income Distribution by Work Experience of the Family Head

Large SMSAs

	Income before Transfers			Transfers			Income after Transfers			No. of Families	
	Amount		Mean	Amount		Mean	Amount		Mean		
Zero weeks	10660.738	5.4%	2352.07	7273.020	57.9%	1604.64	17933.699	8.5%	3956.70	4532.484	18.3%
1 thru 13 weeks	1449.187	0.7%	2461.51	594.215	4.7%	1009.30	2043.413	1.0%	3470.84	588.737	2.4%
14 thru 26 weeks	4211.031	2.1%	4281.71	756.942	6.0%	769.64	4967.906	2.3%	5051.30	983.490	4.0%
27 thru 39 weeks	6310.438	3.2%	5658.12	703.991	5.6%	631.21	7014.406	3.3%	6289.31	1115.289	4.5%
40 thru 47 weeks	10374.387	5.2%	7639.20	542.522	4.3%	399.48	10916.855	5.2%	8038.64	1358.046	5.5%
48 thru 49 weeks	5577.977	2.8%	8189.36	172.561	1.4%	253.34	5750.539	2.7%	8442.72	681.124	2.7%
50 thru 52 weeks	158825.063	79.8%	10325.04	2491.073	19.8%	161.94	161315.938	76.3%	10486.97	15382.504	61.9%
Not available	1499.176	0.8%	7740.36	18.688	0.1%	96.49	1517.865	0.7%	7836.85	193.683	0.8%
Total	198907.938	100.0%	8009.06	12552.996	100.0%	505.44	211460.500	100.0%	8514.49	24835.359	100.0%

Central-City Poverty Areas

	Income before Transfers			Transfers			Income after Transfers			No. of Families	
	Amount		Mean	Amount		Mean	Amount		Mean		
Zero weeks	1163.063	7.4%	1122.06	1626.724	68.1%	1569.38	2789.814	15.3%	2691.47	1036.538	28.4%
1 thru 13 weeks	249.159	1.6%	1732.04	105.567	4.4%	733.85	354.720	1.9%	2465.86	143.852	3.9%
14 thru 26 weeks	692.485	4.4%	2738.65	180.174	7.5%	712.55	872.658	4.8%	3451.20	252.856	6.9%
27 thru 39 weeks	969.479	6.1%	4559.68	100.685	4.2%	473.54	1070.164	5.9%	5033.23	212.620	5.8%
40 thru 47 weeks	1349.016	8.5%	5878.50	88.345	3.7%	384.97	1437.361	7.9%	6263.48	229.483	6.3%
48 thru 49 weeks	502.884	3.2%	5097.18	33.672	1.4%	341.29	536.556	2.9%	5438.48	98.659	2.7%
50 thru 52 weeks	10858.586	68.6%	6504.44	253.812	10.6%	152.03	11112.352	61.0%	6656.44	1669.411	45.7%
Not available	37.671	0.2%	5133.45	0.948	0.0%	129.24	38.619	0.2%	5262.69	7.338	0.2%
Total	15822.336	100.0%	4333.98	2389.927	100.0%	654.63	18212.238	100.0%	4988.62	3650.755	100.0%

"Amount" in millions of dollars.
"No. of Families" in thousands.

family incomes, only the work experience of the head of the family is considered. As may be expected, income distribution and public transfer payment distribution have an inverse pattern; income generally increases with the number of weeks worked during the year, whereas the opposite holds for transfer payments in large SMSAs. Families whose heads work less than 13 weeks receive an average from $1,604.62 (zero weeks worked) to $1,009.30 (1–13 weeks worked). Families whose heads work throughout the year receive approximately $161.94. Average income before transfers increases monotonically as the number of work weeks increases. Transfers create one exception to this pattern: after transfers the average income of families whose heads do not work at all is higher than that of families whose heads work between 1 and 13 weeks. The income share of families whose heads work less than 40 weeks increases from 11.4 percent to 15.1 percent by social welfare payments; the income share of families whose heads work between 40 and 48 weeks remains unchanged (5.2 percent); the share of income of "full-time" workers decreases from 82.6 percent to 79.0 percent.

In central-city poverty areas transfers exhibit a similar pattern. The relative predominance of social welfare payments to nonworkers is even more accentuated. The income effect differs slightly. An "income reversal" takes place between two pairs of groups: after transfers the nonworkers have a higher mean income than 1–13-week workers, and the 27–39-week workers have a lower mean income than the 14–26-week workers. Furthermore, families whose heads work less than 26 weeks have their income share increased from 13.4 to 22 percent by public transfers, whereas the income share of families whose heads work more than 26 weeks decreases from 86.4 percent to 77.7 percent due to public transfers. This pattern is not surprising. Several transfer payments depend on the recipients' absence from work. Furthermore, a large share of Social Security is paid to retired people.

5. The opportunity to work is closely related to a person's skills and training. People who have little education and no training find it hard to secure employment even during an economic boom, and they are the first to be fired during an economic recession. The following patterns in income and transfers distribution across *educational levels of the family head* (table 6) are found: In large SMSAs average income before and after transfers increases monotonically with education of the family head. In central-city poverty areas there is one exception to this rule, which may be a consequence of sampling variability: the average income (before and after transfers) for families whose head completed one or two years of college is lower than that of families whose head completed three or four years of high school. For central-city poverty areas and total large SMSAs average social welfare payments decrease monotonically as education increases. In *large* SMSAs transfers increase the income share of families whose heads have less than eleven years of school from 26.8 percent to 29.0 percent. They decrease the

Table 6. The Effect of Social Welfare Payments on Income Distribution by Education of the Family Head

Large SMSAs

	Income before Transfers			Transfers			Income after Transfers			No. of Families	
	Amount		Mean	Amount		Mean	Amount		Mean		
Primary (0–6)	10135.867	5.1%	4011.42	2491.453	19.8%	986.03	12626.609	6.0%	4997.17	2526.750	10.2%
Primary (7–8)	20140.945	10.1%	5301.00	3243.897	25.8%	853.77	23384.480	11.1%	6154.68	3799.460	15.3%
Secondary (9–10)	23160.766	11.6%	6753.80	2030.776	16.2%	592.18	25191.309	11.9%	7345.92	3429.289	13.8%
Secondary (11–12)	68952.813	34.6%	8148.29	3102.666	24.7%	366.64	72051.928	34.1%	8514.52	8462.238	34.1%
Undergrad (13–14)	24169.914	12.1%	9528.25	817.395	6.5%	322.23	24987.281	11.8%	9850.47	2536.657	10.2%
Undergrad (15–16)	30804.496	15.5%	12312.49	599.741	4.8%	239.71	31404.246	14.8%	12552.21	2501.889	10.1%
Graduate (17–20)	21666.375	10.9%	13722.47	268.534	2.1%	170.07	21934.934	10.4%	13892.56	1578.897	6.4%
Not available	2.689	0.0%	10351.99	0.031	0.0%	120.75	2.721	0.0%	10472.74	0.260	0.0%
Total	199033.688	100.0%	8014.10	12554.477	100.0%	505.50	211583.313	100.0%	8519.41	24835.422	100.0%

Central-City Poverty Areas

	Income before Transfers			Transfers			Income after Transfers			No. of Families	
	Amount		Mean	Amount		Mean	Amount		Mean		
Primary (0–6)	2526.558	16.0%	2950.60	844.476	35.3%	986.21	3371.057	18.5%	3936.84	856.284	23.5%
Primary (7–8)	2671.098	16.9%	3627.57	575.010	24.1%	780.91	3246.114	17.8%	4408.49	736.332	20.2%
Secondary (9–10)	2644.950	16.7%	4144.00	419.513	17.6%	657.27	3064.465	16.8%	4801.27	638.260	17.5%
Secondary (11–12)	4989.500	31.5%	5164.77	437.398	18.3%	452.76	5426.797	29.8%	5617.43	966.063	26.5%
Undergrad (13–14)	942.336	6.0%	5101.60	65.771	2.8%	356.07	1008.106	5.5%	5457.66	184.714	5.1%
Undergrad (15–16)	1166.683	7.4%	7085.90	40.019	1.7%	243.05	1206.701	6.6%	7328.96	164.648	4.5%
Graduate (17–20)	883.355	5.6%	8433.17	7.743	0.3%	73.92	891.097	4.9%	8507.09	104.748	2.9%
Not available	0.0	0.0%	0.0	0.0	0.0%	0.0	0.0	0.0%	0.0	0.0	0.0%
Total	15824.469	100.0%	4334.22	2389.930	100.0%	654.588	18214.328	100.0%	4988.79	3651.046	100.0%

"Amount" in millions of dollars.
"No. of Families" in thousands.

income share of those with an education of eleven or more years of education from 73.1 percent to 71.1 percent.

Social welfare payments to large SMSAs in general and to central-city poverty areas of these large SMSAs in particular are to a slight degree successful in redistributing income from the less needy to the more needy. At income levels after transfers of below $5,000, transfers have the effect of increasing the *absolute and relative* amounts of income received by families. At income levels above $5,000 only an *absolute* increase in income due to transfers can be observed.[13]

Looking at some of the characteristics that influence a family's ability to earn income, it can also be observed that groups who tend to be impaired in their ability to seek or retain gainful employment tend to receive higher social welfare benefits than those who are in economically more advantageous circumstances. Families with female heads of household, with heads who have employment for at most short periods, and/or whose lack of education makes it difficult for them to find or keep jobs tend to receive relatively higher transfers than other groups; their income share is increased in relative and absolute terms.

However, the fact remains that sizable as these transfers appear, they do not suffice in ridding all Americans of the worry of sheer physical survival. A good part is directed to less urgent needs. Furthermore, a sizable group of needy Americans are not helped by social welfare measures, either because they do not know how to avail themselves of sources of income, or because legalistic refinements in social welfare legislation make assistance unavailable to them.[14] Although social welfare payments serve to alleviate some inequities, inspection of distributive patterns alone indicates that there is room for considerable improvement and extension of social welfare benefits.

Distributive Patterns of Social Security and Public Assistance

A detailed study of the *distributive pattern of social welfare payments* will be confined to two groups – Social Security and public assistance programs. These two programs are chosen as representatives because they are

---

13. It would be desirable to separate the net transfer effect by subtracting from the gross transfer amounts distributed in this paper the net tax of given groups. Unfortunately, compatible data for an undertaking of this type are not available.

14. For example, residence requirements for state public assistance not only keeps potential candidates from receiving transfers but also prevents recipients from moving to areas with better job opportunities for fear of losing public assistance before being able to secure a job.

not only sizable in terms of the benefits disbursed, but they also occupy different positions on a scale of classifiers of social welfare programs. Social Security is considered an earned right, whereas public assistance is directed to those in need who have not had a chance to earn any such right. Public assistance payments are based on means tests – that is, the need of the recipient has to be established. Furthermore, the sociopsychological considerations involved in receiving benefits from the two programs are considerably different. Receiving Social Security is far more socially acceptable than receiving public assistance. The receipt of public assistance is usually coupled with social disadvantages that may not only be psychological only but very often are also economic in nature.[15]

1. Distributive patterns of transfers and income for black and white families differ somewhat. The distribution of Social Security and public assistance *by race* shows rather diverse patterns (table 7). White families receive a slightly higher relative share of *Social Security* benefits than black families; the average difference in receipt is approximately $170 per family in large SMSAs. The difference is not significant for the poverty areas. More than 90 percent of all families receiving Social Security in large SMSAs and 63.8 percent in central-city poverty areas are white; 9.1 percent and 34.0 percent are black. In large SMSAs the average receipts of white families exceed the overall mean receipt in central-city poverty areas, as well as that of black families in general. This indicates that the larger share of Social Security benefits accruing to large SMSA residents in nonpoor areas primarily favors white people.

Public assistance shows a distinctly different pattern. Only 59.1 percent of all recipient families are white while 40 percent are black. Considering that 87 percent of all families in large SMSAs are white and 12.1 percent are black, this indicates that a much larger share of black families than white families receive public assistance. The 59.1 percent white families receive 54.1 percent of all public assistance in large SMSAs, which is less than their proportionate share; the 40 percent black families, by contradistinction, receive 44.6 percent of all public assistance, which is slightly larger than their proportionate share. This fact is also reflected in the mean amounts received by black and white families. On the average, black families receive approximately $300 more in public assistance than white families do, but this does not necessarily indicate that black families are made better off by public assistance than white families. A more detailed empirical study may reveal that black families on the average are somewhat larger than white families, and therefore on a per capita basis the black families may still receive less or at least no more than white families.

---

15. The analysis of Social Security and public assistance is confined to the population of recipients only. Families not receiving the particular type of social welfare payment were not included in the estimates of populations and in computations of average amounts disbursed.

Table 7. Distribution of Social Security and Public Assistance by Race of Recipient

Large SMSAs

| | Social Security | | | | Public Assistance | | | |
	Amount		Mean	No. of Families	Amount		Mean	No. of Families
White	7024.555	91.5%	1506.10	4664.066	90.3%	994.326	54.1%	1508.82	659.005	59.1%
Black	623.591	8.1%	1330.07	463.838	9.1%	819.286	44.6%	1840.54	445.133	40.0%
Other	25.192	0.3%	850.12	29.633	0.6%	23.046	1.3%	2286.85	10.078	0.9%
Total	7673.340	100.0%	1486.34	5162.539	100.0%	1836.658	100.0%	1648.38	1114.216	100.0%

Central-City Poverty Areas

| | Social Security | | | | Public Assistance | | | |
	Amount		Mean	No. of Families	Amount		Mean	No. of Families
White	704.886	64.7%	1335.75	527.704	63.8%	348.246	39.8%	1811.47	192.244	38.9%
Black	370.750	34.0%	1319.30	281.020	34.0%	522.790	59.7%	1737.72	300.847	60.8%
Other	13.799	1.3%	732.43	18.840	2.3%	4.725	0.5%	2749.55	1.718	0.3%
Total	1089.435	100.0%	1316.43	827.564	100.0%	875.761	100.0%	1769.89	494.810	100.0%

"Amount" in millions of dollars.
"No. of Families" in thousands.

In central-city poverty areas of large SMSAs 60.8 percent of all public assistance recipients are black, whereas only 38.9 percent are white. In poverty areas white families receive a slightly larger than proportionate estimated share of social welfare payments than black families do; however, the difference is probably not statistically significant.

2. Income other than transfers determines the amount receivable from many programs. Table 8 shows the distribution of Social Security and public assistance *by class of income before transfers.* In large SMSAs the major share of Social Security is received by income classes between $1,000 and $5,000 income before transfers. This indicates that the main beneficiaries of Social Security are usually people with some other small income. Income classes with negative or zero income before transfers receive a relatively lower share of Social Security payments. An inspection of income class means also indicates the same point: The mean receipt of Social Security by families with annual income before transfers between $1,000 and $5,000 is considerably higher than the means of other income classes.[16]

The average amount of Social Security received by a family residing in a central-city poverty area is less than the average for large SMSAs. Furthermore, there is a much smaller concentration of recipients of social welfare payments in the middle-income classes between $3,000 and $25,000. In central-city poverty areas 73.4 percent of the recipients of social welfare payments have an annual income before transfers of under $2,500. These income groups receive 72.8 percent of Social Security benefits paid to residents of central-city poverty areas. The highest average payments are received by families with income before transfers between $1,000 and $5,000. A little less than one-quarter of all residents of central-city poverty areas and of large SMSAs in general receive Social Security.

3. An investigation into the distributive pattern of Social Security and public assistance *by different types of families* (table 9) reveals that families, as compared with individuals, receive a relatively larger share of Social Security. In particular, families with a male head with spouse present receive a considerably higher relative share of Social Security. Families with a male head but with no spouse present receive somewhat less on the average. The difference in the averages may not be statistically significant, however. Families with female heads receive a considerably smaller amount of Social Security. Amounts received by individuals, in turn, are still lower.

Central-city poverty areas exhibit a different pattern. It appears that in those areas only, families with male heads, whether or not the spouse is present, receive a higher than proportionate share of Social Security. Families with female heads receive a somewhat less than proportionate share of

---

16. Estimates for the two extreme income classes – that is, negative income and income above $25,000 – are not as reliable as the other estimates, in view of the fact that the sample in those groups is rather small.

Table 8. Distribution of Social Security and Public Assistance by Income Before Social Welfare Payments

Large SMSAs

	Social Security					Public Assistance				
	Amount		Mean	No. of Families		Amount		Mean	No. of Families	
Negative income	26.892	0.4%	1307.65	20.565	0.4%	11.737	0.6%	2418.99	4.852	0.4%
Zero income	742.525	9.7%	1301.04	570.715	11.1%	1023.867	55.7%	1879.31	544.809	48.9%
$1 thru $599	1274.750	16.6%	1567.84	813.058	15.7%	193.179	10.5%	1912.92	100.986	9.1%
$600 thru $999	582.647	7.6%	1483.52	391.425	7.6%	91.469	5.0%	1525.47	59.961	5.4%
$1,000 thru $1,499	729.148	9.5%	1663.04	437.127	8.5%	66.325	3.6%	1362.12	48.692	4.4%
$1,500 thru $1,999	545.715	7.1%	1572.87	346.954	6.7%	79.768	4.3%	1558.33	51.188	4.6%
$2,000 thru $2,499	460.539	6.0%	1772.40	259.839	5.0%	43.286	2.4%	1004.48	43.093	3.9%
$2,500 thru $2,999	275.586	3.6%	1584.03	173.977	3.4%	37.186	2.0%	2142.42	17.357	1.6%
$3,000 thru $4,999	935.225	12.2%	1549.42	603.594	11.7%	102.015	5.6%	1142.74	89.271	8.0%
$5,000 thru $9,999	1261.739	16.4%	1420.44	888.269	17.2%	134.522	7.3%	1250.57	107.568	9.7%
$10,000 thru $24,999	778.211	10.1%	1280.26	607.851	11.8%	49.590	2.7%	1154.03	42.971	3.9%
$25,000 and above	61.525	0.8%	1236.41	49.761	1.0%	3.764	0.2%	1081.73	3.480	0.3%
Total	7674.484	100.0%	1486.40	5163.133	100.0%	1836.704	100.0%	1648.41	1114.225	100.0%

Central-City Poverty Areas

	Social Security					Public Assistance				
	Amount		Mean	No. of Families		Amount		Mean	No. of Families	
Negative income	5.133	0.5%	1015.89	5.052	0.6%	2.161	0.2%	2085.04	1.036	0.2%
Zero income	257.254	23.6%	1243.81	206.827	25.0%	554.557	63.3%	1878.41	295.226	59.7%
$1 thru $599	231.953	21.3%	1358.35	170.761	20.6%	114.370	13.1%	2264.95	50.496	10.2%
$600 thru $999	84.513	7.8%	1115.81	75.741	9.2%	42.547	4.9%	1531.31	27.785	5.6%
$1,000 thru $1,499	109.670	10.1%	1636.79	67.003	8.1%	28.315	3.2%	1304.08	21.712	4.4%
$1,500 thru $1,999	46.505	4.3%	1221.54	38.071	4.6%	16.219	1.9%	1553.29	10.442	2.1%
$2,000 thru $2,499	56.823	5.2%	1306.34	43.497	5.3%	23.268	2.7%	937.88	24.809	5.0%
$2,500 thru $2,999	42.709	3.9%	1564.80	27.293	3.3%	27.497	3.1%	2407.66	11.421	2.3%
$3,000 thru $4,999	115.699	10.6%	1429.64	80.928	9.8%	26.151	3.0%	1212.63	21.566	4.4%
$5,000 thru $9,999	107.851	9.9%	1223.46	88.152	10.7%	36.885	4.2%	1406.19	26.230	5.3%
$10,000 thru $24,999	30.620	2.8%	1302.94	23.500	2.8%	3.810	0.4%	930.48	4.095	0.8%
$25,000 and above	0.750	0.1%	1001.83	0.748	0.1%	0.0	0.0%	0.0	0.0	0.0%
Total	1089.477	100.0%	1316.47	827.574	100.0%	875.780	100.0%	1769.90	494.817	100.0%

"Amount" in millions of dollars. "No. of Families" in thousands.

Social Security. Furthermore, the difference in average receipts between different types of families is larger in central-city poverty areas than in large SMSAs. The families with male heads with spouses present receive almost as high an average benefit as in total large SMSAs; families with female heads receive considerably less. Receipts of Social Security by individuals, whether primary or secondary individuals, are lower in both subpopulations.

Also under this classification, public assistance shows different patterns. Whereas Social Security seems to favor families with male heads, public assistance clearly favors families with female heads. In large SMSAs 41 percent of all recipients of public assistance are families with female heads. These families receive a total of 50.2 percent of all public assistance disbursed to large SMSA residents. All other types of families receive a less than proportionate share. This is also reflected in the average amounts of public assistance received by different family types. Whereas families with female heads of household receive an average of $2,018.57, families with male heads of household with spouses present receive only $1,554.86 (table 9).

4.   The distribution of Social Security and public assistance *by educational level of family head* is shown in table 10. It is evident that education does not have a very sizable impact on the amount of Social Security received by a family. Families whose heads have an educational attainment of high school completion or less receive slightly more than their proportionate share of Social Security, whereas families whose head is college educated (either undergraduate or graduate) receive less than their proportionate share. The deviations from exact proportions are very small. Families with heads who completed an undergraduate education or less receive between $1,410 and $1,558, approximately, which involves a very small variability between groups.

In central-city poverty areas the distributive pattern is similar. However, only families whose head has an education of eight years of primary school or less would receive a slightly higher average share of Social Security. A considerably lower estimated Social Security receipt can be observed for families whose heads have graduate education; however, the sample for this subgroup is rather small and the estimate may therefore deviate considerably from the population mean.

Public assistance shows an interesting pattern: in general it does not seem to favor families whose heads have low educational achievements, but in particular it favors families whose heads completed between seven and ten years of school. By comparison, families whose heads have less than seven years of schooling receive less than their proportionate share of Social Security, although their share is still somewhat higher than the relative share received by the families whose heads have an educational experience of eleven years or more. As may be surmised, a small percentage of the population of public assistance recipients in large SMSAs can claim a family head with an educational level beyond high school completion. Only an estimated

Table 9. Distribution of Social Security and Public Assistance by Type of Family

Large SMSAs

	Social Security					Public Assistance				
	Amount		Mean	No. of Families		Amount		Mean	No. of Families	
Male head and spouse	4020.413	52.4%	1698.82	2366.591	45.8%	472.398	25.7%	1554.85	303.821	27.3%
Male head no spouse	305.199	4.0%	1640.20	186.074	3.6%	20.088	1.1%	1324.48	15.167	1.4%
Female head	1406.517	18.3%	1556.30	903.756	17.5%	921.219	50.2%	2018.57	456.371	41.0%
Primary individual	1825.219	23.8%	1147.74	1590.266	30.8%	382.517	20.8%	1276.08	299.757	26.9%
Secondary individual	117.095	1.5%	1009.06	116.043	2.2%	40.467	2.2%	1034.86	39.103	3.5%
Total	7674.438	100.0%	1486.50	5162.727	100.0%	1836.688	100.0%	1648.40	1114.219	100.0%

Central-City Poverty Areas

	Social Security					Public Assistance				
	Amount		Mean	No. of Families		Amount		Mean	No. of Families	
Male head and spouse	446.733	41.0%	1614.51	276.698	33.4%	174.903	20.0%	1909.29	91.606	18.5%
Male head no spouse	67.418	6.2%	1491.22	45.210	5.5%	9.331	1.1%	1304.42	7.154	1.4%
Female head	167.167	15.3%	1286.69	129.920	15.7%	482.157	55.1%	2111.56	228.342	46.1%
Primary individual	360.151	33.1%	1091.73	329.888	39.9%	187.532	21.4%	1275.76	146.996	29.7%
Secondary individual	47.990	4.4%	1046.62	45.852	5.5%	21.857	2.5%	1055.03	20.717	4.2%
Total	1089.459	100.0%	1316.45	827.569	100.0%	875.781	100.0%	1769.91	494.815	100.0%

"Amount" in millions of dollars.
"No. of Families" in thousands.

Table 10. Distribution of Social Security and Public Assistance by Work Experience of Family Head

Large SMSAs

	Social Security					Public Assistance				
	Amount		Mean	No. of Families		Amount		Mean	No. of Families	
Primary (0–6)	1667.164	21.7%	1410.03	1182.357	22.9%	447.875	24.4%	1514.82	295.661	26.5%
Primary (7–8)	2207.954	28.8%	1557.59	1417.537	27.5%	444.670	24.2%	1762.32	252.320	22.6%
Secondary (9–10)	977.889	12.7%	1517.58	644.373	12.5%	475.474	25.9%	2055.04	231.369	20.8%
Secondary (11–12)	1773.995	23.1%	1558.97	1137.927	22.0%	376.770	20.5%	1408.65	267.467	24.0%
Undergrad (13–14)	488.101	6.4%	1342.57	363.557	7.0%	70.371	3.8%	1338.82	52.562	4.7%
Undergrad (15–16)	364.182	4.7%	1423.08	255.910	5.0%	20.607	1.1%	1434.25	14.368	1.3%
Graduate (17–20)	195.143	2.5%	1210.75	161.085	3.1%	0.944	0.1%	1992.51	0.474	0.0%
Not available	0.031	0.0%	120.75	0.260	0.0%	0.0	0.0%	0.0	0.0	0.0%
Total	7674.449	100.0%	1486.43	5163.000	100.0%	1836.712	100.0%	1648.430	1114.219	100.0%

Central-City Poverty Areas

	Social Security					Public Assistance				
	Amount		Mean	No. of Families		Amount		Mean	No. of Families	
Primary (0–6)	456.012	41.9%	1317.17	346.204	41.8%	265.993	30.4%	1647.57	161.445	32.6%
Primary (7–8)	311.286	28.6%	1422.00	218.907	26.5%	177.891	20.3%	1719.02	103.484	20.9%
Secondary (9–10)	97.946	9.0%	1231.89	79.509	9.6%	239.250	27.3%	2194.78	109.008	22.0%
Secondary (11–12)	171.763	15.8%	1277.96	134.403	16.2%	169.262	19.3%	1664.26	101.704	20.6%
Undergrad (13–14)	32.486	3.0%	1146.04	28.346	3.4%	20.745	2.4%	1272.92	16.297	3.3%
Undergrad (15–16)	18.568	1.7%	1189.48	15.610	1.9%	2.657	0.3%	922.41	2.880	0.6%
Graduate (17–20)	1.396	0.1%	304.12	4.589	0.6%	0.0	0.0%	0.0	0.0	0.0%
Not available	0.0	0.0%	0.0	0.0	0.0%	0.0	0.0%	0.0	0.0	0.0%
Total	1089.456	100.0%	1316.45	827.568	100.0%	875.796	100.0%	1769.93	494.818	100.0%

"Amount" in millions of dollars.

"No. of Families" in thousands.

6 percent fall into this group. In central-city poverty areas the pattern described for public assistance in large SMSAs is slightly more accentuated. Whereas in large SMSAs families whose heads have education between seven and ten years receive relatively higher average public assistance, in central-city poverty areas this can be said only about families whose heads have between nine and ten years of education.

5.   The distribution of Social Security and public assistance by work experience is depicted in table 11. The largest share of Social Security recipients – 62.2 percent – do not work at all. This group of families receives approximately 65.7 percent of Social Security benefits accruing to residents of large SMSAs. It is somewhat surprising that the next largest share accrues to the group of families whose head works full-time. The 21 percent of all families whose heads work between fifty and fifty-two weeks a year receive 18.5 percent of Social Security benefits. (Those groups of recipients who work part of the year constitute a relatively small part of the population.)

A similar pattern is observed in central-city poverty areas, where 70 percent of all Social Security recipients are families whose heads do not work at all. These families receive 71 percent of Social Security benefits accruing to central-city poverty areas. The next largest group are families headed by a person who works throughout the year. This group constitutes 14.4 percent of all families and receives 13.1 percent of all Social Security benefits. No excessively large variation between group means can be observed, although some of the differences may be significant.

The right half of table 11 shows the distribution of public assistance by work experience of the family head. The pattern in this group is very similar to that of Social Security distribution. The largest share of public assistance benefits is received by families whose heads do not work during the year, followed by the group of families whose heads work throughout the year. As in the case of Social Security, a slightly larger than proportionate share is received by the former group, and a slightly less than proportionate share is received by the latter. Group averages for public assistance show higher variability than those for Social Security. In central-city poverty areas the pattern is very similar except that the share of full-time workers who receive public assistance is relatively smaller.

In summary, the results of this section indicate that Social Security programs help those who are strong enough to help themselves. The right to receive benefits is earned on the basis of employment and contributions. The main support of this $22 billion program goes to white families, to low-income groups (however, not to the very poorest), to families with male heads, and finally, a sizable share goes to full-time workers. Although the major share benefits nonworkers, the absence of the retired from the labor force is socially accepted.

The sad fact remains, however, that even in "the land of the free and the home of the brave" not all are able to provide for themselves or even to *earn*

Table 11. Distribution of Social Security and Public Assistance by Education of Family Head

Large SMSAs

	Social Security			Public Assistance		
	Amount	Mean	No. of Families	Amount	Mean	No. of Families
Zero weeks	5042.477 65.7%	1570.10	3211.550 62.2%	1365.307 74.3%	1871.64	729.470 65.5%
1 thru 13 weeks	346.869 4.5%	1627.50	213.129 4.1%	78.068 4.3%	1283.97	60.802 5.5%
14 thru 26 weeks	316.355 4.1%	1410.60	224.268 4.3%	87.074 4.7%	1569.77	55.469 5.0%
27 thru 39 weeks	280.774 3.7%	1315.84	213.380 4.1%	45.639 2.5%	940.07	48.548 4.4%
40 thru 47 weeks	202.588 2.6%	1179.78	171.716 3.3%	47.281 2.6%	1243.50	38.022 3.4%
48 thru 49 weeks	62.047 0.8%	1432.84	43.304 0.8%	17.279 0.9%	892.87	19.352 1.7%
50 thru 52 weeks	1422.962 18.5%	1311.15	1085.272 21.0%	196.035 10.7%	1205.93	162.558 14.6%
Not available	0.0 0.0%	0.0	0.0 0.0%	0.0 0.0%	0.0	0.0 0.0%
Total	7674.059 100.0%	1486.46	5162.613 100.0%	1836.682 100.0%	1648.40	1114.221 100.0%

Central-City Poverty Areas

	Social Security			Public Assistance		
	Amount	Mean	No. of Families	Amount	Mean	Weighted Cases
Zero weeks	776.660 71.3%	1340.73	579.281 70.0%	714.467 81.6%	1953.00	365.830 73.9%
1 thru 13 weeks	54.773 5.0%	1331.83	41.126 5.0%	34.084 3.9%	1161.65	29.341 5.9%
14 thru 26 weeks	56.145 5.2%	1588.10	35.353 4.3%	32.516 3.7%	1266.48	25.674 5.2%
27 thru 39 weeks	32.176 3.0%	1237.04	26.010 3.1%	11.058 1.3%	957.55	11.549 2.3%
40 thru 47 weeks	17.974 1.6%	976.64	18.404 2.2%	27.483 3.1%	2439.71	11.265 2.3%
48 thru 49 weeks	9.086 0.8%	1095.28	8.295 1.0%	9.556 1.1%	759.57	12.580 2.5%
50 thru 52 weeks	142.617 13.1%	1197.49	119.097 14.4%	46.602 5.3%	1208.09	38.575 7.8%
Not available	0.0 0.0%	0.0	0.0 0.0%	0.0 0.0%	0.0	0.0 0.0%
Total	1089.430 100.0%	1316.42	827.567 100.0%	875.765 100.0%	1769.88	494.813 100.0%

"Amount" in millions of dollars.
"No. of Families" in thousands.

their right for help from others. Public assistance programs are designed to help these groups. They benefit the black, the very poor, the poverty areas, families without a male head, the uneducated, and those who cannot find work. Even these programs, however, require some knowledge and sophistication in their utilization by potential recipients; the uneducated often seem to lack that knowledge. Furthermore, it has been argued that society at large imposes a "tax" on recipients of public assistance by keeping them in dependence and by treating them as low-quality citizens. Economically, public assistance does little better than it does socially; benefits are barely sufficient for physical survival, depend on means tests that are too low, and frequently are bought at the price of human dignity. Finally, many needy are unable to receive assistance.

The Poverty-Reducing Role of Social Welfare Payments

The five groups of public transfer payments under investigation belong to the so-called "income-maintenance programs." One way of measuring their effectiveness is in terms of a "target" income; income before and after transfers can be compared with this target income.

Two such target income levels shall be investigated: (1) the economy poverty cutoff level (henceforth called *poverty line*), and (2) the low-cost poverty cutoff level (henceforth called *low-cost line*). Both income levels constitute modifications of the poverty and low-cost cutoffs published by the Social Security Administration, priced as of December 1966 to adjust for a change in the price index.[17]

According to the two income cutoffs the population may be classified as (1) poor (below the poverty line), (2) low-income (between the poverty line and the low-cost line), or (3) nonpoor (above the low-cost line). Inclusion of the income effect of transfers on the poverty classification of a family, and the breakdown into recipients and nonrecipients leads to nine groups: (1) poor who do not receive transfers ("poor bef & aft non"), (2) poor who receive public transfers but are not lifted out of poverty by transfers ("poor bef & aft rec"), (3) poor who receive public transfers and are lifted to low-income ("poor bef & low-inc aft"), (4) poor who are lifted out of poverty above the low-income line by public transfers ("poor bef & nonpoor aft"), (5) low-income groups who do not receive any public transfers ("low-inc bef & aft non"), (6) low-income families who receive public transfers but are not lifted above the low-income line ("low-inc bef & aft rec"), (7) low-income families who become nonpoor because of public transfers ("low-inc bef & nonpoor aft"), (8) nonpoor who do not receive transfers ("nonpoor bef &

---

17. A further discussion of poverty and low-cost cutoffs may be found in the Appendix.

aft non"), and (9) nonpoor who receive transfers ("nonpoor bef & aft rec").

1. Of the 24.8 million families residing in large SMSAs 18.8 percent have an income below the poverty level before receiving transfers (table 12). Of these 18.8 percent 5 percent do not receive any social welfare payments at all. Although a further 5.3 percent are recipients of social welfare payments, they are not lifted out of poverty. Of all families 2.6 percent are shifted from the poverty level to the low-income level, and 5.9 percent become nonpoor because of social welfare payments. A rather small percentage of the population can be found at the low-income level – that is, with income above the poverty line but below the low-income line. Approximately 59.3 percent of all families have an annual income above the low-income line and do not receive public transfer payments. However, 17.9 percent of the population who have an annual income above the low-income line are recipients of social welfare payments.

Among poor families a considerable variability in income can be observed. For example, the mean income of a family who is poor and does not receive social welfare payments is $1,332.71. By comparison, the average income before transfers of poor families who receive transfers but are *not* lifted out of poverty by them is only $390.73. The average income of poor families who are lifted out of poverty by social welfare payments is, by comparison, higher than $390,74, but, on the other hand lower than the average income of poor families who do not receive social welfare payments. This would suggest that families who are poor – but not the very poorest – would tend not to receive social welfare payments, whereas the poorest families generally would receive welfare payments. For the poorest of the poor, however, this does not suffice to lift them out of poverty. This pattern is only partly confirmed for families at the low-income level. Whereas the nonrecipients of social welfare payments have a higher average income than the recipients, it appears that those with a relatively lower income tend to receive larger social welfare payments that lift them out of poverty. As may be expected, the mean income of families with an income above the low-income line who do not receive social welfare payments is considerably higher than that of families who do receive transfer payments.

Even though the largest share of social welfare payments is received by the poor, social welfare payments were not primarily designed to reduce poverty. In fact, 42 percent of all social welfare payments to large SMSAs considered in this analysis are received by families who are *not* poor. The average social welfare receipts of nonpoor people are considerably lower than the average receipts of poor families; in particular, those groups, that are lifted into a different poverty class receive higher transfer payments. Thus social welfare payments have a redistributive effect. Whereas the nonpoor receive 96.3 percent of income before transfers, their share of income *after* transfers is only 93 percent. The income share of the 18.8 percent families who are poor *before* transfers is increased from 2 percent before transfers to 4 percent *after* transfers.

Table 12. The Poverty-Reducing Effect of Social Welfare Payments

Large SMSAs

	Income before Transfers			Transfers			Income after Transfers				
	Amount		Mean	Amount		Mean	Amount		Mean	No. of Families	
Poor bef & aft non	1641.958	0.8%	1332.71	0.0	0.0%	0.0	1641.958	0.8%	1332.71	1232.043	5.0%
Poor bef & aft rec	518.148	0.3%	390.73	1607.723	12.8%	1212.37	2125.894	1.0%	1603.12	1326.096	5.3%
Poor bef & low-inc aft	462.925	0.2%	705.94	1236.102	9.8%	1885.00	1699.042	0.8%	2590.97	655.754	2.6%
Poor bef & nonpoor aft	1480.344	0.7%	1010.47	3686.991	29.4%	2516.72	5167.211	2.4%	3527.11	1464.997	5.9%
Low-inc bef & aft non	1925.252	1.0%	3817.38	0.0	0.0%	0.0	1925.252	0.9%	3917.38	504.337	2.0%
Low-inc bef & aft rec	164.030	0.1%	3083.87	38.453	0.3%	722.93	202.483	0.1%	3806.81	53.190	0.2%
Low inc bef & nonpoor aft	1151.398	0.6%	2782.77	716.250	5.7%	1731.08	1867.663	0.9%	4513.88	413.759	1.7%
Nonpoor bef & aft non	152144.625	76.5%	10324.73	0.0	0.0%	0.0	152144.625	71.9%	10324.73	14735.934	59.3%
Nonpoor bef & Aft rec	39437.004	19.8%	8863.09	5268.273	42.0%	1183.99	44706.117	21.1%	10647.28	4449.570	17.9%
Total	198925.563	100.0%	8009.67	12553.785	100.0%	505.47	211480.188	100.0%	8515.18	24835.660	100.0%

Central-City Poverty Areas

	Income before Transfers			Transfers			Income after Transfers				
	Amount		Mean	Amount		Mean	Amount		Mean	No. of Families	
Poor bef & aft non	620.574	3.9%	1429.31	0.0	0.0%	0.0	620.574	3.4%	1429.31	434.176	11.9%
Poor bef & aft rec	169.045	1.1%	343.04	623.401	26.1%	1265.07	792.436	4.4%	1608.10	492.777	13.5%
Poor bef & low-inc aft	153.283	1.0%	737.56	420.469	17.6%	2023.21	573.747	3.2%	2760.75	207.823	5.7%
Poor bef & nonpoor aft	202.193	1.3%	753.85	679.600	28.4%	2533.80	881.785	4.8%	3287.63	268.213	7.3%
Low-inc bef & aft non	494.843	3.1%	3630.95	0.0	0.0%	0.0	494.843	2.7%	3630.95	136.284	3.7%
Low-inc bef & aft rec	35.659	0.2%	2768.84	19.039	0.8%	1478.30	54.697	0.3%	4247.16	12.879	0.4%
Low-inc bef & nonpoor aft	259.153	1.6%	2922.28	121.441	5.1%	1869.39	380.592	2.1%	4291.64	88.682	2.4%
Nonpoor bef & aft non	10839.316	68.5%	6955.82	0.0	0.0%	0.0	10839.316	59.5%	6955.82	1558.907	42.7%
Nonpoor bef & aft rec	3048.783	19.3%	6749.83	525.985	22.0%	1164.50	3574.804	19.6%	7914.41	451.682	12.4%
Total	15822.844	100.0%	4334.05	2389.935	100.0%	654.63	18212.789	100.0%	4988.68	3650.819	100.0%

"Amount" in millions of dollars.

"No. of Families" in thousands.

The lower half of table 12 shows the corresponding figures for *central-city poverty areas*. In this subpopulation 38.4 percent of all families can be classified as poor with respect to their income before transfers. A very sizable share – 11.9 percent – of these poor families do not receive any social welfare payments at all. Although 13.5 percent receive social welfare payments, they are *not* lifted out of poverty by these payments. The remaining 13 percent change poverty classification due to the receipt of social welfare payments. Even in poverty areas a sizable percent of the population is not poor and receives no transfer payments (42.7 percent). This is considerably less than in total large SMSAs, but it still comprises more than two-fifths of the population. Approximately one-eighth of the population (12.4 percent) are nonpoor and receive transfer payments. The percentage of the population in the low-income range is rather small even in this subpopulation. The average income of the *nonpoor* in poverty areas is considerably lower than average income of the nonpoor in total large SMSAs. Inspection of the percentages of social welfare payments to different poverty groups indicates that in poverty areas relatively more social welfare payments are paid to poor people than in large SMSAs as a whole. A study of the mean amounts of social welfare payments, however, indicates that this is not the case; the higher percentage share only reflects the fact that there is a considerably larger share of the poor in those areas. The 38.8 percent of families who can be classified as poor with regard to their income before transfers receive a total of 7.3 percent of income before transfers. Transfers increase their share of income to 15.8 percent after transfers. *Thus transfers have the effect of doubling the share of income of poor people.* On the other hand, the relative share of the 55.1 percent who can be classified as nonpoor – that is, with income before social welfare payments above the poverty line – are reduced from an income share before transfers of 87.8 percent to one of 79.1 percent. Under the poverty classifications employed, 15.7 percent of the families residing in large SMSAs and 28.9 percent of all families in central-city poverty areas change poverty classification due to transfer payments.

2. Another way of assessing the effectiveness of social welfare payments in reducing poverty is by the measurement of what may be termed the *poverty gap*[18] and the *low-income gap*. A poverty gap before transfers is defined as the difference between income at the poverty line and actual income before transfers, when that income is below the poverty line. For income above or equal to the poverty line, the poverty gap equals zero. The poverty gap after transfers is the difference between poverty-line income and actual income after transfers, when income is below the poverty line; the gap is zero otherwise. The low-income gap before transfers, correspondingly,

---

18. Robert J. Lampman, "Approaches to the Reduction of Poverty," *American Economic Review* 55, no. 2 (May 1965): 523.

Table 13. The Distribution of the Poverty Gaps before and after Social Welfare Payments by Poverty Class

Large SMSAs

	Poverty Gap before Transfers			Poverty Gap after Transfers			No. of Families	
	Amount		Mean	Amount		Mean		
Poor bef & aft non	1396.667	21.5%	1133.61	1396.667	61.2%	1133.61	1232.043	5.0%
Poor bef & aft rec	2493.801	38.4%	1880.55	885.991	38.8%	668.12	1326.096	5.3%
Poor bef & low-inc aft	1046.741	16.1%	1596.24	0.0	0.0%	0.0	655.754	2.6%
Poor bef & nonpoor aft	1554.563	23.9%	1061.13	0.0	0.0%	0.0	1464.997	5.9%
Low-inc bef & aft non	0.0	0.0%	0.0	0.0	0.0%	0.0	504.337	2.0%
Low-inc bef & aft rec	0.0	0.0%	0.0	0.0	0.0%	0.0	53.190	0.2%
Low-inc bef & nonpoor aft	0.0	0.0%	0.0	0.0	0.0%	0.0	413.759	1.7%
Nonpoor bef & aft non	0.0	0.0%	0.0	0.0	0.0%	0.0	14735.934	59.3%
Nonpoor bef & aft rec	0.0	0.0%	0.0	0.0	0.0%	0.0	4449.570	17.9%
Total	6491.766	100.0%	261.38	2282.658	100.0%	91.91	24835.660	100.0%

Central-City Poverty Areas

	Poverty Gap before Transfers			Poverty Gap after Transfers			No. of Families	
	Amount		Mean	Amount		Mean		
Poor bef & aft non	478.777	21.8%	1102.72	478.777	56.3%	1102.72	434.176	11.9%
Poor bef & aft rec	994.913	45.3%	2018.99	371.500	43.7%	753.89	492.777	13.5%
Poor bef & low-inc aft	361.737	16.5%	1740.60	0.0	0.0%	0.0	207.823	5.7%
Poor bef & nonpoor aft	361.622	16.5%	1348.26	0.0	0.0%	0.0	268.213	7.3%
Low-inc bef & aft non	0.0	0.0%	0.0	0.0	0.0%	0.0	136.284	3.7%
Low-inc bef & aft rec	0.0	0.0%	0.0	0.0	0.0%	0.0	12.879	0.4%
Low-inc bef & nonpoor aft	0.0	0.0%	0.0	0.0	0.0%	0.0	88.682	2.4%
Nonpoor bef & aft non	0.0	0.0%	0.0	0.0	0.0%	0.0	1558.307	42.7%
Nonpoor bef & aft rec	0.0	0.0%	0.0	0.0	0.0%	0.0	451.682	12.4%
Total	2197.048	100.0%	601.79	850.276	100.0%	232.90	3650.819	100.0%

"Amount" in millions of dollars.
"No. of Families" in thousands.

is the difference between income at the low-income level minus income before public transfers, when that income is below the low-income line. The low-income gap is zero for income equal to or above the low-income line. The low-income gap after transfers is the difference between income at the low-income level minus income including public transfers. When the income lies above that low-income line, the low-income gap equals zero.

A comparison of income gaps before and after transfers indicates the effectiveness of the transfers in reducing poverty. Table 13 shows the poverty gaps before and after public transfers for the two subpopulations under investigation. As income figures in the previous tables would suggest, the largest average poverty gap before transfers can be observed for those families poor before transfers that received transfers but were not lifted out of poverty. Table 12 shows that their mean income is lower than that of other groups; consequently, their average poverty gap before transfers is largest. In this respect the same overall pattern may be observed for large total SMSAs and central-city poverty areas, with one exception. The average poverty gap before transfers in central-city poverty areas is that of poor families who do not receive any transfers. This is not the case for total large SMSAs. In the latter group, the smallest poverty gap can be observed for families who are poor before transfers but are lifted out of poverty by transfers.

This reflects the fact that public assistance constitutes a relatively large share of Social Security benefits in central-city poverty areas. The income level on which its availability is made dependent would appear to be too low to effectively alleviate poverty. In large SMSAs transfers reduce the poverty gap from approximately $6.5 billion to roughly $2.3 billion. Total transfer payments to large SMSAs amount to approximately $12.6 billion. These $12.6 billion, however, result in a reduction of the poverty gap by only $4.2 billion. This indicates that *approximately one-third of all transfer payments achieve the elimination of poverty*. This performance score can hardly be considered very impressive

Central-city poverty areas receive about $2.4 billion in social welfare payments. The poverty gap before transfers amounts to approximately $2.2 billion. Transfer payments reduced this poverty gap to approximately $850 million. This amounts to a poverty-gap reduction of approximately $1.3 billion.

3.   Inspection of the poverty line and low-income line (in the Appendix) shows a monotonic relationship between the two. The low-income gaps (table 14) consequently exhibit essentially the same patterns for poor before transfers as the poverty gaps.

The large mean low-income gap observed in central-city poverty areas for families who are recipients of transfer payments but are not lifted above the low-income level represents a coding error. It is impossible for the low-income gap of families in the low-income range to exceed low-income gaps of families with income below the poverty line.

Table 14. The Distribution of the Low-Income Gaps before and after Social Welfare Payments by Poverty Class

Large SMSAs

	Low-Income Gap before Transfers			Low-Income Gap after Transfers			No. of Families	
	Amount		Mean	Amount		Mean		
Poor bef & aft non	2148.650	22.3%	1743.97	2148.650	50.6%	1743.97	1232.043	5.0%
Poor bef & aft rec	3217.788	33.4%	2426.51	1609.966	37.9%	1214.06	1326.096	5.3%
Poor ber & low-inc aft	1443.616	15.0%	2201.46	207.513	4.9%	316.45	655.754	2.6%
Poor bef & nonpoor aft	2370.390	24.6%	1618.01	0.0	0.0%	0.0	1464.997	5.9%
Low-inc bef & aft non	230.605	2.4%	457.24	230.605	5.4%	457.24	504.337	2.0%
Low-inc bef & aft rec	84.804	0.9%	1594.36	46.351	1.1%	871.42	53.190	0.2%
Low-inc bef & nonpoor aft	134.708	1.4%	325.57	0.0	0.0%	0.0	413.759	1.7%
Nonpoor bef & aft non	0.0	0.0%	0.0	0.0	0.0%	0.0	14735.934	59.3%
Nonpoor bef & aft rec	0.0	0.0%	0.0	0.0	0.0%	0.0	4449.570	17.9%
Total	9630.551	100.0%	387.77	4243.082	100.0%	170.84	24835.660	100.0%

Central-City Poverty Areas

	Low-Income Gap before Transfers			Low-Income Gap after Transfers			No. of Families	
	Amount		Mean	Amount		Mean		
Poor bef & aft non	748.342	23.7%	1723.59	748.342	47.8%	1723.59	434.176	11.9%
Poor bef & aft rec	1273.947	40.3%	2585.24	650.510	41.6%	1320.09	492.777	13.5%
Poor bef & low-inc aft	497.895	15.8%	2395.77	77.425	4.9%	372.55	207.823	5.7%
Poor bef & nonpoor aft	503.704	15.9%	1878.00	0.0	0.0%	0.0	268.213	7.3%
Low-inc bef & aft non	70.480	2.2%	517.15	70.480	4.5%	517.15	136.284	3.7%
Low-inc bef & aft rec	36.686	1.2%	2848.59	17.647	1.1%	1370.29	12.879	0.4%
Low-inc bef & nonpoor aft	28.892	0.9%	325.78	0.0	0.0%	0.0	88.682	2.4%
Nonpoor bef & aft non	0.0	0.0%	0.0	0.0	0.0%	0.0	1558.307	42.7%
Nonpoor bef & aft rec	0.0	0.0%	0.0	0.0	0.0%	0.0	451.682	12.4%
Total	3159.946	100.0%	865.54	1564.405	100.0%	428.50	3650.819	100.0%

"Amount" in millions of dollars.
"No. of Families" in thousands.

4. Previous analysis of social welfare payments showed that Social Security and public assistance exhibit distinctly different distributive patterns. Because the programs were designed for different purposes, this is quite understandable. Table 15 presents the poverty reduction of Social Security and public assistance for large SMSAs and central-city poverty areas.[19] Of the 18.8 percent families *in large SMSAs* who are poor before receiving public transfers 4.1 percent are lifted to an income level above the low-income line by Social Security; the income of 1.9 percent of all families is raised to the low-income level. The largest part of the poor, however, are not removed from poverty: 8.4 percent do not receive Social Security, and 4.4 percent remain poor despite the transfer. Of the 77.2 percent who are not poor, 9 percent receive Social Security. In large SMSAs 40.4 percent of all Social Security benefits are received by the 81.2 percent of the population who are not poor. They constitute 43.4 percent of all Social Security recipients. Seven percent is received by families with income between the low-income line and the poverty line. The remaining 52.5 percent of Social Security benefits are received by the poor.

Public assistance programs are primarily designed to provide income to the needy. We would therefore expect that public assistance payments are received almost exclusively by the poor. Survey of Economic Opportunity (SEO) data, however, indicate that in large SMSAs approximately 10.6 percent of public assistance is received by families who are not poor before transfers. This constitutes 0.7 percent of all families residing in large SMSAs. Whereas this percentage may be biased on the high side, sample data would indicate that a sizable amount of public assistance is not received by poor families. In fact, according to the SEO estimates, 16.3 percent of all recipients are in the nonpoor group. Of the 18.8 percent families who are poor before transfers, 15.3 percent do not receive any public assistance; 2.5 percent (54.7 percent of all public assistance recipients in large SMSAs) remain poor even after transfers. Only 1.1 percent are lifted out of poverty. Although most public assistance programs are geared to the truly needy, we can observe that Social Security lifts approximately 6 percent of all families (28.7 percent of recipients) out of poverty. Only 1.1 percent (or 24.5 percent of all recipients) are lifted out of poverty by public assistance. On the other hand, we can see that a much larger share of public assistance recipients who are poor before transfers are not lifted out of poverty. For the poor, average Social Security payments are somewhat lower than average public assistance payments; the reverse holds true for the nonpoor. In the low-income group, those who are lifted out of the low-income range into the nonpoor range receive higher mean Social Security benefits. Those who remain in the same poverty class, on the average, receive lower Social

---

19. Poverty classification in table 15 depends *only* on the poverty-reducing effects of Social Security and public assistance, respectively.

Table 15. The Poverty-Reducing Effect of Social Security and Public Assistance

Large SMSAs

	Social Security					Public Assistance				
	Amount		Mean	No. of Families		Amount		Mean	No. of Families	
Poor bef & aft non	0.0	0.0%	0.0	2095.538	8.4%	0.0	0.0%	0.0	3795.571	15.3%
Poor bef & aft rec	1135.851	14.8%	1030.83	1101.875	4.4%	849.715	46.3%	1393.13	609.932	2.5%
Poor bef & low-inc aft	754.205	9.8%	1636.20	460.947	1.9%	366.861	20.0%	2610.83	140.515	0.6%
Poor bef & nonpoor aft	2137.543	27.9%	2094.83	1020.389	4.1%	350.255	19.1%	2646.25	132.359	0.5%
Low-inc bef & aft non	0.0	0.0%	0.0	634.223	2.6%	0.0	0.0%	0.0	921.017	3.7%
Low-inc bef & aft rec	11.100	0.1%	646.18	17.177	0.1%	23.947	1.3%	1368.17	17.503	0.1%
Low-inc bef & nonpoor aft	533.400	7.0%	1667.47	319.884	1.3%	51.776	2.8%	1580.24	32.765	0.1%
Nonpoor bef & aft non	0.0	0.0%	0.0	16942.352	68.2%	0.0	0.0%	0.0	18998.559	76.5%
Nonpoor bef & aft rec	3102.346	40.4%	1383.37	2242.599	9.0%	194.140	10.6%	1071.72	181.148	0.7%
Total	7674.441	100.0%	309.01	24834.973	100.0%	1836.693	100.0%	73.97	24829.344	100.0%

Central-City Poverty Areas

	Social Security					Public Assistance				
	Amount		Mean	No. of Families		Amount		Mean	No. of Families	
Poor bef & aft non	0.0	0.0%	0.0	830.385	22.7%	0.0	0.0%	0.0	965.583	26.4%
Poor bef & aft rec	335.857	30.8%	984.08	341.288	9.3%	457.524	52.2%	1455.72	314.292	8.6%
Poor bef & low-inc aft	179.341	16.5%	1633.29	109.803	3.0%	185.426	21.2%	2746.65	67.510	1.8%
Poor bef & nonpoor aft	235.756	21.6%	1940.20	121.511	3.3%	163.689	18.7%	2943.94	55.602	1.5%
Low-inc bef & aft non	0.0	0.0%	0.0	174.611	4.8%	0.0	0.0%	0.0	218.456	6.0%
Low-inc bef & aft rec	4.068	0.4%	922.93	4.408	0.1%	14.991	1.7%	1984.24	7.555	0.2%
Low-inc bef & nonpoor aft	80.425	7.4%	1367.19	58.825	1.6%	9.977	1.1%	843.22	11.832	0.3%
Nonpoor bef & aft non	0.0	0.0%	0.0	1818.148	49.8%	0.0	0.0%	0.0	1971.790	54.0%
Nonpoor bef & aft rec	254.027	23.3%	1324.88	191.734	5.3%	44.170	5.0%	1161.64	38.024	1.0%
Total	1089.473	100.0%	298.427	3650.710	100.0%	875.776	100.0%	239.89	3650.639	100.0%

"Amount" in millions of dollars.
"No. of Families" in thousands.

Security benefits than the corresponding group of public assistance recipients.

In central-city poverty areas 38.3 percent of all families can be classified as poor before transfers; of these families 22.7 percent do not receive Social Security, and 9.3 percent are not lifted out of poverty by the amounts they receive. Social Security succeeds in raising the incomes of 6.3 percent of all families in poverty areas above the poverty line. Even in poverty areas 5.3 percent of all Social Security recipients are nonpoor. Average Social Security benefits for almost all poverty classes are lower in poverty areas than in total SMSAs.

Only a small proportion (11.9 percent) of the 38.3 percent of poor residing in poverty areas receive public assistance. The predominant number of poor recipients do not receive a sufficient amount to lift them out of poverty. On the other hand, 1 percent of central-city poverty area residents are nonpoor and receive public assistance. (This 1 percent constitutes 7.7 percent of all public assistance recipients.) The 6.5 percent of the residents in central-city poverty areas whose income before transfers is between the low-income and the poverty lines receive a smaller relative share (2.8 percent) of public assistance. There is evidence that public assistance payments to poor families in central-city poverty areas on the average are higher than to poor families in large SMSAs as a whole. The reverse can be said about families with incomes before transfers above the poverty line.

The elimination of poverty certainly does not provide the most impressive success of social welfare payments to large SMSAs in general, and to central-city poverty areas of these large SMSAs in particular. Not only do 42 percent of all social welfare benefits to large SMSAs benefit the nonpoor, but furthermore, only one-third of the benefits are directed toward elimination of the poverty gap. It appears surprising that the "income-maintenance programs" serve, in fact, to maintain the predominant share of poor social welfare *recipients* below the poverty line. It also comes as a shock to observe that public assistance, the programs for the most needy, lift an even smaller proportion of poor out of poverty than social security.

Conclusion

The empirical analysis of the effect of transfer payments to large SMSAs on income distribution in general, and on poverty reduction in particular, leads to many surprising patterns. These cast a clear light onto the current debates on the need for reform of the welfare system and the need for the institution of new income-maintenance programs:

1. Of the seemingly massive cash benefits disbursed under social welfare programs, only a small fraction (7.44 percent) goes to the urban poor.

2. Whites receive higher incomes before these transfers, whereas blacks receive slightly higher transfers. But the effective redistribution from whites to blacks is minute.

3. The distribution of income and transfer payments by income class including transfers indicates that the redistributive effect of transfers is slight. The income of the groups with income below $3,000 increased from 1.7 to 3.3 percent in large SMSAs and from 6.5 to 11 percent in poverty areas.

4. The distribution of income and transfers by family head indicates that: (a) families with male heads have the highest income and the lowest transfers; (b) families with female heads have low income and higher transfers; however, these transfers are not enough to equalize the income of families with male and female heads; and (c) poverty areas are characterized by many more families headed by females or consisting of single individuals than the rest of the large SMSA.

5. The distribution of income and transfers by work experience suggests that the fewer weeks the family head worked, the lower was his (her) income and the higher were public transfer receipts.

6. Distributing income and transfer by level of education of the recipient reveals that: (a) income increases with the level of education, and (b) transfers decrease with the level of education of the recipient.

7. The pattern of distribution of Social Security and public assistance follows: (a) whites receive more Social Security than blacks, particularly in the nonpoor areas of central cities; (b) public assistance is disbursed more to blacks than to whites.

8. The major share of Social Security and public assistance payments goes to individuals with an income before transfers ranging from $1,000 to $5,000.

9. Families with male heads with spouse receive more Social Security, whereas families with female heads receive more public assistance. The poverty areas exhibit larger differences in group averages than the other areas.

10. Families living in large SMSAs whose heads had seven to ten years of education, or similar families living in poverty areas whose heads had nine to ten years of education receive higher amounts of public assistance, whereas those with a lesser education receive slightly less. Few families whose head had obtained education at the level of high school completion or beyond receive public assistance.

11. Nonworkers received the highest Social Security payments, followed by full-time workers. The same pattern holds for public assistance.

12. The poverty-reducing effect has some surprises in store: (a) a sizable proportion of social welfare payments (42 percent in large SMSAs and 22 percent in poverty areas of large SMSAs) go to the nonpoor; (b) a large number of poor families do not receive social welfare benefits; (c) the predominant share of poor recipients remain poor

even after transfers; (d) although the relative income share of families poor before transfers is doubled by social welfare payments, the relative income share of the 18.8 percent poor in large SMSAs is only 4 percent after transfers.

13. Although more than one-half of all transfers are disbursed to poor before transfers, the more than $12 billion social welfare payments to large SMSA residents reduce the poverty gap by only one-third of this amount.

14. Although public assistance is more directed toward "socially under-privileged" groups and poor people, it has an almost negligible effect in eliminating poverty: only 1.1 percent of the families in large SMSAs and 3.3 percent in poverty areas are moved out of poverty by public assistance. The major share of public assistance maintains recipients in the same poverty class.

The empirical analysis of social welfare payments to large SMSAs and to poverty areas of central cities of large SMSAs suggests that some degree of redistribution to the needy is achieved by these public grants. However, they fall a long way short of (a) achieving any sizable degree of reduction of income inequality and (b) complete reduction of poverty. A wide scope for the extension of benefits and the reform of existing methods of conveying benefits is indicated.

Appendix

"[The Survey of Economic Opportunity] files contain information collected in sample surveys in the spring of 1966 and 1967. The Bureau of the Census conducted the surveys for the Office of Economic Opportunity in order to supplement the information regularly collected in the Current Population Survey (CPS) for February and March of each year. The common items in the SEO and the CPS include personal characteristics (age, race, sex, family relationship, marital status), last year's work experience, and income.

"In addition, the SEO provides information on dimensions of poverty not usually obtained between the decennial census years (such as on housing) or obtained even less regularly such as the data on assets and liabilities. . . .

"The SEO sample of 30,000 households is made up of two parts. The first is a national self-weighting sample of approximately 18,000 households, drawn in the same way as the Current Population Survey Sample. In order to obtain better information concerning the poor – particularly the non-white poor – 12,000 additional households were also included in the SEO by drawing a sample in areas with large nonwhite populations."[1]

---

1. 1967 Survey of Economic Opportunity Codebook Introduction.

The SEO file contains four segments: (1) household, (2) interview unit, (3) person, and (4) adult segments. Distributions presented in this paper contain aggregations of the "interview unit" (that is, family) level. The classifying characteristics of race, education, and work experience were derived from the "person" record of the family head. Only the SEO file 1967 (containing data on the year 1966) were used.

Poverty classification on the SEO file presents a modified form of the Social Security Administration's economy poverty cutoff levels[2] priced as of December 1965. For nonfarm families the poverty line is at 99.5 percent of the following figure.[3]

Family Size	None	1	2	3	4	5	6 or More
			Number of Related Children under 18				
		Nonfarm					
Male head							
1 under age 65	1758						
65 or over	1579						
2 under age 65	2198	2462					
65 or over	1973	2462					
3	2559	2642	2792				
4	3374	3424	3306	3473			
5	4071	4121	3988	3888	3971		
6	4670	4686	4587	4487	4354	4421	
7 or more	5882	5932	5816	5716	5584	5384	5335
Female head							
1 under age 65	1626						
65 or over	1559						
2 Under age 65	2031	2217					
65 or over	1949	2217					
3	2476	2359	2609				
4	3240	3356	3341	3306			
5	3888	4005	3988	3955	3822		
6	4537	4620	4587	4553	4404	4270	
7 or more	5699	5783	5766	5716	5567	5451	5184

Farm cutoffs are set at 85 percent of nonfarm cutoffs. The low-income line is set at 97.7 percent of the Social Security Administration's low-cost poverty cutoff level, priced as of December 1966, which is shown below for nonfarm families. Farm cutoffs are 85 percent of nonfarm cutoffs.[4]

---

2. Molly Orshansky, "Counting the Poor: Another Look at the Poverty Profile," *Social Security Bulletin* (January 1965): 3–29.

3. Survey of Economic Opportunity Codebook, 1967.

4. Ibid.

Family Size	Number of Related Children under 18						
	None	1	2	3	4	5	6 or More
Nonfarm							
Male head							
1 under age 65	2138						
65 or over	1926						
2 under age 65	2969	3158					
65 or over	2676	3158					
3	3384	3469	3554				
4	4417	4467	4315	4400			
5	5296	5348	5161	5026	5059		
6	6025	6092	5923	5804	5635	5618	
7 or more	7581	7648	7479	7344	7174	6887	6802
Female head							
1 under age 65	1973						
65 or over	1880						
2 under age 65	2740	2865					
65 or over	2611	2865					
3	3282	3367	3351				
4	4264	4332	4298	4197			
5	5095	5178	5128	5043	4856		
6	5889	5940	5889	5787	5618	5432	
7 or more	7412	7462	7412	7310	7123	6955	6617

6

Irving Leveson: Strategies against Urban Poverty

Introduction

Watts was the Black Tuesday of the urban crisis, at the core of which are problems of poverty and race. But the urban crisis can be viewed as only one part of a larger social depression in which the efficiency and

Presented at the Symposium on the Grants Economy held between the Association for the Study of the Grants Economy and the American Association for the Advancement of Science, Boston, Mass., December, 1969. Reprinted by permission of the author. The author is director of research, Office of Comprehensive Planning, New York City Department of City Planning. He has benefited from conversations with members of the Comprehensive Planning staff of the New York City Department of City Planning, particularly from discussions with Barney Rabinow, Hank Sirlin, and Bruce Zellner, and also from discussions with Jon Wiener and Nora Piore. The views expressed are those of the author and need not represent those of the City Planning Commission, the Community Renewal Program, or any of their affiliates or consultants.

responsiveness of our social institutions are in question. Poverty policy cannot ignore these issues.

Until recently antipoverty efforts have been erratic and fragmentary. A particularly serious deficiency has been the lack of a framework within which to consider the merits of broad policy alternatives. Even when it is agreed that the success of a program will be measured by its ultimate impact on the well-being of the population, empirical and often theoretical analyses have focused on a single indicator of well-being at a time. A more useful framework for policy decisions would simultaneously examine the impact of a number of programs on a whole set of indicators. We make an effort to develop such a framework and to consider the relative attractiveness of major antipoverty policy alternatives when viewed through such a frame-work.

We begin by examining the meaning of well-being and poverty. A class of measures of poverty for analytical uses is proposed. A social index which measures well-being is defined, and its relationship to social indicator–production functions is laid out in an econometric model view of the system. The approach is placed within the technology of consumption framework of Kelvin Lancaster's "New Approach to Consumer Theory." The model provides the core of a framework for determining the implications of a number of major directions and strategies.

The Meaning and Measurement of Well-Being and Poverty

Past Treatment of Well-Being and Poverty

For a long time income has been the dominant measure of the well-being of people. With the systematic development of the National Income Accounts, per capita income has emerged as the primary measure of the state of economic development in international comparisons, and the growth of income has become the yardstick of domestic progress. The measurement of income has presented many methodological difficulties which on the whole tend to result in an overstatement of the rate of improvement of well-being over time.

In the last several years attention has shifted from measures of the level of income appropriate for concern about economic growth and business cycles to measures of the distribution of income relevant to concern for the problems of poverty and race. Initially the Lyndon B. Johnson administration used the proportion of persons in families with incomes below $3,000 in 1960 dollars as its measure of poverty. More recently the

Council of Economic Advisors has adopted the "Orshansky Index," which takes into account family size, farm-nonfarm residence, and in the case of one- and two-person families, whether the household head is over or under age sixty-five. The index includes a set of incomes for each family size for classifying persons as "near poor."[1] Many other measures of poverty have been proposed, including numerous income–family size schedules implicit in various income maintenance proposals.

There have been a number of suggestions of ways of supplementing income so that it would continue to provide a single overall measure of well-being, including proposals to formally incorporate information on assets into a combined measure,[2] as the National Income Accounts already do by inputing rent to owner-occupied housing. Many researchers have recommended including in income the value of goods and services received through social welfare programs,[3] and adjusting income for differences in family size. James Morgan further suggests that we combine income with information on the amount of effort involved in attaining that income, and that poverty be defined to include persons below one-third of the national average of his "index of well-offness."[4] S. M. Miller and Frank Riessman have put forth the concept of "command over resources," in which they include the value of pension rights as well as free services. In addition, they favor the concept of "inclusion" in economic, political, psychological, and social processes,[5] a factor that may instead be treated as a means of achieving improvements in well-being rather than as a direct measure of it.

---

1. M. Orshansky, "Counting the Poor: Another Look at the Poverty Profile," *Social Security Bulletin*, January 1965, pp. 3–29.

2. B. L. Weisbrod and W. L. Hansen, "An Income-Net Worth Approach to Measuring Economic Welfare," *American Economic Review* 58, no. 4 (December 1968): 1315–29.

3. President of the United States, *Economic Report of the President* (Washington, D.C., 1969), p. 161 and unpublished supporting tables prepared by D. Ott for the Council of Economic Advisors; and R. J. Lampman, "Transfer Approaches to Distribution Policy," *American Economic Review* 60, no. 2 (May 1970): 270–79.

4. J. N. Morgan, "The Supply of Effort, the Measurement of Well-Being, and the Dynamics of Improvement," *American Economic Review* 58 (May 1968): 31–39. Morgan proposes assuming that the indifference curves between income and leisure are rectangular hyperbolas, in which case the product of income and leisure provides an index that is an ordinal measure of the combined utility. The problem with Morgan's measure is that it assumes that a person would be as well off as before if he suffered a 1 percent loss in income that was accompanied by a 1 percent increase in leisure. One intuitively feels that leisure has a lower value, particularly for the poor. Morgan's own evidence, cited earlier in his paper, that many poor desire more work than they are able to obtain supports this notion. Furthermore, there may be additional utility derived from the receipt of earned income rather than having a dependency status if self-sufficiency is valued. Such a measure could be amended to include some value for self-sufficiency. See M. L. Skolnick, "A Comment on Professor Musgrave's Separation of Distribution from Allocation," *Journal of Economic Literature* 8, no. 2 (June 1970): 440–42.

5. S. M. Miller and F. Riessman, *Social Class and Social Policy* (New York: Basic Books, 1968), chap. 1.

The Need for Improved Concepts and Measures

Poverty can be defined most comprehensively as the existence of a low level of utility. Differences among groups in utility are not sufficiently reflected in income alone, even if they are adjusted for assets, family size, and effort. More generally we want a measure of well-being that incorporates the values of both the stocks and flows of all physical and human resources used in both market and household production and consumption. But these are just inputs into processes by which more basic wants are satisfied. We prefer to define poverty so that it is related to the effectiveness of those processes in satisfying basic wants. Before this is formally done, let us first enumerate some of the sources of differences in utility that may be important and which an income measure would not explicitly reflect. We shall argue that the net result of these factors is that income tends to overstate the relative well-being of the poor.

It has generally been regarded that the impact of restrictions that affect allocative efficiency is small.[6] However, union effects and occupational licensing tend to exclude the poor from employment, and import quotas and minimum quality restrictions raise their costs, acting like a regressive tax. The impact of these factors on income distribution may be sizable. It also appears likely that the poor bear disproportionate shares of the costs of economic growth in terms of such problems as pollution, crime, and labor-market dislocation.

The well-being of the poor may also be lower than indicated by incomes because of conditions in the markets in which they deal. Some examples are: (1) There are important economies of scale related to average transaction size in supermarkets that cannot easily be realized in the ghetto. (2) The size of the market makes it more difficult to get a physician when needed. (3) Costs of credit to the poor are high because of high costs of more finely distinguishing risk classes. The poor tend to be relatively inefficient consumers and producers of household activities.[7]

The most discussed factor that could make utility vary differently than in proportion to money income is the possibility of a diminishing marginal utility of money. Although economic theory has advanced without reliance on such a proposition, the absence of diminishing utility is by no means universally accepted.[8]

---

6. H. Leibenstein, "Allocative Efficiency vs. X-Efficiency," *American Economic Review* 56, no. 3 (June 1966): 392–415.

7. For example, see D. Caplovitz, *The Poor Pay More* (New York: Free Press, 1968).

8. "Use value was rejected as the cause of exchange value by ignoring that men buy water and diamonds by increments and not all-or-none. It took the best minds a century to discover that wants are progressively satiable . . . and the diminishing utility of money is still questioned, in defiance of common sense" (F. H. Knight, "Laissez Faire: Pro and Con," *American Economic Review* 57, no. 6 [December 1967]: 78). See H. Theil and R. Brooks, "How Does the Marginal Utility of Income Change When Real Income Changes?", University of Chicago Center for Mathematical Studies in Business and Economics, Report No. 7012, March 1970.

Variability of income can have important consequences for social problems such as family stability, crime, and mental health. When we consider the process of adjustment of the poor to fluctuations in income, it is apparent that there can be socially undesirable consequences. Reactions to negative transitory incomes may be a reduction in the stock of human capital or its rate of growth, such as by taking a job that is detrimental to health or by leaving school in order to work. Increased participation in the labor force of women may adversely affect child development. One form of adjustment may be through criminal activity. Because some of the adjustments to transitory income and costs may be irreversible, it is quite possible that for the poor, positive transitory income is valued far less than if an equal negative transitory income is disdained. Because gross differences in income include both the permanent and transitory components, this phenomenon could produce effects for gross income differences that strongly resemble the effects we would observe from diminishing marginal utility of money.

The irregularity of incomes of the poor may be part of a more general phenomenon whereby nonpecuniary labor market factors make the poor even worse off relative to middle-income persons than indicated by monetary factors. The poor tend to receive jobs that have the most undesirable hours of work and physical conditions and that are often considered boring, degrading, and so on. Closely related to this is the absence of as much utility derived from expectations of higher future incomes than those with more promise or a longer time horizon might enjoy. The net effect of these considerations is that income, even with many of the adjustments that have been proposed, appears to be an inadequate measure of the well-being of the poor.

Poverty and Social Indicators

In order to overcome the inadequacies of measures of well-being and poverty based on income alone, we use information on income in conjunction with other measures such as infant mortality and juvenile delinquency. There has generally been no attempt to see that those represent a complete set in the sense that together they reflect all major elements – such as security, comfort, and so on – that enter the utility functions of broad population groups. In spite of the absence of any formal framework in which to select and structure separate indicators, their use to collectively measure the well-being of a population involves an *implicit* choice of weights with which they are combined into an overall index.

There is no uniquely correct social index. Conceptually we desire a set of measures that includes anything that enters into anyone's utility function. Empirically we would prefer a small group of measures upon which there is some general agreement. In going from the one to the other the preferences of the decision maker or the technician inevitably enter. The choice of indicators may reflect the concerns of a particular group or the kinds of problems they have power to influence; there can be subgroup social indices for major problem areas. There is no unique set of weights to be assigned. The problem of whose social welfare function is to be optimized will not be solved here, but in the political arena. It is there that problems of interpersonal comparisons of utility are also resolved.

Decision makers can assign their own weights either implicitly or explicitly. The researcher can assist by indicating the weights implicit in any overall index and the way choices would vary with alternative sets of weights. The value of a social index primarily depends on its usefulness in an actual decision-making process. There are advantages for keeping the choice of weights flexible, because their negotiation is an important part of the political process. At the same time formal analysis can be facilitated by the construction of overall social indices and poverty measures based on them. These provide the dependent variable for analyses of the impacts of alternative policies. Analysis can be conducted with alternative weighting schemes and empirical results based on alternative weights presented in terms of choices, such as between a high safety-security strategy and a high consumption strategy. Some notions about how a composite measure of well-being might look can be discerned by examining the way other social indicators vary with income. We summarize these measures for convenience into an overall social index (SI).[9]

We define a social index as follows: the change in a social index (ΔS) can be viewed as a weighted average of changes in separate indices (Δs_j), each measuring some aspect of health, safety, comfort, and so on, that enter directly into utility functions. The values $\bar{\mu}_j$ indicate the social value of increments in Hs_j. Thus

$$\Delta S = \sum_{j=1}^{m} \Delta s_j \, \bar{\mu}_j. \tag{1}$$

The $\bar{\mu}_j$ are averages here because, rather than being applied to small changes in s_j, they are being used to value changes over a range that may be sizable. Although, for simplicity we treat these values as fixed, in principle they could easily be made a function of the level of component indices.

The relationships between measures of well-being and income have

---

9. Indices of socioeconomic status (SES) appear to have the same objectives as a social index. Rather than attempt to sort out independent effects of a large number of highly correlated measures, a small number that are important and partially independent (particularly income, education, and occupation) are chosen to represent a broad range of conditions.

been found quite generally to have the shape of the curve in figure 1a.[10] Some examples include the income pattern of many physical health measures and some mental health measures, the high unemployment rates of those with lowest levels of education (a measure of permanent income), and the tendency of the lowest income areas to have more crime and addiction, poorer sanitation, and high functional illiteracy. The use of a poverty line, on the other hand, is equivalent to assuming that the level of utility is discontinuous, with a jump at the poverty line as in figure 1b.[11]

A Proposed Measure of Poverty

Recently there have been attempts to define poverty in terms of the difference between one's income (y_i) and some minimum or average level (L). This would imply that in the relevant range utility differences are proportional to income differences as in figure 1c. For example, the Council of Economic Advisors and others concerned with the costs of income-maintenance proposals have relied heavily on the "poverty income gap" proposed by Robert Lampman.[12] The poverty gap is the amount of money necessary to bring all poor up to the poverty line. If n_i is the number of individuals with income of $y_i < L$, the poverty gap G is

$$G = \sum_{i=0}^{n} (L - y_i) \, n_i. \tag{2}$$

But as we have indicated, well-being probably tends to increase more than in proportion to income at low levels and less thereafter. Let L represent some minimum standard of income. This could be defined as the point above

---

10. The shape of the curve may simply reflect the inadequacy of income as a measure of utility. It may also be the consequence of diminishing returns in the production of gains in social indicators. On the other hand it may stem from a prevalence of neighborhood effects or interaction effects at low levels of income, which makes problems more difficult to deal with. In the case of health, Richard Auster, Irving Leveson and Deborah Sarachek have suggested that occupation and consumption choices are made in part as a result of rising income and in part in order to achieve increases in income. Therefore, because they produce other satisfactions, choices will be made even though they may be detrimental to health. See R. Auster, I. Leveson, and D. Sarachek, "The Production of Health, An Exploratory Study," *Journal of Human Resources*, Fall 1969, pp. 411–36.

11. For a discussion of the inadequacies of a single poverty line, see T. I. Ribich, *Education and Poverty* (Washington, D.C.: The Brookings Institution, 1968), chap. 2. Ribich proposes the use of two poverty criteria such as the Social Security Administration's *poor* and *near poor* designations. In effect he approximates a curve with a three-level step function in the interest of simplicity. However, Ribich, who is critical of the use of income alone, suggests that cultural factors be introduced into the measure. Here we bypass the need to specify the determinants of a low level of well-being by measuring their consequences directly in a social index.

12. R. J. Lampman, "Approaches to the Reduction of Poverty," *American Economic Review* 55, no. 2 (May 1965): p. 523.

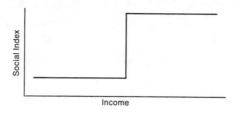

Figure 1a.

Figure 1b.

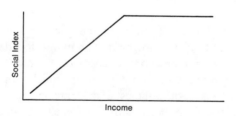

Figure 1c.

which the social index is essentially flat if our representation is correct. Define σ_{ij} as the change in jth social indicator per dollar that income changes when income is below L at y_i. Let μ_{ij} be the marginal utility of a unit change in the jth social indicator when income is at y_i. The μ_{ij} could allow for many factors, including emphasis placed on any particular indicator by different individuals, diminishing marginal utility of money, the way interdependencies among social indicators affect the utility of the individual, or the inter-dependencies between the utility functions of members of society.

The set of weights given to different deficiencies in income is

$$w_i = \sum_{j=1}^{m} \sum_{i=0}^{L} \sigma_{ij} \ \mu_{ij}. \tag{3}$$

We can define a new measure, a poverty differential (D), as a transformation of the poverty gap, which allows for the way in which utility varies with money income:

$$D = \sum_{i=0}^{n} w_i \, (L - y_i) \, n_i .$$

(4)

Because a poverty differential is a weighted sum of income differences; it includes the poverty gap as a special case. D is identical to G when all $w_i = 1$.

In determining changes in a poverty differential over time it would be necessary to adjust L for changes in the cost of living, if it is to be used as absolute poverty measures are used now. We may instead judge that the well-being of the poor deteriorates when they obtain increases in income concomitant with increases in the price level alone. The ability to share in the gains from technological change may depend on the maintenance of an income position relative to society. We can utilize D as a relative measure of poverty by increasing L at the average rate of income growth for society.

The Production of Well-Being

The development of systematic policies for dealing with problems of urban poverty has been hampered by a lack of agreement on a definition of what the problem is. Each definition of the problem and implied policy responses has something to be said for it. The nation has developed a set of policies that borrows fragmented components from each of these approaches. However, we have evolved to a point at which much can be gained from the development of a set of policies and strategies within a conceptual framework that integrates the key features of each alternative. In order to deal with the kinds of problems posed it is necessary to formulate a model of how the system works. We focus on the system by which skills and effort are translated not only into incomes but also into more basic improvements in well-being. The concern is with long-term effects, including those that may not appear until the next generation.

The process by which changes in social indicators come about can be usefully understood within the framework of Kelvin Lancaster's "New Approach to Consumer Theory."[13] In the model *goods* are used in more fundamental *activities* such as "going to the movies," and the activities are undertaken because they produce desired *characteristics* such as relaxation. The set of functions that indicate the amount of characteristics produced by activities is designated the "technology of consumption."

Generally activities produce more than one characteristic. The amount

---

13. K. Lancaster, "A New Approach to Consumer Theory," *Journal of Political Economy*," April 1966, pp. 132–57, and "Change and Innovation in the Technology of Consumption," *American Economic Review* 56, (May 1966): 14–23.

of each characteristic that can be obtained from a given expenditure on an activity can be compared with the amounts that can be obtained from an equal expenditure on another activity. An activity that produces less of each characteristic than another with an equal expenditure can be ruled out as an inefficient choice. The choice of relative quantities of the remaining activities then depends on the relative preferences for alternative characteristics. That is, the consumer "makes an efficiency choice in rejecting goods which do not enable him to reach an efficiency frontier and a private choice in finding the preferred point on the frontier."[14]

The counterpart of Lancaster's characteristics in our analysis is the social indicators which measure various aspects of well-being. The analog of activities is life styles. Life styles define an aggregate set of activities or an aggregate production function. In that vein we classify different circumstances as different life styles only if they have major consequences for differences in well-being. The level of well-being is determined by the level of income, the distribution of families among life styles, and the efficiency with which resources are used within life styles.

A life style strategy can operate in one of two ways. It can either increase the consumer's knowledge about production alternatives or it can change his opportunities so that a life style becomes more or less attractive than before. An example of the former is educating youngsters about the harmful effects of drug addiction in order to discourage drug abuse. Parenthetically, the reason we would consider this a life style strategy but would not treat an antismoking campaign the same is not because consumer ignorance is greater in one case than in the other but because addiction has such enormous consequences for so many aspects of the person's well-being.

A schematic representation of an illustrative model in which well-being of the poor is determined is presented in figure 2. A social index depends on income per adult equivalent person in the family given by M, where adult equivalence of children is determined by the typical consumption of children relative to adults. The index also depends on the distribution of families among life styles (L) and the efficiency (E) with which resources are used within life styles to produce well-being. Triangles represent policy multipliers, the triangle above M indicating the direct effect of a unit change in M on S. Lines coming together indicate that a basic mathematical operation is occurring. For example, M is equal to the ratio of total family income (Y) to the number of adult equivalent family members (N), and family income is the sum of its components-earned income (Ye) plus property income (Yp) plus transfer payments in cash or in kind (T) less depreciation in the stock of human capital (Dh) and depreciation in the stock of physical and financial capital (Dp). Life styles and efficiency depend on equality of opportunity (O) and the stocks of human physical and financial capital, as do earnings

14. "Change and Innovation," p. 17. Also see G. S. Becker. "Consumption Theory: Some Criticisms and a Suggested Approach," unpublished (1968).

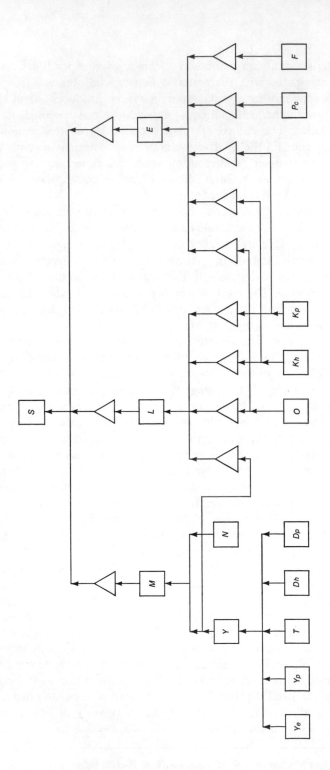

Figure 2. Structure of the Central Model

(not shown). Income has an impact on life styles that produces a secondary effect on well-being in addition to its direct effect. Efficiency of consumption also depends on the efficiency of markets for goods and services and on family structure. We have illustrated the structure of only the central portion of a much more complex model in order to illustrate a way of viewing a complete process in which the variable and their policy multipliers interrelate to influence a composite measure of well-being.

The ratio of the social index to the level of income is designated "social productivity," and it is with the determinants of social productivity that much of the following discussion will be concerned.

Some Questions of Efficiency

Inflation and Quality in Public Programs

A set of problems is the subject of widespread concern. Professional opinion begins to congeal around a particular solution and gains momentum. Pilot projects demonstrate the validity of the program concept. A large scale program is mounted. Costs soar, quality is poor, and underutilization appears where the unmet need was considered vast.

Inflation

A rapid rise in the costs of service as a consequence of the infusion of large amounts of public funds into a sector is a situation that is most likely to occur when a number of conditions are present:

1. *The expansion of funding is very large.* The greater the expansion, the greater is the difficulty of attracting, training, and organizing personnel and other resources, because it is necessary to draw on resources that are increasingly less suitable or less willing to shift to the sector being expanded.

2. *The expanding sector is comprehensive.* If a small sector is expanded it may be possible to attract resources from a number of other sectors using similar resources. When all such sectors are expanding it becomes more costly to draw resources from elsewhere.

3. *The sector uses highly specialized resources requiring a long period of training or construction.* If the resources are highly specialized it is less possible to attract them from other sectors. The increase in demand will result in a bidding up of wages and prices until new supplies are available. In some industries this period of adjustment of supply can be as long as ten years or more.

There are three ways of avoiding the inflationary impact of expansions of public funds, and perhaps all of them should be tried concurrently:

(1) Demand increases can be gradually phased in so as to allow time for the development of additional services. (2) Funding of increases in manpower training and facilities construction can begin years before the funding of services. The funding of services can be timed to the new resources coming into the market. (3) It may be possible to alter the conditions of production so as to permit a rapid expansion of output without extensive inflation. One approach is the method used by Operation Breakthrough, which seeks to transform housing production on a mass production basis. The essence of mass production is the breaking down of tasks into routine components that can be performed by less skilled persons. The principles of mass production seem applicable not only to physical commodities but also to services.

Another approach is to reduce the amount of bureaucratic restriction, including effects of unions and regulatory agencies. The essence of bureaucracy is the inability to respond to change. When demand increases occur, the bureaucratic supplier will respond less at a given cost increase in a given period of time. The implication is that it is necessary to restructure an industry *before* funds are infused.

These considerations suggest that we may have to give heavy weight to the responsiveness of supply in determining which programs to fund. Furthermore, the more downwardly rigid wages are, the more permanently we will have to live with the cost increases. We should also note that income maintenance, because it goes for similar services, is not exempt from the possibility of a sizable inflationary impact either.

Inefficiency also results from rapidly establishing new operations, because of the political incentives for the funding agency to show rapid progress and because of the desire of recipients to take advantage of the availability of funds. There is a tendency for municipalities to consider federal money as "free" to them, for example, and not to consider costs to taxpayers of other parts of the country. If the resources are sufficiently cheap, their use in highly inefficient operations is permitted, and too frequently, there is no competitive mechanism to weed out wasteful operations. Part of the effects of haste would be relieved if programs were implemented gradually. Also, the locality should be made to consider the true cost of the funds as the loss of alternative uses. This can be done by a block grant or revenue-sharing program in which the amount of funds available to the area is known and the alternatives remain within the area. The feasibility of this approach depends on the ability to develop alternative mechanisms to satisfy the desire for accountability of funding agencies and legislative bodies, which now rely on categorical grants as a control mechanism.

Any effort to define quality necessarily involves an effort to convert it into quantity terms. It is useful to develop a definition along the lines suggested by Lancaster. In his framework we can define "what is often meant by an overall improvement in quality" as what will "happen if the new goods, for the same outlay, give more of all characteristics in approximately the same proportion as the old. . . . In other cases, a quality improvement may correspond rather to an increase in some characteristics, with the others unchanged."[15]

To understand quality it is necessary to go one step further. We are usually concerned with comparisons among products that involve more of some characteristics but less of others. However, we should not become lost in the problem of arbitrating preferences when we are designing program choices and mixes, for that role will be performed in the political arena.[16] The following pages examine possible causes of low quality in publicly funded services, drawing heavily on a theoretical analysis of the problem.[17] Low quality may come about in a number of ways, and these tend to suggest that low quality might be a fundamental outcome of the way decisions are made.

Assuming that it costs less to produce a low-quality service than a high-quality service, society may intentionally choose low quality in order to be able to reach a larger number of people. It appears that the desire for equity is frequently pushed to the point where services produced are of such low quality that they lead to very little if any improvement in well-being. The improvement in quality using a given technology requires greater resources *per person served*. However, a budget increase need not by itself raise quality if the preferences are heavily skewed toward equity in the availability of services.

The problem of low quality due to emphasis on equity can come about as a consequence of a fragmented decision-making process. As an example, assume that there are ten programs and that each person in a population is served equally by each program. Suppose that if more resources were allocated to fewer persons it would be possible to produce a higher quality level for any one service. If the number served were limited to permit an increase in quality, there would still be a loss to those persons who did not continue to receive service. Instead, assume there were an authority responsible for allocating resources in ten different services. The authority could direct the same level of resources to each individual as before; however, it could provide each person with only some of the ten services, but at higher quality than before. Equity would be maintained, and if under the first scheme services were of such low quality as to have been highly ineffective, all might be better off under a consolidated plan. Such opportunities could be developed through decentralization of service decisions to the community level.

Another source of low quality in the process by which resources are

15. Lancaster, "Change and Innovation," p. 22.

16. See J. Coleman, "The Possibility of a Social Welfare Function," *American Economic Review* 56, no. 5 (December 1966): 1107–8.

17. See I. Leveson, "Quality Determination in Public Programs," unpublished manuscript, May 1968.

allocated among programs derives from the way the recipients of grant funds view their opportunities. A locality receiving a categorical grant treats the resources as free because the resources will go to other areas if they are not used locally. There is an incentive to go forward with projects of low quality even if the benefits are far less than the costs, because the recipient does not bear the costs. With a block grant to the locality, the value of the funds in a particular use is gauged against their value in an alternative project within the locality. The argument against revenue sharing has been that divorcing taxation from spending would reduce efficiency, but the effects of the use of categorical grants appears to have been far worse. A block-grant approach may be a very powerful means of increasing quality.

An increase in resources per person served with a fixed budget by a single program can come about only by instituting a selection process among potential consumers. It is where the scarcity of resources has not been recognized and universal eligibility has been permitted that quality has deteriorated. More efficient providers may produce higher quality services at lower costs. If casual observations of a tendency for more efficient providers to produce at both low costs and high quality are valid, it might follow that an increase in efficiency of existing providers is an important method of raising quality.

The involvement of community groups in planning creates an interesting challenge. Although they will often seek high quality, they may be more likely to choose equity when faced with broad community pressures. Whether community efforts will result in a sufficient increase in efficiency or in the availability of resources to make it possible to reach more residents without further lowering quality is not clear.

Utilization

Low utilization of services follows directly from low quality, particularly if we define quality to include amenities to the consumer. Even if services are provided free to the consumer, he bears costs in forms such as travel, waiting, and service time. Furthermore, the value of the services to him depends on their "quality," and the lower the quality the less he will use them.[18] The main method to try to improve utilization has been consumer education, and although this is often desirable, there is no reason to believe that increased knowledge of the availability of services will appreciably increase utilization unless the services are of an acceptable quality.

---

18. For a fuller discussion see I. Leveson, "The Demand for Neighborhood Medical Care," *Inquiry*, December 1970, and "Access to Medical Care: The Queensbridge Experiment," *Inquiry*, September 1971.

Income Transfers or Funding Individual Services?

The direct transfer of income to the poor has a number of possible advantages. It gives the consumer free choice among providers of service, which allows greater freedom for consumers to express their tastes or to respond to changing opportunities. Direct transfers are also expected to offer the advantage of much lower administrative costs. Because income transfers permit choice among providers of care, they allow competition as a mechanism to maintain cost efficiency. A particularly important aspect of this competition may be in freeing the consumer from reliance on government providers where they are inefficient and where private production is possible. Where public funding has created large increases in demand, however, there may be few such competitive opportunities in the face of great shortages.

The alternative to income maintenance is government funding of selected goods and services. The individuals will make consumption decisions in accordance with their private benefits. The provision of funds for particular purposes makes it possible to encourage instead the consumption of goods and services that yield a high social return.[19] A major direct benefit is through satisfaction derived by the nonpoor from improvements in the well-being of the poor. Other benefits to the nonpoor may include reduction in crime against the nonpoor and the savings of public assistance and other program costs through alleviation of poverty. There are benefits to poor persons who do not participate directly in programs, as well as to those who do. A particularly important route by which funding of services can have an impact may be by encouraging expenditures on development of skills or on investments that can have a high payoff in the future.

The notion of income maintenance is closely linked with issues of insurance. The insurance area has been cited as an outstanding case of market failure because of the "moral hazard" – the tendency of high-risk persons to enroll first. Moral hazard necessitates premiums that are too high to attract persons who are the best risks. This, together with the high cost of identifying differences among individuals in the size of risk, means that there are many types of risk against which it is not possible to insure. This line of reasoning supports government provision of many types of social insurance. In fact, it has been suggested that the welfare system ought

---

19. Theoretical analyses of this problem have compared a free-choice situation with public selection of all goods and services and have derived the proposition that greater well-being arises from choice. For example, see L. Foldes, "A Note on Redistribution," *Economica* 34 (May 1967): 203–5. However, when we consider public choice of individual commodities, the same result need not hold. For a recent effort to consider opportunities for individual commodities see M. C. McGuire and H. Garn, "Problems in the Cooperative Allocation of Public Expenditures," *Quarterly Journal of Economics* 83, no. 1 (February 1969): 44–59.

to be operated as an insurance system, with the possible benefit that people would be more likely to leave the welfare rolls voluntarily if they knew they could get back on when they needed to.[20]

The concept of income maintenance seeks to avoid singling out particular groups for assistance. When goods and services for the poor have been publicly funded there has been emphasis on programs providing investment in human beings – raising future well-being through improving skills and health. For those least able to benefit from such programs (such as the aged and severely disabled) a maintenance effort has been considered more appropriate. When insurance considerations are added, the appropriateness of selecting eligible individuals from the many persons who might be served becomes even greater. The rationale for providing public funding of medical services is that different individuals require different amounts of maintenance that depends on their health and incomes and that the amounts can be effectively differentiated through health insurance.[21]

An income-maintenance system providing only direct financial assistance and based on income and family size alone will not concern itself with developing abilities to earn future incomes or with the provision of insurance. It implicitly assumes that a socially desirable level of education and training and other human investments will be forthcoming without public aid. It depends on a simplistic conception of well-being that does not take into account differences in well-being which do not vary directly with income alone (such as health) or the extent to which poverty is caused by inequality of opportunity (rather than simply inadequate productivity).

Income maintenance can have a variety of adverse effects on incentives, particularly on work incentives.[22] It can adversely affect educational performance by reducing a child's expected time in the labor force. It may also influence family composition, criminal activity, and the geographic distribution of the poor.[23]

---

20. E. Durbin, *Welfare-Income and Employment* (New York: Frederick A. Prager, 1969).

21. In this vein arguments that medical care should be provided free as a matter of right have been criticized as conflicting with the scarcity of resources when applied to all commodities. Instead, one could make a case for use of *full* medical insurance to compensate for *part* of the losses of well-being sustained as a result of poor health.

22. See C. T. Brehn and T. R. Saving, "The Demand for General Assistance Payments," *American Economic Review* 54, no. 6 (December 1964): 1002–18; and D. H. Greenberg and M. Kosters, *Income Guarantees and the Working Poor: The Effect of Income Maintenance Programs on the Hours of Work of Male Family Heads* (Santa Monica, Calif.: The RAND Corporation, 1971).

23. The impact of payment methods on family structure has been noted by Moynihan and others. It is always possible to adjust the payment formulae to encourage families to stay together, but this becomes an additional cost that must be considered, and society has not yet shown a willingness to bear that cost.

It has also been contended that payment on the basis of the number of children will encourage childbearing. There is some controversy over the empirical evidence for this. International comparisons are of limited accuracy, and such payment systems may

A large number of forms of income maintenance have been proposed to deal with the problems of work incentives. There are two predominant effects: (1) the larger the income one receives without working, the less likely he will be to work (income effect); and (2) the larger the proportion of earnings he can keep, the more likely he will work (substitution effect). The Family Security Plan permits retention of half of earnings and thus creates greater work incentives than the present welfare system, but it has greater disincentive effects than some other alternatives. The demogrant or fixed payment per capita avoids the disincentives of substitution effects by making payments independent of employment. It also avoids high administration costs and stigmatizing the poor; however, it may have an appreciable income effect on incentives.

A wage-subsidy plan could let persons of low income keep, for example, 150 percent of what they earn by a government contribution of fifty cents for each dollar earned. This plan makes it possible to skew incentives in favor of work through the substitution effect, offsetting any disincentives of income effects from concurrent lump-sum payments. A wage-supplement plan would have to include a basic allowance for those who do not work.

The acceptability of any of these plans hinges on ability to restructure the existing pattern of free and subsidized services to overcome inequities

---

be more frequently instituted where birth rates are low. Furthermore, the welfare system may simply slow down the rate of decline of birth rates of persons moving from rural to urban areas. What is relevant but not always realized is that any payment on a per-child basis works in the direction of encouraging childbearing relative to a labor market in which nothing extra is paid to a worker as a result of his having an additional child. Yet family size is an important source of differences in well-being between the poor and nonpoor, for those with more children with a given income will of necessity spend less per member of the family. Half of the poor are often children, and society tends to take some responsibility for their welfare. It may be that the efforts of income maintenance on family size have not been great because of the limited extent to which the poor now exercise free choice, and therefore as family size becomes determined on an increasingly voluntary basis, the impact of basing a payment on the number of children (and the evidence of an impact) will increase.

It has also been maintained that the provision of income maintenance standards in accordance with the income of the state or city would encourage migration to high-benefit areas. (For some evidence see R. Reischauer, "The Impact of Redistributional Programs on Geographic Mobility" [Columbia University Labor Workshop Paper, 1970].) Migration could result in an uneven distribution of the fiscal burden of poverty and could also aggravate the problems of poverty by concentrating the poor in a few locations. Some areas may desire to have benefits above a national minimum well beyond those necessitated by the cost of living. The question of geographic differences in benefits has been raised primarily in connection with incentives to interregional migration. In the future equalization may be of increasing concern when it acts as a deterrent to suburbanization of the poor.

Discussions of incentives have centered on nonparticipation in the labor force. The evidence of the effects of unemployment from crime studies suggests that we will have to broaden the analysis to include other adverse effects of nonworking populations on society. In addition to effects on criminal activity, poor employment opportunities for persons of dependency status may result in greater sanitation problems, false alarms, fires, vandalism, and housing deterioration. The costs from these sources have yet to be carefully assessed.

and particularly to avoid situations in which persons fare less well by working than by not working.

Income maintenance provides freedom of choice, allowing the consumer to avoid ineffectively provided services and creating the possibility of competition among providers. However, for the most part it does nothing to change the inadequate service delivery patterns that are already too often rigidly structured as a result of past approaches. Under these circumstances, expansion of income maintenance could easily lead to expansion of inadequate systems to a size that makes them more difficult to change, a result that could be accompanied by extensive inflation as well. Funding of services does not provide the same degree of choices of commodity or ease of administration as income maintenance does, but it does permit encouragement of consumption of goods and services with high social benefits, and it could be set up to permit competition and freedom of choice of provider.

The Government as Provider

The decision to employ public funds to accomplish social objectives involves separate considerations from the question of whether or not the funding body should itself carry out the effort. The most important issue is whether the provider should be any government unit rather than a nonprofit or private firm or set of firms. Even when the decision has been made to go outside government, too often there has been reliance on a single provider or a limited group without recognition of the opportunities in an entire market. The usual practice is to fund the producing unit rather than to give the consumer a credit to use at the acceptable provider of his choice. The decision to let the government provide precludes opportunities for competition as a mechanism to promote efficiency. Selection of nongovernment providers does not guarantee the operation of competitive forces, but it offers the possibility of doing so.

It is possible to make only indirect inferences about the possible advantages of government production of publicly funded services. The advantages that are sometimes assumed would seem to stem from the greater possibility of control over the content and costs of production. The government unit presumably has direct control over the details of its own operations. Control is much more difficult to effect over the operations of a contractor because of the difficulties of foreseeing all possible circumstances and because of the costs and uncertainties of enforcement. We would expect direct production to occur most often when uncertainty is important and enforcement difficult.

In service operations with great flexibility in choice of output mix, the funding unit might be particularly prone to determine the specific services to be provided and their quantities and quality levels. It might want to direct the process of client selection and to see that there is appropriate matching between clients and services. There is also a possible cost rationale for government production, which usually contains some implicit form of wage and price controls through its direct decisions about prices and through a personnel system designed to prevent abuses.

The same arguments that apply to government production apply to the choice of a small number of providers. Few providers are easier to control, and the issue of choice of provider boils down to the issue of the effectiveness of market forces, direct controls, and various combinations. Unfortunately there seems to be a large gap between the possible advantages of government production and the situation in practice. In a government-run process, the system of checks and balances designed to prevent misuse of funds frequently results in substantial reduction in efficiency.[24] One example is that more money is spent to validate public assistance claims than is likely to be misspent if an honor system were used. The rigidities of processes in municipal watchdog agencies result in both immediate inefficiency and a cumulative long-run impact on the growth of productivity by discouraging innovation. Bureaucratic procedures raise the cost of government action, delay the response of government, and seriously block new activities, which require the greatest number of approvals to get into operation.

Furthermore, state and local governments have recently been arenas for the rapid growth of union power. Studies have suggested that the union impact on wages has been substantially higher than previously believed. In the public sector the possibilities for raising costs are probably even greater because of the dependence of political organizations on union support and the fact that wage gains have a smaller percentage effect on costs than on profits. Unions tend to preserve and enhance their relative wage position, job security, and work environment by work rules and entry restrictions that, on the whole, reduce the rate at which productivity can advance. Experiences in the transportation, construction, and other fields suggest that attempts to maintain a relative wage advantage produces a loss in the *rate* of productivity growths resulting in an *increasing gap in efficiency* relative to other industries.[25]

Rigidities in both the operations of government and the rules enforced by unions and licensing agencies have generally produced an extensive underinvestment in innovation. The tendency for private firms to underinvest in research and development because of their inability to capture all the benefits of that research is well known. The difficulties of either producing or adequately supervising such activities in a government setting has been in part responsible for the rapid growth of the nonprofit sector.

---

24. See New York City Planning Commission, *Plan for New York City, Vol. I: Critical Issues* (New York, November 1969), chap. 4.

25. Economists have not been willing to discuss interindustry differences in the level of productivity because of the noncomparability of different outputs. However, we can view final products as being produced in intermediate steps, many of which are common to different industries. When we compare the efficiency with which individual steps are performed, it is apparent that productivity differences among industries are great.

Forces that tend to make governments inefficient as a provider of service can also limit their efficiency as purchasers with responsibilities for overseeing contractors. Inefficiencies in government have led not only to a thrust toward income maintenance but to efforts to limit the role of government, even if problems remain unsolved. A more moderate approach is to permit government funding of private providers under mechanisms that tend to automatically encourage efficiency and innovation.

Components of Income Generation

Human Resource Programs

Manpower training, and education programs have been areas of large government financing and production of services because of the particularly large external benefits and because of the imperfect availability of credit for education. Programs dealing with manpower and education have the problems of quality encountered by other service programs, and they also have additional problems that merit explicit attention. Although rates of return to investments in education are moderately high and do not decrease over time, studies of special programs aimed at the urban poor provide far less encouraging results.[26] The payoff to manpower training programs may be limited because employment experience over the long term will likely be far less satisfactory than in the immediate follow-up period. For example, measures of benefiting a cyclical upswing will not reveal that a subsequent recession results in loss of work habits or show the effect of future increases in income maintenance that reduce participation in the labor force. The special education programs, notably the Head Start program and the Neighborhood Youth Core, lack effectiveness, based on the limited evidence available. One could question the possibility of success of dropout-prevention programs for a group whose family structure does not demonstrate the link between education and employment and whose public assistance alternatives significantly lower the private rate of return to education,[27]

---

26. For example, see R. A. Levine, "Evaluating the War on Poverty," in *Perspectives on Poverty, II: On Fighting Poverty*, ed. by J. L. Sundquist (New York: Basic Books, 1969), pp. 188–216; and G. G. Cain and R. G. Hollister, "Evaluating Manpower Programs for the Disadvantaged," in *Cost-Benefit Analysis of Manpower Programs*, ed. by G. G. Sommers and W. D. Wood, Reprint No. 47 (Madison, Wis.: University of Wisconsin, Institute for Research on Poverty).

27. This point deserves more than passing attention. The effect of compulsory education with limited returns stemming from irregular labor force attachment is to reduce those aspects of quantity that are less tightly controlled (homework, attendance) and to reduce quality (that is, less effort through less attention). If we require education in terms of accomplishments rather than longevity, a variable attendance period may be more effective, but it would then lose its impact without appropriate teenage employment opportunities.

especially in an educational system in which dropping out might be a rational response to training considered irrelevant.

In spite of these considerations there appears to be widespread belief that education and training programs have potential effectiveness. The consequence of the evidence that Head Start had little effect was not reconsideration of the theories that led to its existence but rather concentration on even younger children. The concept of "potential effectiveness" has not been defined. Surely there are many other programs that would also pay off if they were able to accomplish what they had set out to do. It would nevertheless appear that decisions based on potential effectiveness are reasonable when the goals and relevance of the entire educational system are being questioned.

We have to start by questioning the meaning of skill and the value of skill components. When dealing with the poor it becomes clear that basic work habits, including showing up regularly and on time, staying sober, not fighting with other workers, plus basic literacy and other ingredients often taken for granted, must be established before training begins. For many it is not a retraining process but a first attempt. The absence of appropriate habits can also greatly impede the elementary education process.

The success of the educational system has depended on its ability to meet the needs of the bulk of society. Arthur Jensen reminds us that modern intelligence tests are rooted in efforts to predict success in staying in school for the European system at the turn of the century.[28] It would seem that one useful interpretation of the "potential effectiveness" concept is that if the educational system devoted its energies to the production of skills that are appropriate for the poor in a modern American urban society, it could have the payoff that traditionally existed for much of society. Formally, variables describing the consumer are efficiency parameters in production functions for educational performance in such a way that the greater the adaptation between the kind of student and the kind of technology used, the more efficient that process. The potential is the increase in efficiency possible through change in the distribution of technologies among students.

Physical Resource Programs

The acceleration effect of population growth during the periods of heavy immigration before 1925 produced an enormous expansion of physical facilities in many large cities. We are now becoming aware of the need for large-scale replacement and modernization of these facilities. And although incomes are now higher, construction costs have also risen sharply relative to other prices, and we no longer have the luxury of building on

28. A. Jensen, "How Much Can We Boost IQ and Scholastic Achievement?" *Harvard Educational Review* 39, no. 1 (Winter 1969): 1–123.

vacant land when replacement is necessary. The replacement demand is superimposed on the demand arising from the economic expansion of the 1960s and the demands from new technologies. Consequently the fiscal and social effort required to deal with the problem is as great as when the facilities were first built.

Massive construction of physical resources has begun in transportation, education, and health, but even in these areas many physical plants are still in poor condition. In addition, substantial efforts will be necessary for many other types of structures – firehouses, police stations, libraries – and huge expenditures will be required for sewage and other projects and for telephone and electric power. But the greatest deficiency in the level of resources needed to make significant improvement in conditions is in housing. The impermanence of the rapid construction undertaken to meet the expansion needs of the past, tendency for low levels of maintenance in geographically high mobile populations, rising construction costs, and tight credit conditions have combined to produce a crisis of major proportions.

Equality of Opportunity

The concept of equality of opportunity includes the development of skills, the earning of income, and the use of income and skills to improve well-being. Basic to the concept is the notion of exclusion of alternatives that would not have been excluded for someone of the same race, for example. When we look at the effects of exclusion in terms of the consumer production model we find an interesting paradox. Because the consumer seeks combinations of characteristics (outcomes), when one activity is precluded we might expect the effect to be minimized by the possibility of engaging in other combinations of activities that lead to a similar mix of characteristics. Why then is discrimination viewed as such a problem? One possibility is that an entire class of goods – goods that are the only good source of certain characteristics – is excluded.[29] Such a class may be all "quality" housing or "quality" education. Implicit in this notion is that the budget constraint does not frequently permit going to unusual sources for these goods. Segregated schools and job discrimination would seem to be as serious as they are because they exclude the best means of producing income, upon which many satisfactions depend.

---

29. Lancaster distinguished two types of substitution effects. Changes in relative prices can influence the relative importance of activities; but there can also be an efficiency switching effect in which some activities become ruled out by changes in relative prices regardless of tastes. The fewer the number of activities, the less often this switching occurs. As a result, lower price elasticities of demand characterize simple economies. In the same way exclusion reduces the number of activities possible and can lead to low price elasticities, which can reduce the effects of public policies. See K. Lancaster, "A New Approach to Consumer Theory" and "Change and Innovation."

Equality of opportunity cannot be defined without a simultaneous specification of the goals of society. One useful definition is no differences in the production functions for social indicators associated with race, religion, and so on. Such differences may arise because of a lack of equality of access – that is, a difference in the probability of receiving service conditional on an event such as illness or robbery. Some would go further and compensate for past neglect, so that equal health would be necessary for equal opportunity to earn income.

Gary Becker has argued that there is no inherent difference between discrimination against one group and preference for another.[30] Observed differences between groups in part reflect the fact that persons do tend to discriminate in favor of their own. Exclusion can occur because of effects of past discrimination against one group, which does not give them an equal opportunity to be discriminated *in favor of* now.

Although exclusion based on race is not a perfect concept, it seems useful for analyzing such problems as housing segregation and treatment of all Negroes in the same risk class for credit and insurance. Restrictions such as union entry rules may have the same effect, and can be analyzed the same way.

There is little information about the effectiveness of alternative policies to improve equality of opportunity. Open housing legislation appears to have accomplished little or nothing. William Landes' work on fair employment practice laws does not give much cause for optimism about this route.[31] The impact of federal funding on urban school systems may offer some opportunities, but there are limits to possibilities for improving educational opportunities without major reductions in housing segregation. Other attempts to equalize opportunity have either been associated with compensation for past disadvantages or combined with other efforts, such as attempts to improve manpower training, placement, and advancement.

Mixed Strategies: Neighborhood Service Innovation

There are two closely related ingredients in the development of a comprehensive strategy – concentration of resources among geographic areas or programs, and coordination and integration of production processes. It would seem that a great deal more could be done to combine program types. If increased income-maintenance benefits are associated with additional leisure, they could be coupled with increased recreation. If they raise

---

30. G. S. Becker, *The Economics of Discrimination* (Chicago: University of Chicago Press, 1967).

31. W. Landes, "The Economics of Fair Employment Laws," *Journal of Political Economy* 76, no. 4 (July/August, 1968): 507–52.

the demand for housing, additional construction could be coordinated with demand. There are many possibilities.

The merits of combining programs into overall strategies depend on the way in which the cost-effectiveness of programs varies with their scale of effort and on the interdependencies in production and outcomes among programs.[32] In addition, it is necessary to weigh the trade-offs between the equity of a more equal distribution of resources and any efficiencies associated with the concentration of resources among particular clients or neighborhoods against society's preferences for equity relative to efficiency.

Concentration of Resources

For a single program, the question of whether resources should be concentrated among selected target groups and geographic areas depends on the importance of neighborhood effects. A classic example is the nonlinear relationship between the probability of contracting a contagious disease and the proportion of persons in the community who are immunized. After a certain proportion is immunized the payoff to additional resources becomes low. This sort of epidemiological property may be fairly widespread in social phenomena. Concentration may be particularly worthwhile when we consider not a single program but a set of closely related programs such as narcotics prevention, rehabilitation, and enforcement. For program combinations that do not bear so directly on the same problem area, the existence of forces that makes the geographic concentration of resources desirable is more conjectural.

Let us consider the question of whether resources should be concentrated among a few programs or spread among many. First we must examine the way in which the marginal cost-effectiveness, measured by the change in a social index per additional dollar spent, varies with the level of expenditures for various programs. An important case occurs when the marginal cost-effectiveness curve for one program is a function of the amount of resources devoted to another program. The overall level of the aggregate curve then depends on its composition, and more than one combination of programs might produce the same payoff. At each level of spending there will be a different aggregate marginal cost-effectiveness depending on which program is increased. If some programs are positively related to each other, the payoff will be higher if these are chosen as a set. The efficacy of concentrating resources among a few programs will depend on the strength of these relationships. The efficacy of concentrating resources, either because of neighborhood effects or program interactions, is an empirical question whose answer is crucial to the design of large-scale efforts.

---

32. Some theoretical considerations are developed by P. E. Vincente, "Reciprocal Externalities and Optimal Input and Output Levels," *American Economic Review* 59, no. 5 (December 1969): 976–84.

The Economics of Coordination

A recent approach is embodied in such programs as the War on Poverty and the Model Cities program. The Model Cities program attempts to deal with problems of fragmented financing, inappropriate client-selection processes, and lack of coordination among producing units whose outputs are components of a more complex set of services. We will designate this an *urban innovation strategy.*

Economists studying the service industries have often noted that outputs that are locally produced and cannot easily be transported to another location or stored for future consumption and outputs for which there is great uncertainty about the quantity and qualities that will be demanded at any given time or place tend to be produced by small producing units. The outstanding example of these is personal services, for which the consumer must be present and is an integral part of the production process.[33]

Services provided for the poor are particularly susceptible to fragmentation among producing units because of the number and variety of problems at which they are directed. Even when these are produced by nonprofit organizations, the attempt to adhere to some sort of efficiency criteria seems to lead to this tendency. However, the production of services is only part of a more general system of nested production functions in which, at each stage, services are highly interrelated. The extent of improvement in health, for example, depends not only on the gross quantities of health services but also on the combinations of types and qualities used and their time sequence. Although efficient production of service output requires small producing units that are often isolated from other services, the achievement of more ultimate objectives requires extensive coordination and often consolidation.

Coordination and consolidation of services is not readily fostered by market processes. Personal services are often subject to consumer and producer ignorance about their effectiveness in accomplishing more ultimate goals and by a divergency between private and social benefits, so that even if one set of producers is more effective, there is no automatic tendency for them to thrive more readily than others. For services to the poor, as a consequence of shortages induced by subsidies, there is often pressure on every producer to expand services – and the pressure is not necessarily greater only on producers who are more effective in attaining end results.

We have then a conflict between the requirements for efficient production of goods and services and those for efficient production of improvements in

33. See M. Friedman and S. Kuznets, *Income from Independent Professional Practice* (New York: National Bureau of Economic Research, 1954); and George Stigler, *Trends in Employment in the Service Industries* (Princeton, N.J.: Princeton University Press, 1965).

end results.[34] There are a number of alternatives for improving the coordination of services.[35] One is to provide additional information about the effectiveness of services to the consumer and to the producer; direct planning efforts can improve the match between services and consumers. Another possibility is to change the locus of decision making to a group that is not subject to the pressures for service efficiency that produce fragmentation. Hopefully one could also change the incentives of the decision maker to make rewards more a function of ultimate outputs. These approaches have been implicit in the growth of consumer organizations.

Consumption of services in the past, through its impact on outcomes, is for example, a determinant of the demand for services in the future.[36] A promising possibility is therefore to make the financial rewards of the producer greatest when he can avoid the need for future services, which he may do by emphasizing prevention, more appropriate services and qualities, or outreach. This notion is the basis for efforts to provide comprehensive medical care by payment of a capitation rate (or single annual sum per capita) to the producer regardless of the amount of services used.

We can make some limited observations about the effectiveness of an urban innovation strategy based on experience with the Model Cities program in New York City, which is still in its relative infancy. First, the costs of coordination of separate programs are exceedingly high. Second, the prospects for achieving integrated production processes appear to be limited in the near future, and any extensive changes will come slowly. However, the program is essentially a demonstration project, requiring current resources to build up experience that can facilitate large-scale action in the future. We do not yet know which activities can be usefully integrated into multiservice centers, neighborhood health centers, educational parks, or other combined forms. The process is one of development of new technology, which will undoubtedly yield a sizable share of both false starts and unexpected benefits if it is given enough time and money to mature. Perhaps the most important impact to date is the development of groups of professional project implementors and program coordinators.

---

34. Many researchers have been concerned with the simulation of market mechanisms to achieve more efficient production of services in nonprofit organizations. Although such efforts are desirable on the grounds that they free resources for other uses, greater efficiency in the production of services may mean additional fragmentation leading to less efficient production of ultimate outputs if it is not accompanied by increased coordination. The net effect of simulating market mechanisms in the production of goods and services on the efficiency of providing ultimate outcomes is open to question. The very existence of the nonprofit sector is based on the inadequacies of market mechanisms in some circumstances. The critical problems is to create incentives for systems efficiency in the production of end results.

35. See H. Leibenstein, "Organizational or Functional Equilibria, X-Efficiency, and the Rate of Innovation," *Quarterly Journal of Economics* 83, no. 4 (November 1969): 500–623, and "Allocative Efficiency vs. X-Efficiency."

36. See I. Leveson, "The Econometrics of Reduced Hospitalization," unpublished manuscript, December 1970.

Mixed Strategies: Population Distribution

The scale of the problem leads naturally to the consideration of alternatives outside the central city.[37] Lower population densities, less unionization, and less established bureaucracy tend to produce lower costs in the fringes of suburban areas, especially for housing, a resource in which the central city is becoming increasingly deficient. The prospect of increased suburban opportunities for the poor makes further sense when we consider the advantage of low costs of space for a group with above-average family size. The middle-class suburbanite often pays a high premium for his location in terms of high costs and time devoted to commuting; the poor could share the benefits without this major cost.

Manufacturing firms have been leaving the central cities, often for suburban locations. Although their number has not been large, these are often firms that are about to undergo rapid expansion of employment. The blue-collar growth has taken place in the suburbs, and the white-collar growth has tended to occur in the central city. The urban poor are frequently already trained for or oriented to the disappearing blue-collar jobs. Four alternatives present themselves. We can subsidize the manufacturing firms to remain, but this is likely to be expensive in view of the high costs of land assembly and rental of urban land.[38] We can build expensive transportation networks to connect the ghetto with the suburb. We can prepare the disadvantaged for employment in the office sector, which is growing where they are. This alternative requires a reorientation in training, a change in attitudes about the masculinity of white-collar work, and the development of social skills, which may take a long time. This avenue needs to be thoroughly explored, but the behavior of the free market to date is not encouraging. Finally, we can relocate the poor to suburban areas where the jobs they would take are more plentiful.

Subsidies to homeowners have been a traditional means of aiding the poor, who typically spend an above-average share of their incomes on housing. However, through the mechanism of the progressive income tax, subsidies to homeowners operate to the advantage of those with the highest incomes. As private homes have become more and more expensive relative to other goods, subsidies to homeowners have become more often subsidies to the middle class rather than to the poor. At the same time, as the central cities have become crowded and housing has become expensive, subsidies for homeownership have become subsidies for the middle class to leave the

---

37. See J. E. Kain and J. J. Persky, "Alternatives to the Gilded Ghetto," *The Public Interest* 14 (Winter 1969): 74–87.

38. Closely related to this is the policy of subsidizing firms to enter the ghetto, which in addition to presenting even greater land assembly problems, does not appear likely to have a large impact on ghetto resident employment based on the few preliminary studies now available.

central cities for the suburbs. The result has been an erosion of the tax base of the central cities and an increasing racial division between city and suburb.

After the massive migration from farm to city has nearly ended we are just beginning to consider seriously the legislation of an income-maintenance program intended to reduce the flow.[39] Yet rather than extend the application of this understanding that the concentration of poor in large cities is costly both in economic and social terms, we concern ourselves almost exclusively with efforts to maintain and service the poor in an urban environment. We cannot wait until the central cities are all black and the problems of concentration of poverty and race multiply before we begin to extensively redistribute the population. Delay will allow changes in land use to raise costs of relocation to the point where they prohibit meaningful action. If we must decide on the basis of what we know now, it would appear that the amelioration of urban poverty requires a massive-scale effort.

Ideas for population redistribution have been around for a long time, but the need for them has never been so urgent. A national population policy should combine housing output and locational plans into a comprehensive strategy. The trend is now toward shifting power from the federal government to the cities and states so that local approaches will be developed. However, a national population policy would require federal and other interstate authority, which would make it possible to override local zoning ordinances and other restrictions. Such action would be necessary on a large scale so that a few localities would not bear an unequal tax burden for supporting services.

Zoning changes alone would not be enough. These would have to be coordinated with mortgage guarantees, subsidization of down payments and moving costs, and changes in the tax advantages of homeownership so as not to disproportionately favor those with higher incomes. The feasibility of such efforts depends also on reducing the dependence of local school financing on the property tax. Without these provisions the cities would be emptied of the more able blacks, leaving only those black workers least able to help themselves. Furthermore, redistribution need not be encouraged through single-family homeownership alone. Forms such as cooperative and condominium apartments should be considered. Supportive services will have to be simultaneously developed.

There will undoubtedly be opposition to such changes; however, it must be recognized that the residents of the communities that exclude housing the poor can afford are now paying heavily for public assistance, Social Security, Medicare, Medicaid, housing subsidies, and other programs. A population-redistribution program might greatly reduce such costs at the same time as the poor are aided.

---

39. See especially J. Tobin's article in *Agenda for the Nation*, ed. by K. Gordon (Washington, D.C.: The Brookings Institution, 1968).

Conclusions

The major theme of this paper has been that if we wish to improve the well-being of the urban poor, income is not enough. It is also necessary to shift families into more productive life styles, and welfare reform and population redistribution can contribute substantially to the purpose. It is further necessary to improve the efficiency of resource use. This can be advanced by a number of changes in the financing and production of service components and by the integration of services at the neighborhood level. Restructuring of revenue sharing, income maintenance, and health insurance can assist in these directions.

3

Transfers and Participation in the Labor Force

A major means of reducing the number of the poor over the last several decades has been the exchange economy; the average level of income in the economy has gone up, largely due to the general rise in wage rates. Income redistribution effects have thus occurred through the market system even though the markets must be recognized as vehicles which generate wide disparities in incomes. On the other hand, if we consider the effect public welfare payments have on the ghetto economy, we may ask how far they tend to discourage the use of this avenue of advancement by the residents of urban poverty areas. More specifically, how far do public transfers act as a disincentive to participation in the labor force of able-bodied males and females? If this disincentive effect is very large, a very strong case can and must be made against the use of public transfers to improve the position of the urban poor. If public transfers have an incentive effect, however, one traditional argument against the expansion of the public grants economy falls by the wayside.

In the first paper of this part Christopher Green and Alfred Tella estimate the effect of nonemployment income and of market-determined wage rates on the work incentives of the poor. They thus look at a general category of nonexchange income and a specific category of exchange income from labor. The specific focal point is an investigation of "nonemployment income on the hours worked per week, weeks worked per year, and the labor force participation rates of families with a nonaged male head." They test the hypothesis that under a negative income tax plan that provides for positive transfers, "workers in families covered by the negative tax would be expected to reduce their hours worked in response both to the supplementation of income ('supplementary' income effect) and to the reduction in the marginal wage (substitution effect)." On the basis of their analysis the authors conclude: "We can interpret our data in terms of income-transfer plans that simultaneously raise family income in amounts ranging from about $600 to $1,000 while reducing the marginal wage rate by anywhere from 25 to 50 percent. We found that the resultant income and substitution effects would produce a reduction in average annual hours of work . . . in response to the combination of a lower marginal wage rate and the addition to income (a result of the receipt of nonemployment income). . . . Approximately a $1.2 billion initial reduction in GNP would result from the induced reduction in hours of work produced by adopting a modest-sized negative income tax."

David Elesh, Jack Ladinsky, Myron Lefcowitz, and Seymour Spilerman examine the same problem and others by means of some preliminary findings from the first field experiment with an income-maintenance program, the New Jersey and Pennsylvania negative income tax experiment. They start by noting that structural approaches to poverty problems – involving alterations in monetary and fiscal policies, education, and training – may not be effective "at least for the current generation in poverty. The poor have large families, broken homes, physical and mental handicaps, and other problems which are generally untouched by higher minimum wages, better employment services, antidiscriminatory legislation, economic progress, or a larger gross national product. . . . Second, . . . structural solutions are long term and not always successful. They involve restructuring labor markets and creating new training systems. Meanwhile the poor must survive. Only distributive programs can guarantee decent standards of survival in the short run."

All three types of distributive programs – social insurance, income subsidy programs (for example, public assistance and veterans' pensions), and income-in-kind programs (such as food stamps, medicaid, and public housing) – "are either irrelevant, grossly inadequate, or detrimental to the present status of the poor," the authors conclude. They then proceed to a discussion of alternative income-supplement strategies – guaranteed employment, children's allowances, and the negative income tax – in terms of a set of evaluation criteria.

The authors discuss the objectives and initial results of the New Jersey-Pennsylvania study, emphasizing that their findings are preliminary and that "it would be inappropriate to draw strong inferences from them." Nonetheless, they contradict the views stated by Green and Tella. Five measures are taken of the work effort response to the negative tax payments: (1) changes in the size of the average payment, (2) relative change in [family] head's earnings for the experimental and control groups, (3) relative change in family earnings (husband's plus wife's earnings) for the experimental and control groups, (4) relative change in head's hours worked for the experimental and control groups, and (5) relative change in wife's participation in the labor force for the experimental and control groups. The authors conclude: "Based on fifteen months' experience in Trenton, Paterson, and Passaic (these cities contain about 37 percent of the sample), we can say that there is little indication that wage earners are leaving the labor force. . . . About 9 percent more of the experimental group than of the control group family heads increased their earnings over the fifteen-month period. However, . . . there is no difference between groups in terms of family earnings. . . . Heads in the experimental group increased their hours worked about 5 percent more than heads in the control group. Finally, . . . experimental group wives, although they were no more likely to leave the labor force than control group wives, were about 9 percent more likely to be housewives at both points in time, and 8 of the 9 percent difference is accounted for by control group wives who entered the labor force during the fifteen-month period. Possibly their entry was due to the deepening of the recession during this period. . . . Thus the most appropriate conclusion to draw . . . is that as yet *there is little evidence of either disincentive or incentive effects.* Given the widespread expectation of disincentive effects, this conclusion is surprising and comforting to the supporters of a negative tax. . . . In addition, there is no evidence that families have treated the payments as a windfall. . . . Fears of spending sprees or unusual expenditures have not been justified. It appears that families budget the payments as they do any other item of income."

The Green and Tella findings are based on property income, which strictly speaking represents a deferred exchange and not a true transfer because individuals may work to acquire income for investment in property, with the expectation of working less thereafter. One may therefore conclude with Elesh, Ladinsky, Lefcowitz, and Spilerman that if the results of the New Jersey-Pennsylvania experiment "prove useful, the nature of social policy making in this country may undergo a radical change." Such a change will have profound effects on poverty and other problems of the urbanized economy.

7

Christopher Green and Alfred Tella:
Effect of Nonemployment Income
and Wage Rates on Work
Incentives of the Poor

Proposals that the United States adopt a negative income tax have aroused concern about work (dis)incentive effects. There is theoretical justification for concern because a negative income tax device assures a minimum income, adds to the eligible unit's disposable income, and reduces its net wage. Economic theory suggests that the resultant income and substitution effects will be adverse to work effort. But *how* adverse is the important question, the answer to which has eluded economists and policy makers. The New Jersey Negative Income Tax project is attempting to measure the incentive effects of alternative levels of income transfer and negative tax rates by direct experimentation with a sample of low-income families. However, the experiment is in its early stages and conclusive results are not yet available.

Purposes and Theory

Our study attempts to provide new insight into the incentives issue. Drawing on existing Census Household Survey data, we investigate the effect of nonemployment income on the hours worked per week, weeks worked per year, and the labor force participation rates of families with a nonaged male head.[1] Because a negative income tax would add a substantial

From *Review of Economics and Statistics*, Vol. LI, No. 4, 1969, pp. 399–408. Reprinted by permission of the publisher and authors. Mr. Green is assistant professor of economics at McGill University, and Mr. Tella is director of the Office of Labor Force Studies, The President's Commission on Income Maintenance Programs. The authors wish to thank Otto Eckstein, Margaret S. Gordon, and Robert M. Solow for their helpful suggestions. The authors also benefited from numerous conversations with Michael Barth, Bruce Gardner, David Greenberg, Terence Kelly, and Dorothy Tella. The views expressed in this paper are the authors' own.

1. In our study nonemployment income primarily consists of non-work-related income, largely property income. It is desirable that work-conditioned or welfare-related nonwage income be excluded in order to better capture the voluntary labor supply effects of having a type of income that can be taken as a proxy for a guaranteed income transfer. Although there may be some unemployment compensation in our nonemployment income data, the amount is probably small because the level of nonemployment income was not very different in families where the head worked part year or in families where the head did not work as compared to families where the head worked the full year. The amount of welfare income received by families with a nonaged male head in the period under analysis was negligible. The adverse influence of inadequate demand on labor supply is minimized by restricting the analysis to a high-employment period.

amount of nonemployment income to the disposable income of families eligible to receive negative taxes, it is relevant to compare the labor supplied by low-income families for whom nonemployment income is a substantial portion of total income, with the labor supplied by families that have little or no nonemployment income.

A negative income tax plan (as designed along the lines of the New Jersey experiment, for example) would pay out a supplement equal to a specified percentage of the difference between a family's pretax income, including earnings, and a given break-even income level. Such a plan has a twofold impact on eligible families: It increases the total disposable income that a family can attain with any given level of work effort, and at the same time it reduces both the potential gain in disposable income from increased work effort and the potential loss from decreased work effort. A negative tax plan that pays a supplement equal, for example, to 50 percent of the difference between pretax family income, including earnings, and a given cutoff level in effect places a 50 percent tax on marginal earnings, or reduces the net marginal wage rate of working members of the family by 50 percent.

Clearly the supplement paid out under a negative tax plan carries by itself a leisure-inducing effect. Total income increases for the same amount of work effort, and workers do not directly experience any withholding of wages. The tax rate on marginal earnings carries further leisure inducement. Because the gain from increased work is reduced, a worker is less likely to increase his hours than in the absence of the tax, and because the loss from decreased labor force activity is reduced, he has more incentive than in the absence of the tax to reduce his hours. In sum, under a negative tax plan workers in families covered by the negative tax would be expected to reduce their hours worked in response both to the supplementation of income ("supplementary" income effect) and to the reduction in the marginal wage (substitution effect).

By this interpretation the negative tax rate produces only a substitution effect. Where there is a positive tax rate both the marginal and average rates are positive. Negative tax rates – as proponents of negative income taxes use the term – imply a positive marginal and a negative average rate. That is, under a negative tax plan incomes rise, thus suggesting a negative average rate. However, because even under a negative tax plan the net marginal wage is less than the gross marginal wage, the marginal tax rate is positive. In economic analysis the average tax rate is associated with an income effect, whereas the marginal tax rate is associated with a substitution effect. In a negative income tax system the income effect associated with the average tax rate is produced by the income supplement or transfer (which we call the "supplementary" income effect). For any initially given level of work effort and pretransfer income there is an associated income supplement, or transfer, the size of which can be made independent of the marginal tax rate. What the negative tax rate does is change the conditions of work – that is, it alters the wage gains and losses associated with an incremental change in hours of work. Thus, once the income effect has been produced by the income supplement, the negative tax rate carries only a substitution effect.

Let us be more explicit about what kinds of labor supply response we expect to find. At a first approximation we draw on standard (comparative static) economic theory. Figure 1 reproduces the traditional income-leisure diagram, which presents in graphic form the substitution and income effects produced by a negative income tax plan. YL is the budget constraint before negative taxes, and $YDBL$ is the budget constraint after the adoption of a negative income tax plan. A family with a single earner who works L_oL hours and consumes OL_o hours of leisure will receive OY_o wage income. Assuming that the family has no other income, it will be eligible for AE in negative income tax payments. By increasing the family's disposable income, the negative income tax payments produce an income effect represented by a downward movement along line PR to a point such as Ey, if leisure is a normal good. The negative tax rate, however, reduces the slope of the budget constraint (by 50 percent in the case shown) in the relevant range. The substitution effect produced by the reduction in the net marginal wage is a rightward movement along DB, which is similar to the pure substitution effect illustrated in figure 1 as a movement along ST to a point such as E_s. The two responses combine to produce the labor supply change induced

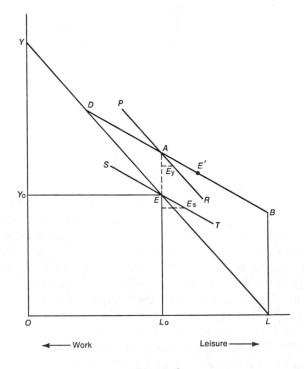

Figure 1.

by negative taxes. The new equilibrium levels of work, leisure, and income are given at a point such as E'.

Our study attempts to directly estimate substitution and "supplementary" income effects, which can be shown to be analogous to those effects produced by a hypothetical negative income tax plan. By combining the estimate for the substitution effect with the estimate for the income effect, we will arrive at a total estimate of the average change in hours of work of male family heads that would be produced by a modest-sized negative income tax plan. We are then able to make a rough calculation of the loss of GNP produced by the labor supply response to the negative income tax.

The Findings of Empirical Studies

The literature on work incentives and disincentives is growing and has an increasingly empirical content. The relevant studies are of three types: (1) investigation of the reaction to high (positive) tax rates; (2) studies of the willingness of social security and public assistance recipients to work; and (3) actual attempts to simulate the labor supply response to a negative income tax using existing data sources.

Studies of the labor supply response to high tax rates indicate, in general, that persons subject to high average and marginal rates do not significantly reduce their hours of work.[2] However, these studies do not provide reliable information about the probable magnitude of the labor supply response of the poor to negative income taxes because: (a) differences in job appeal and the amount of status and power associated with different jobs suggest that low-income and high-income persons may not respond to high marginal tax rates in the same way, and (b), as we have shown above, a negative tax rate produces only a leisure-inducing substitution effect, whereas a positive tax rate produces both a substitution effect and a partially or wholly offsetting income effect.

Studies of the incentive effects of existing income-maintenance plans fall into two groups: (1) those that investigate the response of the aged to the social security retirement test, and (2) those that investigate the demand for public assistance. The former suffer from the fact that the aged are likely to respond differently than the nonaged, whereas the latter are unable to separate out the response to implicit 100 percent "tax rates," which eliminate all monetary gains from work.[3]

---

2. T. Sanders, *Effects of Taxation on Executives* (Boston: Graduate School of Business Administration, Harvard University, 1951); G. F. Break, "Income Taxes and Incentives to Work: An Empirical Study," *American Economic Review* 47 (September 1957): 529–49; R. Barlow, H. E. Brazer, and J. N. Morgan, *Economic Behavior of the Affluent* (Washington, D.C.: The Brookings Institution, 1966).

3. For example, see L. Gallaway, *The Retirement Decision: An Exploratory Essay*, Department of Health, Education, and Welfare, Research Report No. 9 (1965). C. T. Brehm and T. R. Saving, "The Demand for General Assistance Payments," *American Economic Review* 54 (December 1964): 1002–18.

The two attempts to simulate a negative income tax produce interesting but widely divergent results.[4] The labor supply response coefficients in the negative tax rate study by Lowell Gallaway are estimated from the response of the aged to social security payments. They also appear to depend importantly on which region of the country is selected for investigation.[5] The simulation by Jane Leuthold of a negative income tax indicates that on the average the labor supply response to negative income taxes is small but tends in a *positive* (work-increasing) direction. The Leuthold results are puzzling and may be the outcome of very special assumptions about the utility function she maximizes or may be due to data limitations.[6]

Description of Data

The data at our disposal came from special tabulations of the Census' Current Population Survey for the income years 1965 and 1966 (both relatively high-employment years). The sample of families we investigated were those with a married civilian male head between the ages of twenty-five and sixty who is neither ill nor disabled. Approximately nine out of ten male family heads in each income class were of prime working age (twenty-five to fifty-four years). Only families with a wife and one to four children present were included in the sample. In addition, all families with negative total income and incomes above $7,000 were omitted from the analysis. The accepted families were subdivided into families in which only the head was working and those in which there was also a working wife. The families were further separated by income bracket and by whether or not they received any nonemployment (non-work-related) income during the year in question. Some of the tabulations subdivided the families with nonemployment income into families for which nonemployment income was more than and less than 30 percent of total family income.

Approximately 2,000 families met the specifications described above. One-third of these had nonemployment income. Families with incomes less than $4,000 accounted for about one-third of the total sample. The number of self-employed family heads in the sample was small.

4. L. Gallaway, "Negative Income Tax Rates and the Elimination of Poverty," *National Tax Journal* 19 (September 1966): 298–307; J. H. Leuthold, "An Empirical Study of Formula Income Transfers and the Work Decision of the Poor," *Journal of Human Resources*, Summer 1968, pp. 312–23.

5. M. Taussig, "Negative Income Tax Rates and the Elimination of Poverty: Comment," *National Tax Journal* 20 (September 1967).

6. Leuthold's model includes minimum income and minimum leisure constraints, which are asymptotes for the "rectangular hyperbola" indifference curves that follow from the Cobb-Douglas utility function that she maximizes. Because of the constraints, the model that Leuthold estimates includes a peculiar wage effect term that would not appear if she had not included constraints. Moreover, it is unclear how Leuthold dealt with families whose income was less than the constraint, posing the problem of taking the logarithm of a negative number.

For each group of families in the sample we have data on the number (and percent) of heads who worked full-year (48 weeks or more) or part-year (47 weeks or less), and those who normally worked full-time (35 or more hours a week) and those who worked part-time (less than 35 hours a week). The weeks and hours information were converted into estimates of annual hours of work. It was estimated that the mean number of weeks of part-year workers (less than 48 weeks of work) was 35 weeks and the mean for full-year workers was 50 weeks.[7] The means for part-time and full-time hours per week were provided by the Bureau of Labor Statistics; they were 24 and 45 hours a week, respectively.[8]

Presentation and Analysis of Estimates

Table 1 shows the percentage of male heads of single-earner families who worked full-year full-time in 1965 and in 1966 (that is, 48 or more weeks and usually worked full-time hours). Within a given family income bracket, we are interested in how these "full-year's-time" labor force participation ratios vary among families with different amounts of nonemployment income. As column (4) shows, low-income families with nonemployment income had substantial amounts of this type of income; substantial, at least, relative to total family income. Differences between columns (1), (2), (3), and column (5) [as shown in columns (6), (7), (8), and (9)] of table 1 indicate, in general, that the higher the percentage nonemployment income is to total family income, the lower is the percentage of families whose head was a full-year's-time labor force participant. The few exceptions may be the result of weak cells – that is, groupings with too few sample observations. (Whereas the standard errors associated with sampling variability are generally low, in the weakest cell the error is as high as 7 percent.)

Because the estimates in table 1 are organized by income brackets and because the population we are concerned with is relatively homogeneous with respect to age and family situation, it would appear that the presence of nonemployment income is at least a partial explanation for the differences in the labor force participation ratios. However, as the following analysis will show, wage rate differences also have to be accounted for.

Even though we have selected a relatively high-employment period for

---

7. Bureau of Labor Statistics data indicate that the mean weeks worked of part-year (worked 1 to 47 weeks) workers is between 35 and 40 weeks. (At the end of the paper we provide estimates assuming a mean of 30 and 40 weeks.) U.S. Department of Labor, Bureau of Labor Statistics, *Work Experience of the Population in 1965*, Special Labor Force Report, No. 76, table A–9, p. A–14.

8. U.S. Department of Labor, Bureau of Labor Statistics, *Labor Force and Employment in 1965*, Special Labor Force Report, No. 69, tables D–4 and D–7, pp. A–30 and A–32.

Table 1. Percentage of Civilian Married Male Family Heads (with Nonworking Wife) Who Worked Full-Time Full-Year, by Income Bracket and Amount of Nonemployment Income

Income Bracket	(1) All Amounts	Family Has Nonemployment Income as a Percent of Total Family Income		(4) Avg. Amt. of Nonemployment Income ($)	Family Has No Nonemployment Income	Percentage Point Change in Full-Time Full-Year Labor Force Participation Associated with Nonemployment Income			
		(2) Less Than 30%	(3) More Than 30%		(5)	(6) (1)—(5)	(7) (2)—(5)	(8) (3)—(5)	(9) (3)—(2)
1965									
Under 3,000	40.00	45.58	35.99	829	64.80	—24.80	—19.22	—28.81	— 9.59
Under 2,000	34.09	23.60	35.94	906	57.21	—23.12	—33.61	—21.27	+12.34
2,000–2,999	45.93	50.38	36.12	773	71.48	—25.55	—21.10	—35.36	—14.26
3,000–3,999	78.78	78.05	81.06	944	90.16	—11.38	—12.11	— 9.10	+ 3.01
4,000–6,999	75.64	78.14	27.90	550	93.82	—18.18	—15.68	—65.92	—50.24
1966									
Under 3,000	40.78	55.73	30.21	619	66.77	—25.99	—11.04	—36.56	—25.52
Under 2,000	34.02	24.34	35.60	593	63.03	—29.01	—38.69	—27.43	+11.26
2,000–2,999	46.87	61.72	17.89	633	70.94	—24.07	— 9.22	—53.05	—43.83
3,000–3,999	53.03	66.17	7.85	537	82.00	—28.97	—15.83	—74.15	—58.32
4,000–6,999	82.22	83.90	43.52	583	92.55	—10.33	— 8.65	—49.03	—40.38

our analysis, inadequate job opportunities and other impediments to employment for particular groups of workers may still have suppressed the level of some of our labor supply estimates. But there is little reason to believe that workers with nonemployment (non-work-related) income versus workers without nonemployment income who come from *similar* low-income classes would be very differently affected by demand or other involuntary factors. For example, the amount of nonemployment income of low-income families with, versus low-income families without, a full-year's-time working head was not greatly different, indicating that family heads working less than full-year's-time did not receive significant amounts of work related income (such as unemployment compensation). This suggests that the employment opportunities facing the two groups of workers may not have been very different. Although the calculated differences in the labor force participation of workers from families with and without non-employment income who are in similar total income brackets may not be seriously biased, the level of labor force participation rates between *low-* and *high*-income groups are probably less comparable. It should also be pointed out that the level of participation rates in table 1 is considerably constrained by the fairly stringent full-employment criterion we have used to define workers.

The estimates in table 1 nevertheless provide some evidence that persons who receive nonemployment income work less on the average (that is, are less likely to be full-time full-year workers) than persons with no nonemployment income.[9] However, table 1 gives no clear indication of the amount by which work effort is affected either by receipt of nonemployment income or by possible differences in wage rates.

In table 2 we have estimated the annual hours of work of the heads of families with and without nonemployment income. These estimates of average annual hours are arrived at by multiplying the mean weeks worked by the mean hours of work per week for each income bracket. For all income brackets shown, families without nonemployment income work more hours than families with nonemployment income. We would expect the hours-worked differential to fall as income rises because the ratio of nonemployment income to total family income tends to fall as total income rises. (Note that the absolute levels of nonemployment income shown in column (4) of table 1 do not rise significantly as total income rises.) This expectation is fulfilled for 1965 but strangely is not met for 1966 in the three lowest income brackets (see columns (7) and (8) in table 2). Nevertheless, the directions of change are those predicted by the traditional income-leisure model.

Reference to a negative income tax raises the question whether the

---

9. Nearly all the difference in full-year labor force participation rates can be accounted for by a shift from full-year's-time to part-year's-time work (that is, by a reduction in annual hours), as is shown in the tables that follow.

Table 2. Mean Annual Hours of Work Differentials, Male-Headed Nonworking-Wife Families with and without Nonemployment Income, by Income Bracket

Income Bracket	Families with Nonemployment Income			Families with No Nonemployment Income			(7) Difference in Annual Hours Worked (3) − (6)	(8) Percent Change in Annual Hours (7) ÷ (6)
	(1) Average Weeks Worked Per Year[a]	(2) Average Hours Worked Per Week[b]	(3) Average Annual Hours (1) × (2)	(4) Average Weeks Worked Per Year[a]	(5) Average Hours Worked Per Week[b]	(6) Average Annual Hours (4) × (5)		
				1965				
Under 3,000	43.32	41.13	1,782	45.14	43.89	1,981	−199	−10.04
Under 2,000	43.56	39.69	1,729	43.72	44.11	1,928	−199	−10.32
2,000–2,999	43.09	42.47	1,830	46.40	43.69	2,027	−197	−9.72
3,000–3,999	47.48	44.29	2,103	48.76	44.64	2,177	−74	−3.40
4,000–6,999	46.74	44.62	2,085	49.18	44.91	2,208	−123	−5.57
				1966				
Under 3,000	43.36	42.62	1,848	46.01	43.00	1,978	−130	−6.57
Under 2,000	43.94	41.05	1,804	45.72	41.85	1,913	−109	−5.70
2,000–2,999	42.98	43.76	1,880	46.33	44.30	2,052	−172	−8.38
3,000–3,999	44.82	42.42	1,901	47.59	44.30	2,108	−207	−9.82
4,000–6,999	47.57	44.93	2,137	49.02	44.82	2,197	−60	−2.73

aThose working 1–47 weeks per year worked an estimated 35 weeks; those working 48 or more weeks a year worked an average of 50 weeks a year.

bThe average hours per week estimate of part-time workers was 24 hours, and average hours of full-time workers was 45 hours per week.

hours change shown in column (7) of table 2 reflects the kinds of income and substitution effects produced by a negative income tax plan and described above in the theoretical section of the paper. We will attempt to show that the figures in column (7) of table 2 reflect a substitution effect due to an income compensated change in the net wage rate, so that after the wage reduction and after the resultant reduction in hours, total income remains at the same level.

The hours differential for families with and without nonemployment income within an income bracket cannot be attributed directly to the receipt of income transfers (nonemployment income). Total income is the same for the two groups (assuming that the mean within-bracket incomes are also the same), but the wage rates are distinctly different – that is, lower for families with than for families without nonemployment income. For 1965–66, the wage rate differences for all but the highest income class vary between 15 and 50 percent, with the two lowest income classes having about a 50 and 25 percent difference. For example, look at columns (3) and (6) in table 2 and pick out the $2,000–$2,999 income bracket. Families with nonemployment income who have total family income between $2,000 and $3,000 had $773 of nonemployment income in 1965. Suppose mean total family income for both the with and without nonemployment income groups is $2,500. Then in 1965 the mean hourly wage of those families without nonemployment income is $1.23 ($2,500 ÷ 2027 hours). The mean hourly wage of families with nonemployment income is $0.94 [(2500 − 773) ÷ 1830].

The difference between the two wage rates could be looked at as a 24 percent reduction [(1.23 − .94) ÷ 1.23] in the net wage compensated for by a lump-sum income payment. Thus the income effect of a reduction in the wage is compensated for, and the resultant change in hours is a measure of the substitution effect.[10] In terms of figure 2, the movement from E to F – or a 197-hour annual reduction in work – is a picture of the substitution effect (or compensated wage effect) we have measured.

A negative income tax does more than simply compensate for the reduction in the net wage rate; it supplements family income, the amount depending on the plan's income guarantee and the offsetting rate. To measure the "supplementary" income effect, we need to compare the annual hours of work of families with the same wage rate but with different amounts of nonemployment (total) income. We are able to make this comparison in a rough way with our tables. We find that the average wage rate of heads in families with nonemployment income is not very different from that of heads in families without nonemployment income in the next lower income bracket. As an approximation, then, we can attribute any related difference

10. Marvin Koster has attempted to isolate the compensated price effect (or substitution effect) produced by an income tax, using nonemployment income and nonemployment income plus spouse's earnings to compensate for the income loss due to a lower net wage. See "Income and Substitution Effects in a Family Labor Supply Model" (Ph.D. diss., University of Chicago).

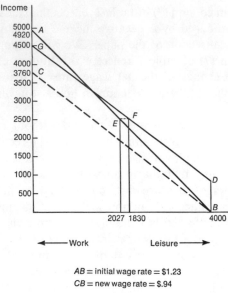

AB = initial wage rate = $1.23
CB = new wage rate = $.94

Figure 2.

in hours to the income effect resulting from the receipt of nonemployment income.

Figure 3 diagrams what we have just described verbally. It shows mean annual hours of work when family income is $2,500 and $3,500, holding

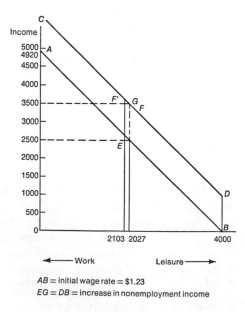

AB = initial wage rate = $1.23
EG = DB = increase in nonemployment income

Figure 3.

the wage approximately constant. If leisure is a normal good, theory predicts that hours of work should fall when some "lump-sum" income is added to family income, say a movement from E to F in figure 3. In the case shown here, hours actually increased slightly, but not nearly enough to offset the hours decrease produced by the substitution effect.

Table 3 presents our estimates of the change in hours due to the income and substitution effects for 1965 and 1966 and an average of the two years combined. The changes in hours due to the substitution effect are all in the predicted direction. For 1965 and 1966, taken separately, the hours change due to the income effect is negative in four out of six cases; when an average for 1965 and 1966 is taken, all changes are in the predicted direction. Our estimates also indicate that the income effect is smaller than the substitution effect, suggesting that the impact on work effort of a negative income tax may depend more on the negative tax rate than on the size of the basic income guarantee.

The estimates suggest that a negative tax plan with a 25 percent rate, which adds from $600 to $1,000 to the income of full-time full-year workers in the $2,000–3,000 income bracket, would produce (in the absence of dynamic effects not considered here) about an 11.5 percent reduction in annual hours of work. But what would a plan with a considerably higher marginal rate – say 50 percent – do? Our estimates suggest the reduction in hours would be only slightly larger with the same guarantee if the net wage were reduced by about 50 percent. (Nevertheless, under both tax rates the reduction in hours due to the compensated wage effect remains larger than the reduction due to the supplementary income effect.) In table 3 note the estimated change in hours for families with less than $2,000. Suppose the mean family income of this group is $1,500. The data show that for this income group nonemployment income averages about $750 for 1965–66. The wage rate of those with nonemployment income is approximately half the wage rate of those without nonemployment income. The annual hours reduction, however, is not much larger for this 50 percent wage rate difference than for the 25 percent wage rate difference.[11]

Up to this point we have considered only families with a nonworking wife. We can briefly report our estimates of how the annual hours of the male head of a family with a working wife change when his family receives nonemployment income. The estimates are presented in table 4, where we only show the 1965–66 average change. The estimated changes are in the predicted direction and are similar to those in the bottom part of table 3. However, in the under-$2,000 income group in table 4, the decline in hours produced by the supplementary income effect is larger than that produced by the substitution effect. Not surprisingly, in both tables 3 and 4 the hours

---

11. It would be interesting to know what form of utility function is implied by the results shown in tables 3 and 4. The authors are attempting to determine this and will report their findings in a subsequent paper.

Table 3. Income and Substitution Effects: Families with Male Head Age 25–60 and Nonworking Wife

Income Bracket	(1) Average Annual Hours, Families with NEYa	(2) Average Annual Hours, Families without NEYa	(3) Change In Annual Hours Due To Substitution Effect (1)−(2)	(4) Change in Annual Hours Due to "Supplementary" Income Effect (See Arrows)	(5) Total Change in Annual Hours (3)+(4)	(6) Percent Change in Annual Hours (5)÷(2)
1965						
Under 3,000	1,782	1,981	−199	−98	−297	−15.40
Under 2,000	1,729	1,928	−199	+76	−121	− 5.97
2,000–2,999	1,830	2,027	−197	−92	−166	− 7.62
3,000–3,999	2,103	2,177	− 74			
4,000–6,999	2,085	2,208	−123			
1966						
Under 3,000	1,848	1,978	−130	−33	−142	− 7.42
Under 2,000	1,804	1,913	−109	−151	−323	−15.74
2,000–2,999	1,880	2,052	−172	+28	−180	− 8.53
3,000–3,999	1,901	2,109	−208			
4,000–6,999	2,137	2,197	− 60			
1965–66 Average						
Under 3,000	1,815	1,979	−164	−66	−220	−11.46
Under 2,000	1,767	1,921	−154	−37	−221	−10.84
2,000–2,999	1,855	2,039	−184	−32	−173	− 8.07
3,000–3,999	2,002	2,143	−141			
4,000–6,999	2,111	2,202	− 91			

aNonemployment income.

Table 4. Income and Substitution Effects: Families with Male Head Age 25–60 with Working Wife; Change in Male's Hours of Work 1965–66

Income Bracket	(1) Average Annual Hours, Families with NEY[a]	(2) Average Annual Hours, Families without NEY[a]	(3) Change in Annual Hours Due to Substitution Effect (1) − (2)	(4) Change in Annual Hours Due to "Supplementary" Income Effect (See Arrows)	(5) Total Change in Annual Hours (3) + (4)	(6) Percent Change in Annual Hours (5) ÷ (2)
Under 3,000	1,780	1,942	−162			
Under 2,000	1,841	1,918	− 77	−168	−245	−12.77
2,000–2,999	1,750	1,974	−224	− 55	−279	−14.13
3,000–3,999	1,919	2,115	−196	− 52	−248	−11.73
4,000–6,999	2,063	2,168	−105			

[a] Nonemployment income.

reduction due to the substitution effect in the $4,000–$6,999 income bracket is not as large (about three-fifths as great) as in the lower income brackets.

Some investigators of family labor supply models include a variable for the income effect of the spouse's earnings on the husband's hours. Our estimates indicate that a small effect may be present (compare columns (1) and (2) in table 3 with columns (1) and (2) in table 4), but our data are probably not reliable enough to go beyond the statement that our estimates do not conflict with the hypothesis that the wife's earnings influence the husband's annual hours. Moreover, except for the lowest income bracket, table 5 indicates that in male-headed low-income families, receipt of non-employment income does not appear to influence the *wife's* decision to become a labor force participant.

Table 5. Labor Force Participation Ratios of Wife (Working Head Present) by Income Bracket and Whether Family Has Nonemployment Income

Income Bracket	Families with Nonemployment Income			Families without Nonemployment Income		
	(1) *1965*	*(2)* *1966*	*(3)* *1965–66 (Average)*	*(4)* *1965*	*(5)* *1966*	*(6)* *1965–66 (Average)*
Under 3,000	37.5	54.0	45.7	38.4	50.1	44.3
Under 2,000	24.0	50.4	37.2	40.1	47.3	43.2
2,000–2,999	44.3	56.1	50.2	36.9	52.6	44.8
3,000–3,999	32.8	39.4	36.1	37.1	37.9	37.5
4,000–6,999	42.6	40.7	41.7	54.0	39.8	46.9

Output Effects of the Reduction in Labor Supply

We would like to know how much output is lost if and when hours of work are reduced in response to a negative income tax plan. Because we have not estimated the hours change in response to an actual negative income tax plan, we must make inferences from the estimate we have made above. As we have already indicated, *we can interpret our data in terms of income-transfer plans that simultaneously raise family income in amounts ranging from about $600 to $1,000 while reducing the marginal wage rate by anywhere from 25 to 50 percent.*[12] *We found that the resultant income and substitution effects would produce a reduction in average annual hours of work – our estimates indicate an 11.50 percent reduction – in response to the combination of a lower marginal wage rate and the addition to income (a result of*

---

12. The 1965–66 average amount of nonemployment income of families with non-employment income who have less than $4,000 of total family income was $750.

the receipt of nonemployment income).[13] Thus we will assume that, on the average male-headed families receiving negative tax payments will reduce their annual hours of work by about 11.5 percent. At this level of work reduction we estimate that about 30 percent of the increase in income possibilities at the initial level of work is consumed in increased leisure, and about 70 percent is consumed in increased money income.

We must now convert the hours reduction into an estimate of the change in output. Our method of doing so is necessarily ad hoc. We have chosen to look at the earnings of the poor as a measure of their contribution to the economy's total output. In 1964 the poor are estimated to have earned approximately $8 billion.[14] Not all of the $8 billion was earned by nonaged persons in male-headed families. We estimate that about 75 percent, or $6 billion, was earned by poor persons whose average labor force response is similar to the response of the group whose hours change we have measured. Thus, the initial reduction in earnings (GNP) from providing poor male-headed families with negative income tax payments that average around $800 per family per year and reduce the net marginal wage rate by from 25 to 50 percent is $690 million (11.50% × $6 billion). To the $690 million we would have to add the response of other groups that would be likely to reduce their work effort, notably females in female-headed families and the aged. The percentage of annual hours response of these groups is likely to be larger than for nonaged male family heads. On the average, if they reduced their annual hours of work by 25 percent in response to a negative income tax plan, their earnings (GNP) would fall by about $500 million. Adding this reduction to our estimate of $690 million for nonaged male-headed families suggests that approximately a $1.2 billion initial reduction in GNP would result from the induced reduction in hours of work produced by adopting a modest-sized negative income tax.[15]

At this point it would be useful to examine the sensitivity of our estimated labor supply (annual hours) and output response to variations in the mean number of weeks worked by part-year workers and nonworkers (those males working less than 48 weeks per year). We used 35 weeks on the basis of the data available to us. However, because we could have used a figure slightly lower or higher than 35 weeks, we think that confidence in our estimates of labor supply and output changes will be enhanced by presenting a range of estimates that assume that the mean number of weeks worked by

---

13. The calculation was made using an unweighted average of the mean hours differentials for each income bracket up to $4,000 for both the nonworking and working wife categories.

14. This estimate was made by one of the authors for a monograph: C. Green, *Negative Taxes and the Poverty Problem* (Washington, D.C.: The Brookings Institution, 1967), p. 141, table 9–1, footnote k.

15. A universal negative tax plan roughly consistent with our data would be one carrying a 50 percent tax rate, a $1,500 guarantee, and a $3,000 break-even level. The initial transfer cost of such a plan in 1966 would have been approximately $6 billion, which would have allowed a reduction in public assistance of about $2 billion.

part-year workers was alternatively 30 weeks and 40 weeks. The estimates are presented in table 6. If the mean is 30 weeks, the unweighted mean percentage reduction in annual hours is 14.19 percent; if the mean is 40 weeks, the unweighted mean percentage reduction in annual hours is 8.87 percent. These estimates of labor supply response imply $851 million and $532 million reductions, respectively, in GNP. When the roughly estimated $500 million output loss due to the response of other groups of workers to a modest-sized negative tax plan is added to these figures, we may still conclude that the initial total GNP loss is somewhat in excess of $1 billion.

Table 6. Percentage Reduction in Annual Hours Worked under Alternative Assumptions about the Mean Weeks Worked of Part-Year (Worked Less Than 48 Weeks) Workers

Income Bracket	Mean = 30 weeks	Mean = 40 weeks
	Families with Nonworking Wife	
Under 2,000	—13.61	— 9.46
2,000–2,999	—13.59	— 8.27
3,000–3,999	—10.21	— 6.03
	Families with Working Wife	
Under 2,000	—16.08	— 9.64
2,000–2,999	—17.17	—11.25
3,000–3,999	—14.45	— 8.60
Unweighted grand mean percentage reduction in hours worked[a]	—14.19	— 8.87

[a] Overall income brackets and both classes of families.

8

David Elesh, Jack Ladinsky,
Myron J. Lefcowitz, and Seymour
Spilerman: The New Jersey-
Pennsylvania Experiment: A Field
Study in Negative Taxation

The fight against poverty has become one of the most important items on the agenda of this country. In reaction to widespread dissatisfaction with traditional welfare programs, the antipoverty innovations of the 1960s emphasized direct action and involvement of the poor, which gave rise to the community action programs. More recently, reflecting the realization that such programs can at best meet the needs of only a small proportion of the poor, attention has turned to income maintenance both for humanitarian reasons and to break the cycle of poverty. This paper reports some preliminary findings from the first field experiment with an income-maintenance program, the New Jersey and Pennsylvania negative income tax experiment.[1] Before moving to a discussion of the experiment, however, it is appropriate to place it in the context of alternative income-maintenance programs.

Alternative Income-Maintenance Programs

The United States already has a substantial system of income maintenance and public assistance that derives essentially from the Social Security legislation of the 1930s. It is necessary to briefly review these programs and evaluate their past effectiveness in combatting poverty to properly understand the many problems a new and comprehensive income-maintenance program must solve.

Presented at the Symposium on the Grants Economy held between the Association for the Study of the Grants Economy and the American Association for the Advancement of Science, Boston, Mass., December, 1969. Reprinted by permission of the authors. The authors are professors of sociology at the University of Wisconsin. The research reported here was supported by funds granted to the Institute for Research on Poverty at the University of Wisconsin by the Office of Economic Opportunity, pursuant to the provisions of the Economic Opportunity Act of 1964.

1. The experiment is a joint effort of the Institute for Research on Poverty at the University of Wisconsin, MATHEMATICA, and the Office of Economic Opportunity. Responsibility for the experiment is thus shared with others; responsibility for the accuracy of this report is ours alone.

Structural Versus Distributive Programs

As James Tobin has pointed out, the United States has dealt with low income in two ways [Tobin, 1968]. First, *structural* remedies – such as altering monetary and fiscal policies, encouraging education, and providing training and rehabilitation – have been sought. These programs attempt to alter the earning capacity of the poor by raising their skill levels and by increasing the demand for labor. Second, *distributive* remedies have been used to make up income deficiencies through cash or in-kind payments or by subsidies to productivity or employment.

Structural programs can be further divided into *market* solutions and *individual* solutions to poverty. Market solutions to low income are attempts to end market imperfections. Among these are the manipulation of monetary and fiscal policy to maintain a high level of aggregate demand, antidiscrimination legislation to end discrimination in employment or restrictions on entry into the organized craft occupations, minimum wage legislation, and attempts to increase the size and efficiency of the employment service system in matching employers with job vacancies and potential applicants. Individual solutions take the form of building up human capital through programs in health, education, and skill training.

Structural Programs   There are many who feel that structural solutions are the most adequate for solving the problem of poverty because they deal directly with failures of the economy or the causes of low earning power. Unfortunately experience reveals that there are two major weaknesses to such solutions. First, there are certain obstacles that limit the effectiveness of structural solutions, at least for the current generation in poverty. The poor have large families, broken homes, physical and mental handicaps, and other problems which are generally untouched by higher minimum wages, better employment services, antidiscriminatory legislation, economic progress, or a larger gross national product. Distributive mechanisms are necessary to meet the needs of the poor who are not reached by these endeavors. Second, given our current knowledge of economics and education, structural solutions are long term and not always successful. They involve restructuring labor markets and creating new training systems. Meanwhile the poor must survive. Only distributive programs can guarantee decent standards of survival in the short run.

We have had substantial experience with economic development and manpower development programs, and it is clear that they fall far short of serving the needs of the poor. Although the number of persons in poverty decreases as aggregate demand rises, the hard-core poor remain substantially untouched. For example, about the same number of persons in female-headed households were poor in 1966 as in 1959 [Orshansky, 1968]. Almost all the decrease in the poverty population in the 1960s was among male-headed households. Reduction of unemployment is also accompanied by inflationary trends that further reduce the value of the earnings of poor households. Perhaps most significant is the possible policy reaction to inflation, which increases unemployment and disproportionately burdens the poor.

Minimum wage legislation, an important feature of American economic policy, rarely helps the poor, who either work less than full-time or have large families. At present or future minimum wage levels their incomes would not be sufficient to keep them above the poverty line. Moreover, minimum wage increases can work to the detriment of the poor, if employers, faced with paying higher wages, release low-skilled workers to increase efficiency. Thus greater industrial coverage under the minimum wage law could well mean greater unemployment and underemployment for the working poor.

The results of manpower development programs have been disappointing. The Department of Labor estimates that there are 11 million poor for whom work is a feasible way out of poverty. Only some 4.5 million have been enrolled in federal manpower programs since 1962, of which about 3 million have been in work experience programs like Neighborhood Youth Corps. These programs emphasize payment for services performed rather than intensive training for work outside the programs. Of the 4.5 million, only 1.4 million, less than one-third, were in intensive training under the Manpower Development and Training Act (MDTA), Job Corps, or similar programs. Not all finished the training, nor were all who finished placed in jobs. Of the 1.4 million in these structured work-training programs, only 50 percent, or 700,000, completed the programs and were placed in jobs [President's Commission, 1969:246]. Manpower and economic development programs undoubtedly play an important role in aiding the poor earn more and hold respectable jobs, but alone they are not a solution to poverty in America.

Distributive Programs   There are three general forms distributive programs take in America today:

1. *Social insurance programs*, such as old age, survivors and disability insurance (OASDI, or Social Security), and unemployment insurance. These programs cover risks that are predictable and outside of individual control; they replace lost earnings from retirement, unemployment, death, or disability. All are in some way tied to work and earnings in that they are financed by employee and employer taxes or contributions specified by law.

2. *Income subsidy programs*, such as public assistance and veterans' pensions. With few exceptions these programs provide cash income transfers only to particular categories of needy persons who are deemed worthy of public assistance – the blind, disabled, and dependent children. The overwhelming majority of income-subsidy programs are financed jointly by federal, state, and local governments; all are administered at the state and local level. None are mandatory programs. The federal government grants matching funds to states meeting a small number of requirements

but does not require that states pay benefits at federally determined levels. According to the Heineman Commission there are "over 300 separate programs of cash public assistance receiving federal funds, covering different categories of the population under widely varying standards" [President's Commission, 1969:286].

3. *Income-in-kind programs*, such as food stamps, Medicaid, and public housing. In-kind programs for the poor exist for two reasons. First, it is argued that certain services, such as housing, will not be provided to the poor by the private market in the quantity and price that they can afford. Second, it is argued that the poor will not allocate their money properly, so it is necessary to control choice and quality. Some in-kind programs provide full subsidy (surplus commodity distribution and Medicaid); others provide only partial subsidy (public housing, rent supplement, food stamps, and Medicare).

Evaluation of Distributive Programs   All three distributive programs are either irrelevant, grossly inadequate, or detrimental to the present status of the poor. First, let us consider social insurance programs. The failures here are twofold. Because the poor have irregular work histories and low earnings, they gain little from Social Security or unemployment insurance. Moreover, few insurance programs provide adequate payments even for workers who have had a solid work history and adequate earnings. Unemployment insurance is particularly unsatisfactory, because it is not universally available and is often not available for long enough periods of time. In 1968 nearly two-thirds of the unemployed were not covered by unemployment insurance, primarily because of benefit expirations [President's Commission, 1969]. Although we recognize that social insurance does keep many people out of poverty, it is not relevant to our current problem.

There are two major problems with income-subsidy programs: inadequate benefits and inadequate coverage. In 1965, of all households that received cash transfers and were below the poverty line before receiving them, 56 percent were *still* below after receiving them. Thirty-two percent of the pretransfer poor received *no* government payments at all [Orshansky, 1968:28]. Average payments per recipient for AFDC equaled $43 per month in January 1969, ranging from $10 in Mississippi to $65 in Massachusetts [President's Commission, 1969]. The poor with intact families cannot qualify for coverage in most states. AFDC-UP does provide for unemployed able-bodied male heads, but less than 100,000 families are covered by this component of public welfare [President's Commission, 1969:22].

The lack of any program for the working poor with intact families appears to have three dysfunctional side effects: it creates work disincentives; it encourages family disruptions; and it has a deleterious social effect because some broken families can qualify for categorical relief and have incomes that exceed those of intact, working families with the same needs.

There are other unfortunate aspects of the public assistance system. Administrative costs are high, in part because the program is decentralized and in part because so much effort is put into screening and surveillance for eligibility. The means test and rules regarding expenditure of benefits deny recipients freedoms other citizens enjoy, and often regulations impose constraints most citizens could not meet. Finally, the program lacks uniformity and clarity, and it grants a great deal of discretionary power to local administrators that is often misused. On this point, Harold Watts has stated [Watts, 1969]:

> Much of the dissatisfaction with our current welfare system stems directly from discretion at the lower levels of authority. The inequities resulting from uneven and sometimes capricious use of this discretion are bad enough, but it can also be argued with some merit that the experience of face-to-face dealing with one who has the authority to withdraw or grant a principal means of support itself encourages and even promotes the very habits and attitudes of dependency our society is at some pains to eliminate.

In-kind programs are the least satisfactory of all distributive schemes; many are demeaning, wasteful, and ineffective, and they falsely assume that the poor lack proper values. The Heineman Commission has recommended that special programs providing food to poor families be phased out in favor of cash assistance. It found that surplus food is often thrown away because people do not like it and that eligible families often do not buy food stamps because they have to give up too many nonfood purchases to do so [President's Commission, 1969:367]. The Commission also has expressed a preference for gradual elimination of housing programs when income supplements approach adequate levels and the private market can meet the demand for low-cost housing [President's Commission, 1969:22].

Alternative Income-Supplement Strategies

Because of the deficiencies of present income-maintenance programs, attention has turned to consideration of various comprehensive income-supplement strategies that would provide nationwide minimum annual incomes to all Americans based on family need or an alternative criterion. The three most widely discussed schemes are: (1) *guaranteed employment*, a program that would make the federal government the employer of last resort for those who could not find jobs; (2) *children's allowances*, which would provide to families a specified grant of money for each child; and (3) *negative income tax*, the program of concern in this paper, which provides specified supplements to annual income based on family size and includes a financial incentive to work feature that reduces payments by some fraction of a dollar for each dollar earned, to insure that those who work always have more income than those who do not.

Criteria for Evaluating Programs   In order to properly evaluate the relative advantages and disadvantages of each scheme, we need a set of criteria applicable to all. Scholars in the field of income maintenance have emphasized a variety of criteria [Marmor, 1969; Weisbrod, 1969; President's Commission, 1969]. In the absence of a generally accepted set, we offer the following tentative list of factors that most would consider a minimal guideline in evaluating any new income-maintenance program:

1. *Adequacy of benefits.* How near or above the poverty line will the poor be after payments, or what percent of lost earnings will be replaced by the program?

2. *Scope of coverage.* What percent of the poor or the risk population will be covered by the program?

3. *Leakage.* How efficient is the program in terms of the percent of total costs spent on administration and in payments to nonpoor as opposed to direct benefits to the poor?

4. *Cost.* How much will the program cost the taxpaying public?

5. *Dignity and restraints on behavior.* Does the program dispense funds without disagreeable surveillance or screening procedures? Does the program restrict freedom of movement or choice in the labor or consumer market?

6. *Adverse side effects.* Does the program have inadvertent consequences such as disruption of family organization, discouragement of participation in the labor force, or encouragement of withdrawal from the labor force in order to qualify for funds? Does the program interfere with other programs or create undesirable patterns of migration?

7. *Clarity of application and minimization of discretionary power.* Does the program minimize, if not eliminate, the power of administrators to determine final treatment of recipients? Are there clear and precise rules that specify the allocation of benefits in the program?

8. *Equity.* Are there precise rules for horizontal equity – that is, the equal treatment of all who are equally placed? Are there rules for vertical equity – that is, clear-cut and reasonable criteria by which groups are differentiated in terms of needs?

9. *Automatic flexibility.* Is there built into the program anticipation of changing statuses of recipients and economic conditions which provide for automatic shifts in benefits?

10. *Economic stability.* Does funding or operation of the program have adverse effects on the economy or labor markets?

We have not attempted to make this list exhaustive. We have intentionally avoided listing specific program attributes having to do with definition of income and family unit, benefit structure, length of the accounting and payment period, how the program shall be paid for, and other features that are obviously critical in the final operation of a program. At present it is not possible to know with any certainty the outcomes for each program on each criterion listed, much less for details not listed. We lack precisely the kind of evidence for program evaluation that is being collected in the New Jersey-Pennsylvania experiment. However, it is possible to make some estimates of how each program might fare in terms of the above criteria so long as we keep in mind the possible influences of variations in program details.

Space does not allow a detailed application of these criteria to the three comprehensive income maintenance schemes. We present instead a brief summary of the most important weaknesses and strengths of each program.

Guaranteed Employment   The major advantages of a guaranteed employment program are its utilization of manpower and the fact that income would be dignified by work rather than stigmatized as "given away." The major weaknesses of a guaranteed-employment program have to do with adequacy, scope, and adverse side effects. Unless a guaranteed-employment program were tied to a generous wage-supplement scheme, it could not provide the occupationally unskilled poor with incomes above the poverty line. Nor would making the federal government an employer of last resort assist the one-third of poor families who simply do not have employable members. Finally, if, as employer of last resort, the federal government paid unskilled workers wages or supplements sufficient to bring incomes above the poverty line, these jobs might very well attract many low paid semi-skilled and unskilled workers from the private sector, an undesirable side effect that would require the imposition of restrictive eligibility rules and tests of need for qualification. These weaknesses appear to outweigh any social gains from linking income to work.

Children's Allowances   The major advantages of a children's allowance program are that it sets up a simple, easily administered, and dignified right to income based on size of family, a criterion that is not considered by employers in setting wages of workers. However, there are a number of weaknesses with respect to adequacy, leakage, and adverse side effects. A good deal depends on the size of the allowance. If payment per check is as low as in Canada and most other nations (excluding France), it would be inadequate to lift most poor families out of poverty. The major weakness, however, is that children's allowances are very inefficient in eliminating poverty because most of the transfers go to the nonpoor. To make the program efficient most of the payments to the nonpoor must be recovered through positive taxation. One major side effect of the program is the possibility that some persons may withdraw from the labor force if benefits rival wages [Green, 1967]. This is particularly important because the program does not encourage participation in the labor force. These disadvantages are sufficient to suggest that, despite its several merits, a children's allowance is not an efficient means of alleviating poverty.

Negative Income Tax   This scheme has many obvious advantages. It would be universal in coverage, would provide a dignified way to transfer funds to the poor without screening or surveillance, would avoid possible disruption of family organization, and, with the work incentive factor built in, would encourage voluntary participation in the labor force. It also minimizes the discretionary power of administrators and provides clear, precise rules of horizontal and vertical equity. As in the federal income tax system, shifts in the organization of the program or recipient status vis-à-vis the program could be easily and automatically accommodated.

The major problems with a negative income tax program have to do with adequacy, cost, and adverse side effects. Adequacy would depend entirely on where the break-even points are set. Most programs now being discussed would not do away with poverty. They are seen as needed minimal supplements to earned income. To wipe out poverty via the negative income tax would be expensive – in the neighborhood of $25 billion. Insofar as benefits rival wages, a negative tax program, like a children's allowance, may contain work disincentives. But because payments are keyed to earned income, the disincentives should be smaller than under a children's allowance program.

Experimental Objectives of the New Jersey-Pennsylvania Study

Whatever the presumed benefits of a negative tax scheme, there are a variety of questions that must be answered before its adoption. With some oversimplification, they can be reduced to one: What is the cost of a negative tax program? To answer this question we must specify a particular program – a particular tax rate, a guarantee level, and a set of eligibility criteria – and examine empirically the work effort under the program.

If tax rates, guarantee level, and eligibility criteria were all that were needed to calculate cost, empirical research would be unnecessary, aside from the determination of the number of eligibles. Nor would research be required if it were possible to determine the work response of participants from theory. But neither economic nor sociological theory is sufficiently developed to provide quantitative forecasts in these areas. Both economic and sociological theory will give us qualitative predictions: we expect some people to choose less work as the cost of not working decreases, but we cannot say by how much. We need to know how the response will vary with the tax-rate–guarantee level combination and within combinations, by labor market status, age, race, ethnicity, education, residential location, family size and composition, occupational history, values, and so on.

The usual types of economic and sociological data – government and private censuses and surveys – are not adequate for answering these questions, for it is extremely unlikely that we could find natural analogues of sufficient size and permanence to be comparable to the exogenously induced changes in a family's unearned income that would be provided by a negative tax program. What evidence we have on the unearned part of a family's income indicates that it is of little consequence for families of low annual income [Weisbrod and Hansen, 1967]. Consequently, we are led to an experimental design for research into the response to a negative income tax.

The particular experiment reported here is chiefly concerned with the broad question of effects on work effort. The dimensions of this question are extremely complex, and we shall list just some of the major issues with which the experiment is concerned. This list by no means exhausts all of the important questions associated with work-effort response. There are many issues that the experiment, by design, cannot address. We shall return to this problem later.

First, if cash transfers carry with them work disincentives, how do these vary by tax-rate–guarantee combinations? Second, will primary and secondary wage earners respond differently? Theory would lead us to expect that wives working as secondary earners will leave the labor force more readily than their husbands, because half their income typically goes to cover the costs of working [Addiss, 1963]. Does this happen and does it happen differentially by transfer treatment? Third, if job opportunities are scarce, do benefits induce migration to areas of tighter labor supply? Fourth, do the guarantees stimulate job changes that produce a fuller utilization of available skills or enhancement of skills or both in order to command a higher price? Fifth, do the guarantees stimulate enrollment to training courses for the purposes of upgrading skills?

Cross-cutting these five issues are questions of response by race, ethnicity, education, age, occupational history, and values. Because the poor are neither uniform in their characteristics nor a random sample of the United States population, estimates of costs must take their composition into consideration. We must learn whether different groups respond in the same way to a particular transfer scheme. We are likely to find that no one program minimizes the disincentives for all groups. If this is the case, examining the intergroup variation in response should provide a basis for constructing ancillary programs to fill in the deficiencies of whatever scheme seems most feasible in terms of the largest group of the poor. And even given the same net aggregate response for two different transfer schemes, we may want to choose, for exogenous policy reasons, the scheme that would minimize the disincentive in one group and maximize it in another. For example, we might want to minimize the disincentive among the young and maximize it among the nearly retired.

Still other questions refer as much to the social as to the fiscal costs associated with a negative tax. For example, we want to know the effect of the transfers on family structure, particularly among blacks. If job-conditioned income instability contributes to marital conflicts and disruptions as currently thought, we want to know if a transfer scheme will reduce them.

On the other hand, it is possible for the transfers to increase marital conflict and disruptions. Because the transfer income does not stem from the activities of an individual, questions may arise regarding rights to it. How this potential conflict will be resolved, and how the resolution will differ by ethnic and racial group are also of interest to us.

In addition, we are examining consumption and savings patterns, use of time, fertility and spacing of children, political consciousness and participation. Because of their importance, some of these issues are being researched even though the experiment is not designed to address them efficiently. For example, although we look into the issues of fertility and spacing of children, these questions really require an experiment of greater duration. And although we examine the impact of income transfers on the economic and political structures of the sampled neighborhoods, the problem truly requires an experiment that supports all of the eligibles in an area, which the present one does not.

The Design of the Experiment

Because the major purpose of the experiment is to assess work-effort response and because most of the poor are in intact families in urban areas, the experiment is restricted to families with nonstudent male heads, eighteen to fifty-eight years of age, able to work, and with normal[2] family incomes no more than 150 percent of the poverty line for each family size. The sample has been drawn from poverty tracts in Trenton, Paterson, Passaic, and Jersey City, New Jersey, and Scranton, Pennsylvania. The first part of the sample was drawn in Trenton in August 1968; the final segment was selected in Scranton in September 1969. Our experience is that roughly 80 percent of the eligibles will fall between 100 and 150 percent of the poverty line.

The basic design contains one experimental and two control groups. Once eligibility is determined from a special screening interview, families are randomly assigned to one of eight negative tax plans, which together define the experimental group, or to one of the two control groups. The experimental group contains 659 families; the first control group consists of 650 families, the second of 100 families.

The eight tax plans are combinations of tax rates and guarantee levels that, in our judgment encompass the area of greatest policy interest. Tax rates range from 30 to 70 percent, and guarantee levels vary from 50 to 125

---

2. "Normal" income refers to an empirical approximation to a long-run income concept such as Friedman's Permanent Income. A regression is being developed to describe the average relation between family income and a fairly eclectic set of household characteristics; they are fitted to give a good approximation at the low end of the income distribution. "Normal" income is an interpolation between (1) a household's income as predicted by this and (2) its actual income over the most recent year as reported in a special screening interview.

percent of the poverty line (thus for a family of four, the range of guarantees currently run from $1,741 to $4,352).[3] Table 1 shows the combinations selected for experimentation; table 2 gives the guarantee levels by family size.

After families have been assigned to groups, all, experimental and control, receive a preenrollment interview. The purpose of this interview is to obtain baseline data in a variety of areas uncontaminated by knowledge of the experiment or the inception of transfers. Subsequently, the experimental families are visited by enrollers who explain the program to them and solicit their cooperation. If cooperation is obtained (fewer than 7 percent refuse), they receive payments for three years. Their only obligation is to report their income and family composition each month and to submit to quarterly interviews.

The first control group is also interviewed quarterly. The size of this group (650 families) reflects a concern for attrition, which grew as sampling and interviewing progressed.

One of the most difficult methodological problems in studies of this kind is the possibility that the transfer effects that are observed are due to the experiment rather than to the payments. Because we are asking people quarterly about their work (and if they are not working, whether they have looked for work), it is possible that our interviews might stimulate work-related responses. We cannot eliminate such effects, but we can measure them by means of the second control group, which will be interviewed annually. Initially it will be selected from the same list of eligibles as the other groups. However, no effort will be made to maintain the same group over the three years. It would be extremely difficult to do so, given the once-a-year contact, and not really necessary. A comparable sample is all that is required, and it can be drawn freshly each year.

Because of a concern for ethnic and racial difference in responses, an effort was made to balance the sample in terms of the variables. We employed a form of stratified random sampling to ensure adequate numbers of black, Puerto Rican, and white families. Had this not been done, there would have been an excess of Puerto Ricans and too few whites. Currently, the sample composition is 37 percent black, 29 percent Puerto Rican, and 34 percent white.

Finally, our design recognizes that the experiment exists in competition with current welfare programs, and during its existence these programs may provide higher support levels. The likely result of such a situation is that some families will elect to receive welfare in preference to the experiment's benefits. Rather than simply drop these families from our program and lose all of the effort invested in them and information obtained from them, we chose to continue these families as part of the experimental group, but to

---

3. Our transfers are periodically adjusted for changes in the cost of living.

Table 1. Negative Income Tax Plans in the New Jersey Experiment

	Tax Rates		
Guarantee levels	30%	50%	70%
.50 poverty line ($1,741)[a]	X[b]	X	
.75 poverty line ($2,611)	X	X	X
1.00 poverty line ($3,482)		X	X
1.25 poverty line ($4,352)		X	

[a] Figures in parentheses are guarantee levels for a family of four.

[b] X marks plans in use.

pay them only the minimum benefit. It would, of course, be of little use to pay them more, because welfare would only cut their payment an equivalent amount. We do not believe this is by any means an optimal solution to the problem, but as yet we do not know of a better one.

Findings and Methodological Issues

Although detailed statistical analysis of the data collected thus far is yet to be undertaken, our experience does permit us to report some preliminary findings relevant to a national negative tax program and to current and future experiments. The findings are of two types: (1) those that relate to both possible national programs and to other experiments, and (2) those that refer more directly to other experiments. In the latter section we shall also address some methodological problems with experiments in general and our experiment in particular. The preliminary nature of the findings

Table 2. Guarantee Levels by Household Size

	Household Size						
Guarantee levels	2	3	4	5	6	7	8 +
.50 poverty line	$1,055	$1,450	$1,741	$1,952	$2,136	$2,294	$2,426
.75 poverty line	$1,582	$2,175	$2,611	$2,928	$3,204	$3,441	$3,639
1.00 poverty line	$2,110	$2,901	$3,432	$3,904	$4,273	$4,589	$4,853
1.25 poverty line	$2,637	$3,626	$4,352	$4,880	$5,341	$5,736	$6,066

cannot be overemphasized; it would be inappropriate to draw strong inferences from them.

National Programs and Experiments

The critical experimental question is, of course, the work-effort response to the negative tax payments. Five measures of this response are currently available: (1) changes in the size of the average payment, (2) relative change in head's earnings for the experimental and control groups,[4] (3) relative change in family earnings (husband's plus wife's earnings) for the experimental and control groups, (4) relative change in head's hours worked for the experimental and control groups,[5] and (5) relative change in wife's participation in the labor force for the experimental and control groups.[6] If wage earners drop out of the labor force and substitute negative tax payments for earned incomes, then the size of the average payment should rise over time – net of cost of living increases – and the remaining four measures of effect should all show a decline in the experimental group relative to the control groups.

Almost all theorists predicted a substitution of experimental benefits for earned income, particularly for secondary wage earners. The important policy question was the estimation of the cost of a national program, given the amount of substitution observed in the experiment. There were a few venturesome souls (including some of us) who felt that the strength of the work ethic in this society might be enough to limit the disincentive effects to secondary wage earners, but they were a distinct minority.

Although at this point conclusions must be considered tentative, the data appear to give some support to the minority position. Based on fifteen months' experience in Trenton, Paterson, and Passaic (these cities contain about 37 percent of the sample), we can say that there is little indication that wage earners are leaving the labor force. Average payments have been quite stable over time and are at an average annual rate of about $1,000. Table 3 gives the relative changes for the other four variables measured at the preenrollment and fifth quarterly interviews.

Panel A shows that about 9 percent more of the experimental group

---

4. The variable is based on the head's report of earnings from all jobs held during the past week.

5. The variable is based on the head's report of the total number of hours worked during the past week.

6. The variable wife's participation in the labor force was obtained from the following question asked at both points in time: What were you doing during most of last week – working for pay, keeping house, looking for work, or what? If a respondent replied that she was "working for pay," "with a job but not at work," or "looking for work," she was coded as in the labor force. If she replied, she was "keeping house," she was coded as a housewife. If she said she was "disabled" or "other," she was coded "other."

Table 3. Measures of Experimental Effect by Experimental Status,
Preenrollment and Fifth Quarterly Interviews

	Experimental	*Control*
A. Change in head's earnings		
Increased by more than $25	38.5%	29.7%
Stayed within $25	39.5	46.5
Decreased by more than $25	22.0	23.8
Total	100.0	100.0
$N =$	(286)	(101)
B. Change in family's earnings		
Increased by more than $25	39.2%	38.6%
Stayed within $25	34.6	35.6
Decreased by more than $25	26.2	25.7
Total	100.0	100.0
$N =$	(286)	(101)
C. Change in hours worked		
Increased	44.8%	39.6%
Stayed the same	20.6	27.7
Decreased	34.6	32.7
Total	100.0	100.0
$N =$	(286)	(101)
D. Change in spouse's labor force participation		
In labor force at t_1 and t_2	7.6%	6.5%
In labor force at t_1, housewife at t_2	7.2	8.7
Housewife at t_1, in labor force at t_2	8.7	15.2
Housewife at t_1 and t_2	64.8	55.4
Other	11.7	14.1
Total	100.0	100.0
$N =$	(264)	(92)

than of the control group family heads increased their earnings over the
fifteen-month period. However, panel B indicates that there is no difference
between groups in terms of family earnings. Consistent with the changes in
head's earnings, panel C shows that heads in the experimental group increased their hours worked about 5 percent more than heads in the control
group. Finally, panel D indicates that experimental group wives, although
they were no more likely to leave the labor force than control group wives,
were about 9 percent more likely to be housewives at both points in time,
and 8 of the 9 percent difference is accounted for by control group wives
who entered the labor force during the fifteen-month period. Possibly their
entry was due to the deepening of the recession during this period.

Independent tests of the significance of the above findings are not appropriate because of the definitional relationships among the measures, but it is possible to test the differences simultaneously using the multivariate analysis of variance. Such a test was performed and it revealed that the pattern of findings was well within the bounds of chance.

Thus the most appropriate conclusion to draw from table 3 is that, as yet *there is little evidence of either disincentive or incentive effects.* Given the widespread expectation of disincentive effects, this conclusion is surprising and comforting to the supporters of a negative tax. But it should also be seen as very tentative, as it is based on only part of the sample and a time period representing less than half of the three-year duration of the experiment.

In addition, there is no evidence that families have treated the payments as a windfall, even during the first payment periods. Fears of spending sprees or unusual expenditures have not been justified. It appears that families budget the payments as they do any other item of income.

From the standpoint of national program cost, another important experimental issue is the likely participation rate of the eligible population. Projections of program costs vary markedly depending on the particular tax rate, guarantee level, and population groups the estimator chooses to incorporate. But all estimates assume complete participation of the eligible population. This is a perfectly reasonable assumption if a national program is structured to make payments automatically. For example, benefits might be computed and paid as a result of filing the annual tax return. However, if application for benefits is discretionary, then the assumption is not viable, and current cost estimates may be excessively high.

Because participation in the experiment is voluntary, we did not assume full participation of the eligible population. Given the percentage of the eligibles utilizing current welfare programs, unemployment compensation, and tax rebate procedures, this just did not seem reasonable. Rather, we expected that families whose normal income was close to their break-even point, or whose income fluctuations brought them close to their break-even point, might not find the size of the payment worth the bother to apply for it. And as income rose, we expected that an increasing number of families with self-definitions as nonpoor would reject the payments.

Thus far these expectations have been confirmed, and the results are observable in terms of the families who have dropped out of the experiment or who have refused to participate. As of mid-November, 47 of the roughly 650 experimental families had withdrawn from the experiment. Of these 47, 41 were at or above their break-even point just before quitting the program. Five of the 6 families who were below their break-even point – that is, who received more than the minimum payment – dropped out either because they moved and could not be located[7] (one case) or because they moved out

---

7. Families are considered to have dropped from the experiment if they move without leaving a forwarding address and if an elaborate search procedure we have developed fails to reveal their whereabouts.

of the continental United States (four cases).[8] For only 6 of the 41 families at or above their break-even point was a move the basis for attrition. (Of these 6, 4 moved and could not be located; this figure should be compared with the 1 withdrawal among the 6 receiving more than the minimum payment, which involved a family that moved and could not be located.) Although evidence based on such small numbers is suggestive at best, it seems reasonable to propose that families receiving the minimum payment may not believe as strongly as families receiving higher payments that keeping the experimenters informed of their whereabouts is worth the bother. Analysis of the refusals provides further substantiation for the general point. Over all cities, 71 percent of the families who refused to participate (54 families) would only have received the minimum payment in any case. Of the remainder, virtually all were families on welfare who did not feel it to their advantage to change to our programs.

Altogether, the number of families who have dropped out is roughly 7 percent of the experimental group and 14 percent of those receiving the minimum payment. It would be extremely difficult to project these figures into estimates for a national program. Families whose incomes exceeded the experimental criterion when eligibility was determined but whose incomes subsequently dropped below it are excluded. Thus net attrition may be less than 7 percent. On the other hand, the exigencies of the research design have required that we make every effort to persuade families to remain in the experiment. Matters are further complicated by the fact that those who withdrew are spread across eight experimental tax plans, so no plan contains enough cases for reliable estimates. Nonetheless, it is clear that if participation in a national program is voluntary, there may well be significant underutilization – as is the case with other voluntary transfer programs.

Experiments   However valuable it may be for an estimate of national program participation, attrition is a serious problem for an experiment. Not only may samples become too small to permit reliable estimates of effects but if attrition is at all selective (and we have seen that it is), the estimates that can be calculated on those remaining in the experiment may be greatly biased. The problem is particularly acute in the control groups, because there are fewer benefits to induce cooperation. Thus far, we have lost 44 control group families out of 650.

The experiment began with payments to all families, experimental and control, of $5 per interview, in the rather naive (it now appears) hope that this amount would be sufficient to hold the cooperation of the main control group. It was not. Moreover, the minimum payment of $5 a month did not seem to be enough to sustain the cooperation of many experimental families.

---

8. We make no effort to follow families who leave the continental United States.

Therefore a decision was made to substantially increase the incentives. Now the main control group is paid an $8 per month "filing fee" for keeping our office informed of their addresses, and the minimum experimental payment is $20 per month. Although we are hopeful that these solutions will alleviate the problem, it is too early to judge their effects. Admittedly, the remedy slightly distorts the experimental approximation to reality, because it can be said that now all families are receiving payments. However, the problem does not appear to be significant. The amount involved probably is not large enough to affect estimates, and in any event, responses are likely to be more readily observed in terms of the variation in payments than in terms of their absolute levels.

For the experimental group, information is another means to minimize attrition. The program was explained to sample families at some length before their enrollment, but a substantial amount of ignorance, confusion, and suspicion remained, and further explanations were made in a number of cases. Although most of the suspicion appears to have been allayed, a recent sampling of families revealed that a great deal of ignorance still exists. Such ignorance does little to motivate cooperation, and consequently we are considering making new explanations to everyone. If such knowledge or the lack of it affects participation in the experiment, it is likely to affect participation in a national program.

Also related to the question of attrition is the length of the period between income reports and payments. Originally families were asked to report their incomes monthly, and payments were made biweekly. But we quickly discovered that many families, particularly those receiving the minimum payment, found the schedule onerous. Fearing – and finding – attrition we attempted to ease the situation by requiring only those receiving minimum payments to report their incomes every three months. Interestingly, we found more opposition to the new plan than to the old. Investigation revealed that with the reduced contact under the new plan, families perceived the requests for data as even greater disruptions of their normal scheme of things than they had under the old plan. In addition, because we require each family to submit their pay stubs along with their income reports, we found that they had difficulty keeping track of them over the three-month period. As a result we returned to the monthly schedule.

Despite their deficiencies, these procedures do represent an improvement over those developed during the planning stage of the experiment. It was intended that both reports and payments would be made on a monthly basis, but pilot interviews suggested that the families would find the schedule bothersome. So we asked ourselves how we could emphasize the benefits of the program and concluded that we had to make the program more visible and salient to the families. One way to accomplish this is simply to increase rather than decrease contact. But to increase contact by increasing the frequency of the required income reports is to emphasize a negative aspect. Accordingly, we decided to shorten the payment interval, and payments are now made every two weeks rather than monthly. Reaction to the change has been remarkably good. Most of the families are paid their earnings weekly or every two weeks, and many have told us that the schedule helps them to integrate our payments into their budgets. Judging from reactions like these, the payment schedule may well have avoided a source of attrition.

More generally, our experience suggests that the length of the interval between payments may significantly affect participation in national programs or future experiments. Keying the transfer interval to the prevailing job payment period could be beneficial.

A number of additional questions of interest to both economists and sociologists derive from the conditions of a negative income tax experiment rather than from negative taxation per se. These problems are of three types: (1) the relationship between the experiment and competing welfare programs, (2) the difficulties of applying different experimental treatments simultaneously to families in a single locale, and (3) the problems associated with supporting only part of the eligible target population in a neighborhood.

Negative tax experiments must exist in the context of alternative welfare programs that they cannot control and which may offer competing benefits. Changes in these competing programs therefore may seriously affect the behavior of experimental families. For example, during this past summer New Jersey raised the support level of its AFDC-UP program. As a result, the AFDC-UP payments now exceed the benefits in a number of tax plans in the experiment. This situation has led a number of families to drop our payments in favor of New Jersey's. Although almost all of these families continue to be interviewed, the loss of these families from our tax plans clearly endangers the validity of the estimates we hope to make about the effects of these plans. Moreover, the loss of families is likely to be systematic, because differences in the educational attainment and sophistication of families imply that the distribution of knowledge about alternative welfare programs is not random. Thus, estimates made on the basis of families remaining in the tax plans may well be biased. It is entirely possible that our experiment and others like it, could be seriously impaired by current competing welfare programs.

Another set of problems derives from the possibility of communication among persons on the experiment. As described earlier, some of the tax plans are considerably more generous than others. Obviously individuals are disturbed when they learn that their families are being supported at a lower level than their neighbors. One family quit the experiment for this reason. Related to this phenomenon is the case of the employer who, discovering that one of his employees was receiving benefits from us, decided the man did not need his job and fired him. Many of these problems are less likely to occur or, if they did, would have little significance in a national program of negative taxation. However, they are endemic to experimentation in this area, and they do make the problem of obtaining experimental guidance for a national program more difficult.

Some of the difficulties associated with supporting only a proportion of the eligible population in a neighborhood relate to our ability to predict community effects that may emerge under an income-maintenance program. A range of neighborhood responses to the infusion of financial resources into poor areas is possible. Services that are currently lacking in these areas may improve; the quality of housing may be raised; or, alternatively, the exploitation of the poor may simply become more rewarding. Similarly, it is possible that with an increase of resources in poor neighborhoods, the ability to maintain self-interest organizations will improve, possibly resulting in a multiplier effect whereby poor neighborhoods translate some of their new income into political power.

However, many of these effects cannot be adequately studied because only a proportion of the eligible population in any neighborhood is supported by the experiment. Some of the possible neighborhood responses may require a minimum critical value of disposable income before they can occur. The aggregate amount of money provided to a neighborhood may be too low to allow us the opportunity to study community organization effects.

Another kind of problem deriving from support of only a proportion of the eligible population stems from pressures that have been exerted to place specific individuals under the support program. In a few instances organized political groups have viewed the experiment as a potential source of favors for important constituents. Pressure has been exerted to admit particular individuals into the experiment or onto the program staff. Fortunately we have been able to resolve these problems without affecting the integrity of the experiment. However, the potential for such interference will have to be considered in planning future experimental research on income maintenance.

Conclusion

Experimentation with income maintenance is important for two reasons: First, there is the significance of the specific policy decisions for which it attempts to provide guidance. How much will it cost? How should it be structured, and so on? Second, and perhaps of greater long-run importance, income-maintenance experiments are a first attempt to guide significant social policy decisions by experimentation. Their importance is highlighted by the generally unexpected failure to find any disincentive effects thus far in the Pennsylvania-New Jersey experiment. If they prove useful, the nature of social policy making in this country may undergo a radical change. But whatever the potential of experiments, we must recognize that they are enormously difficult to execute successfully. It is for this reason that we have noted here a number of the difficulties that have arisen in the course of the New Jersey-Pennsylvania experiment.

Of course we have not and cannot cover all the issues here. Some are being addressed elsewhere. Three projects covering other topics are currently underway, although they are at earlier stages of the experimental process. The first is a replication of the New Jersey-Pennsylvania experiment in a rural setting. The study is being conducted in Iowa and North Carolina under the direction of D. Lee Bawden of the University of Wisconsin's Poverty Institute. Although a major question is the response of rural residents to differential tax rates and guarantee levels, this study also will examine the residential mobility response to these same experimental variations. As a result, the sample is more nearly representative of the poor in its area and includes female-headed households and unrelated individuals. More importantly, however, provisions have been made to include persons who spin off from the experimental families and establish households of their own. At this point the experimental households have just been chosen and payments started.

Another important question currently under investigation is the extent to which work response to a negative tax system would interact with a manpower program. This study is being conducted in Seattle, Washington, in cooperation with the Model Cities program. At present it is still in the design stage, so it is not possible to describe the specific structure of the experiment. In the third experiment, located in Gary, Indiana, particular attention is being given to the impact of negative taxation on family stability and structure. In both Seattle and Gary the experimental samples will be representative of the cities' poor populations.

In closing, we would like to mention a critical issue that heretofore has received little attention: the ethical questions in social experimentation. One set of problems arises from the fact that we are intervening in major ways into the lives of human beings – even if it is ostensibly for their betterment. For example, do we have any responsibility for what happens to persons in the experiment after the payments have ended, when they know, or at least were repeatedly told, that the benefits will only be paid for a given time period? More specifically, if, for those eligible for welfare, there is a time gap between the end of our payments and the start of welfare, do we have a responsibility to assist them financially? What are our obligations if families develop patterns of life that cannot be sustained without the experimental payments?

A second set of issues stems from the need to minimize nonexperimental stimuli. For example, the press has been extremely interested in the details of the experiment. One part of this interest is a continual request to talk with experimental families in order to add "human interest" to their stories. But to meet these requests would be to make publicity yet another experimental stimulus. After some initial difficulties, we have been able to persuade them to report less personalized stories. But it is clear that the problem of the relationship between the needs of social experiments and institutions such as the press is a general one, and new standards must be worked out. The public does have a "right to know," but successful social experiments also require a limit to that right.

We raise these issues as warnings to future experimenters rather than as problems capable of universal solutions. We note only that we hope to report at a later time on our particular solutions.

References

Addiss, L. K. "Job-Related Expenses of the Working Mother." *Children*, November–December, 1963, pp. 219–23.

Green, C., *Negative Taxes and the Poverty Problem*. Washington, D.C.: The Brookings Institution, 1967.

Marmor, T. R. "Income Maintenance Alternatives: Concepts, Criteria, and Program Comparisons." University of Wisconsin, Institute for Research on Poverty, Discussion Paper No. 55, 1969.

Orshansky, M. "The Shape of Poverty in 1966." *Social Security Bulletin*, March 1968, pp. 3–31.

President's Commission on Income-Maintenance Programs, *Poverty Amid Plenty: The American Paradox*. November 1969.

Tobin, J. "Raising the Incomes of the Poor." In *Agenda for the Nation*, edited by K. Gordon, pp. 77–116. Garden City, N.Y.: Doubleday & Co., 1968.

Watts, H. W. Testimony before the Committee on Ways and Means, House of Representatives, U.S. Congress, on H.R. 14173, "Family Assistance Plan." 1969.

Weisbrod, B. A. "Collective Action and the Distribution of Income: A Conceptual Approach." University of Wisconsin, Department of Economics, 1969.

Weisbrod, B. A. and Hansen, W. L. "An Income-Net Worth Approach to Measuring Economic Welfare." University of Wisconsin, Department of Economics, 1967.

4   Tax Transfers and Educational Policy

In the long run the key to the reform of the ghetto economy and, more specifically, to participation in the labor force of the urban poor is education. By changing attitudes toward work and by providing the verbal and other skills required for functioning in an industrial, urbanized economy, education becomes the major element that may break the established patterns of poverty.

The role of taxes and transfers in implementing the objectives of educational policy is thus of major importance. In the present institutional setting, public schools depend on local as well as on state and federal sources of finance to meet the increased demand for high quality education. The papers in this part report on the role of state grants in helping to increase the financial resources of metropolitan schools. They point out that the tax base is being shared by local governments and that one level's decision to increase taxes to raise educational finances is not independent of other levels' efforts. Furthermore, the flow of state and local taxes among states and between levels of government leads to *implicit* grants and taxes, as any one state may shift the burden of providing education to other states or to the federal government. Finally, federal funding to help hard-pressed school districts is not a straightforward problem of allocation: It generally entails resource mobilization or "strategic" behavior on the part of the recipients; and the federal government exercises imperfect de facto control as it operates under imperfect information.

Byron Brown discusses the effect of state grants on the equality of opportunity in education. He notes that both the federal government and several states administer grants-in-aid programs that have as one objective the encouragement of equality of opportunity in elementary and secondary education. Although it is obvious that these grant plans have not nearly achieved perfect equality, either in expenditures or in educational quality, the question remains whether they are at least a move in the right direction. Brown analyzes the causes of inequality of opportunity in education and determines the effects on equality of opportunity of a widely used plan of state aid to local school districts. In addition, the unique educational problems that confront many large cities motivate him to use a model to explore the effects of this aid plan for urban school districts.

He contends that the quality of education in a school district is the relevant basis of comparison to determine equality of opportunity. On the basis of his model he shows that attempts to lessen differences in educational quality between districts through changes in the policy parameters at the disposal of the state government are likely to be unsuccessful and indeed may work to widen existing differentials. There are two related reasons for the failure of grants to achieve the goal of narrowing quality differences: (1) The aid plan virtually ignores variations in the variable it is supposed to influence – namely, quality. (2) If we want to influence the level of quality, we should gear grants to differences in the factors that determine quality. But of the multitude of factors we could identify, including prices, tastes, and the conditions of production, the grant plan focuses on only two – resources and the number of students. Obviously, variations in the factors that are ignored could subvert any efforts at control of quality through these two factors. Examples emphasize these points. The author notes that large city school systems have several unique features: low quality persists in parts of many urban school systems; resources, particularly as measured by property values, differ from surrounding suburban areas, as do the number of students per district. He concludes with a discussion of how these factors operate within the context of the aid plan to work for or against equality of opportunity in urban school systems.

Thomas Muller estimates the impact on income redistribution of state grants to public schools in Delaware. He notes that resistance to the use of the local property tax to meet accelerating education costs has increased sharply in recent years. Therefore, a number of proposals have been submitted to increase grants to local school districts by state governments. These additional grants are designed to reduce the burden of lower-income residents and thus presumably will result in income redistribution. He examines the spatial redistribution among local districts caused by the education grant structure and evaluates the impact on income redistribution of proposed legislation.

In Delaware the tax structure is characterized by a progressive personal income tax, a sizable corporate tax shifted to residents of other states, and the absence of any sales tax. As the result of the progressive tax structure and the concentration of wealth, one small area of the state, which contains about 53 percent of the population, contributes about 90 percent of the funds for state primary and secondary education. The result is a redistribution of income from the more affluent to poorer school districts amounting to over $100 per capita. However, a proposal to further reduce the local tax burden by a matching state-local contribution formula based on the size of the property base would provide more relief to affluent districts than to the lower-income districts designated as beneficiaries of this aid. Part of this phenomenon is attributed to the lack of positive correlation between income and property value in Delaware. The new proposal can thus result in an increased local tax bundle.

The author concludes that "substantial income redistribution" takes place at the intrastate level as a result of state grants for primary and secondary education distributed on a flat-grant, "nonequalizing basis." Equalizing for income or property value in Delaware would not result in significant shifts between urban and rural areas. The examination of alternative criteria for distribution of state grants indicated that the income redistribution impact of alternative need measures vary considerably by location. The application of fiscal need measures by the state, in fact, results in a net outflow of income from the city. Apparently, the concentration of poverty among nonwhite, large-city residents requires additional educational resources not reflected in per capita income or per pupil property value statistics. Use of educational criteria would result in income redistribution from suburban districts to central cities and, to a lesser degree, to rural districts.

Charles Waldauer's paper is an empirical analysis of the external effects of grants-in-aid to schools in the Syracuse SMSA on the taxes and expenditures of the villages and towns with which these schools share tax bases. The hypotheses tested are that: (1) local governments are fiscally interdependent through the nexus of shared tax bases; and (2) the fiscal impacts of aid are transmitted from aided to neighboring governments via changes in the fiscal pressures on these shared bases. The study is undertaken with the hope that some insight into the external effects of aid can be gained and that knowledge of local fiscal behavior can be extended.

Previous empirical studies of the tax and expenditure effects of aid on local governments examined only the responses of the *aided* governments; no attempt was made to investigate the spatial interrelationships embodied in the responses of other governments with which the aided governments share tax bases. By overlooking the external effects, these analyses provide a limited picture of the impacts of aid, and they reflect a partial equilibrium approach to what is essentially a general equilibrium analysis. The stepwise approach to ordinary least-squares regression analysis on a cross-sectional basis is the statistical method used by Waldauer. The effects of both the levels of aid for a single fiscal year and the incremental changes in the levels of aid from one year to the next are examined.

The major findings are: (1) local governments sharing the same tax bases are sensitive to each other's fiscal decisions; and (2) the tax and expenditure effects of aid are transmitted to unaided governments through changes in the fiscal pressures on the shared tax bases, as long as the changes are significant and the fiscal operations of the aided governments are not so great as to completely dominate the unaided governments. The implications of this study are twofold: (1) the fiscal interdependence among local governments must be taken into account before making any normative judgments about proposed or existing aid programs; and (2) all grants to local governments should be considered in their full spatial context, avoiding a piecemeal approach to developing and administering aid programs.

Donald Phares analyzes one facet of the grants economy that deserves greater attention: the impact that geographical tax flows exert on the fiscal structure of the state-local systems. State boundaries, although they are quite effective in defining legal, budgetary, institutional, and functional arrangements, do not serve as barriers to the flow of state-local taxes among states and between levels of government. The openness of the economy prevents taxes levied in any one state from necessarily remaining within that state. Likewise, the features of federal tax law permit tax burdens to flow between levels of government (state-local to federal, for example). Both of these spatial tax flows represent an implicit form of grant among states or between levels of government. To the extent that any given state can shift some of the burden of providing public goods to other states or to the federal government, its position has improved. This is, of course, simultaneously true of all fifty states.

Phares makes explicit the grant character of spatial tax flows by showing "the impact that [these] flows ... exert on the tax structure of each state-local system." His "approach is to investigate the impact of state-local taxes at their final geographical resting place, not just taxes levied within a particular state – that is, geographical incidence rather than geographical impact." He estimates that "the range in percent of total taxes exported is from a high of 49.0 percent in Nevada ... to a low of 15.8 percent in New Hampshire. ... The estimated $8.3 billion in exported state-local taxes represents a geographical shifting of the burden of taxation to residents of other systems. ... The net effect is a partial rearrangement of the support of public goods for any particular state and for all states."

He observes that of the $8.3 billion in exported taxes, $3.046 billion is borne by the federal revenue structure through the deductibility provisions of the federal tax law, and $5.25 billion remains "a burden on residents of the state-local systems in the form of various state-local taxes imported into the state." He allocates the latter to states on the basis of their proportion of total national consumption expenditures. Thereafter he estimates the impact of spatial tax flows on state-local tax incidence by means of a regression model that relates income and tax burden. Based on these estimates he notes that "(1) the local sector exerts a regressive influence in every state-local system; and (2) spatial tax flows also exert a regressive influence on state-local incidence. The combined effect of these two forces raises some interesting questions pertaining to the continued financing of education by the local sector and proposals for shifting the financial responsibility for education upward in the government hierarchy. ... When one contrasts the responsibility for providing public education with the resources available to meet this responsibility, there emerges a rather perverse pattern. The level of government with the most responsive revenue source – the federal government – has assumed a small portion of the financial burden. The level of government with the least responsive revenue source – local government – has assumed the major burden. ... The spill-over effects of the provision of education suggest that local fiscal responsibility is highly inappropriate. ... If education is also accepted as at least partially redistributive in nature, local financing becomes even more untenable. The federal government is the only level of government that can possibly internalize the benefits from any form of redistribution. ... The current fiscal responsibility for education seems to run counter to many ideas of economic common sense."

David Porter and David Warner examine the operation of federal aid to education with regard to economic and organizational factors. They note that as federal aid programs have rapidly expanded, congressmen and federal executives have confidently "justified" increases by pointing to the presumed impact on the programs aided. But to what extent do these funds reach the specifically intended programs? Are there "legal diversions" that conventional control procedures do not reveal? And to what extent do discretionary grants distort the allocation of resources by the grantee, who is often more involved in mobilizing outside resources than he is in allocating his own resources effectively?

A key but often unwritten premise of much of the current literature on budgeting and federal aid is that money from federal aid programs flows through the channels prescribed by congressional and executive allocators. This premise assumes that the grantees passively receive the resources allocated to them and maximize their output within the federal regulations. Or alternatively, the premise posits "perfect control" based on "perfect information" by the federal allocators. Challenging these assumptions, Porter and Warner clarify economic and organizational factors that may result in *imperfect control* of the flow of resources resulting from official allocations of federal aid and *imperfect information* about the impact of this aid.

A framework for identifying and analyzing the salient economic and organizational factors leading to imperfect control and information is developed in a theory of resource mobilization. The basic premise of this theory is that people actively seek resources; they do not, as is implicit in many theories of "resource allocation," wait passively for resources to be handed to them for use as instructed. At every level of organization decision making seems to be at least as oriented toward mobilizing resources as it is toward allocating these resources. Even the so-called grantor is often as concerned with mobilizing additional resources to grant in the next round as he is in allocating his grants efficiently in this round.

Some of the conclusions are: For much of the United States categorical aid to education is the only aid that will not be "mobilized" by teachers' unions in pay increases; federal aid is the only source of compensatory and remedial programs in most school districts; aid for experimental programs often operates to compensate suburban districts that do not receive aid for poor children; the timing and administration of federal aid to education at both the state and federal levels vitiates much of its potential effectiveness; and many school administrators feel that they are judged in good part on their ability to mobilize outside money.

Part 4 provides some insight into the complexities of the structure of the public grants economy in meeting educational needs. Although many problems remain, some reorganization of this structure appears to promise improvements in this vital determinant of the human ecology of urban life. The next part is addressed to yet another basic qualitative aspect of urban existence – the physical ecology of life, which is threatened by pollution and environmental deterioration.

9

Byron W. Brown: State Grants
and Inequality of Opportunity
in Education

The inequality of opportunity that exists in public schools represents one of the basic failures of our social system. The relative educational deprivation of the poor and of blacks and other minority groups and the subsequent effects on the class structure and distribution of income are documented by J. S. Coleman [6], T. W. Schultz [13], G. S. Becker [1], B. A. Weisbrod [15], and others.

One purpose of giving state aid to local school districts is to promote equality of opportunity. I question to what extent these aid plans can be expected to promote equality of opportunity and answer that they cannot be expected to do much in achieving equality. To arrive at the answer in a rigorous and systematic way, I treat in the following pages: (1) the general question of local school district behavior, and how a district reacts to outside attempts to influence its educational choices; (2) the question of defining equality of opportunity in education in terms of the behavioral characteristics of school systems; and (3) the question of the means by which current aid plans try to influence district behavior and thereby fail in promoting equality of opportunity.

In the next two sections I take up the first question by proposing a model to explain school district choices of educational outcomes. Then I briefly discuss some of the reasons for state aid and the details of the particular aid plan I analyze using the model. After attempting to establish a meaningful notion of increasing equality of opportunity, an investigation of the full model of district behavior yields the conclusion that the aid plan is not in general equalizing. I present evidence to support these conclusions as a practical and as a theoretical reality. The last section contains some comments on what form improvements in the present system might take.

School District Educational Objectives

In this section I outline a model to explain the nature of the choices involved in a school district's decision about the kind of public education

Printed by permission of the author. All rights reserved. Mr. Brown is a member of the department of economics, Michigan State University.

The author is indebted to David Cohen, director of the Center for Educational Policy Research, Harvard University, and C. Waldauer for helpful comments. Responsibility for the heresies in the paper is my own.

system it desires. The school district is chosen as the unit of analysis not only because almost all earlier research follows this pattern but also because it is the relevant legal unit for state aid decisions. One result of this abstraction from the family as the decision unit is to submerge many of the important differences that exist within real-world districts. Consideration of the district as a homogeneous unit also obscures the political processes by which collective decisions are achieved. The less homogeneous a district is in its socioeconomic characteristics, the greater becomes the danger that I neglect in my abstraction some truly important facets of the educational problem. With these caveats, I believe enough of the baby remains without the bathwater so that the model I propose provides some valuable new insights.

Assume that each school district has a utility or social-choice function that reflects the value to the district (U) of the consumption of education (E) on the one hand and the composite of all other goods and services (G) on the other.

$$U = F(E, G) \tag{1}$$

This function is assumed to have all the properties economists usually attribute to individual utility functions, including convex indifference curves and the possibility that the form of the function may vary from one district to another.

The other goods and services are assumed to be a composite commodity, because the only substitution possibility I consider is with education itself. Districts will try to maximize their collective satisfactions by choosing values of G and E, subject to a set of constraints on behavior that will be specified in the next section.

With these preliminary details out of the way, an important question still remains in determining the meaning of the education output variable, E. The families in a school district desire education presumably because it will inculcate in their children certain characteristics that will help assure their "success" in adult life and that will contribute in substantial measure to their children's future "happiness."

What characteristics make up the educational output? Some are certainly cognitive skills that could be measured by achievement tests. Others might be characterized as affective traits, reflecting complex psychological characteristics that are either instilled or developed within the school system. Examples would be the ability to concentrate on given tasks for extended periods or the acceptance of desirable attitudes and responses to established authority. Finally, we might expect the school system output to include cultural factors such as national pride and identity, devotion to national institutions thought to be desirable, and class characteristics.

Whatever the meaning of output, two things remain abundantly clear. First, E is a vector of characteristics, in which the number of elements is large, and many, if not most, are not easily measured. Second, it is not realistic to suppose that school district administrators sit down and in some rational fashion decide on the value they would like for each component of output. If realism were the goal, we might better choose as a measure of output the percent of high school seniors who go to college, because that is what many districts seem most concerned with. The difficulty is fundamental. Districts do indeed choose an "educational output." Moreover, it is the result of a choice between that and some other ways of consuming resources. I am sure that districts even make their decisions in the maximizing context implied above, recognizing the implications of choice. But the razor only cuts so fine, and we must be aware of the complex statement we are making when we say that "the quality of education is greater in one district than another."

Economists have generally found intractable this kind of capital specification problem. My goal is not to try to make a contribution to the pure theory of capital, however, so I must settle for some simplifying assumptions once more. The most important assumption for this paper is that Q, the quality of education, is a scalar quantity. This amounts to saying that the various educational output components can be aggregated into an index.

The above discussion relates to the quality of education. The output of education in a school district has an additional component, however – the "through-put" of students. Of two districts with identical output quality vectors, the one that educates the larger number of students has a larger output (see [4]). We might then write the total quantity of education as the product $S \times Q$, where Q is the assumed scalar measure of educational quality and S is the number of students.

Constraints on District Behavior

One of the advantages of choosing the school district as the unit of analysis is that it clarifies a unique aspect of the problem of educational choice: each school district is both the producer and the consumer of the educational output. Therefore, in attempting to maximize satisfactions through choice of education versus other goods and services, the district is subject to two constraints, the traditional income or resource constraint of value theory on the one hand and the production function for education on the other.

The resource constraint is simply:

$$X + V = p_G G + p_T T, \qquad (2)$$

where X is the amount of district resources after taxes, V is the amount of the educational subsidy the district receives from the state, T is the composite commodity of inputs needed in the production of education in schools, and p_G and p_T are the prices of G and T, respectively. The prices are assumed to be exogenous for district decisions. T is a composite commodity, made up, in fact, of various teacher services and other raw material inputs, because input substitution possibilities are not of direct concern here.

My definition of V corresponds to the foundation plans used in most states to redistribute educational resources. Charles Benson [2], and J. E. Coons, W. E. Clune, and S. D. Sugarman [8] discuss the nature and history of the plan. Thomas Johns [10] gives the details of all state aid plans for the school year 1968–69. Although details vary widely among states, the basic formula for the foundation plan is

$$V = k_1 S - k_2 X, \tag{3}$$

where k_1 is the basic subsidy granted to each district for each student, k_2 is the amount by which a district's subsidy is reduced for each dollar of resources it possesses, and S and X are defined above. Stated another way, the subsidy per student received by a district (V/S) is an amount k_1, adjusted for the district's resources per student (X/S).

Certain features of the foundation plan as I have presented it are worthy of special note. First, in (3) X is the total resources of the district, whereas in practice it is usually the equalized property tax base.[1] My version is probably closer to the intent of the plan, in that districts with greater "ability" should receive a lower subsidy per student.

Second, equation (3) is only a prototype of plans actually used in several states. Politically and economically motivated variations make some plans quite complicated, as in Michigan, where both k_1 and k_2 are functions of X, or in other states, which set k_2 equal to zero. The prototype contains the essential elements of almost all state plans, however.

Finally, I emphasize that in what follows attention is paid only to the effects of distributing funds under the foundation plan. The means of collection and the distribution of the tax burden are abstracted. Certainly the total effect of any state plan for aid to education depends on the distribution of the tax burden as well as on the revenue benefits. The reason I separate the two issues for analytical purposes is that the revenue decisions of state legislatures are often separate from the equalization provisions inherent in any one aspect of state expenditures.

---

1. It is well known [9] that wealth (or assets) and income are not perfectly correlated with each other, so the distinction between these two resource measures must be carefully maintained for statistical purposes. The differences are not important for our purposes, however.

For the second constraint on district behavior I write the production function for education as

$$E = f(S^*, T), \tag{4}$$

where S^* is the number of students who pass through the educational system, weighted for the educational characteristics they have already acquired outside the school system. This adjustment in the "student input" is necessary if the production function is to reflect only the contribution of the school system, through application of the inputs, T, and their interaction with S^*, to the final educational output. In a comparison of two school districts, one with a high value of S^* will, for given amounts of other inputs, have a higher output, E, in terms of final characteristics. The higher value of S^* is a reflection of the fact that the students received more education outside the school system, with the result that they represent a more "enriched" input from the point of view of achieving any final output.[2] I assume that S^* is an exogenous variable for school district decisions, at least in the short run, and furthermore that it is a costless input in the sense of not requiring out-of-pocket expenditures.

All the warnings expressed in the previous section about the nature of output apply here. Although some work has been done in developing educational production functions with multidimensional outputs (see [11]), we again seek refuge in the assumption that a meaningful index of output is possible. I will return to this assumption once again in the discussion of proposals for reform of state aid plans.

The Notion of Equality of Opportunity

I now take a slight detour from the presentation of the model and turn to consideration of the general notion of equality of opportunity. It is essential to formulate a clear definition of equality of opportunity in education in the context of the model, so that the effects of state aid in this regard can be understood. I define an increase in equality of opportunity as follows: *a state aid plan increases equality of opportunity if it decreases the differences in educational quality,* Q, *among school districts.*

---

2. There is more than one way to handle this problem. An alternative would be to define Q in terms of the *change* in characteristics due to formal education, with the number of students (unadjusted) appearing as both an input and an output. The initial characteristics of students entering the school system do not then appear explicitly in the problem – only as the component of a difference. I chose the method in the paper because it makes quite explicit that the initial student characteristics are *inputs* into the school system, as well as more generally recognized factors as teachers, chalk, and books.

To understand the rationale for this definition, which is formulated in terms of the output of the educational system, I offer two related reasons for state intervention: the protection of children and the breaking down of rigidities in the socioeconomic class structure. The protection of children is the rightful role of the state. This paternalism extends not only to protection from physical harm and abuse, even from parents, but also to the parents' failure, for any number of reasons, to provide enough of some essential commodity for the child. State aid to local school districts seeks to protect the child and thereby to promote equality of opportunity through the provision of education, even if his parents are too poor to purchase education or are simply disinclined to do so.

The argument runs much deeper, however, for we must ask why education is so critical a commodity in this regard. Obviously the state is content to let children (and everyone else) consume widely varying amounts of most other goods. The answer lies in the alleged link between education and economic or social mobility or both. Education permits an individual the opportunity for greater economic advancement, and at the same time it breaks down rigidities in the social class structure.[3] Education is the means by which individuals can accumulate in themselves "human capital." Equality of opportunity, it would seem then, must relate to the output of education, insofar as that variable is a critical one in influencing the socioeconomic class structure. Indeed, to determine whether the state aid promotes or retards equal opportunity, it is then sufficient to look at differences in the educational output variable.

Certainly equality of opportunity in this sense cannot mean giving each child the same amount of "human capital," even if that were possible. But equality can reasonably mean the absence of large, sustained geographical, racial, or socioeconomic differences in education. Using the school district as the unit of analysis provides a convenient scale for judging the effects of state aid on equality of opportunity.

The definition used here is necessarily inadequate, however. The notion of equality of opportunity is a total societal concept that describes the bases for interclass mobility with respect to the entire range of the existing public and private social structure and institutions. The term "equality of *educational* opportunity" can be understood in this context as reflecting the role of only one set of institutions in advancing total equality. Two important implications of viewing educational equality of opportunity as a part of a larger concept are first, that absolute equality of opportunity in education cannot be defined in a vacuum apart from the operation of other institutions, and second, that the general problem of equality of opportunity cannot be solved by the educational system alone.

---

3. That education really has these benefits may be seriously questioned. That the benefits of education in achieving these social objectives have been seriously overestimated is certain.

With respect to the definition of equality of educational opportunity used in this paper, educational output, Q, can and must still be the indicator. But some care should be exercised when it comes to equating equal outputs with equal opportunity, as this may not be strictly correct from the total societal standpoint. Recall that my definition classifies an aid plan as equalizing if it diminishes differences in output. As will soon become apparent, however, this difficulty will interfere in no way with the conclusions of the analysis.

Solution of the Model

In this section I bring together the threads of the model and give an answer to the question of how school districts decide on an amount of education to produce and consume. The principal elements of the model are: (a) each school district's utility or social-choice function, (b) the production function for education, and (c) the resource constraint, taking into consideration subsidies available under the foundation plan. Each district tries to maximize its collective satisfactions subject to the two constraints, or

$$\text{Maximize } U = F(E, G),$$

$$\text{subject to } E = f(S^*, T),$$

$$X(1 - k_2) + k_1 S = p_G G + p_T T,$$

where $k_1 S - k_2 X$ has been substituted for V. The variables S, S^*, p_G, and p_T are assumed to be exogenous. I put off for a moment the condition that $E = Q \times S$.

Form the Lagrangian expression

$$L = F(G, E) - m_1 [E - f(S^*, T)] \tag{5}$$
$$- m_2 [X(1 - k_2) + k_1 S - p_T T - p_G G],$$

where m_1 and m_2 are Lagrangian multipliers. Using subscripts to denote partial derivative of the functions, the first order conditions for maximization of U are the two constraints and $F_E \times f_T/p_T = F_G/p_G$. This has the usual interpretation that the additional satisfaction per dollar spent on educational inputs should equal the additional satisfaction per dollar spent on all other goods and services. If a school district is to succeed in maximizing satisfactions, it must allocate its resources accordingly between the two commodities.

Assuming that all functions are twice differentiable, the sufficient conditions for a maximum require that the determinant of the bordered Hessian matrix

$$
\begin{bmatrix}
0 & 0 & p_T & p_G & 0 \\
0 & 0 & f_T & 0 & -1 \\
p_T & f_T & m_1 f_{TT} & 0 & 0 \\
p_G & 0 & 0 & F_{GG} & F_{GE} \\
0 & -1 & 0 & F_{EG} & F_{EE}
\end{bmatrix}
$$

be negative and its first principal minor be positive. This is assured if

$$
F_E, F_G, F_{EG}, (F_{GG}F_{EE} - F_{GE}^2) > 0; \; F_{GG}, F_{EE} < 0,
$$

and $f_{S*}, f_T, f_{S*T} > 0; f_{TT} < 0,$

which are the restrictions usually imposed on utility and production functions.

The first order conditions enable us to write the school district demand functions for E and T.[4]

$$
\begin{aligned}
E &= e[X(1 - k_2) + k_1 S, \, S^*, \, p_G, \, p_T] \\
T &= t[X(1 - k_2) + k_1 S, \, S^*, \, p_G, \, p_T]
\end{aligned}
\tag{6}
$$

Each school district demands values of the dependent variables according to the amount of its resources (including subsidies), the (weighted) number of students to be educated, and the two price variables. Insofar as the utility and production functions vary among school districts, the functional forms of the demand curves will also vary among districts. Under the assumption that $E = QS$, the district's demand for quality is simply $e(.)/S = q(.)$. This analysis identifies the dependent (endogenous) variables in the problem, and in addition clarifies to a great extent the most important independent (exogenous) variables.

It is a simple though tedious matter to find the signs of the partial derivatives of (6). Assuming the second order conditions for a maximum are satisfied, and letting $y = X(1 - k_2) + k_1 S$, the signs are

$$
e_y, t_y, e_{S*} > 0;
$$

$$
e_{p_T}, t_{p_T} < 0; \text{ while}
$$

$$
e_{p_G}, t_{p_G}, t_S{}^* \text{ have indeterminate sign.}
$$

---

4. There is also, of course, a demand function for G, but it is not of direct interest here.

I reserve for the next section examination of the effects of changing k_1 and k_2. Note that an increase in a district's total resources, $X(1 - k_2) + k_1 S$, always increases the demand for education, whereas an increase in price of inputs will work in the opposite direction. A final point is that nothing can be said a priori about the effects of increasing the (weighted) number of students, S^*, on the optimal level of resource use in producing education. S^* measures outside-of-school cultural and educational preparation of students, and this result means that better prepared pupils might have either more or less inputs devoted to them. The crucial factor is what happens to the "effectiveness" of teachers and schools as the outside-of-school factors change.

The Effects of State Aid

In this section I explore the effects on educational quality (characteristics) of a state changing its aid to local districts under the foundation plan. Because state legislatures write policy for state aid through their choice of values for k_1 and k_2, I examine the differential effects on quality in two school districts, i and j, of varying these parameters.

The attempt to investigate the effects of aid on quality is a different approach to analysis of state aid. Other works on this subject, for example, Benson [2] and Coons, Clune, and Sugarman [8], all concentrate on the effects of aid on educational expenditures. Although their approach may be interesting for some purposes, it is a misleading one for gaining insights into equality of educational opportunity as I have defined it.

After division by S the districts' demand functions for quality may be written

$$Q_i = q_i[X_i(1 - k_2) + k_1 S_i, S_i, S^*{}_i, p_{T_i}, p_{G_i}], \qquad (7)$$

and similarly for district j. The effects of aid on equality of opportunity measured by $Q_i - Q_j$ can be seen in three special cases:

(a) *Variations in* k$_1$, *all else constant.* An increase in k_1 will increase the total resources of both districts, and because education is not an inferior good, quality will increase in both districts. But clearly the *differential effect* depends on the other factors determining quality and each district's elasticity of demand with respect to the resource change. In figure 1 district i always increases quality more than district j for a given increase in k_1. The solid lines show increases in k_1 at first equalizing, then unequalizing. The dotted line illustrates the possibility of increasing k_1 always being unequalizing. This possibility exists because of the other factors (relative input prices, variations in S^*, etc.) that enter into the determination of output.

(b) *Variations in* k$_2$, *all else constant.* The same analysis holds for changes in k_2, the allegedly equalizing feature of the foundation plan. Increases in k_2

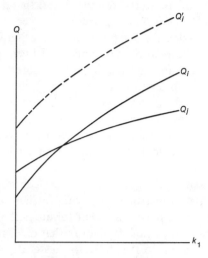

Figure 1. The Effects on Educational Quality of Changing k_1

Q_i' differs from Q_i because of the effects of the other factors influencing Q. Increases in k_1 may be equalizing, as with Q_i and Q_j, or always unequalizing, as with Q_i' and Q_j.

will decrease resources and therefore quality in both districts. But even though there is a larger reduction in resources in the richer district, absolutely nothing can be said about relative effects of the change for the same reasons outlined under case (a).

(c) *Variations in* k_2, *given the total subsidy to all districts together.* This is the most interesting case because it clearly illustrates the redistributive possibilities inherent in the foundation plan for a fixed quantity of aid to be spread among all districts. Let total subsidies to the two districts be

$$V = k_1(S_i + S_j) - k_2(X_i + X_j).$$

When V is constant ($dV = 0$) we can write k_1 as a function of k_2,

$$k_1 = \frac{V + k_2(X_i + X_j)}{S_i + S_j}.$$

It follows that

$$Q_i = q_i\left[X_i + V\frac{S_i}{S_i + S_j} + k_2\left(\frac{X_i + X_j}{S_i + S_j}S_i - X_i\right), S_i, S^*{}_i, p_{T_i}, p_{G_i}\right],$$

and similarly for Q_j.

The term $[S_i(X_i + X_j)/(S_i + S_j)] - X_i$ will be positive or negative as district i is either below or above average in resources per student. Increases in k_2 (given $dV = 0$) will increase the resources and therefore the quality of education in districts with below-average resources per student. This in no way guarantees that the redistributive policy of increasing k_2 will be equalizing. Figure 2 illustrates the possibilities. The solid lines, Q_i and Q_j, show increases in k_2 having an equalizing effect. Q_j is the poorer, with less resources per student. But if quality in district j is given by Q'_j, increases in k_2 serve only to make quality more disparate. Sufficiently large variations in the other factors determining quality could bring this about. For example, the poorer district may have relatively lower teachers' salaries or very high tastes for education, permitting the residents to demand a higher level of educational quality.

In all the cases presented above it is perfectly clear why aid plans of the foundation type are hopeless instruments through which to achieve equality of opportunity. The apparent reason for their failure is that the plans ignore the effects of many, indeed most, of the factors that determine the quality of education. Where the solution to the difficulty lies is the subject of the last section of this paper. But first I turn to some empirical observations that emphasize the practical importance of the problem and that suggest the seriousness of the theoretical possibilities already discussed.

Some Evidence

In this section I present evidence that lends support to the rather gloomy hypothesis put forth – that is, that there is reason to suspect present aid plans

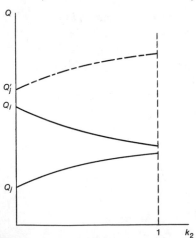

Figure 2. The Effects on Educational Quality of Changing k_2, Total Aid to Both Districts Held Constant

District j is the poorer in resources per student. Q'_j and Q_i differ because of the effects of the other factors influencing Q. Increases in k_2 may be equalizing, as with Q_j and Q_i, or unequalizing, as with Q'_j and Q_i.

of the inability to promote equality of opportunity. The argument rests on the observation that a multitude of factors enters into the determination of educational quality, and only a few of these are ever taken account of in the distribution of state aid. If I can show that the determining factors do in fact vary widely among school districts, then our worst fears can certainly become a reality. The variability of these factors is almost too obvious to require further comment, and my impression is one of stalking a fly with an elephant rifle. Yet the facts must be stated.

Present Differentials in Educational Quality

The work of James S. Coleman [6] and the report of the U.S. Civil Rights Commission [12] have effectively destroyed any vain hopes that equality of opportunity exists in our schools today. Equality of opportunity remains out of our grasp, if not beyond our reach. It is, furthermore, the cities, with their high concentrations of minority groups and low levels of socioeconomic status, that are at the lowest end of the quality distribution.

Variations in Resources (Wealth)

The measure of resources in the determination of state aid is almost always assessed value of property. The foundation plan *does* seem to account for differences in the ability to finance education, but the choice of the particular measure of property valuation yields some noteworthy perversions. These often arise because cities are "rich" when measured by assessed valuation and "poor" by other standards. Therefore, a program to penalize the "rich" in terms of property is largely a way to give less to the central city and more to the suburbs. M. Spitzer, M. C. Burstein, and J. T. Hudman [14, p. 9] write:

> In this connection, the operation of the New York State aid plan is illustrative. . . . The award [to a district] is "equalized" by a formula involving assessed valuation of property per pupil . . . . The overall effect of these formulas is an allocation to Buffalo of 27.7 per cent below and to New York of 24.4 per cent below what each city would have received if the aid were to be distributed on a per student basis.

Variations in Teachers' Salaries

Few aid plans take into account regional variations in the costs of providing equivalent service. Salaries are of course the largest part of all expenditures for education. If a plan fails to take into account wide variations in salaries, it discriminates against areas where higher levels prevail. Table 1 presents data on thirteen large cities for which salary data are available, along with the state average in each case. In every city except Baltimore teacher costs are higher than the average for the state. In one instance, Philadelphia, average instructional staff salaries were $3,000 greater than for the state on the averages. If we consider average classroom teachers' salaries within a state, the presence of substantial variations is apparent. Table 2 presents salaries for large school systems in Michigan for 1966–67. The range in the average salary of the systems shown, all with enrollments of over 12,000, is in excess of $1,200 per year. Of the systems shown in table 2, Detroit, the largest system, has the second highest average salary – some evidence, perhaps, of the high cost of education in large cities.

Variations in Student Input

One of the noteworthy conclusions of the Coleman Report [6] was the fact that average class and socioeconomic status in schools has an important influence on school outcomes. In the language of this paper the characteristics of the student input, S^*, are a critical part of the educational quality of a school. The fact of segregation by race and socioeconomic group, particularly

Table 1. Average Annual Salary of Instructional Staff
in 13 Cities and States, 1969–70

City/ State	Salary	City/ State	Salary
(1) Baltimore	$ 9,346	(8) Milwaukee	$ 9,700
Maryland	9,885	Wisconsin	9,150
(2) Boston	9,500	(9) New Orleans	7,950
Massachusetts	9,175	Louisiana	7,220
(3) Chicago	11,990	(10) New York City	10,300
Illinois	9,950	New York	10,200
(4) Cleveland	9,410	(11) Philadelphia	12,000
Ohio	8,594	Pennsylvania	9,000
(5) Dallas	9,400	(12) St. Louis	10,171
Texas	7,503	Missouri	8,091
(6) Houston	7,954	(13) San Francisco	11,100
Texas	7,503	California	9,980
(7) Los Angeles	10,600		
California	9,980		

Source: B. H. Barr and B. J. Foster, *Statistics of Public Elementary and Secondary Schools, Fall 1969*, U.S. Office of Education, National Center for Educational Statistics.

Table 2. Average Salaries of Classroom Teachers
in Large Michigan School Systems, 1966–67

City	Salary	City	Salary
Detroit	$8,580	Wayne	$7,621
Flint	7,755	Birmingham	8,222
Grand Rapids	6,720	Waterford Twp.	7,539
Lansing	7,647	Bay City	7,790
Pontiac	8,309	Farmington	7,286
Saginaw	7,831	Port Huron	7,176
Warren	7,251	Jackson	8,394
Dearborn	9,687	Garden City	7,421
Royal Oak	7,740	East Detroit	8,087
Kalamazoo	7,566		

Source: *23rd Biennial Survey of Public-School Professional Personnel, 1966–67: Data for Systems with Enrollments of 12,000 or More,* National Education Association, Research Division, Research Report 1967-R12.

Note: The school systems are ranked in descending order of enrollment, October 1966.

evident in cities, creates great variability in the amount of "student input" for a given number of students. I judge this to be the single most important deterrent to achieving equality of opportunity under a foundation plan or any other aid plan linked to costs or expenditures.

Variations in Other Factors

There remains an entire group of related factors that influence the amount of education a district may choose. Some of these might fit under one of the above categories. A report on the California school system [3] lists the following factors as unique to urban schools:

In school districts that serve urban areas a larger proportion of the pupil population than in other districts is enrolled in vocational and technical classes, and this adds to the cost of the educational program.

School districts that serve urban areas have more than the normal demand for special education services for handicapped pupils. . . .

The majority of the foreign born immigrants that come to California settle in urban areas, and the school districts that serve those areas must, therefore, establish and maintain many classes to teach English, elementary subjects, and citizenship to non-English-speaking pupils. [A point closely related to the quality of student input.]

In school districts that serve urban areas vandalism is high, and security officers are required and employed to protect the property of the districts.

A foundation plan would take no account of such variations among districts. Problems of the handicapped often elicit special support from states, but most of the other problems listed are usually ignored.

A related urban problem is that of "municipal overburden," which is discussed by Benson [6] and Coons, Clune, and Sugarman [8]. The basic idea is that cities require such a large amount of other "essential" public services that the ability to finance a satisfactory educational program is impaired. The importance of this financial pinch is undeniable for some cities.

In this section I have tried to show by giving empirical evidence and the views of experts in educational finance that the factors cited earlier as important in the determination of educational quality do indeed vary from school district to district. The evidence is overwhelming that such variation is widespread.

Conclusion and the Question of Reform

The general conclusion stated previously remains valid: increasing aid under the foundation plan (or any cost or expenditure based plan, for that matter) is not an effective means of increasing equality of opportunity. This conclusion follows directly from the recognition of factors other than costs or wealth that enter into the determination of educational quality. Much of the analysis I presented was directed to demonstrating the importance of these other factors. Because they are not, and almost certainly cannot be, compensated for, equality of opportunity is an impossible goal under the present scheme of allocating aid.

Two important questions remain. First, in the face of these facts, known to everyone in the field, why does the view persist that equality of opportunity can be achieved in terms of expenditures per student? Second, what kind of aid plan is suggested by the model I have presented as an improvement over present schemes?

I have not resolved the first question completely in my own mind, but I can offer some insights. It might be argued that experts in school finance have stuck to revisions in cost-based systems because these are politically more feasible. "Make recommendations, and more important, tailor your analysis, to yield reforms which are realizable in the near future." Some of this might reasonably occur in a field, but the degree of conformity is uncomfortably high. If the scientific community has any function at all, it is not to tell the politicians what is politically possible.

This might also explain why some authors recommend a patchwork approach to some of the problems raised in this area. By suggesting aid supplements on the basis of "task units" or some other need criterion, they still maintain the basic aid plans. Few suggestions are given on how the "task units" might be scientifically determined, however; so this remains merely a recognition of part of the problem. As an illustration, Coons, Clune, and Sugarman [8, p. 241] write: "Municipal overburden correction is something like task unit adjustment for particular kinds of pupils: it is important to think about, but not essential to act upon, at least until we have a proper power equalizing system the operation of which can be evaluated."[5] This approach is a bit disingenuous.

The deemphasis on all the factors other than wealth in determining aid may also explain an easy confusion about the true meaning of equality of opportunity. "Equality of opportunity means (roughly) equal services, which in turn can be achieved from (roughly) equal inputs, which can be purchased by giving districts (roughly) equal financial resources." The explanation for making such an argument may rest on the fact that the model implicit in the minds of the investigators was never set down and solved as in this paper. Explicit solution makes all the variables important, in principle; so it is harder to selectively deemphasize some on the basis of past experience or analytical convenience.

Other investigators have failed to come to grips with the ideological and institutional realities implicit in true equality of opportunity. Benson [6, p. 181] is acutely aware of all the problems we are discussing:

> Clearly, the same number of dollars buys different amounts of education (in the real sense) in the various school districts. Some differential costs, such as transportation, can easily be taken into account in an equalization formula, but others such as costs of teachers' services, cannot. This is a more complex problem than simply recognizing that the cost of living varies from one part of the state to another. An old industrial city, cost-of-living adjustment aside, may have to offer many more dollars than a pleasant upper-income suburb to attract the same quality of teachers. Next, even assuming that some ideal formula to account fully for differences in cost of education exists, there is no reason to think that a count of children in ADA is fully representative of educational need. Depressed areas may need more educational services than rich areas, in order to compensate for the effects of cramped home environments. It is now becoming quite plain that pupil inputs, one of the most important variables determining school output, varies greatly from one district to the next, but so far the determination of what volume of real educational resources is required to adjust for differences in pupil inputs eludes our grasp.

Having made the above statement, how he can still advocate a percentage equalizing aid plan, even though it is "patched up" to account for some of the factors he mentions, is a little strange. Coons, Clune, and Sugarman [8, p. 213] are a bit more direct:

> If poor districts tax lower than that percentage [set by the state in order to spend a certain number of dollars] because their voters do not care as much about education as those in other districts, under the rules of power equalizing they deserve less and get less: the system is working properly.

---

5. The power-equalizing scheme is a variation on Benson's percentage equalizing, which in turn is a plan linked to assessed valuation and costs.

They go on to state [p. 237]: "We are not prepared to scrap free enterprise; one of the driving principles behind our initial demand for equal educational opportunity is the fair operation of the free-enterprise system."[6]

The essence of free enterprise is inequality – those who have greater wealth are able to buy more goods and services. But the ideology of equal opportunity is to protect children by giving all the same amount of something, even against the "tastes" of some voters and parents. When the state interferes to assure standards, it undertakes to do what local districts cannot or will not do for children. If the higher authority of the state is used, local control in any meaningful sense is impossible. This point must be faced. The issue is conveniently avoided by reverting to aid plans that are based on costs or wealth, which affect quality only indirectly and which therefore cannot guarantee equality of opportunity. Ultimately the issue is resolved against equality of opportunity.

Finally, the preoccupation with cost- and wealth-based plans is partly the result of the faith our materialistic society places in the ability of sufficient money to solve any problem. "If you want schools to be more equal, give more money to the 'bad' ones to bring them up to snuff." But given the class structure of school districts and the importance of the student input, there is a dimension of the problem money might not solve. The "money solution" is the motivation behind the so-called compensatory plans for school aid. The underlying philosophy is that bad schools can be isolated like a disease and cured with sufficient innoculations of money. The model used in this paper makes clear the importance of the student input, and in so doing it emphasizes the essential frustrations a compensation plan will encounter.

These points lead directly to some observations about how equality of opportunity might or might not be achieved. First, any aid plan that achieved even perfect equality in expenditures per student would fail the test of equality of opportunity for reasons developed at length in this paper. Second, although the emphasis of any program of equality of educational opportunity should be on the outcomes of education, this is clearly not a problem money alone can solve. If, as I assume (and all evidence supports this view), the student input is important, no amount of money alone is capable of solving the problem.

Consider finally the institutional implications of the state guaranteeing levels of educational quality throughout its jurisdiction in order to achieve equality of opportunity. Local control would in fact vanish. The rich would not be allowed to purchase more "human capital" for their heirs than dictated by the state. These are institutional changes not likely to be greeted with enthusiasm in our country today or anytime in the very near future. Alas, equality of opportunity in education is an idea whose time has not yet come.

---

6. Even the most politically conservative economist must smile to himself when the specter of free enterprise is conjured up to justify what is admitted by all to be a government-controlled (although decentralized) monopoly.

References

1. Becker, G. S. *Human Capital*. National Bureau of Economic Research, 1964.
2. Benson, C. S. *The Economics of Public Education*, 2d ed. Boston: Houghton Mifflin Co., 1968.
3. California State Department of Education. *Recommendations on Public School Support*. 1967.
4. Cohn, B. "Economies of Scale in Iowa High School Operations." *Journal of Human Resources*, 3, no. 4 (Fall 1968): 422–34.
5. Coleman, J. S. "The Concept of Equality of Educational Opportunity." In *Equal Educational Opportunity*, ed. Harvard Educational Review, pp. 9–24. Cambridge, Mass.: Harvard University Press, 1969.
6. Coleman, J. S. et al. *Equality of Educational Opportunity*. U.S. Office of Education, 1966.
7. Conant, J. B. *Slums and Suburbs*. New York: Signet Books, 1961.
8. Coons, J. E.; Clune, W. E. III, and Sugarman, S. D. *Private Wealth and Public Education*. Cambridge, Mass.: Harvard University Press, Belknap Press, 1970.
9. James, H. T.; Thomas, J. A.; and Dyke, H. J. *Wealth, Expenditure and Decision-Making for Education*. School of Education, Stanford University, 1963.
10. Johns, T. L., ed. *Public School Finance Programs, 1968–69*. U.S. Office of Education, 1969.
11. Levin, H. M. "A New Model of School Effectiveness." Stanford Center for Research and Development in Teaching, Memorandum No. 63, May 1970.
12. *Racial Isolation in the Public Schools*. A Report of the U.S. Commission on Civil Rights, 1967.
13. Schultz, T. W. "Investment in Human Capital." *American Economic Review* 51 (1961): 1–17.
14. Spitzer, M.; Burstein, M. C.; and Hudman, J. T. "State Public School Finance Programs in Perspective." Mimeographed, undated.
15. Weisbrod, B. A. "Education and Investment in Human Capital." *Journal of Political Economy* 70, no. 5, part 2 (supplement) (1962): 106–23.
16. Weisbrod, B. A. *External Benefits of Public Education: An Economic Analysis*. Industrial Relations Section, Department of Economics, Princeton University, 1964.

10

Thomas Muller: Income Redistribution Impact of State Grants to Public Schools: A Case Study of Delaware

The growing fiscal needs of local government and the resulting demands for federal and state revenue sharing with municipalities have been the subject of considerable discussion in recent years. Particular attention has focused on expenditures for public education, which rose faster than any other local service except welfare between 1960 and 1970. Rising revenue needs financed primarily from local property taxes have accelerated pressure to increase non-locally generated funds for primary and secondary schools. This pressure has taken the form of public dissatisfaction with present methods of financing education, as reflected in recent voting patterns.[1] A more drastic response has been legal action, starting with the 1971 *Serrano* v. *Priest* decision in California, which was followed by similar court decisions in Minnesota, Texas, and New Jersey. State and federal courts have ruled that differences in property wealth result in gross fiscal inequities, which can in turn produce inequities in educational opportunity. The courts are therefore requiring the states to develop alternative fiscal arrangements to reduce expenditure differentials between districts, which will likely result in redistribution of the tax burden among districts. In response to public sentiment President Nixon appointed a Commission on School Finance charged with the responsibility to "examine alternative sources of money as well as alternative distribution of these funds to meet the educational needs of children in urban, suburban and rural schools."[2] The Nixon administration also pledged in early 1972 to relieve the burden of the local property tax for education. Although this implies an increase in federal funds from a national tax, it remains likely that state government will have to assume a greater share of the education cost compared to the present fiscal arrangements.

Public sector income redistribution is generally concentrated at the

Presented at the Symposium on the Grants Economy held between the Association for the Study of the Grants Economy and the American Association for the Advancement of Science, Chicago, Illinois, December, 1970. Revised January 1972. Reprinted by permission of the author, who is on the senior research staff at Urban Institute, Washington, D.C.

1. In a five-year period ending with the 1968–69 school year voter approval of school bonds dropped from 80 percent to 44 percent. A number of suburban school districts in Missouri and city districts in Ohio could not obtain additional funds from increases in property taxes during 1970, and were thus temporarily shut.

2. President's Commission on School Finance, press release of November 6, 1970.

federal program level, where, it is argued, this function can be accomplished most efficiently. However, just as federal grants tend to redistribute income among states, grants by states to local school districts can lead to substantial redistribution within a state. The extent of redistribution is a function of the interaction among four variables: (1) size of state grant relative to locally raised revenue; (2) structure of the state tax base providing source of grants; (3) distribution formulas for state grants; and (4) differences in income distribution between school districts.

This paper examines the level of income redistribution resulting from state grants to primary and secondary education in Delaware, where in 1968–69 the state provided 76 percent of total nonfederal revenues to local school districts, compared to a national average of 44 percent. The fiscal importance of these education grants can be demonstrated by the fact that they constitute almost half of Delaware's total expenditures derived from state taxes.

Characteristics of Delaware

Delaware has consistently ranked as one of the three states in the nation that provide the highest share of state grants to local school districts. These grants have accounted for 70 percent or more of total primary and secondary school expenditures since 1955, exceeding 85 percent in some years. On a per capita basis, only five states spend more state funds for education than Delaware.

The state typifies the socioeconomic characteristics and problems associated with large industrial states. The largest city, Wilmington, shows a 13 percent loss of population between 1960 and 1970. The migration out is concentrated mostly among middle-class white families, particularly those with school-age children. The city's taxable property base, despite rapidly rising public-sector service costs, has remained relatively constant in the past decade, and the value of tax-exempt property has risen rapidly. The public school system was predominantly white in the 1960s. In 1970 the pupils were about 74 percent black, although blacks constituted only 45 percent of the city's 1970 population. The suburban districts of Wilmington, which contain one-half the state's population, are with few exceptions affluent, with an aggregate nonwhite school enrollment of less than 4 percent. Unlike Wilmington, where the school district boundaries are coterminous with city boundaries, the two other cities in Delaware form only parts of school districts. The balance of districts in the state contain communities of less than 10,000, with black enrollment ranging from 11 percent to 35 percent. Income in these low-density districts is sharply below the state average, although Delaware's overall per capita income is one of the highest in the nation. Manufacturing is Delaware's dominant economic sector, with the DuPont Corporation employing 25,000 workers, over 15 percent of the state's total labor force.

Structure of the Local and State Tax Base

The tax structure at the state level has a considerable impact on income redistribution. As shown in table 1, three tax categories provide over 90 percent of revenues from taxation of Delaware's general fund, the source of all state grants for education: the state individual income tax, corporate taxes, and excise taxes on selected goods. State taxes are grouped in table 1 into those that are progressive, such as the personal income tax, proportional to income, and those that are regressive, such as the motor fuel tax. The dominance of progressive taxes, which account for 52.9 percent of all tax revenue, explains why Delaware is the only state found to have an overall progressive tax structure.[3]

State individual income taxes range from 1.5 percent for taxable income under $1,000 to a maximum of 11 percent for income over $100,000. The effective tax rate for a household earning $25,000 is estimated at 4.9 percent, a rate exceeded by only four states. An indication of both the progressive tax structure and income concentration in Delaware is that in 1965, 4.1 percent of those filing state returns, representing adjusted gross income over $20,000, comprised 24 percent of all income and 56.9 of total state income tax payments.[4] The effective tax rates for high-income taxpayers are reduced substantially by federal tax offsets. The personal income tax provides 60 percent of all taxes paid directly to the states by its residents. Two other progressive taxes, inheritance tax and estate tax, are concentrated among high-income residents. In fiscal 1969, 1 percent of all taxable estates paid 80 percent of total inheritance and estate taxes levied. The importance of the inheritance tax can vary sharply from year to year. For example, when Pierre S. DuPont died in the early 1960s, taxes from his estate equalled 15 percent of the general fund, compared to 2.3 percent from this source in 1968.

Delaware is one of the few states without a sales tax, but the state imposes excise taxes on specific items. In this category are the gasoline tax, cigarette tax, and alcohol tax. These taxes provide about 24 percent of taxes paid directly by state residents. The balance of revenues to the general fund, as shown in table 1, are corporate franchise and income taxes and minor taxes. The franchise tax is levied almost exclusively on out-of-state corporations incorporated under Delaware's liberal laws. The corporate tax is at a flat 6 percent rate, similar to the level of contiguous states. The highest share of corporate franchise and income taxes of any state are shifted to out-of-

---

3. D. Phares, "Impact of Spatial Tax Flows as Implicit Grants on State-Local Tax Incidence" (Paper delivered at the Grants Economy Symposium AAAS, Chicago, December 1970, published in this volume, pp. 258–275).

4. In 1965, 4.1 percent of all federal tax returns represented income earned in the state above $20,000, as shown in U.S. Department of Treasury, *Statistics of Income 1965* (Washington, D.C.: U.S. Government Printing Office, 1968). Taxpayers filing their returns paid 57.0 percent of all Delaware federal individual income taxes, almost the identical share paid from state tax returns with incomes above $20,000.

Table 1. Structure of State General Funds 1968–69[a]

Tax Category	Source of tax revenue		Tax burden on state residents	
	Amount of Revenue (In Thousands)	Percent of Total Revenue from Taxes	Amount of Revenue (In Thousands)	Percent of Total Revenue from Taxes
Progressive				
Personal income	$ 66,335	45.6	$ 66,335	60.0
Inheritance	3,090	2.1	3,090	2.8
Estate	3,294	2.3	3,294	3.0
Race tracks	6,596	4.5	2,196	2.0
Proportional				
Alcoholic				
beverages[b]	3,102	2.1	3,102	2.8
Realty transfer	2,077	1.4	2,077	1.9
Regressive				
Corporate				
franchise	17,611	12.1	704	0.6
Corporate income	15,078	10.4	1,508	1.4
Motor fuel	17,457	12.0	17,457	15.8
Cigarette sales	6,338	4.4	6,338	5.7
All other	4,422	3.1	4,422	4.0
Total	$145,400	100.0	$110,523	100.0

[a] Excluding revenues from nontax sources.

[b] Although expenditures for alcoholic beverages are proportional to income, tax payments may be regressive within higher income classes because tax is on quantity purchased.

state residents.[5] It is assumed that in addition to corporate taxes, only the racing track is shifted to out-of-state residents. Although tourists and other visitors no doubt also purchase goods in the state, these tax receipts are considered to be minor.

At the local level the property tax, limited in Delaware to real property, is the major local funding source for both schools and other public services. In addition, a number of low-income school districts impose a flat capitation tax on each resident over twenty-one years of age. In 1969 revenues from the

5. C. M. McLure, Jr. ("The Interstate Exporting of State and Local Taxes: Estimates for 1962," *National Tax Journal*, March 1967) estimates that Delaware exports 91 percent of the corporate income and franchise tax. This appears to be a conservative estimate. Approximately 96 percent of the franchise tax and 90 percent of corporate taxes is shifted to out-of-the-state residents. If these values are used, 22.6 percent of the taxes forming the state tax base are exported.

Although the magnitude of imported taxes in Delaware is not estimated in this paper, it is obvious that exports exceed imports. D. Phares ("Effects of Implicit Grants") estimates that in 1962 Delaware exported $41.2 million in taxes, whereas it imported $14.2 million.

property tax in Delaware comprised only 15.7 percent of total state and local funding for public services, the lowest percentage in the nation.

Income Redistribution from Existing State Grants among Districts

The income redistribution impact of education grants is examined spatially among school districts in this paper. All districts in the state are grouped into one of the following four categories:

(1) central city (Wilmington); (2) suburban districts (balance of New Castle County districts, less Newark and Appoquinimink districts); (3) districts with cities over 10,000 residents (Newark and Dover); and (4) districts with communities of less than 10,000 population (Kent and Sussex counties, with the exception of Dover).

The income redistribution effect of the existing flat-grant state distribution formula is initially examined under the assumption that school district residents contribute only 77 percent of total general fund revenues generated.[6] The balance of revenues, as shown in table 1, is implicitly provided by out-of-state residents (consumers, shareholders) via the exported share of corporate and race track taxes.

Table 2 shows the share of payments by residents of school districts into the state general fund utilized for primary and secondary education compared with the state grant payments back to those school districts.[7] The difference between the outflow of tax revenues and grants received is shown in the third

---

6. The state distribution formula is based on a flat payment reflecting elementary and secondary school enrollment units for all categories of current expenses. Because the statewide salary schedule reflects differences in education and experience of teachers, this results in state grant differentials among districts. The state also contributes 60 percent toward capital expenditures.

7. Total payments are computed by estimating the percent of state tax payments to the state general fund collected from residents of each school district. Income statistics are derived from relating the five-digit zip code location of each school within districts in the state with adjusted gross income reported for each of the three income classes shown on the computer tape of U.S. Department of the Treasury, *1966 Statistics of Income* (Washington, D.C.: U.S. Government Printing Office, 1969). Five-digit zip code maps for Delaware were utilized to estimate school district boundaries.

Delaware state income, estate, and inheritance taxes by school districts are based on county level state income tax payments derived from data in the state of Delaware's *Annual Report 1966–67* (Wilmington, Del.: Delaware State Tax Commissioner, 1968). Tax payments in each school district were apportioned among the three income groups by relating federal income tax incidence from *Statistics of Income 1966* to state tax incidence from state sources. Realty and cigarette taxes were calculated by apportioning, among school districts in each county, payments to the general fund by the three income classes. For motor fuel and alcoholic beverage taxes, total state payments to the general fund were again apportioned by the three income classes. Tax incidence for each income class was estimated from statistics in U.S. Department of Labor: *Consumer's Expenditure and Income, 1960–61* (Washington, D.C.: U.S. Government Printing Office, February 1965).

Table 2. Redistribution of Income Resulting from Existing
State Education Grants 1968–69
Tax Shift Assumption

School District	State Education Grant (In Thousands)	Payment to General Fund by State Residents (In Thousands)	Total Net Transfer (In Thousands)	Per Capita Net Transfer
Central City				
Wilmington	$ 7,866	$ 6,918	$ 948	$ 11.00
Suburban districts (Balance of New Castle County except Newark and Appoquinimink)				
New Castle—G.B.	3,472	1,763	1,709	58.00
Claymont	1,452	1,221	231	14.00
Conrad Area	2,778	2,539	239	6.00
De La Warr	2,021	950	1,071	66.00
Alexis I. DuPont	1,416	5,697	−4,281	−404.00
Alfred I. DuPont	4,822	7,099	−2,277	− 50.00
Marshallton-McKean	2,690	2,532	158	9.00
Mt. Pleasant	2,656	2,577	79	4.00
Stanton	1,978	1,221	757	54.00
Total	23,285	25,599	−2,314	39.00
Cities of over 10,000				
Newark	6,282	4,205	2,077	42.00
Dover (capital district)	2,750	1,357	1,393	50.00
Total	9,032	5,562	3,470	44.00
Under 10,000 and rural (Kent and Sussex counties except Dover)				
Appoquinimink	1,171	723	448	35.00
Hartly	142	45	97	54.00
Lake Forest	1,378	407	971	78.00
Milford	1,737	669	1,068	68.00
Smyrna	1,346	407	939	92.00
Caesar Rodney	2,380	769	1,611	86.00
(Sussex county)				
Delmar	389	226	163	31.00
Indian River	3,573	904	2,668	115.00
Laurel	1,089	317	772	89.00
Cape Henlopen	1,709	678	1,031	73.00
Seaford	1,864	814	1,050	53.00
Woodbridge	965	271	694	89.00
Total	17,743	6,230	11,512	$ 76.00
State total payment	57,926	44,309		
Out of state tax shift	—	13,617		
Total revenue	57,926	57,926		

column. The final column computes per capita net income transfers for each district individually and by category. Aggregating school district fiscal flows by type of district, all categories except suburban are net beneficiaries of state grants to education. However, the level of per capita transfers among suburban districts varies considerably. As a result of the out-of-state tax shift, only two suburban districts are receiving less in state grants than their payment to the general fund. The highest income school district in the state shows a net transfer outflow of $4.2 million. An additional $13.6 million is implicitly distributed to school districts by out-of-state residents through exported tax burdens. Wilmington benefits relatively little from the present grant system – unlike the two noncentral cities, each of which are net recipients of over $40 per capita. Districts containing small communities are net recipients of between $3 and $115 per capita from state education grants.

Net transfers have also been computed on the assumption that no tax shifts to out-of-state residents occur. This alternative increases state resident tax payments by $13.6 million. This computation is useful, at least for comparative purposes, because it reflects the fiscal situation in larger states which cannot shift a substantial part of their taxes to out-of-state residents. It may be argued further that there is a limit to the level of taxes which can be exported even by a small state such as Delaware without counter-measures by other states. As shown in Table 3, Wilmington would show a net fiscal outflow if, in fact, part of the tax burden for education were not shifted. In addition, given this assumption, six suburban school districts show a net outflow of funds.

Net transfers to and from school districts as a percentage of per capita income are shown in table 4. In the district with the largest net outflow, the net transfer represents 4.6 percent of 1966 per capita adjusted gross income. In rural districts, net inflow of funds from state education grants ranges from 1.6 percent to 8.7 percent of per capita income.

Table 3. Redistribution of Income Resulting from Existing State
Education Grants
No Tax Shift Assumption

	State Education Grant (In Thousands)	Payment to General Fund[a] (In Thousands)	Total Transfer (In Thousands)	Per Capita Net Transfers
Central city	$ 8,014	$ 9,033	$— 1,019	$—14
Suburban districts	23,690	33,761	—10,071	—41
Cities over 10,000 populations	9,193	7,315	1,878	22
Under 10,000 and rural	18,032	8,820	9,212	70

[a] Taxes paid by state residents.

Table 4. Net Transfers Resulting from Existing Delaware
Distribution Formula as a Percent of Per Capita Income
(Shifting Assumption)

District	Adjusted Gross Per Capita Income 1966	Per Capita Net Transfer (From Table 2)	Percent Net Transfer as Percent of G.A.I.
Central city			
Wilmington	$2,794	$ 11	0.39
Suburban districts			
New Castle	2,576	58	2.25
Claymont	2,718	14	0.52
Conrad Area	2,576	6	0.23
De La Warr	2,374	66	2.78
Alexis I. DuPont	8,775	−404	−4.60
Alfred I. DuPont	4,301	− 50	−1.16
Marshallton-McKean	3,709	9	0.24
Mt. Pleasant	3,735	4	0.11
Stanton	2,173	54	2.49
Total	3,429	39	1.14
Cities over 10,000			
Newark	2,875	42	1.46
Dover (Capitol district)	2,064	50	2.42
Total	2,627	44	1.67
Under 10,000 and rural			
Appoquinimink	1,746	35	2.00
Lake Forest	2,225	78	3.51
Milford	2,123	68	3.20
Smyrna	1,064	92	8.65
Ceasar Rodney	1,982	86	4.34
Delmar	1,901	31	1.63
Indian River	1,817	115	6.33
Laurel	1,993	89	4.47
Cape Henlopen	2,004	73	3.64
Seaford	2,352	53	2.25
Woodbridge	1,756	89	5.07
Total	1,997	76	3.81

Alternative Allocation of Additional State Grants

Since the late 1950s, the local share of educational expenditures in Delaware increased from 10 percent to 21 percent. Concurrently, local property tax rates to pay for education have risen sharply. For example, the Wilmington school property tax rate increased from $1.14 per $100 assessed value in 1967 to $1.75 in 1970, the highest rate in the state. Suburban and rural districts also increased their property tax rates substantially in recent years. These unpopular tax rate increases were a major cause for the consideration of three alternatives for increased state grants, two of which have been partially implemented:

1. Providing additional grants to school districts on the basis of fiscal need, defined by the state as the per pupil value of the property base, on a matching state-local basis. Under this approach, there is an inverse relationship between the local property base and the share of state grants. Fiscal need is also defined on the basis of per capita income and compared to need defined by property value.

2. Increasing state education grants to a level where the share of local revenues could be reduced. State grants would be distributed on a similar basis as at present – that is, a flat grant formula independent of fiscal or educational need.

3. Providing additional revenues to school districts on the basis of educational, rather than on the basis of, or in addition to, fiscal need. The distribution of funds is discussed while considering both state and federal criteria of educational need.

Although at present only relatively meager funds have been allocated under Delaware legislation for distribution based on both state-defined fiscal and educational need, it is nevertheless relevant to examine the fiscal impact of these alternatives on Delaware's school districts, as these alternatives are under consideration in other states, particularly in view of recent court decisions to reduce expenditure differentials among school districts.

In determining the income redistribution pattern associated with alternative methods of distributing state grants based on fiscal need, it will be assumed that the state will match, on the basis of a formula discussed in the following section, the average per pupil local revenue presently provided from local sources in the county with lowest per pupil expenditures. This amount, in Sussex County, was $109 per pupil during 1968–69. The cost of the program is also estimated if it would match the average 1968–69 local current operating revenues for education, or $166 per pupil.

An alternative is to provide additional, nonmatching aid following the distribution pattern of the existing flat grant personnel unit formula, thus reducing directly the dependence on local property taxes.

In considering educational need distribution criteria, specific sums of grant payments will not be calculated. Rather, the percent payments to each school district will be computed and related to other distribution alternatives. It will be assumed that the state will raise additional revenue by proportionally increasing all major taxes paid by state residents comprising the state general fund. Corporate income and franchise taxes are not increased, as such increases may reduce the likelihood of enterprises incorporating in Delaware.[8]

---

8. The assumption that all taxes will be increased proportionately is questionable. It is more likely that only one or two individual tax rates will be increased, selected on the basis of least political resistance and additional revenues obtainable. It is also feasible that a new tax may be added.

Matching State Aid Based on Fiscal Need

Delaware provides supplementary funds to school districts on the basis of state defined fiscal needs. This need is determined by an index of "relative ability to pay" computed by dividing the per pupil property base in the school district by the state average property base, which has an index value of 100.

$$\text{Local District Share} = \frac{\text{School District Index}}{100} \times 50 \text{ percent}$$

$$\text{State Share} = 100 \text{ percent} - (\text{Local District Share})$$

The legislation specifies that in no case is the state share to be less than 10 percent of the amount authorized. Thus, if a district has an index over 180, it is treated as if the index value was 180. The only beneficiary of this provision is the affluent Alexis I. DuPont District.

To determine differences in the distribution of aid using income as the ability to pay criterion, a supplementary index comparing each district's per capita income to the state average is also computed.

The amount of additional state revenue required to match local funds to raise a total of $107 using the relative property wealth index is $5,700,000. Using income as the ability to pay measure, the state has to raise an additional $6,252,000. The differences in index values using the property wealth and income criteria are shown in table 5. In Wilmington, the income index is 22 percent below the property value index, whereas in suburban districts, the income index is 27 percent above the property value index.

Table 5. Ability to Pay Based on Property Value and Income

	Property Value[a] Index	Income Value Index	Per Cent Difference
Wilmington	128	100	21.9
Suburban districts (all)	97	123	26.8
Alfred I. DuPont	106	154	45.3
Alexis I. DuPont	260	314	20.8
Newark	82	103	25.6
Rural districts	91	71	22.0

[a] State equalized property values

Differences in these ability to pay measures between the central city, suburbs and rural areas are attributable to the following factors:

1. **Assessment practices** The state distribution formula is based on the assumption that assessed value of property is equal to 50 percent of market (or "full") value in the metropolitan area. While this relationship was approximately representative of both the city and suburban districts in the late 1950s, rising per unit property values in the suburbs without parallel increases in the city have changed this relationship. A county government–sponsored study in 1967 shows that in Wilmington assessed value is equal to about 70 percent of market value; in suburban New Castle County, it is only 52 percent of market value.[9]

2. **Differences in type of property** Commercial and industrial property comprise 40 percent of the assessed taxable property base in Wilmington, compared to only 15 percent in suburban school districts. In rural districts farms and acreage form a large share of the tax base.

3. **Public school attendance** Computed per student, property values in Delaware and other states are based on students attending public school, not on the basis of total private and public enrollment. Nonpublic, primarily parochial, school enrollment is higher in Wilmington and other central cities compared to suburbs. Approximately one-third of Wilmington's students are enrolled in nonpublic schools, whereas private school attendance in suburban districts is only 12 percent. In addition, Wilmington, as well as other central cities such as Detroit, has fewer children between the ages of five and fourteen as a percent of total population compared to suburbs, due to the previously noted migration out of families with school-age children.

The impact of these factors on central-city, suburban, and rural property value-based "ability to pay" is shown in table 6.

An examination of the index values in this table, which are based on the previously defined ability-to-pay formula, shows that if only residential

Table 6. Per Pupil Alternative Property Value Indexes
1968–69

Criterion	State	Wilmington	Suburban Districts	Rural Districts
State-defined full value	100	128	97	91
Adjusted full value[a]	100	105	110	95
Residential property only[b]	100	78	144	52
Total school attendance[c]	100	102	98	103

[a] This adjustment reflects assessment to market value ratio of 70 percent in Wilmington.

[b] Adjusted full value excluding industrial and commercial property.

[c] Both public and private schools, and state-defined full value is calculated.

9. J. L. Jacobs and Company, *Report and Recommendation on Assessments for City of Wilmington and County of New Castle, Delaware* (Chicago, September 1967).

property were included in computing per-pupil wealth and if property values were adjusted to reflect current assessed to market value ratios, Wilmington would receive 61 cents of each dollar, raising 39 cents locally, whereas suburbs would receive only 38 cents of each dollar, with the balance comprising the local share of matching funds. Under provisions of existing legislation, which considers all real property and state-defined assessed to market value ratios, Wilmington receives only 36 cents of each dollar provided in matching funds, and suburban districts receive 52 cents, providing only 48 cents locally.

This example illustrates how existing assessment practices and the inclusion of industrial and commercial property are disadvantageous to the central city.[10] A similar pattern is found in Detroit and other central cities, which have stagnant or slowly rising unit property value, a larger proportion of commercial property, and lower public school attendance compared to suburbs. As a result, central cities are at a disadvantage if the distribution aid criterion is per-pupil property wealth.

Net transfers between school districts using both per-pupil value of property and per capita income criteria of ability to pay based on the formula discussed previously are shown in table 7. Columns (1) and (2) combine tax payments by the district to the state, to the general fund, which distributes matching funds, and the local matching funds. Values in these columns represent the total cost to the district under the matching-grant program. Column (3) represents state grants to the district and local matching funds, or $109 per pupil. This is the inflow of additional state and local funds for education. Columns (4) and (5) are resulting net transfers, representing the difference between the inflow and outflow of funds utilizing the two ability-to-pay measures.

Although the use of the income criterion results in increased state matching funds to the central city, Wilmington remains at a disadvantage. This inequality is primarily attributable to the income-distribution structure in Wilmington. Although there is a higher proportion of low-income households in the city compared to the state average, tax payments to the state on a per capita basis are considerably above the state average – a phenomenon attributable to high-income neighborhoods remaining within city boundaries. This suggests a migration of middle-income families from the city, with low-income families and high income families with few children in public schools remaining. Rural districts would be the major beneficiaries of the income criterion, because a considerable part of their wealth is represented by land. Despite underassessment for property tax purposes, agricultural land and farms nevertheless form over 25 percent of the assessed property value in these rural districts.

---

10. Concurrently cities benefit by high concentration of nonresidential property because a high proportion of the tax is shifted to noncity residents.

Table 7. Net Transfers Resulting from Fiscal Need Matching Grant Distribution
(In Thousands $)

School Districts	Tax Payment to State General Fund and Local Matching Share		Local Revenues— State Grant and Local Matching Share	Net transfer	
	(1) Property Value Criterion	(2) Income Criterion	(3)	(4) Property Value Criterion (3 − 1)	(5) Income Criterion (3 − 2)
Central city					
Wilmington	$ 1,858	$ 1,725	$ 1,498	$ −360	$ −227
Suburban districts					
New Castle	473	560	674	+201	+114
Claymont	317	339	345	+ 28	+ 6
Conrad Area	700	650	639	− 61	− 11
De La Warr	272	344	436	+164	+ 92
Alexis I. DuPont	984	1,047	283	−701	−764
Alfred I. DuPont	1,455	1,778	1,024	−431	−754
Marshallton-McKean	549	602	367	−182	−235
Mt. Pleasant	689	745	568	−121	−177
Stanton	767	436	676	− 91	+240
Subtotal	$ 6,206	$ 6,501	$ 5,012	$−1,194	$−1,489
Cities over 10,000					
Newark	$ 1,132	$ 1,328	$ 1,427	$ +295	$ + 99
Dover	521	430	627	+106	+197
Subtotal	$ 1,653	$ 1,758	$ 2,054	$ +401	$ +296

Under 10,000 and rural

Lake Forest	$ 170	$ 151	$ 300	$ +130	$ +149
Milford	233	236	387	+154	+151
Smyrna	174	157	276	+102	+119
Caesar Rodney	273	295	524	+251	+229
Appoquinimink	172	199	243	+71	+44
Delmar	62	54	64	+2	+10
Indian River	457	324	605	+148	+281
Laurel	127	126	214	+87	+88
Cape Henlopen	362	228	366	+4	+138
Seaford	277	274	382	+105	+108
Woodbridge	107	103	206	+99	+103
Subtotal	$ 2,414	$ 2,147	$ 3,567	$+1,153	$+1,420
Total	$12,131	$12,131	$12,131	-0-	-0-

Increased State Aid without Matching Contribution

The basic principle of matching-grant formulas is that local districts are *required* to raise part of the revenue from their own sources. As an alternative, Delaware can increase grant payments to local districts under provisions of the present nonmatching requirement formula. It will be assumed that state grants will be $109, or alternatively, $166 per pupil regardless of the characteristics of the student or teacher. Increasing aid by $109 in 1968–69 would have resulted in practically eliminating both property and capitation taxes for schools in rural districts and in reducing school property taxes in urban districts by over 40 percent. Increasing grants by $166 would eliminate local taxes in all but nine districts of the state. In addition, low-expenditure district revenues, which are contributing less than $166, would be increased above their present level, reducing interdistrict expenditure disparities considerably,[11] in conformity with recent court rulings in other states. Total additional state revenues necessary to increase per-pupil grants by $109 would be $12.1 million, to increase grants to $166 per pupil, $18.5 million, or 12.7 percent of the state general fund.

A comparison of net transfers applying a flat grant of $109 per pupil and the use of property and income criterion matching grants is shown in table 8. The first column shows the difference between revenues provided to the general fund from each school district to raise $12.1 million compared to funds returned to the district on a flat $109 per pupil basis. The second and third columns, based on values from table 7, show the net flow when matching-grant formulas are applied. As the results in the last two columns indicate, both Wilmington and suburban districts are fiscally better off if either the income or per-pupil property value criteria are utilized to increase funds for education compared to increasing revenues by the use of additional flat-grant payments. Nonmatching grants would result in additional net outflow of $1 million, or $30 per capita from the two high-income DuPont districts. Conversely, both smaller cities and rural districts are beneficiaries of flat-grant payments, as their net inflow is increased considerably. Combining the flows resulting from the existing distribution formula (see table 2) and the supplemental grant of $109 would result in an average $49 per capita outflow from the suburbs and $90 per capita inflow into rural districts.

Supplementary Grants Based on Educational Need

One criticism of the "equal per-pupil expenditure" approach is that it may discriminate against students who come from disadvantaged home environments. Both the federal government and Delaware provide grants to

---

11. The coefficient of variation for total current per pupil expenditures among school districts in Delaware during 1968–69 was 0.13, below the level of most states. A flat increase of $109 to all school districts would decrease the coefficient of variation to 0.09.

Table 8. Flat Grant-Matching Grant-Net Fiscal Transfer Differential
(In Thousands $)

School District Type	Interdistrict Transfer Flat Grant Distribution	Net Transfer-Matching Grant Distribution[a]		Difference between Flat Grant and Matching Grant Distribution	
		Property criterion	*Income criterion*	*Property criterion*	*Income criterion*
Central city	$ − 410	− 360	− 227	50	183
Suburban districts	−2,044	−1194	−1489	850	555
Cities over 10,000	510	401	296	−109	−214
Under 10,000 and rural	1,944	1153	1420	−791	−524

[a] Values from table 7.

school districts on the basis of what each define as educational need. These grants are distributed on the premise that such defined groups of disadvantaged students require supplemental revenues. Provisions of Title I of the Federal Elementary and Secondary Education Act of 1965 qualify a school district for federal grants if it has ten or more families earning less than $2,000, and/or such families earning over $2,000 but receiving Aid for Dependent Children (AFDC). In Delaware all but three districts (two wealthy suburban and one low-income rural) receive Title I grants. In urban areas of the state the majority of students who qualify do so on the basis of the AFDC criterion; low income is the dominant factor for participation in rural districts. Unlike the fiscal need measure determined by average income suggested previously, Title I funds are nonmatching, concentrating on grants to students of low-income families independent of the total income structure in the district.

Delaware, under provisions of state legislation SB 171, distributes (as of 1970) nonmatching supplemental grants to school districts that can provide evidence that 20 percent or more of their students in grades three to nine are two or more years below grade level in language arts and mathematics achievement. The legislation authorized $1.5 million over a three-year period, or only 25 percent annually of the amount received by school districts from the Federal Title I program. The legislation further stipulates that Wilmington is to receive at least 60 percent of the total appropriation. A total of seven districts qualify for these grants. It is noteworthy that if SB 171 grants were distributed on a per–qualified student basis (as defined by the state legislation) independent of the 60 percent provision, Wilmington would receive only 36.4 percent of the total amount authorized. Grants to eligible districts vary from $30 to $106 per qualified student, with the maximum per-pupil grant going to Wilmington.

The 60 percent provision is obviously designed to provide Wilmington with additional education revenues it is not qualified to obtain under provision of other legislation. The justification may be twofold: total property tax rates (for both education and other public services) exceed the level of the suburbs, and the high concentration of low-income minority students may contribute to per-pupil expenditures for instructional and noninstructional functions that are considerably above the state average level.

The major conceptual difference between Title I and SB 171 is that the federal legislation assumes an a priori linkage between socioeconomic characteristics of the household (low income and welfare status) and educational need of the student, whereas the state assumes that deficiency in test scores is prima facie evidence of educational need. In reality both are income redistribution devices, with the federal criteria favoring central cities and rural districts, as well as southern states with low family money incomes. Similarly, SB 171 grants are directed toward the central city and school districts in the low-income southern counties of Delaware. From an educational viewpoint Title I criteria are subject to the criticism that they substitute fiscal need for educational need. Thus, students from low-income homes who may not require additional resources qualify as recipients, whereas others who may require supplemental aid but are from neither low-income families nor households on welfare are ineligible. Conversely, the use of the test score criterion, it may be argued, could be rewarding poor quality of instruction, because incentives for improvement in achievement are not specified in the legislation.

Net Transfers between Districts under Alternative Distribution Criteria

A relative comparison of percent payments to the state general fund for education by district and percent grants from this fund for each of the five distribution criteria discussed in this paper is shown in table 9.

Wilmington receives 61.3 percent of all grants under SB 171 but only 9.4 percent of all grants under the matching-grant formula based on property and 12 percent if per capita income or flat payments were the basis for aid. If state supplementary grants were to be provided on the basis of low income and AFDC households (Title I criteria), the city would qualify for 48.1 percent of the state total. As noted previously, however, the city would receive only 36.1 percent if only test scores are used as the criterion of Wilmington's share. Only one suburban district, De La Warr, which has the highest nonwhite enrollment and lowest per-pupil property value of any suburban district, would receive more in grants than its contribution to the general fund regardless of the criteria used.

Of the two cities with populations exceeding 10,000, Dover benefits regardless of the alternative examined, whereas Newark is at a fiscal disadvantage if either of the two educational need criteria is utilized.

Small cities and rural districts, when aggregated, receive between 23.4 percent and 36.7 percent of total grant payments; their share of general fund taxes is only 14.0 percent. If the level of the grants distributed under SB 171 provisions to each district were to depend exclusively on test scores, however, there would be little difference between any of the criteria discussed and the value of grants received by rural areas. For example, under either the per-pupil property value index or Title I criteria these districts would receive about 33.9 percent of the state-distributed total.

Conclusion

This article has shown that substantial income redistribution at the intrastate level in Delaware results from the allocation of state educational grants despite the use of a flat, "nonequalizing" state formula, because the state

Table 9. Share of State Grants to School Districts under Alternative
Distribution Criteria Provisions
Percent of Total Grants 1968–69

School District	Payment to General Fund	Per Pupil Property Value	Per Capita Income	Flat Per Pupil Grant	Title I Criteria	SB 171 Criteria
Central city						
Wilmington	15.6%	9.4%	12.0%	12.0%	48.2%	61.3%
Suburban districts						
New Castle	4.0	7.5	5.8	6.3	3.0	—
Claymont	2.8	3.2	2.8	2.7	0.9	—
Conrad Area	5.7	4.7	5.5	5.1	1.4	—
De La Warr	2.6	5.4	4.0	3.6	3.7	7.2
Alexis I. DuPont	12.6	0.5	0.5	2.3	—	—
Alfred I. DuPont	15.8	8.4	3.8	8.3	—	—
Marshallton-McKean	5.7	2.5	2.0	4.5	0.4	—
Mt. Pleasant	5.8	3.7	3.0	4.6	0.3	—
Stanton	2.7	1.2	6.6	3.9	0.4	—
Subtotal	57.7%	37.1%	34.0%	41.3%	10.1%	7.2%
Cities over 10,000						
Newark	9.5%	14.6%	11.1%	11.4%	2.2%	—
Dover	3.2	5.0	6.3	5.0	5.7	8.1%
Subtotal	12.7%	19.6%	17.4%	16.4%	7.9%	8.1%
Under 10,000 and rural						
Lake Forest	0.9%	3.2%	3.3%	2.4%	3.1%	—
Milford	1.4	4.1	3.8	3.2	4.9	6.6%
Smyrna	0.9	2.7	2.8	2.2	1.9	5.0
Caesar Rodney	1.8	6.1	5.4	6.2	2.5	—
Appoquinimink	1.7	2.9	2.3	1.9	1.6	7.0
Delmar	0.5	0.5	0.7	0.5	0.4	—
Indian River	2.1	4.6	6.5	4.9	7.5	4.8
Laurel	0.8	2.3	2.2	1.7	5.8	—
Cape Henlopen	1.5	1.6	3.7	2.9	2.6	—
Seaford	1.8	3.6	3.6	3.2	3.5	—
Woodbridge	0.6	2.3	2.3	1.2	—	—
Subtotal	14.0%	33.9%	36.6%	30.3%	33.8%	23.4%
Total	100.0%	100.0%	100.0%	100.0%	100.0%	100.0%

provides a large share of total revenues. Increasing state grants by $109 results in an average per capita income outflow of 1.4 percent from suburbs and an inflow of revenues to rural areas comprising 4.5 percent of their income. It has also been demonstrated that equalizing grants on either per-income or property value differentials would not result in any shifts in the redistribution pattern. The level of income redistribution in Delaware is attributable to the progressive state income tax, the high share of state aid, and the concentration of high-income taxpayers in suburban districts. A similar pattern of redistribution can be found in other states that have a progressive income tax and a high share of state aid.[12]

The applications of alternative state distribution grant criteria in Delaware indicated that relative fiscal need criteria in the central city measured by either property value or income did not even approach the level of educational need indicated by the use of socioeconomic characteristics or educational achievement scores. This is a pattern typical of other large Northeastern and North-Central cities, which tend to have high property values relative to suburbs but low achievement scores and high concentrations of low-income minority students. The use of educational need measures would result in Wilmington obtaining almost half of supplemental payments, although its students comprise only 12 percent of the state's public school enrollment. The use of educational need criteria to allocate state funds could therefore result in considerable income redistribution from suburban districts to central cities, and to a lesser degree, to rural areas.

The probable impact of legal and legislative action in the 1970s will be increased state fiscal responsibility for public education, both from its own revenues and from revenues obtained from the federal government. The outcome of these funding changes will be lower per-pupil expenditure disparities among states and particularly within school districts of states. Because the central city–suburban–rural distribution of educational expenditures, property wealth, per capita income, and other population characteristics found in Delaware are typical of most states in the nation, the income redistribution pattern resulting from changes in education finance during the 1970s shown in Delaware is representative of other states where local property taxes are presently the major source of revenue.

---

12. An examination of net transfers between metropolitan and rural school districts in North Carolina shows a redistribution pattern and per capita value of net transfers similar to the level found in Delaware. North Carolina provides 79.5 percent of combined state-local expenditures for education, the highest percentage of any state in 1968–69 except Hawaii, which has a totally state funded education program. In Hawaii there is also redistribution from the metropolitan areas to rural islands.

11

Charles Waldauer: External
Effects of Education Grants on Tax
Base-Sharing Municipal
Governments

Scope of the Analysis

Government officials need to have fuller knowledge of the impacts of grants-in-aid if they are to make intelligent decisions about the allocation of resources through aid programs. In particular, the fiscal interdependence among local governments sharing the same tax bases must be taken into account before normative judgments are made about existing or proposed programs. An inquiry into the nature of this interdependence raises the question of whether the tax and expenditure impacts of grants on aided governments can be transmitted as external effects to other governments. If so, grants to local governments should be considered in their full spatial context, avoiding a piecemeal approach to intergovernmental aid.

This paper presents an empirical study of the influences of grants to schools in the Syracuse, New York, metropolitan area on the taxes and expenditures of the towns and villages that share their tax bases with these schools. The following hypotheses are tested – and confirmed – by examining the external effects of education grants: (1) local governments are fiscally interdependent through the nexus of shared tax bases; and (2) the fiscal impacts of grants are transmitted from aided to neighboring local governments via changes in the fiscal pressures on these shared bases.

Previous empirical studies of the tax and expenditure effects of grants on local governments examined only the responses of the *aided* governments. No attempt was made to investigate the spatial interrelationships that result from the sharing of tax bases and that are reflected in the responses of these coincident governments. These analyses assumed implicitly that local governments that share tax bases act independently of each other in their tax and expenditure decisions.[1] By overlooking the external effects, these studies

Presented at the Symposium on the Grants Economy held between the Association for the Study of the Grants Economy and the American Association for the Advancement of Science, Chicago, Illinois, December, 1970. Reprinted by permission of the author. The author is associate professor of economics, PMC Colleges, Chester, Pennsylvania. A summary version of this paper appeared in the December 1970 issue of the *National Tax Journal* as "Fiscal Interdependence Among Tax Base-Sharing Local Governments: The External Effects of School Aid."

1. An analogy to this assumption of fiscal independence is found in microeconomic theory of the firm under pure competition. In this market situation competing firms act independently of one another in their pricing and output decisions.

provide a limited picture of the impacts of grants, and they also reflect a partial equilibrium approach to what is essentially a general equilibrium analysis.

This study departs from the conventional approach by making explicit the assumption that local governments are very responsive to each other's fiscal decisions when they share tax bases. This hypothesis is based on the belief that these coextensive governments must be sensitive to one another's fiscal decisions, as they affect the levels of taxation because they ultimately derive their tax revenues from the same sources and serve the same constituency. As a result, both the voter-taxpayers and local officials are aware of, and extremely sensitive to, the effects that any tax change by one local government would have on the aggregate local tax burden.[2]

Data Examined

The statistical method used is the stepwise approach to ordinary least-squares regression analysis on a cross-sectional basis. Both the levels of school aid for a single fiscal year (1961) and the incremental changes in the levels of school aid from one year to the next (1960 to 1961) are regressed on the respective taxes and expenditures of the tax-base-sharing nineteen towns and fifteen villages. Time-series analyses of the external effects of education grants are precluded by school district consolidations and changes in town and village budgetary systems – both of which prevent any comparability in the fiscal data over time.

The stepwise approach is employed to produce better estimates of the "net" influences of education grants on town and village tax and expenditure decisions; that is, the impacts that remain after taking into account the corresponding influences of variables that reflect local fiscal capacity and need. First, the tax or expenditure variables are regressed on the aid variables, and then the fiscal capacity and need variables are introduced into the regression equations one at a time in that order.[3] Attention is directed toward any changes in the values of the net regression coefficients of the aid variables and their standard errors.

---

2. This model of fiscal interdependence has its analytical counterpart in micro-economic theory of the firm under oligopolistic competition, where firm pricing and output decisions are mutually interdependent.

3. The basic set of regression equations used in this stepwise procedure is:

$$X_1 = b_2 X_2 + e$$
$$X_1 = b_2 X_2 + b_3 X_3 + e$$
$$X_1 = b_2 X_2 + b_3 X_3 + b_4 X_4 + e,$$

where X_1 represents the tax or expenditure variable; X_2 is the aid variable; X_3 is the fiscal capacity variable; X_4 is the fiscal need variable; the bs are the respective net regression coefficients; and e is the error term (stochastic variable).

In the absence of any income data and because real property is the only broad-based tax available to the local governments studied, *taxable real property values per capita*[4] are used as the variables reflecting town and village *fiscal capacity*. Local *fiscal need* is represented by *dummy variables* that reflect *population size* and *degree of urbanization*.[5] Population density per square mile in 1960 and the percentage population change from 1957 to 1960 were used initially as independent variables reflecting fiscal need, but they were dropped from the analysis because they were not significantly related to the town and village taxes and expenditures.

To avoid the undue statistical influence of government size, the aid, tax, and expenditure variables all are presented in ratio form, expressed in both *per capita* and *per $1,000 of taxable real property* terms. The use of population and taxable property as common denominators for measuring fiscal activity also offers the advantage of presenting the fiscal variables in terms of both the benefits received from and the tax burden costs of the government services provided to people and property.

The following two definitions of external effects are used in this study, and they are based on the premise that the fiscal impacts of grants are transmitted from aided to neighboring local governments in the form of decreased or increased fiscal pressures on the shared tax bases:

1. *Tax and expenditure inducement effects* describe instances in which the receipt of aid by one government is associated with increases in the taxes and expenditures of other tax-base-sharing governments (that is, the net regression coefficients between aid and these taxes and expenditures are significantly positive).[6] Inducement effects are expected in connection with grants that are used by the aided governments to substitute for local taxes in financing their services, because the tax substitution would decrease the fiscal pressures on the shared tax bases. These decreased pressures, in turn, would act to induce the other governments to increase their tax levies to support increased expenditures.

---

4. State equalized to full market values of locally assessed real property for 1961 are used when examining the fiscal impacts of the 1961 levels of aid. These full market values insure comparability among the local governments, because their tax assessment rates and practices vary. However, the 1960 to 1961 changes in locally assessed values are used when examining the incremental changes in the levels of aid from 1960 to 1961. This is necessary to avoid the statistically confounding effects of yearly changes in the state equalization rates, which occur regardless of whether or not there are any changes in the locally assessed values. In this case comparability among the governments is not impaired, because none of them changed their assessment rates or practices during the periods studied.

5. Large and highly urbanized towns and villages are assigned the dummy variable of 1, and the smaller and less urbanized governments are assigned the dummy value of 0.

6. $\dfrac{d(T_i)}{d(A_j)}$ and $\dfrac{d(E_i)}{d(A_j)} = b_{ij} > 0$; where T_i and E_i are the respective taxes and expenditures of the i_{th} unaided local government, and A_j is the aid received by the j_{th} local government. In terms of hypotheses testing, which utilizes the t distribution for small sample size, and setting the alpha risk of rejecting a true null hypothesis (a "type I error") at 5 percent, inducement effects are presumed to occur when the net regression coefficients are greater than zero by about 1.8 times their standard errors.

2. *Tax and expenditure restraint effects* relate to situations in which aid to one local government is accompanied by decreases in the taxes and expenditures of other coincident governments (that is, the respective net regression coefficients are significantly negative).[7] Restraint effects are presumed to result from grants that stimulate the aided governments to increase their expenditures financed from local taxes, because the expenditure stimulation would increase the fiscal pressures on the shared tax bases. As a result, the other governments would feel restrained from increasing their tax levies to finance increased expenditures.

Empirical Results

The major findings are that: (1) local governments sharing the same tax bases are sensitive to each other's fiscal decisions; and (2) the tax and expenditure effects of grants are transmitted to unaided governments through changes in the fiscal pressures on the shared tax bases – as long as the changes are significant and the fiscal operations of the aided governments are not so great as to completely dominate the unaided governments.

A separate study of the school districts indicates that the grants received by these schools tend to substitute for local real property taxes in financing expenditures on education. As a result of this easing of the fiscal pressures on the shared real property tax bases, education grants are expected to induce both towns and villages to increase their tax levies and expenditures to support greater levels of municipal services.

Table 1 presents the variables examined and the data sources. Essentially the same set of variables is used for both the nineteen towns and fifteen villages studied. Tables 2 and 4 give the simple (zero-order) correlation coefficients between the variables for the towns and villages, respectively. Table 3 presents the regression coefficients of school aid from stepwise regressions with the dependent variables town taxes and expenditures; table 5 shows the corresponding values for village taxes and expenditures.

External Effects on Towns

The net regression relationships in table 3 demonstrate that the 1961 levels of education grants induce the towns to undertake greater expenditures and taxes (that is, the coefficients are significantly positive). The inducement effects are reduced when measures of town fiscal capacity and need are included in the regression analysis. These reductions are expected; they arise from the strong equalization provisions contained in the state education

---

7. $\dfrac{d(T_i)}{d(A_j)}$ and $\dfrac{d(E_i)}{d(A_j)} = b_{ij} < 0$. In these instances, restraint effects are presumed to occur when the net regression coefficients are less than zero by about 1.8 times their standard errors.

Table 1. Variables Examined and Data Sources

Variables	Abbreviations
Dependent variables[a]	
Total property taxes per capita	T/C
Total property taxes per $1,000 of full market value of taxable property	T/FV
Total property taxes per $1,000 of locally assessed value of taxable property	T/AV
Total current expenditures per capita (water and electric utility fund expenditures of villages excluded)	E/C
Total current expenditures per $1,000 of full market value of taxable property	E/FV
Total current expenditures per $1,000 of locally assessed value of taxable property	E/AV
Independent variables[a]	
Total education aid per capita[b]	A/C
Total education aid per $1,000 of full market value of taxable property[b]	A/FV
Total education aid per $1,000 of locally assessed value of taxable property[b]	A/AV
Independent variables[a]	
Full market value of taxable property per capita	FV/C
Locally assessed value of taxable property per capita	AV/C
Dummy variable for population size and degree of urbanization (value of 1 is assigned to towns and villages that are large and highly urbanized; value of 0 is assigned to the other towns or villages)	DV

[a] Town and village populations and taxable real property values (both full market and locally assessed) are taken as reported in the *New York State Comptroller's Special Report on Municipal Affairs* (Albany: New York State Department of Audit and Control), an annual publication. Aid, tax, and expenditure data are taken as reported in the respective annual financial reports of the school district board of education, town supervisor, and village treasurer, copies of which must be filed with the New York State Department of Audit and Control.

[b] Total education aid is aggregated on a townwide basis for each of the nineteen towns studied by apportioning each school district's aid to its constituent towns in exactly the same proportion that the district's total taxes are levied on each town. This procedure is necessary because school districts cut across town boundaries; all districts contain more than one town and all towns lie in more than one district. The apportioning of education aid is not required for the fifteen villages studied, because each village lies in one school district only, although each village constitutes less than the total area of the district.

grants.[8] The equalization provisions result in the state grants being relatively more important revenue sources for, and being received in proportionately greater amounts by schools that serve the smaller, less urbanized towns; these schools also possess less fiscal capacity. The inverse relationships between the levels of education aid and town fiscal capacity and need are revealed in table 2 by the strongly negative simple correlation coefficients.

---

8. Both the basic foundation aid program for current expenditures and the capital construction aid programs have allocation formulas that are inversely related to local fiscal capacity, as measured by the full market value of taxable property. For detailed descriptions of all state aid programs to local governments in New York see *State Aid to Local Government* (Albany, N.Y.: New York State Department of Audit and Control), published annually.

Table 2. Simple (Zero-Order) Correlation Coefficients:
Impacts of Education Aid on Towns

1961 Fiscal Levels (Average Fiscal Impacts)[a]				
DV	FV/C	A/C	T/C	E/C
DV 1.000	.119	−.576	−.377	−.343
FV/C	1.000	−.470	.051	.020
A/C		1.000	.533	.493
T/C			1.000	.844
E/C				1.000

	DV	FV/C	A/FV	T/FV	E/FV
DV	1.000	.119	−.661	−.424	−.381
FV/C		1.000	−.829	−.486	−.512
A/FV			1.000	.722	.731
T/FV				1.000	.916
E/FV					1.000

1960 to 1961 Changes in Fiscal Levels (Marginal Fiscal Impacts)[a]				
DV	AV/C	A/C	T/C	E/C
DV 1.000	.479	−.121	.084	.166
AV/C	1.000	−.031	−.275	−.213
A/C		1.000	−.005	−.123
T/C			1.000	.397
E/C				1.000

	DV	AV/C	A/AV	T/AV	E/AV
DV	1.000	.479	−.204	.036	.110
AV/C		1.000	−.145	−.331	−.290
A/AV			1.000	−.024	−.091
T/AV				1.000	.467
E/AV					1.000

[a] See table 1 for explanations of the abbreviations used for these variables.

On the other hand, the net regressions in table 3 give no evidence that the 1960 to 1961 incremental changes in education grant levels have any effects on the incremental changes in town tax or expenditure levels (that is, the coefficients are not significantly different from zero). This is not entirely unexpected, because the incremental changes in education grant levels have very weak impacts on the incremental changes in the tax and expenditure levels of the schools themselves. This result is taken as an indication that there must be significant changes in the fiscal pressures on the shared tax bases before the fiscal impacts of grants will be transmitted to coincident local governments.

Table 3. Stepwise Values[a] of Multiple Determination Coefficients (R^2), Net Regression Coefficients (b), and Standard Errors of Net Regression Coefficients (Ob): Impacts of Education Aid on Towns

1961 Fiscal Levels (Average Fiscal Impacts)

Dependent Variables	Stepwise Order of Independent Variables[b]	Stepwise Values of b and Ob for Education Aid		Stepwise Values of R^2	Dependent Variables[b]	Stepwise Order of Independent Variables[b]	Stepwise Values of b and Ob for Education Aid		Stepwise Values of R^2
T/C	1. A/C	b	0.296[c]	.283	T/FV	1. A/FV	b	0.197[c]	.521
		Ob	(0.144)				Ob	(0.044)	
	2. FV/C	b	0.298[c]	.294		2. FV/C	b	0.140[c]	.563
		Ob	(0.146)				Ob	(0.042)	
	3. DV	b	0.240	.328		3. DV	b	0.114[c]	.578
		Ob	(0.148)				Ob	(0.040)	
E/C	1. A/C	b	0.210[c]	.242	E/FV	1. A/FV	b	0.248[c]	.534
		Ob	(0.106)				Ob	(0.056)	
	2. FV/C	b	0.211[c]	.250		2. FV/C	b	0.183[c]	.568
		Ob	(0.107)				Ob	(0.054)	
	3. DV	b	0.167	.279		3. DV	b	0.160[c]	.588
		Ob	(0.108)				Ob	(0.053)	

1960 to 1961 Changes in Fiscal Levels

T/C					T/AV				
	1. A/C	b -0.034	Ob (0.198)	.000		1. A/AV	b -0.008	Ob (0.070)	.000
	2. AV/C	b -0.005	Ob (0.196)	.034		2. AV/C	b -0.018	Ob (0.070)	.063
	3. DV	b 0.002	Ob (0.198)	.044		3. DV	b -0.017	Ob (0.070)	.072
E/C					E/AV				
	1. A/C	b -0.041	Ob (0.088)	.015		1. A/AV	b -0.018	Ob (0.067)	.008
	2. AV/C	b -0.041	Ob (0.087)	.036		2. AV/C	b -0.024	Ob (0.066)	.065
	3. DV	b -0.038	Ob (0.089)	.050		3. DV	b -0.022	Ob (0.067)	.081

a Coefficient values are corrected for degrees of freedom.

b See table 1 for explanations of the abbreviations used for these variables.

c Statistically significant at the .05 level using the t distribution for small sample size.

External Effects on Villages

Contrary to expectations, the net regressions in table 5 indicate that the 1961 levels of education grants restrain the villages from undertaking greater levels of expenditures and taxes (that is, the coefficients are significantly negative). As is true of the towns, and for the same reason, the external effects of school aid are reduced when measures of village fiscal capacity and need are included in the regressions. The inverse relationships between school aid levels and village fiscal capacity and need are shown by the simple correlations in table 4.

Table 4. Simple (Zero-Order) Correlation Coefficients:
Impacts of Education Aid on Villages

| | *1961 Fiscal Levels (Average Fiscal Impacts)*[a] | | | | |
	DV	*FV/C*	*A/C*	*T/C*	*E/C*
DV	1.000	.686	−.475	.658	.665
FV/C		1.000	−.674	.658	.711
A/C			1.000	−.826	−.742
T/C				1.000	.893
E/C					1.000

	DV	*FV/C*	*A/FV*	*T/FV*	*E/FV*
DV	1.000	.686	−.459	.367	.345
FV/C		1.000	−.710	.149	.132
A/FV			1.000	−.542	−.437
T/FV				1.000	.778
E/FV					1.000

| | *1960 to 1961 Changes in Fiscal Levels (Marginal Fiscal Impacts)*[a] | | | | |
	DV	*AV/C*	*A/C*	*T/C*	*E/C*
DV	1.000	.286	−.106	.134	.161
AV/C		1.000	−.413	.470	−.143
A/C			1.000	−.488	.170
T/C				1.000	−.201
E/C					1.000

	DV	*AV/C*	*A/AV*	*T/AV*	*E/AV*
DV	1.000	.286	−.057	−.031	.057
AV/C		1.000	−.420	.108	−.320
A/AV			1.000	−.144	.217
T/AV				1.000	−.014
E/AV					1.000

[a] See table 1 for explanations of the abbreviations used for these variables.

The observed restraint effects are taken to be an indication that the levels of school finances are so great as to completely dominate and inhibit the fiscal operations of the underlying villages.[9] As a result, village officials feel constrained in any desires to expand municipal service levels despite the tendency for education grants to substitute for local taxes and to ease the fiscal pressures on the shared tax bases. These restraining influences should be more pronounced on the smaller, less urbanized villages, because the levels of school finances are more dominant in rural areas. This dominance is a reflection of the fact that fiscal needs and demands for municipal services are lower in the rural communities (note the positive simple correlations in table 4 between village tax and expenditure levels and the dummy variable for population size and degree of urbanization).

For the same reason as given for the towns, the 1960 to 1961 incremental changes in education grant levels have no apparent effects on the incremental changes in village tax and expenditure levels. As shown in table 5, the net regression coefficients are not significantly different from zero.

Implications

The fiscal implications of these results are clear. The full impact of grants cannot be analyzed and the grant programs themselves cannot be fully evaluated by focusing solely on the aided governments and ignoring the reactions of their tax-base-sharing neighbors. There is a definite need for greater use and further development of general equilibrium models of government fiscal behavior, with special attention directed to the critical role played by the sharing of tax bases. Specifically, further empirical studies are needed to examine the external effects of education grants on municipal governments and the external effects of grants to municipalities on local school districts, as well as other overlapping local governments.

For example, in New York State the fiscal impacts of state welfare and highway grants to counties should be taken into account jointly, along with the impact of state grants to schools, before establishing the allocation criteria for the general purpose state per capita grants to counties, cities, towns, and villages.[10] Any tendency for these welfare, highway, and education grants to substitute for local taxes in financing government services should be reflected in the per capita grant formulas. In particular, measures of

---

9. The ratios of school taxes and expenditures to village taxes and expenditures range from 1.8 to 3.4 for taxes, and from 2.2 to 4.2 for expenditures; with the larger ratios prevailing in the more rural areas. The corresponding ratios for schools to towns are 1.1 to 2.0 for taxes and 1.4 to 2.5 for expenditures, again with the larger ratios occurring in the rural areas.

10. The per capita grants are based on differential rates for each type of municipal government. The rates are further adjusted to equalize fiscal capacity, which is reflected primarily by the full market value of taxable real property per capita.

Table 5. Stepwise Values[a] of Multiple Determination Coefficients (R^2), Net Regression Coefficients (b), and Standard Errors of Net Regression Coefficients (Ob): Impacts of Education Aid on Villages

Dependent Variables[b]	Stepwise Order of Independent Variables[b]	Stepwise Values of b and Ob for Education Aid	Stepwise Values of R^2	Dependent Variables[b]	Stepwise Order of Independent Variables[b]	Stepwise Values of b and Ob for Education Aid	Stepwise Values of R^2
			1961 Fiscal Levels				
T/C	1. A/C	b −0.256c (0.054)	.682	T/FV	1. A/FV	b −0.047c (0.035)	.293
		Ob				Ob	
	2. FV/C	b −0.168c (0.038)	.842		2. FV/C	b −0.070c (0.036)	.314
		Ob				Ob	
	3. DV	b −0.117c (0.029)	.906		3. DV	b −0.066 (0.037)	.337
		Ob				Ob	
E/C	1. A/C	b −0.202c (0.060)	.550	E/FV	1. A/FV	b −0.061 (0.035)	.190
		Ob				Ob	
	2. FV/C	b −0.137c (0.042)	.757		2. FV/C	b −0.057 (0.037)	.212
		Ob				Ob	
	3. DV	b −0.098c (0.035)	.816		3. DV	b −0.054 (0.039)	.234
		Ob				Ob	

1960 to 1961 Changes in Fiscal Levels

T/C	1. A/C	b −0.030[c]		.238	1. A/AV	b −0.015	.021
		Ob (0.015)				Ob (0.024)	
	2. AV/C	b −0.023	T/AV	.325	2. AV/C	b −0.015	.024
		Ob (0.014)				Ob (0.027)	
	3. DV	b −0.024		.333	3. DV	b −0.015	.022
		Ob (0.016)				Ob (0.031)	
E/C	1. A/C	b 0.023		.029	1. A/AV	b 0.098	.047
		Ob (0.031)				Ob (0.126)	
	2. AV/C	b 0.019	E/AV	.035	2. AV/C	b 0.067	.109
		Ob (0.034)				Ob (0.118)	
	3. DV	b 0.019		.040	3. DV	b 0.067	.108
		Ob (0.038)				Ob (0.129)	

[a] Coefficient values are corrected for degrees of freedom.

[b] See table 1 for explanations of the abbreviations used for these variables.

[c] Statistically significant at the .05 level using the t distribution for small sample size.

local fiscal capacity should be adjusted to include other grants received. As indicated in this study, the substitution of education grants for local taxes did ease the fiscal pressures on the shared tax bases sufficiently to induce the towns to increase their overall tax and expenditure levels. In a similar fashion, grants to villages, to towns, and to cities, respectively, should be examined for their external effects on coextensive local governments.

12

Donald L. Phares: Impact of Spatial Tax Flows as Implicit Grants on State-Local Tax Incidence: With Reference to the Financing of Education

---

Geographical Tax Flows as Implicit Grants

The nature of grants in our economy is increasingly being subjected to academic scrutiny. Transfer payments, subsidies, expenditures that have direct benefit for certain classes of persons are explicit unilateral transfers, with the grantor and grantee easily identifiable. Although extent analysis is not always in agreement about the influence of these grants – witness the controversy surrounding federal aid – understanding of their impact and magnitude is improving. Implicit public grants, a second major dimension of the grants economy, are also receiving attention. For example, the similarity to grants of federal tax treatment of homeownership, deductibility of state-local taxes, and expenditures that provide implicit benefits to certain groups are all receiving analytical and empirical scrutiny.

However, another form of implicit grant has yet to receive empirical attention. The system of state-local governments that comprises the American federal system is characterized by the openness of its economic operations. State boundaries, although they are quite effective in defining legal, institutional, budgetary, and fiscal variations, do not serve as effective barriers against the flow of tax burdens and expenditure benefits. The resident of New York who travels to Nevada to gamble pays gambling taxes, which support the provision of public goods to residents of Nevada. In a like manner,

---

Presented at the Symposium on the Grants Economy held between the Association for the Study of the Grants Economy and the American Association for the Advancement of Science, Chicago, Illinois, December, 1970. Reprinted by permission of the author, who is at the Center of Community and Metropolitan Studies, Department of Economics, University of Missouri, St. Louis.

residents of Nevada help support public goods in Michigan by purchasing automobiles on which Michigan has levied taxes. The U.S. economy is characterized by such flows of goods, services, and individuals.

In addition to the flows among states, there is a flow of tax burdens between levels of government. Provisions of the federal tax law that permit the deduction of state-local taxes in determining federal tax liability provide an implicit federal grant to the support of state-local public goods. One manifestation of these flows of tax burdens among states and between levels of government (hereinafter called spatial or geographical flows) is an alteration of the tax incidence configuration in each state-local system. To the extent that state-local taxes can be "shifted" to the federal revenue structure and to the extent that taxes are shifted spatially among states, both the level and incidence of specific taxes and the total tax structure are affected.

The focus of this study is explicitly on the impact that spatial tax flows (as a form of implicit grant) exert on the tax structure of each state-local system. Our approach is to investigate the impact of state-local taxes at their final geographical resting place, not just taxes levied within a particular state – that is, geographical incidence rather than geographical impact. This method makes explicit the grant nature of spatial tax flows. The discussion will develop an empirical approximation to the dollar magnitude of tax flows out of (exporting) and into (importing) each system. Using this data, a more accurate picture of the incidence of state-local taxation can be defined both within a state and across all states.

As Charles McLure has noted, the literature on geographical tax incidence is sadly lacking:

> Although there is an extensive literature on the subject of incidence, most of it is in the context of a closed economy, so that all statutory taxpayers and ultimate bearers of the taxes are residents of the taxing region.[1]

This situation remains despite the fact that a major trait of our system of state-local government is the openness of their economies. Any assumption that taxes levied in a given state remain within that state and that these taxes represent the only tax burden on the residents of the state is conceptually simplistic and empirically untenable. Taxes levied in a given state-local system have repercussions throughout the entire economy, and they become a burden on residents of other states.

The task at hand assumes several dimensions. First, the exporting of taxes must be estimated, by state and by type of tax, which involves determining the flow of taxes among states and the flow of taxes to the federal government revenue structure through federal tax law deductibility features.

---

1. C. McLure, "Commodity Tax Incidence in Open Economies," *National Tax Journal* 17 (June 1964): 187.

Second, the amount of taxes imported into each state (from all other states) must be estimated. Finally, these spatial tax flows must be incorporated into an empirical model designed to estimate the incidence of each state-local tax structure. Only when the model accounts for this flow of tax burdens among states and between levels of government will the resulting estimates be indicative of the "true" pattern.

Historical Treatment of Geographical Incidence

The phenomenon of geographical incidence has been treated analytically in two distinct ways. The first method – the "Michigan approach" – results from the work of Richard Musgrave and Darwin Daicoff. They assume that taxes levied in other states are of no consequence for the state under analysis.[2] In effect, these taxes are assumed to be beyond the control of the state under analysis; only the tax policy of the given state is considered. Fiscal decisions are viewed as unilateral and *not* responsive to forces operating in other state-local systems.

The second method – the "Wisconsin approach" – results from the study *Wisconsin's State and Local Tax Burden* under the aegis of Harold Groves.[3] In this study taxes in Wisconsin are treated in relation to the taxes levied in neighboring states. It is assumed that states do not operate unilaterally in making fiscal decisions but rather are influenced by circumstances in other states.

Each conceptual approach to geographical incidence makes an alternative assumption concerning the nature of the economic environment in which state-local systems operate. The Michigan approach assumes an open economy in which fiscal decisions are made unilaterally; the Wisconsin approach assumes a closed economy in which decisions are made in relation to neighboring systems in an interdependent fashion.

In the Michigan study Musgrave and Daicoff adjust their estimates of incidence for the exporting of taxes out of Michigan (they estimate that $374 million, about 21 percent of Michigan taxes in 1956, is exported), and the calculation of the distribution of tax burdens for Michigan takes this into account. The problem of tax importing is not given explicit analysis, a result of the methodology of the study, which limits analysis to the burden of taxes actually levied in Michigan.[4] The Wisconsin study also accounts for the exporting of taxes (it is estimated that more than 20 percent of Wisconsin taxes

---

2. R. Musgrave and D. Daicoff, "Who Pays the Michigan Taxes?" in *Michigan Tax Study Staff Papers* (Lansing, Mich.: State Secretary of Finance, 1958).

3. University of Wisconsin, *Wisconsin's State and Local Tax Burden* (Madison: University of Wisconsin, School of Commerce, 1959).

4. Musgrave and Daicoff, "Who Pays the Michigan Taxes?"

were exported to the federal government or out of state consumers in 1956 – $156 million out of $727 million). However, as in the other studies, tax importing is dismissed by the assumption that imported and exported taxes are offsetting.[5] A third study done for Minnesota under O. H. Brownlee accounts for exporting of tax burdens through the federal offset and higher prices.[6] No attempt is made to estimate the impact of taxes imported into Minnesota on tax incidence, however.

Each of these studies done for individual states misspecifies the true burden of state-local taxation by an amount that is a function of the degree to which exported and imported taxes do not exactly offset each other. Although this may be acceptable when examining one specific state, analysis of the entire set of state-local systems must take into account the full context of spatial tax flows – exporting and importing.

The only empirical model that accounts for the geographical flow of taxes, both in and out of an area, was developed by Werner Hirsch and his associates in a study of the external costs and benefits of education in Clayton, Missouri.[7] The Hirsch study concentrates analysis on a small municipality and the flow of costs and benefits arising from the provision of education in this community. In examining the cost flows, a spatial tax incidence model was constructed to cope with the spill-in and spill-out of taxes relevant to the financing of education. The methodology of the Hirsch study is much the same as here, but the focus differs. Hirsch was not concerned with the flow of costs among all local governments but rather into and out of Clayton.

Imported taxes by state are a significant factor in the state-local tax structure. Table 1 indicates that this category of (implicit) taxation averages 14.2 percent with, a range between 18.0 percent and 11.1 percent of total taxes. In addition, it is shown that exporting and importing do not offset each other, as assumed in prior models. Having presented the historical context for the present study, attention will now be shifted to the dollar magnitude of spatial tax flows and their incorporation into a model designed to estimate the distribution of tax burdens. The impact these tax flows exert on the incidence of state-local tax structures and the relevance of the findings for the financing of education will then be considered.

The Dimension of Spatial Tax Flows in the United States

The importance of tax exporting for the state-local systems is evident from an examination of table 1, column 1. Based on McLure's estimates for

5. University of Wisconsin, *Wisconsin's State and Local Tax Burden*, p. 45.

6. O. H. Brownlee, *Estimated Distribution of Minnesota Taxes and Public Expenditure Benefits* (Minneapolis: University of Minnesota, 1960), pp. 5–7.

7. W. Z. Hirsch, E. Segelhorst, and M. Marcus, *Spillover of Public Education Costs and Benefits*, 2d ed. (Los Angeles: University of California, Institute of Government and Public Affairs, 1969).

Table 1. Dimensions of Spatial Tax Flows

State	Total Exported Taxes ($ Millions) (1)	Exported Taxes As a Percentage Of Total Taxes (2)	Total Imported Taxes ($ Millions) (3)	Imported Taxes As a Percentage Of Total^a Taxes (4)	Total Federal Offset ($ Millions) (5)
Alabama	$ 89.52	20.5	$ 72.0	17.2	$ 28.46
Alaska	9.85	18.8	6.8	13.8	3.61
Arizona	82.98	25.3	37.3	13.2	23.98
Arkansas	53.51	21.0	36.8	15.5	13.94
California	1,013.15	19.7	539.1	11.6	492.21
Colorado	92.28	19.4	53.6	12.3	43.65
Connecticut	137.48	20.1	93.0	14.6	53.35
Delaware	41.20	36.7	14.2	16.7	2.00
Florida	215.45	20.3	134.5	13.7	45.36
Georgia	120.46	19.2	90.4	15.1	42.49
Hawaii	38.22	22.0	17.3	11.3	13.93
Idaho	28.23	20.7	18.9	14.9	6.99
Illinois	519.45	21.1	324.7	14.3	149.99
Indiana	164.53	17.3	136.1	14.8	22.78
Iowa	116.81	18.3	74.1	12.5	30.93
Kansas	101.64	19.6	60.9	12.8	29.67
Kentucky	93.82	20.1	69.4	15.7	30.21
Louisiana	174.92	26.7	75.1	13.5	15.57
Maine	31.16	15.8	25.7	13.4	7.56
Maryland	151.32	21.2	96.7	14.7	82.44
Massachusetts	259.39	17.6	170.8	12.7	125.42
Michigan	367.86	19.4	234.3	13.3	121.83
Minnesota	166.76	19.2	92.5	11.7	68.33
Mississippi	64.94	20.5	39.4	13.5	15.77

State	(1)				
Missouri	144.07	17.6	119.3	15.0	59.43
Montana	35.49	21.9	19.4	13.3	5.89
Nebraska	46.55	17.2	37.3	14.3	7.28
Nevada	46.64	49.0	10.0	17.1	3.79
New Hampshire	22.84	18.2	18.4	15.2	5.16
New Jersey	293.73	19.4	222.2	15.5	113.63
New Mexico	41.56	22.2	25.7	15.0	7.51
New York	1,112.11	20.4	585.3	11.9	634.30
North Carolina	152.92	20.7	98.8	14.4	68.25
North Dakota	25.23	18.7	14.7	11.8	5.10
Ohio	368.32	18.6	292.1	15.4	104.94
Oklahoma	103.08	22.5	60.9	14.6	26.67
Oregon	83.58	20.0	56.7	14.5	41.45
Pennsylvania	434.42	18.6	356.7	15.8	147.47
Rhode Island	41.89	22.2	26.3	15.2	13.31
South Carolina	64.46	19.5	48.3	15.4	22.62
South Dakota	26.17	17.2	15.8	11.1	3.81
Tennessee	108.83	20.6	81.4	16.3	31.82
Texas	516.37	27.9	250.6	15.8	56.22
Utah	42.87	20.9	35.7	18.0	15.73
Vermont	14.64	15.9	10.5	11.9	5.85
Virginia	108.49	17.4	101.9	16.5	48.46
Washington	125.33	16.5	92.5	12.7	36.46
West Virginia	64.65	21.1	44.7	15.6	6.74
Wisconsin	171.52	17.6	114.0	12.4	102.22
Wyoming	20.65	25.2	10.5	14.6	20.36

Source: Col. (1) derived from McLure, "An Analysis of Regional Tax Incidence." Col. (5) derived from B. Bridges, Jr., "Deductibility of State and Local Nonbusiness Taxes under the Federal Individual Income Tax," *National Tax Journal* 19 (March 1966) : 1–17 and McLure.

[a] Total defined after geographical incidence, i.e., [Total — (Exporting — Importing)].

264 Tax Transfers and Educational Policy

1962, exported taxes represented about 21 percent of total state-local tax revenue – some $8.3 billion out of $42.0 billion.[8] One-fifth of the aggregate burden of state-local taxation is shifted from the state in which it is levied to rest upon residents of other states or the federal revenue structure. The geographical incidence of these taxes has substantial import for the incidence of taxation in any given state and for variation across all states.

The range in percent of total taxes exported is from a high of 49.0 percent in Nevada (due to the importance of gambling and related taxes) to a low of 15.8 percent in New Hampshire. The exporting of specific taxes exhibits even greater variation. The average percent exported ranges from a high of 44.7 percent of corporate taxes (with a range from 80.6 percent in Delaware to 32.7 percent in South Dakota) to 6.2 percent of miscellaneous taxes (with a range from 64.8 percent in Nevada to less than 0.1 percent for states such as Alaska, Iowa, and Kansas); table 2 gives details by type of tax.

The coefficients of variation for the percent of specific taxes exported further accentuate the degree of variation across states. Taxes such as those

Table 2. Range and Coefficient of Variation[a] for Percent of State-Local Tax Revenue Exported, by Type of Tax, 1962

| | Range | | Coefficient of |
Tax	High	Low	Variation
Corporate income	80.6	32.7	.1602
Individual	29.5	14.6	.2213
Property	25.1	11.5	.2196
General sales	32.5	0.0[b]	.2732
Selective sales			
Alcohol	51.7	0.0	.7499
Tobacco	35.9	2.1	.6503
Motor fuel	31.1	16.9	.1322
Public utility	81.2	0.0[b]	1.1910
Insurance	61.8	28.1	.2085
Recreation	59.9	0.0[b]	1.4229
Death and gift	91.6	0.0[b]	.6328
Motor vehicle license	41.1	15.4	.1708
Severance	76.9	0.0[b]	1.2632
Miscellaneous	64.8	0.0[b]	1.7344
Total exported	49.0	15.8	.2532

Source: Computed from data in McLure, *op. cit.*

[a] For states actually using the tax.

[b] Exported tax less than 0.1 percent of total tax revenue.

8. C. McLure, "An Analysis of Regional Tax Incidence, with Estimation of Interstate Incidence of State and Local Taxes" (Ph.D. diss., Department of Economics, Princeton University, 1966).

on severance, recreation, public utilities, and alcohol exhibit a high degree of variation across states (1.26 to .75), whereas corporate income, motor fuel, motor vehicle license, and individual income and property taxes cluster more closely around the mean value for all states (.16 to .22). Not only is there considerable variation across states in the relative amount of exporting of various types of taxes but there is also considerable divergence in this variation. Although there is some variation in the relative amount of exporting of each type of tax, there are some types of taxation in some states that are much more amenable to exporting – for example, gambling taxes in Nevada and severance taxes in Texas. This type of variance in the use and relative importance of specific exported taxes is crucial to delineating the impact of spatial tax flows.

The estimated $8.3 billion in exported state-local taxes represents a geographical shifting of the burden of taxation to residents of other systems. For example, taxes levied in Michigan on the various phases of automobile production are reflected in higher prices for the finished product. The burden of these taxes is thus substantially shifted to residents of other states. In a similar manner, Michigan residents bear the burden of taxes that are levied in other states and reflected in the higher prices paid for out-of-state goods consumed by Michigan residents. The net effect is a partial rearrangement of the support of public goods for any particular state and for all states. To the extent that state A can shift the cost of public goods to residents of other states or to the federal revenue structure, it is receiving an implicit grant. To the extent that state A imports taxes from other states, it is providing an implicit grant to these states. The same is true of all states simultaneously.

This $8.3 billion in exported taxes can be separated into two components: (1) the burden that remains within the state-local system (that is, taxes rearranged among states) and (2) the "burden" on the federal revenue structure in the form of reduced federal tax yields. The latter results from provisions in federal tax law that permit the deduction of state-local taxes in computing federal tax liability. The task becomes one of isolating that portion of the $8.3 billion in exported taxes that is borne by the federal government. The balance represents the burden of exported taxes remaining with residents of the state-local systems as state-local taxes. This component can be treated as a separate category of taxation (a composite of various types of "imported" taxes).[9]

For 1962 the cost to the federal government of state-local nonbusiness tax deductions is estimated as $2.73 billion. The cost of business tax deductions to the federal government – $315 million – is based on McLure's

---

9. A point of clarification is perhaps necessary. The tax burden being considered here is only that of state-local taxes. Of course, residents of states ultimately bear the burden of all taxes. That portion of state-local taxes shifted to the federal revenue structure through tax law deductibility provisions is not relevant to the burden of state-local taxation per se. Assuming constant yield, federal taxes will adjust to make up for the loss due to the deductibility provisions.

estimates of the total local share of corporate taxes (see table 1 for a state-by-state breakdown).[10] The total amount of state-local taxes borne by the federal revenue structure through the deductibility provisions of the federal tax law is estimated as $3.046 billion. The balance of the $8.3 billion in exported taxes – $5.25 billion – is manifest as a burden on residents of the state-local systems in the form of various state-local taxes imported into the state.

Having isolated the magnitude of exported taxes remaining with the residents of the state-local systems from that borne by the federal government, the aggregate dollar amount of imported taxes – $5.25 billion – can be allocated to each state. This allocation must be done on a basis that approximates the relative importation of taxes by state. Taxes that are exported from a state are exported predominantly in the form of higher prices. This implies, of course, that the same taxes are imported into other states in the form of prices. Accordingly, the aggregate amount of imported taxes – $5.25 billion – is allocated to each state on the basis of the state's proportion of total national consumption expenditures. Although this is not a perfect method of allocation, it does approximate the importation, inasmuch as consumption reflects the price effects of spatial tax flows.[11] The result of this allocation is shown in table 1, column 3. It is this amount for each state that must be allocated by income class to complete the estimation of tax incidence. Table 1 provides data, by state, on each major component of the geographical flow of taxes. Given data on each component of the geographical flow of taxes, a model can be developed to determine what influence the spatial flows of taxes exert on the state-local tax incidence.

Geographical Tax Flows and the Incidence of Taxation

The burden of taxation on residents of a given state is lessened to the extent that taxes levied within the state are exported to residents of other states or the federal revenue structure. The burden is increased to the extent that residents of a given state bear the burden of taxes levied in other states. The question of the burden of taxation thus becomes considerably more complex in the context of an open economy where tax burdens are not assumed to remain in the state in which levied. This flow of taxes in and out of state-local systems and between levels of government must be incorporated into any model designed to estimate state-local tax incidence on a state-by-state basis. More importantly, unless spatial incidence is incorporated explicitly, any estimated pattern of tax incidence will be distorted to the extent

---

10. See Bridges, "Deductibility of State and Local Nonbusiness Taxes," and McLure, "An Analysis of Regional Tax Incidence," pp. 256–59.

11. A more desirable allocator would be a series that reflects the flow of goods and services among states, e.g., the amount of goods consumed in a given state, imported from some other state. Such data is not available.

that (1) imported and exported taxes do not exactly cancel each other and (2) the federal government assumes some of the burden in reduced federal tax yields.

Using McLure's estimates, the dollar amount of total taxes exported can be determined, by type of tax, by state (see table 1, column 1). The dollar amount of exported taxes borne by the federal revenue structure can be determined from estimates by Bridges and McLure as outlined in the previous section (see table 1, column 5). The difference between these two magnitudes defines aggregate imported taxes – that is, taxes imported into a state from other states (see table 1, column 3). This data can then be used to refine a standard incidence model to adjust for the spatial flow of tax burdens. To accomplish this, the dollar amount of each specific tax exported is netted out of the total for each state. This provides an initial approximation to the amount of each tax whose incidence remains within the geographical confines of the state in which levied.

The $8.3 billion in exported taxes, however, must become manifest as a burden either in the form of state-local taxes or as reduced federal tax yields. Of the $8.3 billion in exported taxes, $5.25 billion represents a direct burden on residents of state-local systems in the form of imported state-local taxes. The balance, some $3 billion, is "absorbed" by the federal government and, assuming constant yield, is retaxed against the citizenry in accordance with the federal tax structure.

The final task in refining the data for the incidence model is the allocation of imported state-local taxes by income class. Inclusion of this form of taxation provides an exhaustive classification of taxes from which incidence patterns can be estimated. Imported taxes – which represent a composite of several types of taxes – are allocated by income class on the basis of total current consumption. The taxes included in this category are taxes that have been exported through the market in the form of higher prices. It is assumed that consumption expenditures reflect both the price effect and relative consumption, thus providing an acceptable proxy for the incidence of imported taxes.

The basic data used to estimate incidence are effective rates of taxation by income class. The methodology underlying the calculation of such data is lengthy – too lengthy to discuss in the confines of this paper. Needless to say, it involves the use of shifting-incidence assumptions, geographical tax flows (the focus of this paper), and incorporation of the major provisions that characterize state-local taxation – that is, exemptions from general sales taxation, personal and dependent exemptions, standard deduction and rate features of state income taxation, and so on.[12]

To examine the impact of spatial tax flows on state-local tax incidence a regression model was specified to relate income and tax burden (effective rate

---

12. See D. Phares, "The Structure of State-Local Tax Burdens: 1962" (Ph.D. diss., Department of Economics, Syracuse University, 1970), chap. 1–3 for a detailed discussion.

of taxation). The results of the regression analysis permit a taxonomy of states according to an empirically estimated pattern of incidence. Perusal of changes in this taxonomy with the incorporation of spatial tax flows makes explicit the impact that these flows exert on state-local tax structures.

The Regression Model

A least-squares regression relating average income to effective rate of taxation, by income class, produces an equation depicting the average relationship between income and burden of taxation. Using data on the effective rate of taxation by income class, such an equation can be computed for each state. The coefficient of the independent variable (b_j) indicates the average change in the effective rate of taxation per unit change in income. As the coefficient (b_j) is greater than, equal to, or less than 0.0, the system of taxes can be classified as being progressive, proportional, or regressive in incidence, on average.

The model used to estimate the distributional configuration is indicated in equation (1).

$$ER_{ij} = a_j + b_j\,(\bar{Y}_{ij}) \qquad i = 1, 2, \ldots, 9$$
$$\text{(income classes)}$$

$$j = 1, 2, \ldots, 50$$
$$\text{(states)} \tag{1}$$

$$ER_{ij} = (T_{ij}/(Y_{ij})$$

$\bar{Y}_{ij}$ = average income

T_{ij} = aggregate taxes

Y_{ij} = aggregate income

There are nine observations for each regression, one for each income class. Using equation (1), b_j is estimated for each individual state. The results permit a taxonomy of states according to the estimated values for b_j.
The null hypothesis becomes:

$$H_0 : b_j = 0.0,$$

with alternatives hypotheses,

$$H_1 : b_j > 0.0,$$
$$H_2 : b_j < 0.0.$$

Hypothesis H_0 implies proportionality, H_1 progressivity, and H_2 regressivity. Standard tests of significance can be applied to the estimated values for b_j and are used to determine whether hypothesis H_0, H_1, or H_2 is satisfied. The .05 level of significance is used as the cutoff value for rejecting H_0 in favor of H_1 or H_2 because it affords adequate protection against rejection of a correct hypothesis. It must be emphasized that this method examines the *average* incidence pattern across the *entire* income distribution rather than between any pair of income classes. The result should be interpreted accordingly.

The Empirical Results

To delineate the spatial dimension of tax incidence and to relate these findings to problems of financing education, the model in equation (1) is specified in three distinct forms. Changes in the taxonomy of states estimated from each variant of equation (1) serve to emphasize how spatial tax flows relate to the financing of education.

The first stage of analysis applies equation (1) to data on the total effective rate of taxation before adjusting for spatial tax flows (unexported). Table 3, column 1 shows the taxonomy that results. Second, equation (1) is applied to data on total effective rate net of property taxation (unexported). Table 3, column 2 shows the results of this stage of analysis.

An extremely strong defense can be made for using property taxation as a close approximation to the impact of local sector taxation policy. Property taxation provides the major source of tax revenue for local governments and is almost entirely locally collected; it accounted for 88 percent of local tax revenue and 97 percent was locally collected in 1962. In addition, property taxation is the major source of revenue for financing local education. Removing the influence of the property tax from the total effective rate of taxation thus provides an acceptable approximation to the impact of both the local sector and education financing. The analysis is purposely designed to show explicitly the state component, rather than the local component, of tax incidence (that is, the residual effective rate after removal of property taxation rather than the effective rate of property taxation directly). This permits inferences about local tax incidence and explicit examination of state incidence, and it also facilitates the discussion of education financing policy to follow.

Finally, equation (1) is applied to the total effective rate net of property taxation, with the data adjusted to account for the spatial flow of tax burdens (exported). These results are presented in table 3, column 3. Application of the model specified in equation (1) to each of these stages of refinement isolates the following forces operating on state-local tax structures:

Comparison	*Effect Isolated*
Column 1 with column 2	Local sector–education financing
Column 2 with column 3	Spatial tax flows

Table 3. Regression Analysis Taxonomy of State-Local Tax Structures[a]

(1) Total Effective Rate—Unexported

$H_1: b_j > 0.0$ Progressive (n = 1)

Del

$H_0: b_j = 0.0$ Proportional (n = 16)

Ark	Minn	N C
Col	Miss	Or
Id	Mo	Pa
Ky	Mont	S C
Mass	N Y	Vt
		Wisc

$H_2: b_j < 0.0$ Regressive (n = 33)

State		State		State		State	
Ala	3	Ind	26	Nev	22	S D	24
Ak	7	Io	17	N H	11	Tenn	5
Ar	25	Kan	23	N J	19	Tex	16
Cal	18	La	8	N M	28	Ut	20
Conn	12b	Me	13	N D	13	Va	9
Fla	15	Md	6	Oh	6	Wash	29
Ga	2	Mich	30	Okl	30	W Va	4
Haw	14	Neb	21	R I	21	Wy	32
Ill	27						

(2) Total Effective Rate Net of Property Tax—Unexported

$H_1: b_j > 0.0$ Progressive (n = 10)

State		State	
Del	8	N Y	2
Id	1	N C	4
Ky	6	Or	7b
Mass	3	Vt	5
Minn	7b	Wisc	9

$H_0: b_j = 0.0$ Proportional (n = 21)

Ak	Kan	Okl
Ark	Me	Penn
Cal	Miss	R I
Col	Mo	S C
Conn	Mont	Tenn
Ga	N H	Ut
Io	N D	Va

$H_2: b_j < 0.0$ Regressive (n = 19)

State		State		State	
Ala	2	Md	1	S D	5
Ar	8	Mich	13	Tex	10b
Fla	10b	Neb	4	Wash	18
Haw	12	Nev	16	W Va	7
Ill	11	N J	3	Wy	15
Ind	9	N M	17		
La	6	Oh	14		

(3) Total Effective Rate Net of Property Tax—Exported

$H_1: b_j > 0.0$ Progressive (n = 2)

State	
Del	1
Wisc	2

$H_0: b_j = 0.0$ Proportional (n = 20)

Ark	Minn	N D
Cal	Miss	Okl
Col	Mo	Or
Id	Mont	Penn
Io	N H	S C
Ky	N Y	Vt
Mass	N C	

$H_2: b_j < 0.0$ Regressive (n = 28)

State		State		State		State	
Ala	8b	Ill	18b	Neb	9b	Tenn	6
Ak	8b	Ind	17	Nev	19	Tex	14b
Ar	15	Kan	7	N J	7	Ut	11
Conn	5	La	13	N M	23	Va	1
Fla	16	Me	4	Oh	20	Wash	24
Ga	2	Md	3	R I	10	W Va	14b
Haw	18b	Mich	21	S D	12	Wy	22

Source: Derived from b_j values estimated from equation (1).

[a] The number beside the state indicates its ranking based on b_j.

[b] Tied ranking for b_j.

Comparison of column 1 and column 2 isolates the local sector impact on state-local tax incidence. After the property tax is "netted out" the taxonomy of states that emerges reveals progressivity or proportionality in the state component of taxation. The number of progressive states increases from one to ten. For these ten states the estimated values for b_j are significantly greater than 0.0 at the .05 level of significance (that is, $H_2: b_j > 0.0$. is accepted). The range is from a relative high for Wisconsin ($b_j = +.133$) to a relative low for Idaho ($b_j = +.046$). The number of proportional states increases from sixteen to twenty-one, and the number of regressive states declines from thirty-three to nineteen. The range in regressivity ($H_2: b_j < 0.0$) for total burden is from a relative high for Wyoming ($b_j = -.303$) to a relative low for Virginia ($b_j = -.048$). The range in regressivity for the state component of burden is from a relative high for Washington ($b_j = -.188$) to a relative low for Maryland ($b_j = -.026$). Of even greater significance is the fact that the estimated values of b_j for the state component indicate less regressivity in *every* state than b_j estimated when the local sector is included. It must be noted that the values for b_j should not be interpreted as absolute measures of incidence. However, they can be used to facilitate ordinal comparisons across states in relative regressivity or progressivity, which is what is intended.

The difference in classification between column 1 and column 2 indicates clearly the regressive impact of the local sector. In every state the local sector increases the degree of regressivity in incidence. Comparison of columns 2 and 3 shows explicitly the impact of spatial tax flows. It can be seen that spatial tax incidence reduces the number of progressive states from ten to two; the progression indicated in these two states is markedly decreased from that indicated in column 2 (Delaware declines from $+.106$ to $+.032$ and Wisconsin from $+.133$ to $+.070$). The number of proportional states only declines by one, but eight of the ten progressive states in column 2 are classified as proportional in column 3. The number of regressive states increases considerably from nineteen to twenty-eight; nine of the twenty-one states classified as proportional in column 2 are regressive in column 3. The range in regressivity of the twenty-eight regressive states in column 3 is from a relative high for Washington ($b_j = -.194$) to a relative low for Virginia ($b_j = -.030$). It is thus obvious that spatial tax flows also exert a regressive influence on incidence. Perusal of the estimated values for b_j reveals that in every state except Nevada regressivity is increased by the spatial flows of tax burdens – that is, the b_j values estimated to classify states in column 3 indicate more regressivity than those estimated for column 2.

The results of the empirical examination of state-local tax incidence undertaken here reveal that (1) the local sector exerts a regressive influence in every state-local system; and (2) spatial tax flows also exert a regressive influence on state-local incidence. The combined effect of these two forces raises some interesting questions pertaining to the continued financing of education by the local sector and proposals for shifting the financial responsibility for education upward in the government hierarchy. Attention will now be shifted to these areas of concern.

Implications for Financing Education

A major policy implication of this research relates directly to the impact the local sector exerts on the total state-local tax structure. The heavy dependence of the local sector on property taxation as a source of revenue creates a strong regressive force in each state. The implications of this type of taxation are considerable from two points of view: first, the level of effective rate of taxation is by far the highest of any state-local tax; second, the distribution of the tax burden is markedly regressive. The combined influence of these forces has placed the local sector in an increasingly less tenable fiscal position.

Empirical examination of local sector tax incidence serves to make explicit the regressiveness of local taxation policy. In twenty-two of the fifty state-local systems the state component of the revenue system is proportional or progressive (see table 3, column 3). Local taxation exerts a strong regressive influence. The incidence and burden of local sector taxation have substantial import for the capacity of this sector to meet expanding demands for public goods. In a system in which the state assumes relatively greater responsibility for raising taxes (for example, Delaware and Hawaii) the nature of the taxes and the scope of the tax base afford a more autonomously responsive revenue source. At the local level the tax base is narrowly defined, and autonomously responsive forms of taxation are not available.

In addition to the regressive influence of local sector taxation per se, it has been shown that the spatial rearrangement of tax burdens introduces an additional element of regression. This has been demonstrated explicitly for the state component (table 3, columns 2–3), but it holds true for total state-local taxation as well. The interaction of local sector regressivity and "geographical tax-flow" regressivity increases the intensity of the fiscal pressure being experienced by local (as well as state) governments.

In the face of the level and incidence of local sector taxation policy, the capacity of this sector to continue to keep pace with demands becomes increasingly less certain. Despite remarkable past performance, serious doubt must prevail about the continuation of past trends. Perusal of the features of local taxation uncovers a process of constant incremental alteration of the existing tax structure in an attempt to obtain additional tax dollars. Rates are increased, tax bases are defined more inclusively, assessments are redone, exemptions and deductions are revised, and, where politically feasible, new taxes are introduced.

Perusal of the literature on the elasticity of state and local tax revenues does not add to the attractiveness of the situation. At best it can be said that the property tax, as the major source of tax revenue for the local sector, responds slightly less than proportionally to changes in economic activity. McLoone's estimates of property tax elasticity, as reported by Dick Netzer, reveal few states with an elasticity approaching 1.0. The United States average is estimated as 0.79 (see table 4).

Table 4. Elasticity Coefficients by State

Region	.85 +	.75–.84	.65–.74	Less than .65
Northeast	7	2	—	—
Midwest	—	4	3	5
West	1	3	5	2
South	—	6	5	5
Total	8	15	13	12

Source: D. Netzer, *Economics of the Property Tax* (Washington, D.C.: The Brookings Institution, 1966), p. 189.

Much of the past responsiveness of the property tax in keeping pace with demands for public goods, especially education, has been provided by revisions of the tax structure rather than by the autonomous response of the tax base. McLoone's estimates indicate that the elasticity of the property tax is less than 1.0 in most states, in some significantly less. When this is contrasted with the responsiveness of expenditures at the state and local level, the nature of state-local fiscal problems is further delineated.[13]

The responsiveness of expenditures on education is a function of the collective nature of education as a public good. This implicitly reflects increases in the demand for education due to rising levels of income, but it also relates to the social perception of education as a merit good. In other words, increased expenditures on education are not simply a function of income but also of society's perception of the benefits derived from education.

When one contrasts the responsibility for providing public education with the resources available to meet this responsibility, a rather perverse pattern emerges. The level of government with the most responsive revenue source – the federal government – has assumed a small portion of the financial burden. The level of government with the least responsive revenue source – local government – has assumed the major burden. The distribution of responsibility for education does not correspond to tax-raising capacity. This

13. See Advisory Commission on Internal Revenue, *Federal-State Coordination of Personal Income Taxes* (Washington, D.C.: Advisory Commission, 1965), p. 42 for a summary of the empirical studies of tax elasticities. Technically the concept of elasticity does not directly apply to expenditures since there are few cases of expenditures that automatically respond to changes in GNP. Changes in expenditures are more analogous to revisions in a revenue structure than autonomous changes in revenue (see ibid., pp. 45–47). Responsiveness is used here as the expenditure analogue to elasticity for taxation.

is adequately reflected in the emerging literature on fiscal disparities across local governments.

Still another peculiarity of the current government arrangement for financing education is that it is a collectively provided good with major spill-overs. As Netzer has noted:

> The bulk of the benefits from public elementary and secondary schooling are realized outside the school district that originally provided the child's education. In fact, in the aggregate, Americans spend about 80 percent of their post-school years living in communities other than those in which they were educated. This suggests that 80 percent, not 45 percent, . . . of the costs of the public schools should be met from federal and state – rather than local – funds.[14]

The spill-over effects of the provision of education suggest that local fiscal responsibility is highly inappropriate. Such a financial arrangement cannot possibly result in adequate levels of service when the external benefits are very large relative to internal benefits. Voters appear to be increasingly sensitive to levies tied to education, and the trend is strongly in favor of defeat rather than passage. Provision of services with heavy spill-overs within the context of small units of government necessarily results in inefficient decision making and inadequate levels of service.

If education is also accepted as at least partially redistributive in nature, local financing becomes even more untenable. The federal government is the only level of government that can possibly internalize the benefits from any form of redistribution. Also, the federal revenue structure is the logical choice to finance any significant explicit or implicit redistribution. To the extent that education is partially redistributive, this component should be financed at the federal – as opposed to the state and local – level.

The empirical results presented in the previous section cannot by themselves support a binding case for the rearrangement of government responsibility for education. Regressivity in tax incidence, even of the level and severity of that exhibited by the local sector, is not a sufficiently persuasive economic consideration to warrant such drastic shifts in the extant institutional structure. However, when the regressivity of local sector taxation is combined with the lack of responsiveness of the local tax base, severe fiscal disparities among local governments, the redistributive potential of education, the existence of large external relative to internal benefits, and the societal perception of education as a merit good, the case is considerably strengthened.

An additional argument has recently been levied against the use of property taxation for local school financing on efficiency grounds. In a study

---

14. D. Netzer, *Economics and Urban Problems* (New York: Basic Books, 1970), p. 177. See Hirsch et al., *Spillover of Public Education Costs and Benefits*, for a study of spillovers for a particular local unit.

of school districts in Michigan, Robin Barlow has concluded that property tax financing of local schools leads to an inadequate level of output:

> Our analysis of some Michigan data suggests provisionally that if school districts used only the residential property tax, an increase of 26 percent in output beyond the level reached in such a system would be required for the attainment of efficiency. But the addition of business property to the tax base causes output to increase by only 16 percent. Hence, on the average, the property tax leads to an inadequate level of output.[15]

These conclusions are based on the assumption that there are no externalities from the provision of education in a local context. If external effects exist then the underprovision of education is increased relative to a nationally efficient level. Although Barlow's results are provisional, even for Michigan, they do suggest that similar situations might exist in other state-local systems.

The current fiscal responsibility for education seems to run counter to many ideas of economic common sense. It seems obvious that the contemporary financial arrangement is more clearly a function of tradition than any application of rational analysis. Shifting the responsibility for education upward in the government hierarchy would immediately eliminate many of the perversities discussed earlier. The incidence of taxation would be made less regressive, the revenue sources would be more elastic, fiscal disparities would be lessened considerably, and the benefits from the provision of education would be more nearly internalized. Also, if property taxation does lead to inefficient levels of output, shifting fiscal responsibility would lessen the underprovision.

The extent of the upward shift in responsibility for education is certainly open to debate and must necessarily be tempered by some noneconomic factors. The range runs from the proposals of a recent Committee for Economic Development report, which calls for the restructuring of metropolitan government, to Netzer's plea for a substantial increase in federal involvement:

> Since much of the movement of population is interstate, the federal role should be a large one, perhaps 40 percent of the total, rather than less than 10 percent as at present.[16]

The total case for restructuring remains clear. The purpose of this analysis has been to add yet another dimension to critique of the present system for financing local education.

---

15. R. Barlow, "Efficiency Aspects of Local School Finance," *Journal of Political Economy* (September–October 1970): 1038.

16. Netzer, *Economics and Urban Problems*, p. 177.

13

David O. Porter and
David C. Warner:
How Effective Are Grantor
Controls?: The Case of Federal
Aid to Education

A Christmas present sent from a distance can always be exchanged for another at the local store.

Kenneth Boulding
American Economic Association, December 1970

Introduction

The superintendent and his staff had gathered in the superintendent's modern, comfortable office for the interview. The air conditioning had been working sporadically that morning, and the assistant superintendents were muttering over their discomfort. The superintendent was thinking about continuing federal aid programs within the district. There were just not enough of them, he said. His staff people had not been able to spend enough time in Washington or at the state capital to find out where the "extra bits" of money could be mobilized. Also, they should spend more time visiting other districts asking, "How'd you get that federal money?"

This interview typified the findings of our study of federal aid to local school districts. School districts do not passively wait for funds to be given to them; they actively mobilize funds from their many income sources and concentrate their efforts on the most productive sources available. The district mentioned above, located in a progressive, medium-sized southern city, had spent the last five years reevaluating their staff and educational program. During this time the budget had increased over 100 percent, and

Printed by permission of the authors. All rights reserved. David O. Porter is an assistant professor of administration and political science at the University of California, Riverside; David C. Warner is an assistant professor of economics at Wayne State University, currently on leave for one year as a consultant to the New York City Hospital Corporation. This research was supported in large part by a grant (#690-056A) from the Ford Foundation. The authors would also like to thank the Syracuse University Research Corporation Policy Institute, the Center for Urban Studies and the Department of Economics at Wayne State University, the Graduate School of Administration, the University of California, Riverside, and the Educational Policy Research Center of the Syracuse University Research Corporation for supporting various segments of this research. Aspects of this paper were presented in more detail at a joint session of the American Economic Association and the Association for the Study of the Grants Economy and the annual meetings of the American Educational Research Association.

the staff had expanded and improved in quality. In 1965 only one staff member had held a doctorate; by 1970 five staff members held doctoral degrees and two others had nearly completed their dissertations.

But where had the money come from? The superintendent, upon assuming office in 1965, made the judgment that his community was not making an "appropriate financial effort" to support their public schools. He hired a research firm to evaluate the needs of the district and to suggest sources for the resources for improvements. They recommended, not surprisingly, that the local community support a higher quality of education, and through speeches, radio programs, and the expansion of his public relations office, the superintendent began to build local support for a more expensive educational program.

In the early years of this effort little attention was given to the federal government and its programs. The superintendent was not opposed to federal aid, but he could see a much more productive source of income within the district itself. Only after the district administration had succeeded in raising the relatively low tax rate in the district did they look more closely at state and federal programs that were based on formulae other than simple entitlements.

Contrast the relatively tranquil setting in this district with the tension of the superintendent's office in a large district located in the center of a northern metropolis. Its local tax base had been declining for the last decade. The expenses of the school district and city government had been rising steadily as they struggled to serve their increasingly low-income clientele. The city government had preempted the local property tax, as they did not need to submit each increase in the tax levy to the voters for approval. In this situation the school district was forced to look beyond the district for revenues. Instead of building up a strong community relations division (except as required by federal guidelines), they assembled a staff that specialized in proposal writing and lobbying at the state and federal levels of government. Through the 1960s this staff became one of the most vigorous and important components of the district administration. There were still sufficient local funds to provide a base from which to operate, but state, federal, and private grants supplied the funds for any innovative, special, or intensive programs.

These two districts and many others like either of them showed that federal aid must be seen as an integral part of the district's funding structure. Research cannot focus narrowly on the various federal aid programs. Each district has its own unique sets of priorities for programs and sources of revenues. It was our purpose to study how one of these sources of revenue (aid from the federal government) and the priorities it encourages fit into the priorities of other income sources of local districts.

This paper is comprised of three main sections. The next section outlines the basic theory of resource mobilization and how it is applied to questions of federal aid. The following section discusses five broad factors that influence the latitude a school district has in mobilizing funds; the central theme is that several factors other than the formal legislative and executive guidelines have a more potent influence on how federal funds will be utilized by local school districts. The final section summarizes the findings of the paper and suggests adjustments in government policies to accommodate our findings. It also suggests some of the implications of this study for future research on resource mobilization and federal aid to education and other fields.

Mobilization or Allocation

A Theory of Resource Mobilization

Many analyses of grants-in-aid begin with the assumption that the funds are allocated by higher levels of government (a donor) to lower levels (a recipient). Much research is concerned with formulating controls that will ensure that the recipient will use the funds in accordance with the donor's desires.

The focus of our research was to look at the flow of funds from the federal government to local schools to see if the mandates of the federal legislation were being carried out in the local districts. Our primary objective was to discover how local school officials obtained and utilized federal funds. To do this we visited thirty-six school districts located in all major regions of the United States. These districts varied in size from 750 to 500,000 students in average daily attendance and spent from $300 to $1200 in current operating funds per child. We also visited state departments of education in four states and interviewed several officials in the United States Office of Education (USOE). We conducted in-depth interviews with the school personnel who were interested in mobilizing these funds and supplemented the interviews with any written data we could obtain. We focused on the various titles of the Elementary-Secondary Education Act (ESEA) and the National Defense Education Act (NDEA), but looked at other legislation as it seemed relevant. The interviews were conducted in two series: the first in the summer of 1968 by Mr. Porter and the second in the summer of 1970 by Mr. Porter, Mr. Warner, and Mrs. Porter.

The basic finding of our research is that political and economic factors other than the objective requirements of the legislation and the guidelines of the executive branch are more decisive in the mobilization and utilization of federal funds in local school districts. The standard controls of the federal government – such as matching funds, maintenance of effort, and audits – have an effect on how the grants are used locally, but a much smaller influence than often thought. Other, more powerful, factors overshadowed the effect of the legislative and executive controls.

To get a clearer view of these more powerful factors, a different perspective was useful. Instead of examining grants-in-aid from the perspective of the donor, as do most studies of resource allocation, we have looked at grants from the perspective of the recipient. In other words, instead of trying to explain federal grants-in-aid from the "top down," we looked at the process from the "bottom up." In doing so we have relied on a theory of resource mobilization by organizations,[1] not a theory of resource allocation.

The basic premises of the theory of resource mobilization are: (1) organizations try to maintain themselves by meeting what they perceive as their own needs and priorities; and (2) actors in organizations do not passively receive funds allocated to them from above; instead, they actively mobilize funds. Therefore, according to these assumptions, formal subordination to higher levels of government does not preclude vigorous efforts at the lower levels to shape programs, to perpetuate ongoing but related activities, or to modify the officially defined objectives of the aid to meet local priorities.

Three Patterns of Resource Flows

The analysis of resource mobilization in agencies receiving federal aid will be facilitated by three concepts: (1) *symbolic allocation*, refers to situations in which a grant releases other funds that would have been used in aided programs; (2) *catalytic allocation*, occurs when a grant attracts funds from other sources into aided programs; and (3) *perfect allocation*, occurs when the full amount of the aid (and no more) is added to the "normal growth" of a given program. These concepts are formally defined below, and they rest on the assumptions that (a) the federal government does not control all expenditures of school districts; (b) school districts have many sources of income other than federal aid; and (c) the federal government has imperfect knowledge about revenues and expenditures within local school districts.

There is much discussion on the impact of federal aid. Careful statistical studies have proliferated, based primarily on data collected by the United States Bureau of the Census or other federal and state agencies. These studies have tried to determine the impact of federal aid on state and local taxing

---

1. Extensive literature exists relating to resource mobilization by organizations. Amitai Etzioni in *The Active Society* (New York: The Free Press, 1968) surveys much of this literature in his chapter "Societal Mobilization and Societal Change" (pp. 387–427). For a more explicit treatment of the theory of resource mobilization relied on by the authors see chapter 2, "A Mobilization Theory," in D. O. Porter, *Who Slices the Pie?* (Detroit: Center for Urban Studies, Wayne State University, 1970). Porter's analysis draws heavily on B. M. Gross, *The Managing Organizations* (New York: The Free Press, 1968); J. G. Miller, "Living Systems: Basic Concepts," *Behavioral Science* 10 (July 1965); T. Parsons, *Structure and Process in Modern Societies* (Glencoe, Ill.: The Free Press, 1960); and J. D. Thompson, *Organizations in Action* (New York: McGraw-Hill Book Co., 1967).

efforts.[2] The results of these studies have been relatively inconclusive. Hopefully, our analysis of some of the economic and political variables within recipient governments will be more helpful in identifying the effects of federal funds on state and local governments.

Figure 1 presents a static model of alternative patterns of resource flows in grants-in-aid programs. In this two-program budget, the horizontal axis, X, represents an aided program (for example, textbooks and materials), and the vertical axis, Y, an unaided program (teacher salaries). The line AC represents a budget constraint (that is, it borders all combinations of X and Y that may be purchased within a given budget) prior to any grants or loans.

When aid is given to program X, a new budget line, DH, is created. The movement of the budget constraint from AC to DH may change the proportional distribution of the budget in one of the three basic patterns. First, there is the case of *symbolic allocation* (often called *substitution effect*) in which the recipient does not increase consumption of X in proportion to the aid and the previous rates of expenditures for X. Some portion of the resource is released by the grant and used for purchases of more Y. The extreme case of this pattern is illustrated in figure 1 by $Y_3 E X_1$.[3] The second

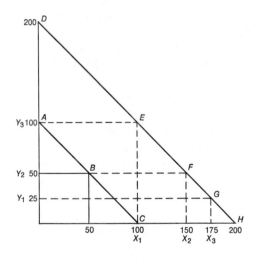

Figure 1.

2. R. W. Bahl, "Studies of Determinants of Public Expenditures: A Review," an unpublished paper prepared while Bahl served as a research fellow with the Metropolitan Studies Program at Syracuse University, summarizes this literature. Illustrative examples of this type of research include G. A. Bishop, "Stimulative Versus Substitutive Effects of State School Aid in New England," *National Tax Journal* 27 (1964); 131–43; A. K. Campbell and S. Sacks, *Metropolitan America: Fiscal Patterns and Governmental Systems* (New York: The Free Press, 1967); and J. Miner, *Social and Economic Factors in Spending for Public Education* (Syracuse, N.Y.; Syracuse University Press, 1963).

3. You must spend at least as much as the amount of the grant on the aided program. Accordingly, in figure 1 a symbolic allocation could not extend into the DE section of the new budget line, DH.

case is *catalytic allocation*, in which the grant-in-aid for X attracts funds in addition to the magnitude of the grant and previous expenditures to program X. Lines $Y_1 GX_3$ illustrate this effect. The attraction of additional funds into program X may be influenced by an increasing demand for the program, the lumpiness of many auxiliary services, or a number of other factors. Third, there is the case of *perfect allocation*, illustrated by $Y_2 FX_2$, in which the total magnitude of the grant is used to purchase more X, with Y remaining constant. This last pattern is one point on the budget line from D through H. Ironically, this is the pattern that is implicitly assumed to occur most frequently by many allocators of federal aid. In summary, symbolic allocation occurs when the impact of aid allocated to specific programs *is not restricted* to those categories. Catalytic allocation occurs when funds allocated to specific programs *attract additional resources* into the aided categories. Perfect allocation occurs when the full impact of the aid *is restricted* to the designated programs.

Figure 1 is based on the assumptions of a 100 percent (or no matching funds) grant and constant relative prices (before and after the grant). Patterns of allocation may be influenced by changing either of these assumptions. Figure 2 illustrates the effect of a 50 percent matching grant. The effect is as if the relative prices of X and Y were changed; each dollar buys twice as much in relation to Y as it did formerly.[4]

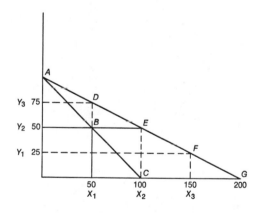

Figure 2.

4. George Break recognized the power of a matching grant to draw other funds into a program by lowering its relative cost when he criticized the 90/10 matching formula for interstate highways. He argued that such a formula makes the money too attractive to turn down, and is "likely to divert state funds from superior uses." G. F. Break, *Intergovernmental Fiscal Relations* (Washington, D.C.: The Brookings Institution, 1967), p. 96. However, in "Federal Highway Grants: A Theory of Stimulation, a Practice of Substitution" (mimeo., February 23, 1967), Thomas O'Brian and William H. Robinson, of the staff of the Bureau of the Budget, using a model similiar to the one developed in this section, found that the 90/10 formula of the interstate highway program allowed local and state governments to reduce their tax efforts for highways.

If the item aided is in short supply, increasing funds for its purchase may increase its price absolutely. Figure 3 illustrates the effect of a 25 percent increase in the price of X. A new budget constraint line, DH, indicates in terms of pregrant dollars the effect of a 25 percent price increase. This line has a steeper slope than DI, the budget line that would have resulted if there had been no increase in the price of X. If there is a nonmatching grant of $100 for X, as is shown here, there will be less incentive to buy more of X, as its price has increased. There will be more incentive, on purely economic grounds, to allocate symbolically – the opposite effect of the situation in figure 2. If a matching grant in combined with an increase in the price of X, the amount of the change is relative prices caused by the matching fund will be diminished. It is possible that an increase in price could cancel out the effects of the matching fund grant completely, or even put X in a worse position relative to Y than it was prior to the aid program.

An important aspect of the dynamics of federal aid programs can be seen when time is considered as a variable in the analysis.[5] There are three possible patterns of expenditure that can result in an aided program as goes from one year to the next: expenditures can increase, decrease, or remain the same. First, assume that both items in the budget have been increasing from year to year by about the same amount. These increases are supported through raises in the tax rate or an expansion of the tax base. In table 1 this situation is illustrated in columns 1 and 2a. The "normal amount of growth"[6]

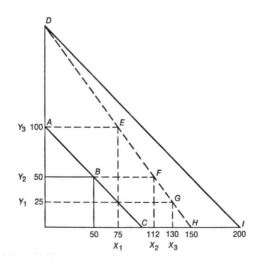

Figure 3.

5. We are indebted to John Henning, professor of economics at Syracuse University, for bringing this feature of the analysis to our attention.

6. Determining a "normal amount of growth," or what expenditures would have been if a grant had not been given, is a very complex problem. An accounting or budgeting technique that has solved this problem has not come to our attention.

Table 1.

	Previous Year	Current Year: with "Normal" Growth	Current Year: Perfect Allocation Plus Growth	Current Year: Perfect Allocation Minus Growth	Current Year: Symbolic Allocation of Growth	Current Year: Catalytic Allocation of Growth	Current Year: "Normal" Decline	Current Year: Perfect Allocation	Current Year: Perfect Allocation Plus Tax Increase	Current Year: Catalytic Allocation
Year / Grants for books	(1) None	(2a) None	(2b) $2,000	(2c) $2,000	(2d) $2,000	(2e) $2,000	(2f) None	(2g) $2,000	(2h) $2,000	(2i) $2,000
Teacher salaries	$8,000	9,000	9,000	9,000	10,000	8,000	9,000	9,000	9,000	8,500
Books	1,000	2,000	4,000	3,000	3,000	5,000	500	2,500	3,000	3,000
Total budget	9,000	11,000	13,000	12,000	13,000	13,000	9,500	11,500	12,000	11,500
Tax decrease				1,000						
Tax increase									500	
Symbolic allocation					1,000					
Catalytic allocation						1,000				500

was $1,000 in each category of expenditure. Now assume that a $2,000 grant is given to the district for books with the assumption of "normal growth"; a perfect allocation is represented by column 2b. Columns 2c, 2d, and 2e show how the budget can be arranged: (1) decrease taxes, (2) allocate symbolically, or (3) allocate catalytically. Each allocation depends on whether "normal growth" is considered and, if so, the value assigned to this growth. Thus several levels of expenditure for teacher salaries, books, or the total budget can all be justified within the restrictions of the grant.

Column 2f shows the case when the "normal growth" of expenditure for books is declining rather than expanding. In this instance, perfect allocation would be $2,500 expenditure for books (column 2g). If the district must use the previous year as a base, they will either have to raise taxes (column 2h) or make a catalytic allocation (2i).

Most of the above discussion dealt with categorical grants-in-aid, the most common type of federal aid program. However, there are a number of general grants, like aid to schools in "federally-affected" areas, and the possible adoption of some form of general-purpose, block-grant programs for states and cities. Further, there are many general aid programs to local units from the states. The difficulty in enforcing any "maintenance of effort" provisos that may accompany block grants can be seen from table 1. The block grants may replace the local tax effort needed to provide the normal growth of programs.

Latitudes of Choice in Mobilizing Activities

Our research found five general categories of variables that affect the latitude of school districts in choosing a symbolic, catalytic, or perfect pattern of resource allocation. Even though these categories of variables were derived from our research in federal aid to education, they are sufficiently general to be applied, with minor modification, to the analysis of resource mobilization in other substantive areas. But before beginning our discussion of these variables, two general observations are appropriate.[7]

First, much of the discussion in this section seems to imply a rationality that is often absent from resource mobilizing. Administrators do not always plan to allocate in symbolic, catalytic, or perfect patterns. Sometimes one pattern or another emerges without plan. Further, the intentions of administrators do not always work out. Faced with a market basket of

---

7. The discussion of these five variables is a condensation of more extended treatments by the authors in an earlier draft of this article, which was presented December 28, 1970, at the joint meetings of the American Economic Association and the Association for the Study of the Grants Economy; D. O. Porter, T. W. Porter, and D. C. Warner, "The Mobilization of Federal Aid by Local Schools: A Political and Economic Analysis" (Paper presented February 5, 1971, at the meetings of the American Educational Research Association); and Porter, *Who Slices the Pie?*

resources with conflicting stipulations, the administrator becomes confused or allocates as best he can.

Second, there is no proper ordering of the variables. Singly, no category of variables explains substantially why one or another of the patterns of resource allocation will be used. Rather, these general categories are highly interrelated. The order of discussion of the variables is arbitrary and is not meant to imply any order of importance.

Technology and Goals

Considerations of efficiency imply, first, that a program has definite goals and, second, that a sufficiently sophisticated technology exists to permit objective evaluations of the impact of an additional or modified input on the outputs of the organization. Unfortunately, most educational programs do not meet these two conditions. No one can specify a single program to "educate" children; there are many life styles, for each of which a different educational approach is appropriate. The choice among these alternatives is based on values and politics. Further, even if a specific goal is agreed upon, theories of learning and teaching are not sufficiently developed to prescribe a series of steps to be followed to arrive at the goal.[8]

Our observations suggest the following proposition as the way factors of technology and goals relate to resource mobilization by organizations: *administrators will have more latitude in choosing patterns of resource allocation as the primary technology they employ becomes less sophisticated and the objectives of the programs become more ambiguous.*

Research verifying that the production function of education is poorly understood is abundant.[9] An examination of the vigorous debate that followed the publication of the Coleman Report[10] shows the relatively low level

---

8. See Thompson, *Organizations in Action*, pp. 83–98, for an excellent discussion of the effects of goals and technologies on evaluation.

9. There is considerable literature dealing with this subject. S. Bowles, "Towards an Educational Production Function," in *Education, Income and Human Capital*, ed. W. Lee Hansen (New York: National Bureau of Economic Research, Columbia University Press, 1970), is perhaps the broadest survey. For other examples see M. Katzman, "Distribution and Production in a Big City Elementary School System," in *Yale Economic Essays* (New Haven, Conn.: Yale University Press, 1969), pp. 201–57; J. Burkhead, *Input and Output in Large City High Schools* (Syracuse, N.Y.: Syracuse University Press, 1967); J. Stark, *The Pattern of Resource Allocation in Education: The Detroit Public Schools 1940 to 1960* (Ph.D. diss., University of Michigan, 1969); S. Balkin, "School Finance and Equal Educational Opportunity" (Department of Economics, Wayne State University).

10. Those interested in that controversy should see J. S. Coleman et al., *Equality of Educational Opportunity* (Washington, D.C.: United States Office of Education, 1966); S. Bowles and M. Levin, "The Determinants of Scholastic Achievement: An Appraisal of Some Recent Evidence," *Journal of Human Resources 3*, no. 1: 3–24; J. S. Coleman, "Equality of Educational Opportunity: Reply to Bowles and Levin," *Journal of Human Resources 3*, no. 2: 237–46; M. S. Smith, "Equality of Educational Opportunity: Comments on Bowles and Levin," *Journal of Human Resources 3*, no. 3: 384–89; Bowles and Levin, "More on Multi-Collinearity and the Effectiveness of Schools," *Journal of Human Resources 3*, no. 3: 393–400. The discussion centered mostly on the extent to which the independent variables were truly independent in determining achievement.

of development in the technologies of education. Inputs, as discussed in this debate, were categorized into three large groups: (1) inputs brought by the student from his innate ability, his experience, and his family; (2) inputs from other students – that is, mostly their socioeconomic characteristics; and (3) the inputs provided by the school, such as teachers, buildings, libraries, and equipment. Attempts to modify these inputs or manipulate them have been frustrated by a lack of consensus on the objectives (due to the localized decision-making processes characteristic of education), because many of the inputs are intractable, and because of a lack of understanding of the effect on outputs of modifications in inputs.

The identification of outputs is at about the same stage of development. The categories of outputs are broad and ill-defined,[11] and the linkages between outputs and inputs are poorly understood.[12] Given this uncertainty, few studies have convincingly shown how the production function of education could be made more efficient.

There were many examples in our interviews of how the ambiguity of goals and the inability of federal evaluators to assess the impact of their inputs allowed greater latitude in the choice of patterns of resource allocation. A review of the evolution of one federal aid program illustrates this point well.

In ESEA I the objective is to help poor children. The formula for distributing the funds is based on the number of children from poor and minority families, and funds are distributed within districts to "target schools" that have the highest concentrations of eligible children. But what services or goods should be purchased with funds from ESEA I to help these children? How can the USOE be assured that the funds are used effectively? How can choices be made among many alternative schemes for teaching poor children? What are the goals of teaching these children – giving them broader cultural experiences or narrowly preparing them for entry into the labor market after they leave school?

These questions were not answered when ESEA I funds entered the budgets of local schools in 1966. Administrators had great latitude in choosing the pattern of allocation because there were so many different programs that could reasonably be conceived of as assisting poor children. Programs included attempts to expose ghetto children to culture by taking them on field trips to museums or bringing art exhibits and string quartets into the schools; the reduction of class size; hiring paraprofessionals to assist teachers; remedial reading, mathematics, and speech programs; extended day programs with sessions after school to provide extra tutoring; summer programs, and many others. With so many choices, a district could choose a symbolic, catalytic, or perfect pattern of allocation at will. For instance, one large district decided to use its ESEA I funds to reduce class

---

11. Bowles, "Towards an Educational Production Function," pp. 20–21.
12. Katzman, "Distribution and Production," pp. 228–29.

size in the target schools, which required hiring more teachers and building "temporary" classrooms; both of these actions were objectives the district had been trying to fund for several years. Another district began a program of remedial reading and mathematics that quickly became larger than could be funded through ESEA I funds alone.

As the program under ESEA I developed, there were growing pressures for concrete results,[13] and the goals were narrowed to increasing the reading and mathematics abilities of eligible children. With these more clearly defined goals, fewer programs could be proposed for support under ESEA I. However, because of the uncertain technology associated with teaching reading and mathematics to educationally deprived children, school districts were still able to adopt widely differing approaches to achieve the new objectives. Thus the districts still had considerable choice in the programs they adopted and the pattern of resource allocation they followed.

Income Sources

A second general factor influencing the degree of latitude exercised by administrators in mobilizing their resources is the number of income sources they have to support their program. Our research suggests the following proposition to explain the effect of the number of income sources on resource mobilization: *administrators will have greater latitude in the choice of a pattern of resource allocation as the number of income sources increases.*

The logic of this proposition is simple. If a district has only one income source, the supplier is able to monitor completely the impact of his contributions. As the number of income sources increases, the ability of any single supplier to trace the impact of his contribution diminishes. The reason can be traced in part to two budgetary strategies practiced, consciously and unconsciously, by almost every administrator we interviewed.

Multipocket Budgeting   The first strategy takes advantage of the varying restrictions placed on income sources. Administrators tend to use resources with the greatest number of restrictions first and to save those with the fewest restrictions until last – that is, as a sort of propensity to conserve all-purpose resources. This strategy, a normal activity for most administrators, is called *multipocket budgeting* in this paper.

Each district has many different accounts from which to finance its activities, and each account has different encumbrances on how it may be used. Federal allocators often assume implicitly that the local administrators plan their "local" programs, fund them, and then turn to the funds available from the federal government only after the local budget has been obligated.

---

13. For example, see Washington Research Project, *Title I of ESEA, Is It Helping Poor Children?* (New York: NAACP Legal Defense and Educational Fund, 1969).

This procedure is usually not followed. More often local administrators follow the strategy of multipocket budgeting. They plan their programs and then review all their income sources, including federal grants, to find the needed resources. This latter procedure tends to promote local priorities at the expense of federal ones.

Federal regulations attempt to keep the programs funded through federal grants separate. Even though many officials at USOE favor the coordination of federal programs by states and local districts, the law has required that the funds not be comingled. All the proposals must finance separate programs. This requirement has frustrated many attempts by state and local officials to coordinate the use of their federal funds, but multi-pocket budgeting exists in spite of the federal regulation. Several examples were found during the interviews with superintendents.

Two southern districts used an informal "programming" approach in their multipocket budgeting as they planned the building of libraries, language laboratories, and science facilities throughout their districts. ESEA I funds, which must be used in "target schools," were used to purchase these programs and facilities for the black schools. (At the time of our interview in 1968 "freedom of choice" was still the approved method of integration, and the target schools were generally the black schools.) NDEA III and ESEA II funds, which may be used anywhere in the district, were combined with local funds and used to put these facilities into the white schools. The procedure was adopted because of the differing encumbrances on each of the sources of income. With this informal programming approach, the superintendents had the opportunity to plan the installation of the facilities throughout the district and to use several sources of income to finance the projects.

The most overt method of multipocket budgeting was developed through what many school administrators are calling "program budgeting." Districts design a number of programs – such as libraries, vocational education, or compensatory education – and seek funds to finance each program. Many different sources of income may be used to support the program. The source of funds is not considered important by the district, merely that the program is fully financed. Program budgeting practices have increased the natural tendency for school administrators to employ this strategy. It encourages them to plan their programs in such a manner that they have more flexibility in choosing symbolic, catalytic, or perfect patterns of resource allocation.

Marginal Mobilizing   A second budgetary strategy relates to the relative productiveness of income sources. Organizations will design their mobilizing efforts so that they will be the most productive on the margin—that is, they marginally mobilize by devoting most of their time to income sources that will yield the highest return for their efforts. This strategy, called *marginal mobilizing* in this paper, was observed in many of the districts we visited, and it explains in part why some districts mobilize more federal funds than others. Some illustrations will demonstrate how this strategy operates.

In districts where the local tax base is productive and expanding (usually middle-income and upper-income suburbs) the efforts of the superintendent's staff will usually be directed more toward cultivating the local voters than toward seeking federal funds. Often such districts will derive less than one-half percent of their budgets from federal sources, even though they may be eligible to compete for substantially more federal funding. Only the federal money that comes to the district automatically and with few strings will be incorporated into the budget. Impressive efforts will be focused on maintaining support for the school's programs in the community, setting up and coaching campaigns for new funds, and working with PTAs and various other citizen groups. The most able men on the superintendent's staff are assigned to these efforts, and incompetence in this area may lead to major shake-ups in the administration.

When local sources of revenue are declining or are not regarded as flexible upward, administrators view these funds as a base from which to work and develop other sources of revenue. In other words, they devote their efforts to the cultivation of income sources that would be more productive on the margin. In one large central-city district, receipts from local property taxes were holding constant or declining slowly. Schoolmen saw little chance of substantially increasing their local revenues because of a long-term erosion of the tax base and vigorous competition from the municipal government for what revenues were available. In this setting the school district assembled a highly skilled, forty-member staff to mobilize funds from the federal and state levels of government; many of the district's personnel are nationally acknowledged as experts in the federal and state support of local schools. Daily contests are maintained with the controllers of funds in the state and federal government. A minimum of effort is devoted to cultivating local financial support for its programs.

In summary, the strategies of multipocket budgeting and marginal mobilizing suggest two ordering procedures in budgeting that may increase the flexibility of an organization in its choice of allocation patterns. First, through multipocket budgeting an organization will obligate its resources in such a way so as to place its own priorities ahead of those of its donors; and second, through marginal mobilizing an organization will concentrate on income sources that are most productive for supporting the activities they hope to continue.

Demand for Education

The demand for educational services varies from school district to school district. Demands for a particular educational service or a package of services may press the administrators of a district to adopt one or another pattern of resource allocation. Our research indicated that *administrators will adopt the pattern of resource allocation that will satisfy the demands of their patrons for educational services.* This proposition may seem obvious, but its impact on the manner in which federal aid to education is utilized is substantial and is sometimes overlooked by analysts of federal aid.

This paper will not analyze all the factors that determine the demand for educational services. However, from our research four broad, interdependent variables seemed to account for most of the variations in demand from district to district. These variables were the past expenditure of the district, the ideology and attitudes of the patrons, the regional location of the district, and the degree of urbanization.

Past Expenditures   When Congress passes legislation to aid a specific educational program, the legislators may be responding to a perceived national need. But some states or districts may already be providing this service adequately. Examples of all three patterns of resource allocation found in the utilization of ESEA II appeared to be rooted in their past expenditures.

Under ESEA II school districts receive aid for the purchase of library materials, texts, and other printed materials. An important requirement is that each district maintain its local effort. Library expenditures, however, are subject to rather uneven increases and vary widely from state to state. The maintenance-of-effort clause penalized jurisdictions that had recently increased their support for libraries and rewarded those that were spending small amounts on these materials. High-expenditure districts were prevented from shifting local funds to areas of higher local priority, whereas districts that had been negligent in providing library materials and services were able to use the ESEA II funds to the fullest extent and could allocate local money, which would have been used to strengthen libraries, for other purposes. In at least one case the federal grant allowed a state to keep its taxes down for another year or two. In this state an officer in the state department of education said that the legislature had been under pressure for several years to provide additional funds for libraries. This pressure subsided after the enactment of ESEA. Similar pressure groups in a neighboring state were successful in getting a bill to aid libraries through the legislature in 1965.

In other jurisdictions, especially in the Southwest, the ESEA II funds served as a catalyst for substantially expanded library programs. Expenditures had been relatively low, and when the federal money became available, administrators designed projects that required more resources than those provided by the federal grant and previous local funds combined.

Ideology and Attitudes   There are two facets to this section: attitudes toward education generally and attitudes toward federal aid to public education.

The first probably has a more significant effect on educational expenditures. The attitudes of district residents toward education seemed to set limits on the level of mobilizing from all sources of income, but particularly on the local level. The patrons of some districts, especially in rural or semirural settings, thought that educational expenditures should be relatively low. In another group of districts, where interest in education was very high, the attitudes allowed substantial expenditures for education without serious dispute; there was a willingness to support unusually high levels of expenditure, irrespective of the source of the funds. A third set of districts were those that had rather extensive local resources but could not exploit them fully because of the unfavorable attitudes toward high educational expenditures held by patrons.

Some districts interviewed refused federal aid on ideological grounds. Two districts in the Southwest would not accept funds through the early NDEA programs but later relented when these funds were supplemented by the ESEA grants. A state official in a Rocky Mountain state reported the same pattern. Several districts in the politically conservative sections of the state had refused to participate in the NDEA programs during their beginning years but were now participating; they had discovered that the federal "strings" were not too tight.

The ideological legacies of many southern districts are a complicated mixture of the desire for racial segregation in the schools and a suspicion of federal control of local schools. The southern districts interviewed were too poor to reject federal aid, however. They accepted the aid, but on the rationalization that integration of their schools was unavoidable, irrespective of whether they accepted federal funds. Segregation, with or without federal aid, is in violation of recent orders of the United States Supreme Court. So the school boards and superintendents concluded that if integration was inevitable, they might as well get as much as they can from the federal government to pay for the integrated system. One southern superintendent expressed satisfaction that he had been able to mobilize over 15 percent of his budget from federal sources. Another was receiving 25 percent of his revenues from Washington. (The national average is under 8 percent.)

Regional Location   Differences in past expenditures and attitudes toward educational expenditures are often reflected in the regional location of the state or district. Thus, the various regions of the United States offer differing combinations and levels of school services. When a national program of federal aid attempts to impose a national priority on these varying regions, there are obvious differences in how the funds will be utilized.

Different mobilization patterns are related to regional variations in expectations about the performance of the school system. In northeastern communities most districts had provided libraries in their elementary and junior high schools several years prior to the passage of ESEA II. Local and state sources of finance had been established to support libraries. Therefore, superintendents in those districts often shifted their ESEA II entitlements toward their relatively tighter construction budgets. In the South and some of the Rocky Mountain States, funds for expanded library programs were just beginning to be available for elementary and junior high schools. The ESEA II funds were used to purchase basic book collections and to hire new personnel. In one district in the South the demands from patrons for library facilities were such that the superintendent indicated that he thought funds for libraries were sufficient prior to ESEA II, even though he had used the ESEA II funds to organize and staff libraries in his elementary and junior high schools.

Urbanization Patterns　Variations in school districts that are rooted in urban, suburban, or rural locations have been rather extensively studied.[14] A number of these variations, but by no means all of the variations discussed in the literature, were observed in the interviews conducted for this study.

The most salient characteristic observed was the shortage of funds in urban and rural districts. Most large central-city and rural districts interviewed were experiencing rather severe financial shortages. The suburban districts, as a group, were relatively better off. The reasons for this financial press in urban and rural districts may be similar – a declining residential and business base on which the local property taxes were levied. These financial shortages had a definite effect on the flexibility of district mobilizers in the patterns of resource allocation they chose. With local resources so restricted, schoolmen had to look to state and federal funds to meet their basic educational needs. Under these conditions, most of the federal grants were used in perfect or symbolic patterns, with almost no opportunity for catalytic patterns to develop because of the inability of the district to provide additional local funds.

Other variations were related to the types of programs emphasized. Urban districts were seeking funds for compensatory programs that came largely from the federal government. Funds for the construction of new plants, the central concern of many suburban districts, come primarily from local bond issues; therefore, federal sources were not seen as an important supplier of funds for one of the most pressing needs of the suburban districts. Many suburban districts hardly bothered with the federal programs, but central-city districts usually had substantial staffs devoting full time to the mobilization of federal funds.

---

14. A. K. Campbell and J. Burkhead, "Public Policy for Urban America," in *Issues in Urban Economics*, ed. H. S. Perleff and L. Wingo, Jr. (Baltimore: Johns Hopkins Press, 1968); A. K. Campbell and S. Sacks, *Metropolitan America* (New York: The Free Press, 1967); Advisory Commission on Intergovernmental Relations, *Fiscal Balance in the American System* (Washington, D.C.: U.S. Government Printing Office, 1967).

Professionalism

Three professional norms are particularly influential in the mobilization of resources in education.[15] First, educators argue, education must be treated as a separate function, both financially and governmentally. School districts were one of the first and are now the most numerous special districts in the United States. Professional educators consistently resist any efforts to combine school districts or their budgets with other local governments. Second, and closely related to the first norm, schools should not be involved in partisan politics.[16] Third, schools must be controlled by professionals.[17]

As a result of these three norms, education is placed apart from other government activities, ensuring that its requests for funds will be considered independently and not in competition with other government services. Local government officials, with their potentially competing priorities, are excluded from authoritative participation in school budgeting; they are both partisan and nonpartisan professional. Even school boards are not able to exert an overwhelming influence on the school budgets because they are not professional educators.

Powerful local, state, national, and university-based institutions promote these professional norms. The National Educational Association (NEA) and the American Federation of Teachers (AFT) have organizations of teachers and administrators that correspond with all levels of government. These organizations serve as bases of organizational and professional power by providing lobbying and bargaining services, by supplying research capabilities needed to generate information with which to do battle with reluctant local taxpayers, the school board, or the legislature, and by controlling the entry of "professionals" into education.

The result of these institutions and norms is that professional schoolmen have an overwhelming influence over the government apparatus that initiates state and federal legislation, works out guidelines for implementation and evaluation of those programs, and initiates and executes the school programs at the local level. Decisions on whether to seek federal aid and which pattern of resource allocation to follow are often based on professional criteria.

An example from our interviews illustrates how professional considerations may affect resource mobilization. Federal aid specialists from several big-city districts had formed a quasi-professional association to plan strategies for mobilizing more funds from the federal government.This group met regularly and often traveled to Washington to present the case of the large-city districts. Their activities included presenting testimony at legislative

15. R. C. Martin, *Government and the Suburban School* (Syracuse, N.Y.: Syracuse University Press, 1963), pp. 6–7, 98.

16. R. A. Dahl, *Who Governs?* (New Haven, Conn.: Yale University Press, 1961), p. 161; H. R. Jones *Financing Public Elementary and Secondary Education* (New York: The Center for Applied Research in Education, 1966), pp. 68–69.

17. R. C. Martin, *Government and the Suburban School*, p. 98.

hearings, placing personnel on committees in the USOE that draft the rules and regulations for federally funded programs, and orchestrating major lobbying efforts, such as the successful campaign to override President Nixon's veto in 1969 of funds for federally impacted areas (P.L. 874). The NEA performs similar functions on a much larger scale.

In the case of the individual administrator, professionalism influences resource mobilization by providing many alternative ways in which he may develop his career. The individual administrator's perception of his role influences his behavior as a mobilizer. The behavior of the person who perceives his business as education and not finance will certainly differ from that of the administrator who considers mobilizing outside resources as a central educational responsibility. For the mobilizer, involvement in federal aid is sometimes considered a way of improving one's professional reputation. Activity in the federal aid network is seen as a way to gain higher personal visibility beyond the local and even state levels in education.

The organizational and environmental conditions surrounding the job of the mobilizer do not entirely determine success or failure at mobilizing. Individual psychological predisposition makes a significant difference in the mobilizing process, and to omit or underestimate it as a factor would be a serious fault. A person who enjoys preparing proposals, actively pursuing federal money by shepherding the proposals through the bureaucracy, and handling larger sums of money than would ordinarily be provided by local and state sources is usually the most effective person at mobilizing federal money. The successful mobilizer is comfortable communicating with various groups within the community as proposals are developed, with schoolmen in other districts from whose experience he can learn, with professional groups for support and suggestions, and with state and federal people in the communication networks developed around federal aid to education. He develops helpful contacts in many places and constantly keeps in touch, seeking and creating opportunities for his district. His energies are not directed only toward the daily affairs of the local district.

The individual personality as a psychological variable lies outside our competence for analysis, but the complex relationship between certain types of personalities and success at mobilizing federal aid deserves further research.

Federal Administration and Regulation

Federal regulations have a more limited effect on the allocation patterns of school districts than is often supposed. *They are important, and administrators are aware of the regulations of each federal program they are participating in; but in spite of the differing requirements of each federal act, symbolic, catalytic and perfect allocation patterns occurred in all of the programs investigated.* Other factors, such as the professionalism of school personnel, the number of other income sources, multipocket and marginal budgeting strategies, the ambiguity of the goals of education, the relatively unsophisticated technologies used, and the demands for educational services are usually a greater influence on how federal aid will be allocated.

The difficulties of evaluating the performance of educational institutions seem to lie at the base of the ineffectiveness of many of the federal controls and regulations. Several federal and state officials lamented that there are no effective tests of the impact of federal aid on learning programs and that most of the tests measuring student performance are culturally biased. When a new program is introduced with the assistance of federal aid, the administrators cannot predict in advance what information to collect so that effective evaluations can be conducted. This contributes to a continuing lack of the information necessary for evaluation of such programs.

Underlying the lack of adequate tests of effectiveness are the unsophisticated and intensive technologies used in teaching and the uncertainty about goals. Without clear or stable objectives and without sophisticated technologies capable of achieving goals that may be selected, evaluation is at best a game of calculated guesswork.

Information and Feedback   Besides the informational problems associated with technologies and the ambiguity of goals, there are a number of important administrative difficulties that make difficult the collection of accurate and meaningful information on the performance of a school district. First, in order to obtain information on which allocation patterns are being followed, evaluators must be intimately acquainted with the activities of the district. Such acquaintance cannot be restricted to the financial records. The evaluator must be familiar with such things as the materials being purchased with grant money and whether these items were purchased with other funds in the recent past. Such questions become very complicated in concrete situations.

A further complicating factor is the large number of school districts in the United States. In 1965–66 there were 26,983 school districts.[18] The in-depth evaluations of expenditures needed to determine the use of federal aid funds in this many districts are not feasible. Further, not only are there a large number of school districts, there are also many sources of income for each district.

State-Federal Relations   Almost all the federal aids to education are channeled through state governments, creating two levels of control. Each state submits a "state plan" to the USOE. Many of these state plans are quite general and are written according to a formula that ensures they will comply with the law provided by the USOE. State plans in two federal programs, though, reflected important additions to the federal guidelines.

---

18. U.S. Office of Education, *Digest of Education Statistics, 1968* (Washington, D.C.: U.S. Government Printing Office, 1968), p. 6.

In ESEA I and ESEA III the size and/or the competitive nature of the programs allowed the states to impose many of their own priorities. For instance, ESEA III was used by some states to channel funds into suburban schools. They viewed the ESEA III funds as a chance to balance the ESEA I money that is tied to the low-income populations of the large central cities. In the ESEA I program, one state stipulated that the money must be concentrated in a relatively few target schools, whereas some other states tried to justify spreading the funds around among as many schools as possible within a district. Federal guidelines allowed both practices.

There are also more general effects of channeling the funds through the state governments. The state department of education, like local school districts, is also mobilizing resources to meet its demands and priorities. Federal funds will be used in symbolic, catalytic, and perfect resource allocation patterns by the state government as they move through to the local district. Thus, the longer the "intermediary chain" between the donor and the ultimate recipient, the more probable it is that the restrictions of the donor will be substantially adjusted to meet the priorities of two or more organizations. Two examples may be cited. Mounting pressures for a Rocky Mountain state legislature to provide additional support for school libraries were abated by the passage of ESEA II. A state in the Northeast was able to meet many of its demands for increased aid to central-city schools with ESEA I. The appropriations from the state for compensatory education stopped increasing after 1965.

Legislative Language   A factor that greatly facilitates a flexible use of federal aid and such strategies as multipocket budgeting and marginal mobilizing is the fact that many of the "categories" for which aid is available are so imprecise and broad that almost any expenditure can be justified. Unsuccessful efforts have been made since the late 1940s to pass a bill that would provide general aid to education. However, proponents of federal aid to education have succeeded in pushing bills through Congress that provide at least some funds for every school district in the United States. Considering the varied needs of these thousands of school districts, the "categorical" provisions of the three or four major acts that distribute this money must of necessity be rather "general." For instance, every school district has science, mathematics, library, and English departments as part of their normal program. It is inevitable that assistance to these programs through the NDEA III will become general aid in part. Programs designed to help the "educationally deprived" also include many general fund activities. Although these grants are concentrated in "target schools," the benefits of these grants are not confined to the poorer students.

Powerful political pressures thwart efforts that might tighten the legislative language of the larger cities. An attempt to review a guideline for ESEA I provides an excellent example. The formula for distributing ESEA I funds is based on the number of children in the district from poor families.

But the intention of the USOE had not been merely to reward jurisdictions that have poor children but also to have some impact on the education of these children. Toward this end, in February 1970 the U.S. Commissioner of Education, James Allen, announced a revised guideline on comparability. He stated that state and local expenditure on each child in a district must be comparable from school to school and that funds from ESEA I must be added to state and local resources. Thus ESEA I money would be truly compensatory and additive as it is supposed to be in theory.

Only in small northern suburbs is ESEA I money currently spent in that manner, usually on after-school or summer camp activities. In no big-city or southern school district did we observe strict comparability.

In addition to defining comparability strictly,

> the new guideline said the state educational agency shall "require" each local education agency to demonstrate that comparability exists or to submit a plan to achieve comparability for the fall of 1970 school term. By April 1, the states were to submit their criteria for judging local educational agencies adherence to comparability. Although the guideline did not mention it, officials made it clear that non-compliance would mean cutoff of funds. . . . Since most of a school budget . . . goes into teacher salaries and the more experienced, higher paid teachers tend to stay on in middle class schools, school districts would have to add some of the more experienced teachers, para-professionals, or some other instructional program to the under-par schools.[19]

The threat to ongoing programs was fantastic. In some Southern districts almost the only money spent on black classes is ESEA I money.

Commissioner Allen's directive was sidetracked in two ways:

> After a hassle that almost gutted the entire comparability require-ment, a little noticed Congressional amendment was passed which undercut the task force definition of comparability in two ways: one, Congress questioned the use of differences in teacher pay based on length of service to figure comparability, and two, the date when noncompliance could mean cutting off funds was pushed back to 1972.[20]

Further, Commissioner Allen was fired early in the summer of 1970, but for reasons unrelated to his educational philosophy.

Thus, the looseness of the language in congressional acts and executive guidelines defining the aided categories, combined with the efforts of administrators to push the federal money into areas of the greatest need for their own districts, converts a large proportion of the categorical grants into

---

19. P. Myers, "The Floundering Effort to Improve City Schools," *City*, June–July 1970, p. 16.

20. Ibid.

general aid. The conversion may result in both symbolic and catalytic allocations or in ambiguous allocations. In order to satisfy the formal definition of symbolic or catalytic allocation, funds must be spent "outside" an aided program or attract additional funds into an aided category. If the boundaries of the aided and nonaided programs are too imprecise, the concepts of symbolic and catalytic allocation lose much of their usefulness.

Maintenance of Effort   The greatest hope of federal allocators is that aid will be used as "seed" money. Unfortunately, only districts with substantial local resources use the federal money in catalytic allocation patterns with any regularity. Most poor districts cannot afford to take advantage of seed money grants. They cannot provide the resources needed to carry a project beyond the initial stage.

It is very difficult to determine if a grant is actually adding to a local budget,[21] partly because of the many problems involving the collection of reliable, current information. But in an effort to circumvent these complexities, some federal regulations select an arbitrary method for determining the "base" from which all the aid given to school districts must be additional. This was the procedure followed in the ESEA II. The average expenditures for the two most recent years are the base from which all ESEA II expenditures must add. The difficulty with such a requirement is that expenditures within the fifty states and 26,000 school districts for libraries and texts do not increase at a smooth and uniform rate. They increase and decrease in fits and starts. Those districts or states that had the lack of foresight to increase their expenditures for libraries in 1965 have been penalized; those that did not have been able to use the federal funds to support an essential item in their school programs.

A second administrative device that has been discussed as affecting the maintenance of local effort is the percent of matching funds required of the receiving agency.[22] Although this question was not explored systematically in our interviews, some of its consequences were observed. First, if local districts were required to provide too high a percent of the funds there was a strong probability that districts would apply for the funds only if they planned to undertake a project even without the aid. The grant covered so small a proportion of any project that it could not provide sufficient inducement or undertake a new program. The same effect was observed when the absolute amount of the grant was quite small, regardless of the matching formula required. Small grants, such as NDEA III or NDEA V-A, tended to be absorbed into the regular operating budgets of the districts.

On the other hand, if the federal share of the grant is too high, there is

---

21. For a more technical explanation of this difficulty, see table I.

22. G. P. Break, *Intergovernmental Fiscal Relations* (Washington, D.C.: The Brookings Institution, 1967), p. 96; T. O'Brian and W. H. Robinson, "Federal Highway Grants," mimeographed (Washington, D.C.: Bureau of the Budget, February 23, 1967).

the possibility that the recipient will be able to shift into other programs local funds that would have been used for that project. Thomas O'Brian and William H. Robinson demonstrated this effect in their analysis of the federal highway program.[23] The same behavior was observed in many of the compensatory programs funded through ESEA I. Several districts and states were able to rely almost completely on federal funds to meet their demands for these programs. Without the federal aid they might have provided at least some local funds or they might have been willing to furnish matching funds.

Categorical versus General Grants   In earlier sections it was suggested that the effects of categorical grants are diminished by the large number of income sources in school districts and such budget strategies as multipocket budgeting and marginal mobilizing. *The combination of these factors seems to support the proposition that as the number of categorical aids increases, the more general these aids become.*

But this feature of categorical grants is heavily influenced by the relative wealth of the district. The poor districts interviewed seemed to prefer categorical grants as long as they are relatively dependable and are not tied to some sort of competition. Categorical grants in this case increase the flexibility of the school district by adding more sources of income and facilitating multipocket budgeting. Because all general support from state and local funds is committed to salaries and maintenance, the poorer districts view the federal government as their only source of funds for innovative or discretionary projects.

Wealthier districts did not appear as interested in categorical federal aid. They will accept funds that can be obtained with little trouble, such as ESEA II or P.L. 874 and P.L. 815, but often refuse to participate in NDEA III and V-A and are less than enthusiastic about ESEA I because of the regulations attached to these programs.

The critical difference between the wealthy and poor districts seems to be that the wealthy districts have enough discretionary funds available from local sources. Local funds do not have as many strings and reports associated with them as the federal grants. Poor districts are more willing to accept the federal strings because of their need for additional sources of income.

The administrators interviewed did not seem to be aware of the specific features of distribution formulae for the federal programs except for the formulae that were based on some attributes of the student population in their districts. Then, the only formulae that influenced how the funds were used was the ESEA I program. Those formulae were used to establish the target schools that received aid. With the other formulae, administrators have little control over the distribution of the funds until they reach the state; then they can sometimes influence how it is distributed.

---

23. O'Brian and Robinson, "Federal Highway Grants."

Timing, Coordination, and Accruals Most of the complaints about federal controls or federal grants at the local level were not about restrictions on objects of expenditure (multipocket budgeting could deal with these), but rather were concerned with: (1) the difficulty of making many different applications to different agencies; (2) the problem of coordinating five to six different fiscal years with the school district's fiscal year; and (3) most important, the rigid duration of grants; because accruals of federal funds were not permitted at the local or project level, tremendous waste was engendered. To the local administrator these are serious deficiencies, which lead to great inefficiencies. The cost of coordinating many sets of applications, stipulations, and deadlines is high.

The most debilitating aspect of many federal grants to every local administrator interviewed was the fact that they often learned whether they would receive the funds at the last moment and that each year's allocation had to be entirely spent by the end of the fiscal year. Nearly every ESEA I or ESEA III project director interviewed recommended that (1) all large programs should be funded initially at a fairly low level for planning purposes and then at a higher level after the "bugs" are ironed out; and (2) that project directors or school boards should be able to learn how much money they will have to spend at least six to eight months in advance.

Why do these funding patterns persist? Why is there a proliferation of deadlines, programs, and unreasonable expenditure requirements, with accruals not permitted? Perhaps the answer lies in the institutional framework of the federal government, which forces grantors of funds to be more concerned with mobilizing the resources for future grants than with the efficient allocation of funds that have already been appropriated. Because the grantor's performance and the importance of his bureau or agency is judged by the relevant House Appropriations Subcommittee to be partly a function of its "base" (the previous year's disbursements and expenditures) and partly a function of the political clout of his clientele (in this case the education establishment), the grantor is under some pressure to make sure many districts get grants and that grant funds are spent by the end of the fiscal year.[24]

Concluding Statements

It is a fruitful thing to start study of any social phenomenon at the point of least prestige. For, since prestige is so much a matter of symbols, and even of pretensions – however well merited – there goes with prestige a tendency to preserve a front of names, of indirection, of secrecy (much of it necessary secrecy). On the other hand, in things of less prestige, the core may be more easy of access.

Everett C. Hughes[25]

---

24. See A. Wildavsky, *The Politics of the Budgetary Process* (Boston: Little, Brown & Co., 1964).

25. E. C. Hughes, *Men and Their Work* (Glencoe, Ill.: Free Press of Glencoe, 1958), pp. 48–49.

Most analyses of budgeting begin with the elitist assumption that the decisions are made at the top of the hierarchy, or in this case, by the federal government. The central orientation of this study has been to reverse this manner of thinking about federal aid. It has focused on the processes of resource mobilization by school districts and attempted to outline a framework for discovering and analyzing some of the important factors that influence their mobilization patterns. No organization passively accepts resources as they are "allocated" to it from above. Rather, organizations actively mobilize most of their resources and attempt, through such strategies as multipocket budgeting and marginal mobilizing, to pursue programs in line with their own needs and demands.

The main finding of our research on federal aid is that factors other than federal regulations and formulae have a greater impact on the patterns of resource allocation used by recipient agencies. A melange of factors, discovered in the interviews with superintendents, influence the emergence of symbolic, catalytic, or perfect patterns of allocation. As yet the models developed in this study do not provide much guidance in predicting how future increments of federal aid will be used by organizations; they do, however, *describe* some of the factors that regularly influence the flow of these funds.

Federal allocators can have only limited control over the final disposition of their funds. Our findings indicate that the ambiguity of the goals, unsophisticated technologies, the number and characteristics of its income sources, strategies such as multipocket budgeting or marginal mobilizing, and professionalism and vested interests of school staffs are the primary groups of factors that influence patterns of mobilization in local school districts.

Most of these factors are not easily regulated or controlled. They are not subject to "rational" or quick changes, if they can be changed at all. No indications were seen that the serious innovations necessary to reduce the number of income sources, to effectively equalize school expenditures *within and among* classrooms, schools, school districts, and states, and to radically increase federal support for education were being planned at any level of government. Rather, most of the activity seems to be centered in the areas promising the least results in terms of "rationalizing" federal aid flows – that is, efforts to introduce revenue sharing, to change matching fund requirements, to add maintenance of effort clauses, or to manipulate the distribution formulae.

Marginal changes in formulae or requirements have not had a significant or predictable impact on the way in which funds are spent at the local level. Federal controls erect a maze of requirements, which, if they cannot be manipulated to fit the local district's objectives, will be ignored, or the money will not be accepted, or it will be diverted in some manner.

The "innovative" or "compensatory" effects of federal aid depend – to a much greater extent than current literature or prevalent thinking on budgeting or resource allocation indicate – on the local administrators, organizations, and communities that receive federal money. Instead of local education being molded by federal aims, it appears that more often local educators are able to mold the federal money and programs to fit their own local priorities and values. More research is needed to describe the process of acquiring and spending federal dollars by local districts. If at times this process should be modified to meet pressing national needs, the process itself must be more fully understood.

Transfers as Instruments of Urban Ecological Policy

In few areas of life have urbanization and industrialization caused such debacles as in the ecology; the very processes that lead to improvements in material welfare have led to pollution of air, water, and land. The papers of this section explore how the successes and failures of exchange or market processes and of grants processes have contributed to the present malaise. They also point out some implications for the use of taxes and transfers as instruments of policies to preserve the urban ecology and for the interaction between both means for financing reforms.

Myrick Freeman examines some implications of grants as instruments and products of pollution-control policies. Special attention is given to the interaction between the grants and exchange sectors of the economy and the ways that grants used for and created by environmental policies affect relative prices and resource allocation. Grants in the form of direct and indirect subsidies to firms for pollution-control activities are compared with charges, and judicial enforcement is compared with sanctions in terms of efficiency and effectiveness in achieving given ambient environmental quality standards.

Because grants do not compare favorably with the alternatives in terms of the proffered criteria, Freeman concludes that it is more appropriate to consider grants as means of redistributing the costs of pollution control. Again, direct and indirect subsidies of pollution-control efforts are considered in terms of their equity, or distribution effects, and the likely costs of achievement. In addition, grants patterned after the "adjustment assistance" provisions of the Trade Expansion Act of 1962 and the Canadian-American Automotive Trade Agreements are discussed. It is suggested that a good case can be made for making adjustment assistance available where pollution-control efforts result in a few bearing large costs through unemployment for the benefit of the many.

The distribution of benefits from improvement in environmental quality is determined by market and pseudomarket mechanisms, which leads to a distribution in which those who have higher incomes tend to get the best environments. In the three cities studied, "air pollution exposure was inversely related to income, and blacks on the average were exposed to considerably lower quality air than whites. . . . Areas with the highest air pollution are also the areas where the proportion of rental-occupancy to owner-occupancy is highest." On the other hand, Freeman notes that if improvement in air quality, in recreation, and in water pollution abatement close to urban concentrations were effected, the distributive results would be more favorable. However, "the most effective way to improve the general distribution of the environment is to improve the basic distribution of wealth." He then concludes: "In sum, I am not enthusiastic about the opportunities for using environmental policies to improve distributional equity."

Thomas Havrilesky discusses the role of technological innovativeness and of grants in the context of the ecological crisis. He emphasizes the fact that a major obstacle to the passage and vigorous enforcement of efficient pollution-control programs is the inadequacy of data on the extent of and dangers from emissions from various sources. Public policy must offset the legal and political impediments to obtaining this information before an efficient program, charging emission fees for the use of a quantity of a common property resource, can be enforced.

After completing this critical summary, he examines the following aspects of the economics of pollution control: (1) There will be a shrinkage in the budgetary purchasing power of individuals, who will devote proportionately more of their incomes to buying goods and services whose prices are forced up by pollution-control programs. He argues that the burden of pollution abatement, as a percentage of income, is borne most heavily by the poor. Environmental quality programs are inconsistent with the war on poverty and must be complemented by a steeply graduated negative income tax. (2) Individuals who feel threatened by pollution cannot use the market or the courts to resolve their problems and must make their plight known either to consumers of products whose production, operation, or packaging are associated with environmental deterioration or to those who can help enact pollution-control legislation. An increasingly well-developed system of unilateral transfer payments from government and foundations allows minority groups to mobilize information-disseminating resources without which their aspirations would be stifled. The change in consumers' tastes and voters' opinions wrought by antipollution minority groups and initiated outside the market's exchange system reflects the role of the grants economy in abetting the participatory revolution of which ecological protest is just a small part. Coming to grips with this aspect of the communication and information market is at least as important for improving the environment as analyses of pollution-abatement programs, which seek a neat balance among the incremental costs and benefits of alternative pollution-control programs. (3) We commonly think of technologists as operating solely on the supply and production side of the pollution-abatement market. Yet the technologist, as he teaches, writes, and speaks about his work, is an opinion maker on the demand side of the market as well. Havrilesky envisions a public policy that encourages informed technologists, individually or as an organized group, to countervail against the producers of environmental "bads" and thereby to increase the flow of environmental information, without which no pollution-control program can efficiently operate. Such a policy would be a major step toward imbuing the technologist with a sense of ethical commitment to the public good. (4) Because they are increasingly aware of the implicit social damages emanating from the unrestrained market-exchange system, many groups in society are becoming increasingly wary of the moralism that the unfettered market-exchange system and its cultural trappings provide optimal social welfare. Indeed, a dominant cultural development, especially among the young, is a growing repudiation of this moralism. Attempts to analyze the ecological crisis ring hollow if they fail to overlook this pervasive trend. He concludes that the emergence of the influential and socially responsible technologist and the institutions operating through the grants economy, publicizing the plight of harmed minorities, constitute major steps toward integrating technological change into the cultural fabric without the continual disruptive side effects associated with the handling of technology by the unrestrained market-exchange system.

Allan Schmid's main focus is on the role of property rights in the context of environmental policy. He notes that the growth of the grants economy of unilateral transfers is in part a response to demands for a different performance of the market economy. Grants are a device to supplement the performance of the market. But it is his judgment that a substantially different result in terms of the environment will not be obtained with the essentially marginal adjustments now possible within either the grants economy or the market economy, given present property rights. Both bilateral and unilateral exchange depend on the underlying property rights, which constitute a directional thrust that shapes the subsequent exchanges. If we are to have nonmarginal improvement in the environment, we shall have to make a nonmarginal change in institutions; and that means adjusting property rights.

Present environmental policy tends toward spreading the cost of improvement on the general taxpayer rather than toward increasing the cost to consumers of goods whose production pollutes. It depends to a large extent on processes like using tax funds to buy out highway billboards or to finance low-flow augmentation reservoirs. (Even municipal sewage treatment plants are financed by general taxes, with low-population and congested areas sharing the bill.) The author notes that present property rights tend to give the right of disposal to those who can appropriate it, and the results can be only marginally modified by public spending or transfers. If present environmental performance is to be substantially redirected, we will need to redefine property rights and to declare prime public claims on certain resources. If public ownership were clarified, it would be possible to utilize the market-exchange process to a greater extent by renting limited use for waste disposal and relying less on police power prohibitions.

The next two papers examine pollution abatement with the aid of the formal body of welfare economics. George Daly and Fred Giertz note that two distinct but related strains have emerged from the substantial body of post-1960 literature dealing with externalities. The first, originally inspired by Coase's classic 1960 article, is that there exists a substantial range of problems involving activities which generate external costs or benefits or both in which Pareto optimality can be achieved through voluntary arrangements (exchange relationships) between the affected and affecting parties. In terms of policy recommendations, the general thrust of this literature has been to suggest minimizing the role of governmental intervention and instead to allow "markets in externalities" to develop. A second feature of this literature (and of earlier literature as well) is the notion that modifications to externality-creating activities, whether voluntary or not, should directly involve the level at which the activity is performed. Thus if a steel factory pours smoke on a nearby laundry, the appropriate topic for negotiation or regulation is the amount of steel (and hence smoke) produced.

Both strains seem to be at variance with real-world approaches to environmental pollution. Here we find increasing public outcries for something to be done about the "pollution problem" and the apparent public and political realization that the solution to the problem will involve increased government intervention in the economy. In addition, we find that in many cases the standards imposed do not directly concern the volume of pollution-generating activity but rather concern abatement measures, which in many cases are designed to allow the primary activity to continue at or near normal levels. For example, most technical research in the area of automobile air pollution has dealt with engine and fuel modifications, the use of filters, and so on rather than with the reduction or elimination of automobile traffic.

Daly and Giertz show that the achievement of Pareto optimality in a world of pollution-type external diseconomies requires an eclectic approach that in general will involve both the curtailment of the primary activity *and* the institution of abatement measures. They note that even when people are aware of pollution and of techniques for reducing it, privately organized activity will result in a greater than optimal level of pollution-generating activity and a less than optimal level of its abatement. Because of problems analogous to the "free-rider" effect of public goods theory, markets in pollution-type externalities will not tend to develop, thus making some type of collective action necessary for the achievement of optimality. They conclude that it is not inconsistent for individuals who are actively engaged in a pollution-generating activity to favor laws that would require the reduction or elimination of this activity or the introduction of compulsory abatement measures or both.

Robert Strotz and Colin Wright examine the following propositions of the classic and more recent literature on the subject of externalities, with special reference to externalities occurring in the form of air pollution:

"1. To equate private and social marginal cost should not be the policy criterion for maximum welfare." They put this objection aside, as they show that their derivation of the classic solution did not require such an approach.

"2. Merger is a solution to the externality problem." Although merger can internalize the externalities that create pollution problems, it is "preposterous" to assume that it is a general or important solution.

"3. In principle, private bribes are as good a solution as the classic tax solution." They show that "allowing B to bribe A, when no tax exists, results in a Pareto optimum and is equivalent to the classic tax solution."

"4. The classic tax solution is unsatisfactory because it does not lead to a Pareto equilibrium." Strotz and Wright distinguish among different situations: (a) "The nonparametric case, in which damaged and damaging parties are well aware of each other. In this case the state can impose a pollution tax on A and pay the proceeds to B as an indemnity; A can bribe B for the privilege of polluting; the state can impose a flat tax on B, effect a transfer payment to A, and then impose a pollution tax on A and pay the proceeds to B as an indemnity; or B can bribe A. Any of the four solutions can take us to a Pareto optimum, and either tax solution will eliminate any incentive for a private bribe. Analytically all four solutions are equivalent." (b) "The parametric case, in which B does not identify A or, in the realistic extension of our model, there are many firms A and many firms B, and private bribes are strategically and informationally unachievable. Here the only available solution is the classic tax solution, and it does not matter whether or not the proceeds are paid to the injured firms as indemnities; in fact, they could be refunded to the damaging firms, provided the refunds are regarded by them as parametric. Certainly in the case of air pollution (and for that matter, for most externalities we think of), the parametric case is generally the more relevant one. This judgment leaves the classic analysis quite intact."

"5. The feasibility of the classic solution depends on whether or not the externalities are separable." Strotz and Wright conclude that "nothing new is introduced into the classic analysis by nonseparability. The Davis-Whinston analysis is best viewed as a critique of bribery solutions for the nonparametric and nonseparable case. Although the production externalities of air pollution are generally nonseparable (at least in the long run, when plant size may be regarded as variable), the nonparametric case is not generally applicable, and hence the bribery solution is not to be expected in any case."

The authors continue by focusing their theoretical insights on policy aspects of pollution control: (1) "Neither merger nor a system of private bribes is a practical solution to the air pollution problem; government intervention is the only recourse if the problem is to be significantly mitigated." (2) "Is it better to tax firms or individuals who pollute or to subsidize the installation of pollution abatement devices? The answer is that there is no analytical distinction from the standpoint of resource allocation between taxing someone for doing something or subsidizing him not to do it." (3) The authors ask further "whether it matters if the tax (or subsidy) is based exclusively on . . . the amount of pollution-creating production or on the use (or nonuse) of . . . the amount spent on pollution-control equipment. The answer . . . is that it does make a difference. . . . In principle one ought not to tax or to subsidize only the production that yields pollution or only the nonuse or use of pollution-abatement equipment. Instead, both should be taxed or subsidized at appropriate rates, or alternatively, the tax should be imposed on the quantity of pollution emitted." (4) "A final comment concerns the practical application of the classic tax-subsidy solution. There is nothing to be sanguine about. . . . The information requirements for the application of the classic theory are excessive from the practical point of view, especially in so complex a network of externalities as that presented by the pollution problem. One can hope that by trial and error the classic solution could be approximated, but other devices may be more suitable both informationally and administratively, especially the use of legally fixed standards for pollution control and the use of zoning."

Strotz and Wright conclude that Pareto welfare economics has nothing to say about the distributive consequences of these measures: a system of transfers presumably can be introduced to achieve a socially desirable income distribution. Nonetheless, they note that "pollution-control measures probably work more to the benefit of the poor, who live and work under polluted conditions, than of the rich, who are better able to avoid pollution, for example, by living in suburbs and by working in air conditioned surroundings. Pollution, aggravating a problem of urban flight, may foster a second round of externalities by encouraging a concentration of the poor in the polluted enclaves of society, where they spin off further external diseconomies on each other."

14

A. Myrick Freeman III: Grants and
Environmental Policy

Introduction

In addition to studying the internal workings of the grants sector, students of the grants economy must also examine the interaction between the grants sector and the exchange sector of the economic system. Grants affect prices and other variables in the exchange sector, and these interactions must be understood before predictions or normative prescriptions concerning grants policies can be offered.

For example, if a public sector grant program is initiated on anything but a random basis, and if the factor that creates eligibility can be acquired through exchange, the private sector market for the goods that bring eligibility will be affected, and possibly rents will be created. To receive agricultural subsidy payments one must own or rent farmland, and the price of farmland has risen as a consequence. Unemployment payments are conditioned on the fact of unemployment. They make unemployment a relatively more valuable status than it would be in the absence of the payments, and they thus raise the price at which an individual would be willing to part with that status – that is, become employed.

In addition to creating or destroying marketable values directly, grants can alter the marginal signals decision makers must interpret, and relative prices and resource allocations can be affected. Also, where the public sector relies on nonmarket resource allocation mechanisms such as grants to achieve its aims, markets may emerge (for example, black markets) or goods may be allocated indirectly via market mechanisms.

In the broadest sense, all the activities of the public sector affect the structure of incentives, rewards, and penalties in the exchange sector of the economy. The task of the policy analyst is to perceive these incentives accurately and to predict the responses of the economic agents of the private sector. This paper will offer some observations on environmental policy, with particular reference to the interactions of the grants and exchange economies. I will first consider grants as instruments of environmental policy, then as products of environmental policy. Finally, I will offer some comments on the appropriate role of equity considerations in environmental policy.

Presented at the Symposium on the Grants Economy held between the Association for the Study of the Grants Economy and the American Association for the Advancement of Science, Chicago, Illinois, December, 1970. Reprinted by permission of the author. Dr. Freeman is associate professor of economics at Bowdoin College.

Grants as Instruments of Environmental Policy

Federal policy toward air and water pollution consists of requiring the states to establish air and water quality standards and to adopt policies to achieve these standards. If the establishment of standards is interpreted as entailing a political choice about gains, costs, and goals, and if the outcome of this choice process is accepted as defining the policy goals, we can direct our attention to the problem of how to achieve these goals.

In this section three alternative policy instruments for achieving environmental quality standards are examined for effectiveness and efficiency. The judgment on effectiveness involves an examination of the underlying incentives and a prediction about whether they will induce the desired action and whether the incentive is strong enough to achieve the standard. The efficiency criterion asks whether the standard will be achieved at the lowest possible social cost.

Effluent or emission charges rank high on both criteria. If the discharge can be measured accurately, and if the charge is set high enough, the incentive is to reduce discharges quickly. Furthermore, if the marginal costs of waste discharge reduction options are equated with the charge and if the costs of the charge are incorporated in output and pricing decisions, dischargers will be led to minimize the social costs of pollution control.

The second pollution control instrument is the threat of judicially imposed sanctions on those whose discharges exceed a prescribed emission standard. This policy instrument results in an excessive social cost to obtain pollution control even if compliance is voluntary and complete and no resources are devoted to inspection and enforcement. This is because inappropriate price signals would go to consumers and to firms. Even after the discharger has voluntarily complied with the posted standards, some residuals would continue to be discharged into the environment. Under a system of emission or effluent charges the cost of maintaining this discharge would be reflected ultimately in the prices of products involved; the higher prices would reduce consumption, which is itself a kind of pollution-control activity. In comparison with charges, reliance on emission standards produces a situation in which too many resources are devoted to production of the goods and too many resources are devoted to controlling the wastes associated with the excess output. In terms of effectiveness also the emission standard approach receives lower marks than charges. The probability of avoiding detection or successful prosecution for violations, the delays inherent in court actions, and the generally low financial penalties for noncompliance all tend to weaken the incentive to comply with standards. In fact, reliance on judicial enforcement tends to distort incentives by making it profitable to hire lawyers rather than pollution-control engineers.

The third policy instrument is grants to dischargers who satisfy certain eligibility requirements by undertaking specified pollution-control activities.

The grants, which can be direct cash payments to dischargers, provide incentives for carrying out pollution-control steps. For example, the government could agree to pay 50 percent of the costs of installing stack gas control devices or secondary waste water treatment plants. Eligibility is established by making the installations. Another form of direct grant or subsidy is the provision of waste treatment services at publicly owned treatment facilities at service charges that are well below cost. Indirect grants can be created by linking favorable tax treatment to desired activities. For example, the real cost of installing pollution-control equipment can be reduced by permitting accelerated depreciation of that equipment for corporate income tax purposes. Also, pollution-control equipment is often exempted from sales taxes and real property taxes.

Grants are likely to be both ineffective and inefficient as instruments of pollution policy.[1] They are ineffective because although they reduce the costs of compliance, they do not eliminate them. They must be accompanied by some other incentive – for example, the threat of sanctions. In fact, the normal incentives for postponing pollution-control activities (the opportunity cost of capital invested in pollution-control facilities, the savings in operating costs by not having anything to operate, and the expectation of cost-saving improvements in the technology of control) may be reinforced by the expectation of a more generous grant program in the future. Grants are inefficient as instruments of pollution control for two reasons: because they reduce the cost of pollution control to dischargers, the total opportunity costs of production are not reflected in the price of the product, and its consumption is higher than optimal; and the relative costs of alternative control techniques are distorted by the firm. Techniques that convey eligibility for grants are made relatively cheaper to the discharger. As a consequence, dischargers may overlook socially desirable processes and equipment changes only because they are not covered by the conditions of the grant.

Grants and Equity in Environmental Policy

As instruments for achieving environmental quality, goals and grants do not compare favorably with the alternatives in terms of the preferred criteria. It therefore seems more appropriate to consider grants as devices for redistributing the costs of pollution control.

First, we should identify the costs of pollution control and their incidence in broad terms, assuming the absence of any policies to alter their distribution. In the long run and in a world of mobile resources, the costs of pollution control will largely be passed on to consumers in the form of higher prices

---

1. For a more detailed discussion, with special attention to water pollution control, see M. J. Roberts, "River Basin Authorities: A National Solution to Water Pollution," *Harvard Law Review* 83 (May 1970): 1530–41.

for goods and services. If pollution control results in changes in relative prices and resource allocations, some part of these costs will be passed back to the factors of production where factor supply elasticities are less than infinite.

However, in the short run there are rigidities and costs associated with shifting resources from one use to another. Firms may incur transitory costs and losses of capital values as they are forced to write off plant and equipment before the planned end of its useful economic life. As some industries contract there may be short-term losses until a new long-term equilibrium is approached. More importantly, some firms may have to reduce their levels of employment or shut down entirely. The result could be severe, prolonged unemployment and fiscal crises for municipal governments where the firms were significant parts of the local economy and where resources, especially labor, are not highly mobile.

There are two categories of grants programs. The first consists of direct and indirect grants to firms, described in the previous section. The second is grants to factors of production, principally labor, that have been adversely affected by the resource reallocations associated with pollution-control policies.

It has been argued that the various forms of direct and indirect grants will spread the burden of pollution control more equitably. According to this argument, the costs of industrial pollution control will be passed on to consumers in the form of higher prices, and the incidence of these costs will be regressive in the style of an excise or sales tax. Also, municipal pollution-control expenditures are financed by regressive property taxes and sales taxes. If the state and federal governments subsidize these activities, they can shift the burden from regressive modes of finance to the more progressive personal and corporate income taxes.

The argument is correct as far as it goes. However, it neglects two important qualifications. First, although cost sharing can change the distribution of the burden between rich and poor, it also increases the total burden because of the adverse economic efficiency effects. Whatever equity benefits are gained by cost sharing come at the expense of higher than necessary treatment costs. Cost sharing is apt to be an expensive way to obtain distributional equity. Conceivably everybody could be made worse off by efforts to redistribute the costs. If subsidies are kept small, the economic cost of subsidies is small, but the impact of the subsidies on equity is also likely to be small; substantial equity benefits are likely to be gained only at the expense of substantial efficiency costs. There must be some cheaper way to improve distributional equity.

As for the second qualification, where the grants go to aid industrial pollution-control efforts, there is some question as to whether the benefits of the subsidy will always be passed on to the consumer in the form of lower prices. For example, if a multiplant firm selling in a national market receives a subsidy for pollution equipment installed in one plant, this is not likely to affect the price at which the product is sold. Hence, the benefits would accrue to stockholders. Subsidies can also produce some interesting interregional transfers. For example, a state subsidy to a municipal treatment plant that is also treating industrial wastes could flow largely to out-of-state consumers or stockholders if the industrial discharger were producing for a national market or if stock ownership were spread across the nation.

Direct grants to factor inputs for the purpose of shifting the burden of pollution control are not presently part of any state or federal environmental program. However, the concept, which is a part of U.S. international trade policy, is applicable as well to environmental policy. Stringent pollution-control efforts (based either on the enforcement of standards or the exchange approach) coupled with liberal doses of direct and indirect subsidies might achieve the desired level of environmental quality relatively painlessly in the sense that there would be little or no dislocation in the production sector – no unemployment, no firms going bankrupt, and so on. However, the excess social cost associated with such subsidy programs could be substantial, perhaps more than we would be willing to bear. Alternatively, if direct and indirect subsidies were ruled out, high-pollution industries would be faced with rising costs, rising relative prices for their products, and shrinking markets. Some firms would leave the industry, plants would be shut down, and labor and capital would be at least temporarily unemployed. The consequences could be particularly severe in areas where factor inputs are relatively immobile – for example, in small towns and one-industry mill towns.

An appropriately designed grants policy could go far toward ameliorating the adverse effects of the pollution-control policy on labor and capital. These grants would have to be designed to assist in and to encourage the necessary economic adjustments and reallocations of resources associated with the pollution-control program.

Certain provisions of the Trade Expansion Act of 1962 and the Canadian-American Automotive Trade Agreement provide a highly useful model. Both of these agreements contain provisions for *adjustment assistance* to localities adversely affected by the lowering of tariffs. According to the Trade Expansion Act, it must be shown that the tariff reductions were a "major" cause of idle facilities, lack of profits, or unemployment. If this can be established, then adjustment assistance is available for both labor and business. Firms can obtain technical assistance in developing new products or lowering costs, or they can obtain low-interest loans or loan guarantees for new equipment or for conversion to a new activity in which market conditions are better. Laborers are able to obtain unemployment compensation and relocation allowances for moving to areas where the prospects of employment are better. Also, workers are eligible for retraining programs and the grants to support themselves while they learn more skills.[2]

Experience with the Trade Expansion Act showed that the eligibility

---

2. J. E. Jonish, "Adjustment Assistance Experience under the U.S.–Canadian Automotive Agreement," *Seminar Discussion Paper No. 13* (Research Seminar in International Economics, University of Michigan, 1969).

requirements were too stringent, and easier requirements were incorporated into the Canadian-American Automotive Agreement. As a consequence, some $4 million in adjustment assistance was dispensed to U.S. workers who were adversely affected by the free trade in automotive parts.

In addition to adjustment assistance for labor and capital, a well-conceived pollution-control adjustment-assistance program should make provision for financial aid to towns that lose tax revenues because of the loss of industry. Finding the conditions of eligibility and providing for an appropriate body to judge that eligibility is a delicate problem; but despite these difficulties, I think that this idea has much to commend it.

In keeping with the theme of the paper, it should be noted that adjustment-assistance programs also alter the marginal signals and incentives faced by economic agents. To the extent that assistance reduces the burden of unemployment, it would tend to slow the reabsorption of labor and capital into gainful employment. However, in contrast to the direct and indirect grants discussed above, the adjustment-assistant grants would be given on a highly selective basis and only where a disproportionate share of the costs of pollution control were being imposed on a small group.

Grants as Products of Environmental Policy

Changes in environmental quality create benefits – that is, grants to beneficiaries.[3] The question is: Are these benefits distributed more equally than the underlying distribution of income or wealth? In other words, do the benefits of environmental improvement policies contribute to the goal of a more equal distribution of welfare, or do they reinforce existing inequalities? The benefits of environmental improvement are enhanced services from the environment – for example, enhanced amenity services, enhanced recreation opportunities, and the improved life-support capacity of the atmosphere. To predict the distribution effects of environmental changes, we need to know by what mechanisms the environmental services are distributed or allocated. I have argued elsewhere that environmental quality tends to be distributed by market and pseudomarket mechanisms so that those with the highest willingness (and, naturally enough, ability) to pay for environmental quality get the best environments. The evidence on the relationship between recreation participation and income, and between air quality and land values both tend to support this hypothesis. I also found that in the three cities I studied, air pollution exposure was inversely related to income, and blacks

3. The material in the next two sections is taken largely from my "Distribution of the Environment," a paper prepared for the Resources of the Future Conference "Research on Environmental Quality: Theoretical and Methodological Studies in the Social Sciences," June 1970. I am grateful to RFF for giving me the chance to work on this problem for a year.

on the average were exposed to considerably lower quality air than whites.

If the rich are getting the best of what is around, does this mean that they will get the best of any environmental improvements? This is not so clear. A lot depends on the circumstances. For example, take the case of air quality. Theory and available evidence would predict that an improvement in air quality over a portion of an urban area would result in higher land values there. If the areas were owner-occupied, the owners would capture the benefits. My studies have shown that areas with the highest air pollution are also the areas where the proportion of rental-occupancy to owner-occupancy is highest. This suggests that the benefits would tend to be passed on to the absentee landlord.

However, the increase in land values is predicated on the assumption that the area with improved air quality would become relatively more attractive to other people and that there would be a net inflow of people and an increase in the demand for land in that area. If land-use patterns are determined by many factors, of which air quality is only one, and if these land-use patterns and density patterns are fairly rigid – that is, they do not respond quickly to a change in only one of these factors – it would appear that the demand shifts necessary to raise land rents would be weak and perhaps nonexistent. If this were the case, the benefits of the cleaner air would accrue to the residents of the area. In other words, it is quite possible that improving air quality over the urban areas might have an equitable pattern of incidence of benefits.

With improved water quality the principal class of benefits is recreation. Recreation participation and income are positively correlated, which would suggest that improved recreation opportunities would tend to benefit the well-to-do. But again, further reflection shows that the outcome is not so certain. It depends on where the new recreation water is located relative to centers of population. One factor that tends to ration recreation use to those with highest incomes is the cost of transportation from the home to the recreation site. If water pollution abatement activities opened up recreation areas close to urban concentrations of low-income population, relatively more low-income people would be able to take advantage of water-based recreation opportunities.[4]

Equity and Environmental Planning

We have showed that it is possible to use grants to shift the costs of pollution control so as to lead to greater equity, and we have showed that the grants inherent in environmental quality improvements may have favorable equity effects. This leads to the question: Should equity considerations

---

4. It should be noted that the other economic barrier to participation is the availability of complementary equipment–boats, fishing rods, and water skis, for example.

play a systematic role in environmental quality planning decisions? There are two aspects to this question. The first is how important is the distribution of environmental quality relative to the overall distribution of income, wealth, or welfare? The second aspect is how important is environmental quality distribution relative to other aspects of the environmental quality management problem? I have argued elsewhere that the distribution of environmental quality is largely the result of the interaction between the distribution of income and wealth and market incentives and market mechanisms.[5] The distribution of the environment is largely a consequence of the broader distribution forces at work in the economic system.

This suggests that the most effective way to improve the general distribution of the environment is to improve the basic distribution of wealth. Many economists would accept the proposition that this is a counsel of perfection and would move on to argue that transfers in kind can be used to adjust the distribution of welfare in the desired direction. The second aspect of the question posed here really relates to the possibilities for accomplishing such transfers through environmental quality management. There are at least two considerations.

First, we must ask whether distributional considerations are likely to significantly alter the rankings of different investments in the environment. For this to occur, there must be differences among investments in the pattern of distribution of benefits and costs. Further, these differences in equity characteristics must be significant relative to the efficiency characteristics of the projects. It seems likely that the equity characteristics of projects *within* broad classifications – for example, water quality, air quality, recreation – will be roughly similar. If this surmise is correct, the ranking of projects within these classes will not be significantly affected by introducing equity considerations. On the other hand, there should be more marked differences in distribution patterns among classes of projects – for example, rural recreation versus urban air quality. In principle, public expenditure decisions should be based on comparisons across all projects of all types. In practice, the political system is much less likely to make consistent comparisons on a systematic basis across dissimilar programs than to make them on similar projects within a single program. In other words, where equity considerations are most likely to have an impact on project rankings, they are least likely to play a systematic, coherent role in the decision process.[6]

A second consideration is the extent to which the physical or financial design of a given project can be altered to achieve equity goals. Given the constraints of the physical systems involved, there is probably very limited

---

5. Freeman, "Distribution of the Environment."

6. For further consideration of this point, see my "Project Design and Evaluation with Multiple Objectives," in U.S. Congress, Joint Economics Committee, *The Analysis and Evaluation of Public Expenditures: The PPB System*, a Compendium of Papers, Washington, D.C., June 1969, pp. 573–77, and references cited there.

flexibility for designing an air or water quality improvement project to achieve distribution goals. The locations of pollution sources and receptors and the dispersion and assimilation processes largely determine what can be done with the system. In principle, the repayment–cost-sharing features of a program provide a high degree of flexibility in distributing project costs and benefits and in influencing the net equity effects. However, it is impossible to alter the financial aspects of the project without altering the marginal price and cost signals governing the actions of private firms and individuals, both residuals generators and receptors. Alteration of these signals to achieve equity goals can be expected to be associated with inefficiency and high social cost.

In sum, I am not enthusiastic about the opportunities for using environmental policies to improve distributional equity. But I must add that there are unexploited opportunities for using grants to redistribute the costs of achieving improvements in environmental quality where these costs are borne by a few for the benefit of the many.

15

Thomas M. Havrilesky:
Technological Innovativeness, the Grants Economy, and the Ecological Crisis

The Economics of Pollution

Introduction

Increasing affluence explains why environmental contamination can no longer be physically confined to poor neighborhoods, the traditional dumping grounds for the indestructible physical mass of residuals inherent in all

Presented at the Symposium on the Grants Economy held between the Association for the Study of the Grants Economy and the American Association for the Advancement of Science, Chicago, Illinois, December, 1970. Reprinted by permission of the author, who is associate professor of economics, Duke University. The article was written while the author was visiting associate professor at Rice University, and he acknowledges the university's support. This paper has benefited from lively discussions with the following economists: Charles McLure and Gordon Smith, of Rice University; David Davies and Jay Salkin, of Duke University; Milton Lower and his wife and Thomas DiGregori, of the University of Houston; John Quincy Adams, of the University of Maryland; and Michael DePrano, of the University of Southern California. They do not necessarily share the opinions expressed here.

production and consumption. Classically, like the communicable diseases of the slums, the spread of filth only begins to concern seriously the federal public health and welfare machinery when it threatens the sanctuaries of the rich and powerful. Moreover, as part of the ecological "revolution," rich and poor alike now more highly value a clean environment.

Nevertheless, we continue to allocate the clean air, clean water, and un- spoiled environments that remain, and are essentially in fixed supply, as though they were practically "free" and their private use or abuse did not impose damages on members of society. The reason for this neglect may seem startlingly distressing to noneconomists – the economic system has not developed institutions that would allow these gifts of nature to be owned and "traded."[1] Clearly, users of a resource who harm others by their behavior should, as a matter of efficiency and equity, pay. When payment is effected, the clean common resource may become available for nondestructive uses. How much should polluters pay? How much of any resource should anyone get? To answer these questions we first examine a basic principle of economics.

The Social Optimum

Economists define a socially optimum allocation of productive resources to obtain where the final increment of any productive resource in each possible employment gives to consumers an equal amount of satisfaction. In a freely competitive market-exchange economy, a social optimum will exist where a direct relationship occurs among all parties to each transaction, thereby allowing all costs and benefits to be reckoned in the market-exchange process.

Some transactions may give rise to benefits and costs, called externalities or implicit social costs, to parties not involved in the transaction. This factor upsets the nice balance and causes a misallocation of resources because some consumers or firms are receiving increments of goods and services (more appropriately labeled "bads" and "disservices") that are not commensurate

---

1. To the reader uninitiated in arid economic nuances this disposition might seem incredibly mercenary. It is not. Ownership of water and air, like land, need not entail profit. For almost a century economists have been familiar with the social ideal that no individual should be permitted to keep the profit (rent) from ownership of a natural resource to the extent that its value to others arises from no effort of his own [8]. For example, the rents accruing to owners of scenically situated mountain property, beach fronts near large cities, or ranches and retreats bordering on public parks all receive rents that, according to this classic ideal, should be confiscated. In the latter case Kenneth Boulding has pointed out that the rent to neighboring landowners may explain why many public parks were established in the first place [4]. See n. 2 and n. 3 for related observations.

Public subsidies for new housing in the form of tax deductions for interest charges, FHA- and VA-insured mortgages, sewer and water services and roads, and the absence of Federal Reserve and Federal Home Loan Bank guidance have encouraged land speculation and suburban sprawl and discouraged central-city renovation. Our land-use policies are a national tragedy.

with the zero incremental sacrifice they make to receive them. Firms or households producing these "bads" and "disservices" neglect them in their decisions because they are not priced in the market.

This reasoning suggests that to solve the problem, emitters of pollution pay receptors of pollution to be allowed to produce these bads[2] (or that receptors pay emitters not to produce the bads). Either way, negative prices are set for the bads produced. If such an exchange could be carried out, a different, and socially optimum, allocation of resources would result as long as markets were freely competitive.

Private Agreements

Thus in principle externalities could be handled by a series of exchanges between the individual parties involved using the courts (or the market[3]) to resolve the conflict. There are three widely recognized obstacles to such a solution. One difficulty in private settlements is that detailed information on the extent of a particular type of pollution at its source is hard to get. *Polluters with inordinate market power in self-interest withhold these data by assorted machinations.* Therefore, pollution can usually be measured only after the pollutant is released into the environment. Because pollutants combine chemically, measurement problems are aggravated. Nevertheless, even if source-by-source data are available, damages to health and life quality from pollution are usually hard to assess. More economic research should be devoted to this problem. [2].

A second predicament in legal redress is that rights to common, as opposed to private, property are difficult to establish in law;[4] owing to the penumbra of uncertainty surrounding the specific causes of the size of the flow of each pollutant and its related social injury, individual legal redress is a formidable task because the law imposes the burden of proof of *harm* on the economically weak, often disorganized, and poorly informed third parties. As a logical extension of the philosophy that the public has an

---

2. Payments to injured parties create incentives for others to move in and to claim injury. As long ago recognized by Professor Coase, this involves knotty problems of equity (e.g., who was "there first," the polluter or the injured party) [24]. To the ecological purist the polluter, of course, can never claim legal priority because he, by definition, always ruptures the ecosystem. Ancient legal doctrine teaches that all natural resources were once held by the government in trust for the people. Following this reasoning, privately owned natural resources may be viewed today as being held in stewardship; it is the government's responsibility to see that these resources are used in the public interest. For a detailed examination of this problem, see A. Allan Schmid's paper in this volume (pp. 340–349).

3. An intermediary (perhaps some government agency) could somehow organize polluters and antipollution groups to "bid" on the rights to a piece of property.

4. If the courts hesitate to establish new precedents (note 2), continue to lag behind public opinion, and in enviromental cases behave as repositories of laissez-faire economic ideology, then private property rights must somehow be assigned and reassigned with redistributive safeguards so that the rich and powerful do not get most of the property.

enforceable right to common property resources (see note 2), the law should impose a greater burden of proof of *safety* [11] on powerful, well-informed polluters and should relax the present stringent restrictions on class action suits against polluters, whether they are industrial firms or government agencies such as the Army Corps of Engineers. To make matters worse, plaintiffs in legal class actions must often prove injury to all members of their class, not just to themselves. Therefore, court negotiations for common property resource damages are exceedingly thorny. With these legal impediments in mind, it is not particularly taxing to envision the imbroglio involved in negotiating with powerful polluters. For example, contemplate the difficulty of proving common property resource damage from the noise pollution and carbon monoxide and nitrogen oxide pollution from passing airliners.

A third problem is that even if the high cost of carrying out private negotiations is everywhere less than the present value of future benefits from the reduction in the externality, a great number of individuals who do not seek redress of damages imposed by emitters cannot be effectively *excluded* from the benefits arising when a small number of others do obtain such relief. For example, if, through the courts, the neighbors of a paper mill make the owner install emission-control equipment, they usually cannot readily induce other benefactors to bear some of their costs of information acquisition and negotiation.

In short, the typical environmental crisis usually involves the confrontation of a mighty economic interest bloc with a large, diffuse, and unorganized group of individuals, each of whom is slightly affected; and under present institutional arrangements the costs to a few individuals of acquiring information, negotiating with the polluter, and making the "free riders" pay are prohibitive.

The costs of negotiation can be reduced by effecting legal and judicial reform to give everyone equal access to the courts, especially in common property resource cases. The high cost of getting information is a classic economic problem in the monopoly power of polluters in the information market. For instance, in parts of Appalachia and other industrial baronies harmed parties are led to believe through years of industrialist propaganda (that is, bad information) that their livelihood depends on disfiguring the environment. The free-rider problem is a knotty one, and alone is sufficient to cause economists to recognize the necessity of collective action. However, in practice, the frustration of resolving all three problems (high information costs, legal obstacles, and free-riders) further explains why collective action is taken.

Therefore, three classes of collective action are often proffered by economists [1, 11, 24, 25]: direct regulation, collectively assessed charges for polluting, and lump-sum[5] subsidies for pollution-arresting processes and

---

5. A unit subsidy for effluents not emitted is a negative charge and has an economic effect similar to the emission charge scheme discussed below. It is not seriously considered by economists, however [1, 11, 24, 25].

equipment. Economists would normally indicate that for any one of these three types of collective action, antipollution programs should minimize the total of the costs of damage from pollution plus the costs incurred in remedying that damage. In a world of certain knowledge about tastes, technology, and social welfare, the quantity of pollution at each source over time should be decreased until the decreasing incremental costs of pollution are equal to the increasing incremental costs of pollution control.[6] Only then will an optimum allocation of resources have been attained.

A major hitch in *any* government pollution-abatement program is that it embroils the government bureaucracy in pollution guideline writing without really solving the problems of high information and legal negotiation costs mentioned above. Because the costs of pollution are often innately hard to assess, the estimation of a (probably concave) functional relationship between damages to life and levels of exposure to various pollutants would alone be an immense chore. But it would be ingenuous to believe that the job could be insulated from the political interference of economically dominant polluters. Furthermore, political favoritism would impede detailed measurement of the quantity of a particular pollutant spewed out by individual firms or industries (not to mention the immense obstacles it would erect to estimating functional relationships between the level of pollution and the level of output of individual firms and industries). Even today, the melange of pollution-control agencies often do not obtain good data because of impediments constructed by their powerful wards and advisers in industry [15]. The dilemma of the regulator becoming the regulated is an ancient, prominent theme in the literature on the public regulation of business. The resemblance between environmental management and other types of regulation is discouraging.

The upshot of this dearth of evidence is that sanctions presently on the books are almost meaningless,[7] and if the nation's spasm of environmental conscience is assuaged, say by a spate of product variations or by the public relations campaigns of industries that think they can clean up their image

---

6. For simplicity of exposition throughout this paper we refer to costs and benefits from pollution control as though they were entirely current. The economically correct approach at all times would be to equate at the margin the *present value* of the future stream of costs and benefits from pollution abatement at each source. Using this approach cogent arguments can be made for *underutilizing* a natural resource, in terms of its present costs and benefits. Once a resource is transformed, it is often impossible or prohibitively expensive to retransform it back into a usable state. This point of view should be incorporated into resource planning programs.

7. Recent hearings [22] are instructive in this regard. Interesting parallels can be drawn with consumer safety legislation. The Pure Food and Drug Laws were enacted about seventy years ago, yet consumer crusaders have long pointed out that the Food and Drug Administration seems to protect profits more than it protects health. Charges are continually made of spies in the FDA, omitted and falsified data, contrived results from commercial testing houses (the industry that pays the piper calls the tune), and even deliberate failure of the FDA to report its findings. Will there be lack of environmental screening and disclosure just as there has been a paucity of disclosure of product safety? The pollution laws presently on the books are so impotent that we have not yet begun to find out.

without cleaning up their backyards [17], the unhappy state of zero enforcement will be imminent. There are sizable costs of organizing and maintaining antipollution lobbying groups, in which each member has a small stake in the outcome. In contrast, polluters generally have a larger economic interest in the outcome and are often already organized for other purposes. Thus, as a general rule, because of lobbying power, political contributions, and day-to-day contact with regulatory agencies, the special interest usually overwhelms the public interest [16]. Like so many social problems, the ecological crisis seems to boil down to the problem of dealing with monopoly power.

Direct Controls

Increasingly, individuals who believe themselves harmed by environmental degradation stemming from economic activity to which they are not a party seek to have lawmakers enact regulations and zoning codes and issue licenses to discharge industrial wastes, which, if not obeyed, result in fixed fines, compulsory public disclosure, compulsory shutdown, or even criminal sentences to polluters. This approach has the advantage of quickly affecting the malaise without onerous debate over alternative levels of emission charges and lump-sum subsidies and their inequities and loopholes.

Ideally, if both pollution costs and pollution-control costs were known precisely, given a set of social preferences and a level of abatement technology, the economically correct level of pollution could be discovered for each pollution source, where the decreasing incremental gain from tightening a pollution standard is just equal to the increasing incremental cost (in terms of measurement and control) of a higher standard. Because of the aforementioned, somewhat contrived difficulty of obtaining data, this source-by-source calculation is not used. Rather, across-the-board standards are set, and fixed fines are supposedly imposed on *all* violators.

In principle, no matter how standards are set, a main disadvantage of this approach is that it does not build in an incentive either not to pollute below the standard or to hold back emissions once the standard has been violated. Also, fixed fines discriminate against firms that have little market power, although Small Business Administration and Economic Development Administration low-interest loans can usually help.

In practice, moreover, this approach metes out anemic doses of "law 'n order" for the violence imposed on individual bodies and minds by the more baneful types and levels of pollution.[8] Again this attitude of permissiveness

---

8. Innumerable cases may be cited. The Agricultural Research Service of the U.S. Department of Agriculture is responsible for pesticide regulation and yet has failed to prosecute a single case in thirteen years. DDT was banned long after production of it declined [12]. In air pollution control, for years all authority was delegated to the states and little progress was made. Moreover, even under the more recent (1967) federal legislation the Department of Health, Education, and Welfare has published scant information

toward violators reflects the economic and political power of well-organized polluters. In standard-setting hearings and informal "advisory" panels far removed from the public eye (such as the administration-sponsored and polluter-dominated National Industrial Pollution Control Council, where complete minutes are not made available to the public), the traditional servitude of government bureaucrats to powerful polluters is painfully apparent [16]. Behind closed doors there is little assurance that the public interest will be represented even by the erstwhile ecological heroes of our regulatory agencies.

For example, the lax penalties for blunders in offshore drilling that result in crude petroleum washing up on our seashores is testimony to the formidable barriers to getting good evidence on the extent of and dangers from oil spills. The petro-mess is also a reflection of the historically casual leasing of public offshore properties by the Department of Interior to private exploiters without releasing data on ecological dangers (even in areas of known geological faults like the Santa Barbara channel), as well as our policy of quotas on oil imports.[9] Giveaways of our natural resources for commercial exploitation are in American tradition grounded in the captivity of government regulatory agencies by private exploiter, and they conjure up a long list of ecological horror stories: the destruction of the buffalo, the dustbowls of the 1930s, overgrazed public ranges, and the scarred Appalachian countryside.

Today offshore oil giveaways, oil import quotas, and heavy oil depletion allowances stand as flagrant subsidies to the oil industry.[10] Controls, taxes, and so on to stop the social damage that arises from these policies represent another class of subsidies. Presumably, policy makers believe that what the grants economy has created, it can also put asunder.

Nonetheless, if they are vigorously enforced, meaningful direct controls will work, albeit inefficiently. It may be assumed that the fines or the costs of

---

on control techniques and air quality criteria, few states have implemented meaningful air pollution control plans, and the National Air Pollution Control Administration has brought only a handful of violators to court. Water pollution control activities have been similarly irresolute. Most notably the Federal Water Quality Administration has been accused of failing to supply the Justice Department with advice or information [18, pp. 164–165]. As mentioned earlier, pollutants in industries are seldom identified on an industry-by-industry basis; where they are, such as in the Houston Ship Channel, the regulatory agency must promise not to use the data for enforcement purposes [5]. Invariably polluters fall back on the excuse that company secrets will be released or that economic development requires disfiguring nature. This fallacious idea is so widespread that many states use lax pollution standards as a means of competing for new industry.

9. Recent Department of Interior actions releasing more Gulf Coast oil lands to private exploitation suggest that the lack of sensible environmental zoning will continue. Reasonable economic arguments can be made to suggest a halt to all import quotas in order to retard environmental degradation. Yet all that we do is allocate public tax funds to encourage the industrialists to clean up their sewers. A rational policy to constrain both offshore drilling and the smog that oil feeds is to tax the internal combustion engine.

10. Does this industry, which now appears to be taking over coal production (thus controlling even more of the energy market) [18], really need a subsidy? For whose welfare does the welfare state operate?

avoiding them will be passed on to the consumer in the form of higher prices; this change in relative prices will shift market demands from social bads to social goods, and direct controls will reallocate productive resources in a desired manner.

Emission Charges

A more efficient way of obtaining this result would be for Congress to levy a system of fees, user taxes, or charges per volume of resource used, as an input or residual depository, commensurate with the danger of the pollutant of each emitter. In effect, this policy means that the control agency would sell quantities of the publicly owned common property resource to the polluter, and the polluter could buy as much as he wanted (see note 3).

The main obstacle to effective policy here too is the difficulty (expense) of obtaining detailed information in a world of changing tastes, changing technology, and shifting geographical distribution of polluters. Recalcitrant polluters would, as discussed earlier, impede the flow of information of the causes, size, and safety of the flow of pollutants.[11] Moreover, in this case the control agency would need even more data on pollution damage because it is tying the fee to the quantity of a common property resource actually used rather than to the violation of a fixed standard.[12]

Nevertheless, unlike direct controls, a system of emission charges requires little knowledge of, and expensive debate, hearings, and lobbying over the costs of abatement; this is left to the polluter. In fact, the main advantage of emission charges is that they build in an automatic incentive for the polluter to reduce his effluent by cutting back on his production, by trying

---

11. James Ridgeway relates a long sequence of water pollution abatement disasters, the theme of which is that federal water pollution control programs concentrate on improving municipal sewer systems but continue to allow industries to dump their filth into municipal sewers on their own terms. He cites numerous case studies of government agencies being misled and uninformed of the quantity and strength of (nonorganic) industrial sewage, which often destroys the bacteria that break down conventional organic wastes. Despite this problem, numerous municipalities refuse to levy additional charges on industrial users [18]. The upshot is that treatment facilities are overloaded, break down, and cause environmental disruption, the cost of which is borne by the taxpayer.

12. This might be done by direct monitoring at the pollution site or, more efficiently, by estimating the flow of pollution as a function of firm output. The pollution control agency might facilitate monitoring by encouraging antipollution groups to act as watchdogs on polluters. Communication with all parties (see note 3) would assist in setting the appropriate schedule of fees roughly commensurate with information about the costs of abatement and the costs of pollution. As mentioned above, fundamental legal precedent must be set to get this data disclosed. Even select congressional committees decry the lack of hard facts [21, pp. 10, 31–32] but hesitate to demand their disclosure [21, pp. 14–16].

One shortcoming of the fee-for-emission scheme is that it exposes the control agency to charges of fee discrimination. In addition, the fee scheme could become very complex, involving fines and subsidies at many stages of production and detailed knowledge of existing and new technology as well as market imperfections (see note 14).

new inputs, or, most likely, by trying new production processes that recover and recycle physical residuals. The incentive system, unlike direct input prescription (or proscription) or output requirements, does not foreclose potential technological innovations. Pollution would be cut back to the point at which the additional cost of not polluting a quantity of the resource equals the fee for buying that quantity.[13]

Despite the shortcomings there are several major areas in which ad hoc versions of this flexible system might succeed. The water meter is an obvious example; surely other low-cost, on-site monitoring is feasible (for example, emission meters). Municipalities could share federal revenues to the extent that their wastes are thoroughly treated, which would induce them to monitor and/or levy added charges on industrial sources of the unassimilable metals, phosphorus, nitrates, acids, and salts that cripple waste-treatment facilities.

In other areas automobiles could be tolled according to their capacity to pollute the air and to congest city streets as they operate and to disfigure the landscape as they are scrapped. (Instead of offering trading stamps, gifts, and lottery tickets for *any* purchase, oil moguls could be induced to issue gift-redeemable coupons [22] for the purchase of lead-free gasoline, and Detroit's auto magnates could be taxed for new car performances and could be induced to sponsor giveaways for customers who regularly have their engines tuned to meet emission standards.) Continuing with some wholly unoriginal hints, manufacturers could be taxed according to the capacity of their product's packaging (for example, beer and soft drink cans) and performance (for example, insecticides and detergents) to leave waste residuals.[14]

Emission charges are costs that will be reflected in product prices. The change in relative prices would cause market demands to shift from social bads to social goods and productive resources would thereby be reallocated in a desired manner.

Direct Lump-Sum Payments for Pollution Abatement

Outright payments to firms that install better pollution control equipment and devote other resources to pollution control are often cited as a means of

---

13. In addition, except in the case of air pollution, revenues can be used to clean polluted resources at the site of the pollution, to reward others who do, or, ideally, to compensate receptors of pollution. Emission fees thus reduce the use of depleted state and local tax revenues to clean the environmental sewers of the polluter.

14. The "materials lost" tax proposal by Robert Ayres [2] is a good example. It is a tax on the waste residual difference between material inputs and material output in manufacturing. A major advantage of this scheme is that it would require a recording of interindustry materials flow data for tax purposes. Given a tax on output residuals (for example, automobile emissions), the incentive to reduce pollution may be passed on to the producer of a pollution-producing input, where the connection between the input and the emission is well known and where the input-producing firm is large enough and *competitive enough* to innovate [16].

directly allocating productive resources to alleviating pollution.[15] These may be viewed as payments to firms for *not* degrading the environment. Naturally they are very popular with polluters [17]. Payments would be in the form of subsidies, tax credits, or accelerated depreciation on pollution equipment, but in principle could be used to subsidize other noncapital costs of pollution control as well.

The arguments against this approach are that it leads to a capital-intensive bias to production in subsidized firms and does not provide sufficient incentive to the producer to use his own methods, such as cutting back his production, substituting inputs that are nonpolluting, or trying a new production process. In the absence of other measures, unless the subsidy is fairly large, the producer will find it profitable to continue to pollute. In addition, the idea of paying a polluter seems inequitable to many (see note 2). Furthermore, subsidies open up inefficient tax loopholes and, unlike other proposals, absorb rather than create tax revenues.[16]

Toward a Broader Resolution of the Pollution Control Problem

Pollution Control: The Poor Pay Any Way

Pollution-abatement legislation that enacts direct controls and emission charges has been shown to "work" indirectly by changing relative prices, which in turn shifts market demands, and hence productive resources, away from social bads to social goods. Legislation that enacts a system of direct subsidies "works" by directly reallocating productive resources. Either way, I now present arguments why these measures are likely to redistribute income away from low-income families.

---

15. Assuming that new equipment will lower operating costs, there will also be an effect on the prices of goods produced by subsidized firms, and resources will be allocated through the shift in demands described above.

16. The preceding discussion has been based on partial equilibrium economics. Treating pollution of different media as separate problems ignores the important tradeoffs that can occur between different types of residuals production and hence different types of pollution. Unlike the partial equilibrium frame of mind, which views nature as consisting of discrete manipulatable categories, a general equilibrium approach to the economics of pollution control is more consistent with a holistic, ecosystematic view of the world. It is consonant with much-needed centralization or regionalization of pollution control agencies. Too long have states demanded their "rights" without recognizing their responsibilities to use (lax) pollution standards as more than just a lure for industrial development. Piecemeal remedies, lack of coordination, and bickering between agencies is well known [18]. Some government agencies (and even some conservation groups) are the captives of industrial interest groups [9]. Furthermore, a general equilibrium approach can more easily deal with the chemical combination among pollutants in any medium (given its temperature, exposure to sunlight, and state of perturbation). Finally, regional regulation lends itself to necessary metering of industrial discharges; as pointed out above, this is a major obstacle to pollution control.

Consider first the income-redistribution effect of direct controls and emission charges. In standard, purely competitive models, as the production costs of polluting firms rise, their output and profits fall in the short run. Because firms leave the industry or fail to expand, the price of their output rises. In imperfectly competitive industries prices rise more directly. Abstracting from input substitutions[17] and technological changes in firms that economize on the now expensive environmental resources, changes in relative prices will effect the distribution of income.

A reasonable hypothesis is that the prices of consumer *necessities* will register more substantial increases than other prices. For example, the prices of nondegradably packaged food and drink (especially those produced with oppressive doses of nitrates and insecticides), electric power produced with high-sulfur fuels,[18] consumer durables which deteriorate rapidly, like cheap furniture and used automobiles (and the gasoline they use), and detergents containing enzymes and phosphates, to name just a few, would increase relative to the prices of many other goods. The relative prices of services, whose production generally would not seem to involve much waste residual, would not rise a great deal. Budget studies [14] show that the lower the level of income is, the greater is the percentage of the total consumption budget devoted to necessities (the food, basic transportation, and shelter categories that contain these items) and the smaller is the percentage of the consumption budget devoted to items with a high income elasticity of demand, whose prices will not be much affected, like personal care services and recreation.[19]

Consider now the policy of subsidizing firms with direct payments to acquire antipollution equipment. Although this may also effect a transfer from taxpayers to consumers (see note 15) and stockholders of subsidized industries, the main redistributional effect would be to transfer dollars away from taxpayers to the firms that produce pollution-control devices. To the extent that the polluting firm is induced to spend something on abatement equipment, a transfer is made to the stockholders and productive factors employed by the firm that produces this equipment, which may be a subsidiary of the polluting firm. As the stockholder is on the average better off than the taxpayer, a reasonable case can be made for the hypothesis that this policy too represents a transfer from the poor to the less poor.

---

17. Substitution of various inputs for the now higher priced natural resources will also redistribute income. Some portion of costs will be borne by factors whose supply elasticities are less than infinite. See the paper by A. Myrick Freeman in this volume (pp. 309–317) for suggestions about grants to firms, workers, and regions adversely affected by pollution abatement programs.

18. The rise in electric power rates because of higher fuel prices may even more directly relate to the rate at which oil oligopolists are gaining control of the nation's coal reserves, thereby wiping out effective interindustry competition. The stifling of new petrochemical uses of coal until sunk costs in oil equipment are realized should be of interest to the UMWA and other Appalachian interest groups [18].

19. Thanks to the regressive burden of pollution measures, recreational activity of the well-to-do is enjoyed in a relatively cleaner, more wholesome setting. See Boulding [4] for some added views on this topic.

Therefore, although more detailed empirical work needs to be done,[20] as a first approximation, it would seem apparent that the war on pollution is inconsistent with a war on poverty and that any pollution program presently considered should be tied to a steeply graduated negative income tax, partly to allay all concern over the income-redistribution effects of pollution control. (See the paper by A. Myrick Freeman in this volume, pp. 309–317.)

There is, however, another side to this issue. Perhaps the poor really will be getting their money's worth. After all, poor neighborhoods have historically been the dumping grounds for the wastes of unfettered capitalism. Noise and air pollution, but probably not water pollution, have been borne largely by people in industrial districts who cannot afford air-conditioned homes in high-income housing developments with swim and golf clubs and vacations at Gstaad and Dubrovnik or even Aspen and Miami Beach. Decent low-income neighborhoods are displaced by fringe area parking and freeways (palliatives for traffic congestion). Today neighborhood groups and some unions are becoming interested in the ecology issue. Their question ought to be: When the offal of industry begins to fall into the scenic playgrounds of the rich, why is it the poor who pay?

The Market for Information

What explains the rapid reallocation of resources for pollution control? The call to arms stems from the systematic manner in which antipollution groups have been able to mobilize public opinion in their behalf. Cynical observers might be inclined to say that our new sense of ecological citizenship has helped transform the poor state of our environment in the public eye from a minor irritation into an authentic eye*sore*.

One may picture environmental information as being supplied to the buying and voting public through the communications media largely by antipollution groups. As mentioned earlier, where the economic and political power of the polluter is formidable relative to that of the antipollution groups[21] there will be a high cost (or shortage) to anyone who wishes to acquire

---

20. The increase in relative prices may thereby measure genuine increases in product quality, which are then reflected in national income statistics. When we introduce the question of measurement on an aggregate basis, our producer-oriented concepts of national income accounting must be severely scored. Gross national product is arrantly "gross." The logical extension of ecosystematic thinking, as well as the myth of consumer sovereignty, requires deductions for both depreciation of human resources (subsistence expenditures) and depreciation of environmental resources. This idea has an intellectual lineage dating back to the eighteenth century French Physiocrats and David Ricardo, but it has barely dented the antic taxonomy to which the corps of national income accountants at the Department of Commerce are devoted.

21. Some conservation groups receive direct industry support. For example, the American Ski Association and the Outboard Boating Club of America supposedly receive substantial financial support from the recreation industry [19].

environmental information. Classically this is a problem in monopoly power and conceivably might be dealt with head on. However, students of government regulation should not be surprised to find out that present public policy seems to treat the problem more circumspectly by subsidizing the communications costs of antipollution groups. Let us examine this process more closely.

Dollar payments to and pressure on the communications media from parties with an economic interest in pollution control stimulate the spread of information. If time and space in the media or in legal environmental information centers are purchased with grants from government, from private foundations with tax-exempt status and a tie-in to industries with an economic interest in sustaining an influence over pollution-abatement legislation under the guise of "efficient resource management," from insurance companies with an eye for improving their actuarial tables, from conglomerate corporations with either growing pollution-control subsidiaries or a desire to engage in ecological puffery, or from any interested individual firm or household seeking tax avoidance, a transfer payment is generated. If time and space are alloted because of government regulation or industry self-regulation (for example, broadcasting good-practice codes) concerning "equal" time, this too constitutes an implicit transfer payment. The communications middleman then takes information from the antipollution minority, perhaps tries to balance it a bit with information either from the public relations departments of polluting private and public enterprises or from "advisory" government panels, organizes it, and disseminates it.

Utilizing the grants economy in this way, the antipollution minority seems to have been able to alter the tastes[22] of buyers and the opinion of lawmakers so cautiously as to avoid the familiar backlash endemic to such strategy. Nascent changes in the tastes[23] of now ecologically literate buyers are transmitted into independent[24] decreases in market demands for products whose stylistic obsolescence, packaging, performance, and disposal give them a high pollution potential. More importantly and dramatically, the opinions of now environmentally responsible lawmakers also change, and pollution-control legislation is passed. Legislated measures do affect relative prices, shift further the market demands for products with a high pollution potential, and so allocate productive resources in the desired manner.

This should not suggest that we have already reached the ecological

---

22. By dint of trained incapacity we economists have a difficult time talking about changes in tastes and their causes. The present analysis deserves a more detailed formulation.

23. In the discussion that follows we remain ambiguous about whether "changes in preferences" refer to changes in the preferences for certain qualities such as privacy, comfort, and socialization or changes in the function that transforms these quality preferences into a set of preferences for goods and services (see note 25). An increased flow of information would alter the latter more readily than the former, which are probably a good deal more stable.

24. Thus, even a laissez-faire policy toward pollution control depends on unilateral transfers encouraged by government policy.

millennium. As pointed out earlier, much remains to be done, especially in improving the efficiency of direct controls, emission charges, and subsidies, by correcting or offsetting impediments to the acquisition of detailed information imposed by economically powerful polluters. Ideally, as abatement measures are strengthened and some firms feel the pinch, polluters themselves may be required to release greater doses of information (see note 14). Perhaps data can be gleaned from the firms that engage in nonprice ecological competition. Presently, however, such possibilities seem unlikely. In fact, in many industries the firms seem so confident that either the ecology craze will recede or that government subsidy will prevail that they devote their resources to ecological advertising and other forms of public relations cosmetic rather than invest in pollution-control technology [17]. In other industries it may be more rational for firms actually to finance an antiecology backlash. Some businessmen feign alarm at the release of their company's "secrets." Already cruel threats have been made to relocate some plants, and the lunatic Right has fulfilled its patriotic obligation by pointing out that Earth Day fell on Lenin's birthday [19].

A Digression on the Information Revolution[25]

It seems that a good number of social ills stemming from the presence of monopoly and monopsony power in the political economy (for example, lack of equal opportunity and intractable externalities) are, as a matter of public policy, handled by subsidies in the market for information. Subsidies in the information market have an enormous impact in effecting the participatory revolution manifested in all forms of social protest, including ecological protest, simply by changing the attitudes of consumers, voters, and lawmakers. The ecological movement and the consumer safety movement

---

25. In a broad sense all markets are instruments for transmitting information among individuals. The traditional marketplace, an institutional arrangement of significant historical durability, is really a means by which one party transmits his given preferences for certain life qualities such as love, health, security, and dominance (conventionally transformed into given preferences for fungible goods and services) to another party and invites him to respond. The historical outcome of such an encounter is a reconciliation of conflicting preferences by exchange in the price system.

The advent of heavy nonprice "competition" and the development of the modern communications industry may be viewed as specialized arrangements for transmitting information that alter the transformation of given preferences for life qualities into preferences for goods and services and even change the life-quality preferences themselves, especially among the young. (See note 23 and the remarks at the end of this section.)

The belief that modern technology must supplement the market exchange process as a means for transmitting individual preferences without endangering freedom is a matter deserving some debate. But whether the market is replaced or not, democrats everywhere must always deter the agglomerations of exclusionist power, acting (perhaps out of cultural self-defense) privately or through the bureaucratic military state, from inhibiting free interchange and the cultural evolution it sustains.

are both manifestations of the rising expectations of many to participate more fully in the economic and political decisions and allocation of public funds.

Let us examine how this process might work. Assume that an individual has a stable demand for information about a social problem like the environmental crisis. Institutional constraints on the supply of such information (discussed earlier) make it fairly costly. Subsidies to communications media increase the supply of information; this lowers the explicit price and increases the quantity of information to the individual, thus perhaps affecting his attitude toward the problem.[26]

When insufficiently subsidized, minority groups aware of the immediacy of exposure and feedback sometimes manage to *stage* their own opinion-molding "news events"; a list of contrived happenings runs the gamut from recent courtroom theater through the panorama of sit-ins, demonstrations, rallies, and protests. Indeed, even the so-called establishment, although it says it really "knows better," has frequently adopted this technique in the same courtrooms, campuses, and streets. When properly modulated, this sometimes entertaining, usually provocative, and occasionally informative innovation is a useful adjunct in the information market.

The subsidy itself presents an interesting phenomenon: the buyers of the information are ultimately bearing the burden of the subsidy. As pointed out in the preceding section, the giving or selling of "equal" time to political and cultural minorities really constitutes a transfer payment from incipiently rebellious middle-American taxpayers and consumers of heavily advertised products to the minority members in question, who are getting more than they "paid for." Doses of information may change tastes and voting habits in a desired manner. When doses of subsidized information are excessive or chafing, the buyer in the medium may very well effect a desire to return to his previous position of high price–low quantity equilibrium – a process of backlash (see note 26).

Let us extend this analysis a bit further. During periods of rejection of older cultural values and a search for new ones, individual demands for

---

26. Further research ought to be done on how significantly these developments on the supply side of the information market actually change tastes and opinions. In the high-income, wants-rather-than-needs economy changes in tastes resemble cognitive-choice responses rather than invidious, Galbraithian, Madison Avenue–conditioned responses. George Katona shows some evidence [10] that, except for times of crisis, aggregate learning patterns are slow.

The added new information changes tastes, and changes in buyers' tastes and voters' opinions may further increase the demand for information, raising its price and encouraging further subsidy to minority groups and technological changes within the communications industry. The dampening factor in this learning epidemic is that each individual has a different tolerance for information available to him at the subsidized market price. Excessive doses may make the disruptive costs of cultural change and the economic burden of the subsidy more apparent. What is labeled as "slanting" of the news by some politicians may really represent a series of dynamic interactions that accelerate the spread of information. Apparently the obsessive fear of permissiveness that troubles some very vocal politicians may be that the public is *permitted* to learn too much.

information surely increase. The rising price of information induces cost-saving technological innovations in communications. The increased speed of information, in common parlance, "makes the world smaller," as dynamic cultural interaction resolves continually newer cultural mixes. (Conversely, one may view the technological innovation as entirely accidental and deduce similar results.) The demise of the weekly magazine and the implementation of new uses for radio, recordings, public concerts, and television are part of this process. One can expect that videotape, cable television, and communications satellites will in the future afford new innovative vehicles. The "establishment" itself would be well advised to innovate in elective, poll-taking, and administrative techniques in order to foster fuller and more flexible participation of dissident groups.

Within the preceding context, the spread of information in general is making many aspiring groups aware of imperfections in our political economy that impede both their ability to resolve problems like environmental externalities and their ability to participate in "the system." Despite the periodic musings of some politicians, many people are becoming increasingly wary of the moralism that the monopoly-dominated market exchange system and the attendant warfare-welfare state, in which public monies are allocated to the vested (military-industrial) interests, who are the best organized and whose fear-rhetoric has the greatest public appeal, is the best of all possible worlds. Indeed, a dominant development is the growing repudiation of this moralism, which I call the *competitive ethic*.[27] As the disenfranchised organize to countervail effectively in the market, avoid taxes, and get their share of government support, the values that dominated the political economy of the past can no longer be sustained.

My view of the ecological crisis incorporates this pervasive trend. The incipient rejection of the competitive ethic in part explains the immense critical demand for information as the individual attempts to reconcile himself to the flux in cultural values. The increased demand for ecological information reflects this development.

When Richard Nixon cultivated the ecology issue as a new, blandly unifying theme to assuage anxiety in this divisive era, he may very well have opened the door to his next "crisis." The revolution among the young

---

27. True-believing economists may chafe at my use of this word to denote a moralizing ceremony rather than the type of market structure (which, together with other factors discussed at the outset of this paper, would provide a socially optimum allocation of resources). Although the educated have long abstractly discussed the unconstrained market system's inequities, they have always been wont to regard them as abnormalities that might even be justified (witness the word *externality*). Meanwhile, "practical" people have proselytized and ritualistically incanted the moralism that our political economy generates the highest social good.

Policy discussions cannot afford to ignore cultural ceremony, especially in the present period of social divisiveness. The growing rejection of the competitive ethic has as much to do with economic analysis of the ecological crisis and other social problems as elaborate input-output tables, interindustry material balances research, and estimates of the implicit costs (shadow prices) of pollution.

idealizes a life style in which the exclusion, secrecy, and manipulative domination over nature, men, and other ("misguided") notions that characterize our present political economy are superseded (perhaps only temporarily) by equal opportunity, openness, and a genuine ecological disposition. The higher value placed on all aspects of the natural environment are in part a manifestation of the profound change in preferences.

The Influential Technologist

The direct controls, emission charges, and direct payments discussed earlier will allocate resources, with varying degrees of efficiency, in a socially desired manner. A social optimum is reached where the marginal increment of a productive resource in each possible employment yields an equal amount of satisfaction to consumers.

Technologists are productive resources. Pollution-control measures will therefore also influence the allocation of the research and development budgets of private and governmental enterprises, including the budgets of the new counterpollution industrial and consulting firms. Firms will seek to adopt a technology that economizes on inputs and residual outputs that because of the system of regulations are viewed as "expensive." Government and foundations, through systems of transfer payments, will redound the efforts of firms in allocating technological resources to pollution control. Technological effort will be allocated in a manner that would seem to be generally consistent with community preferences, reflected in pollution-control legislation. Technologists have an impact on the ecological crisis that transcends their employment on the supply side of the pollution-abatement market. In teaching, writing, and speaking about his work, the technologist affects tastes and helps reconcile individual preferences with the community preferences now attuned to the demands of the antipollution groups. Technologists are more than builders of better mousetraps and better mantraps; they talk about their work, and because of improvements in the information market, the public is better able to listen.

This advocate role of the technologist may really reflect more than technological shoptalk. In the following section I suggest that the value of this information may explain the ethical revolution under way among the ranks of applied scientists and technologists. For the time being, let it suffice to say that the technologist, employed to measure and abate environmental decay, has valuable information and might be induced to speak his mind.

Earlier in this discussion I pointed out that the lack of good evidence on the extent of and injury from pollution explains much of the inefficiency of methods of coping with the environmental dilemma. Citizen groups, frustrated with government ineptitude and inaction are turning to the courts. Expert technological testimony is in strong demand [21]. If we are to approach the ecological crisis intelligently, perhaps our first priority should be to enact legislation designed to encourage the flow of information from the technological community.

Leadership of government pollution-abatement agencies must be held up for review. Corporation-employed and government-employed technologists must be rewarded to blow the whistle on their employers without fear of harrasment. Perhaps the latter can be encouraged by appropriate due process safeguards [15], or perhaps it is no longer unthinkable that technologists, like blue-collar workers, should organize effectively to protect their interests and to promote their own ethical standards, which might include a commitment to the public interest. Professional unanimity need not prevail, but debate and criticism will be useful to community undestanding. The demand for information is there. As Thorstein Veblen long ago predicted [23] and as John Kenneth Galbraith warns today [7], the technologist is the keystone in the contemporary industrial mosaic. As a responsible source of information for society he is invaluable.

Technological Innovativeness and the Competitive Ethic

Technology

Although the benefits of new technology are heralded in modern folklore, there persists at the same time a residue of romantic, pastoralist hostility to technological change. And although technological change may have short- and long-term effects on our cultural and even genetic makeup [16, 20, 21], many of the externalities that so trouble some scientists stem not from the fabled occult demons embodied in technological change itself but from the way we allocate our technological resources.

In the philosophy of science, technology is referred to as the application of accepted theories or rejected theories or the use of rules of thumb not yet amenable to scientific investigation.[28] When technology transcends a tried conventional framework, even in areas where well-tested theories are available, but more often where existing theories are irrelevant, it must proceed by trial and error. The social risk in these cases is problematic; even though pure science and occasionally individuals may act independently of socially prescribed constraints, the technological organization usually may not; its activity, unlike that of the laboratory scientist, usually has discernible effects on the social milieu.

---

28. Technology and the technologist are conceived, in a manner that will appear unusual to economists, as being dissimilar from pure science and the pure scientist but roughly synonymous with applied science and the applied scientist. I have in mind not a strict taxonomy but rather an ordered ranking of scientific activity from one polar extreme (pure science) to another (pure technology).

Why does the technologist step beyond his familiar framework and, at risk to society, try new processes?[29] Foolhardiness is probably not endemic to his vocation. Rather, his behavior today is largely explained by the market-exchange mechanism. Simply stated, the technologist is hired by the highest bidder – the bidder who believes he stands to benefit from the abilities of the technologist.

For example, because of the space race technologists are prodded beyond their workaday domain. This imposes certain risks (externalities) on society – for example, the risk of moon bugs returning with the astronauts. Therefore, although space scientists may have an unfalsified theory well in hand and astronauts may feel confident about their space vehicle, numerous precautions and regulations reduce the external costs involved in the bilateral economic transactions that place men and vehicles on the moon. On the other hand, any ground to space ventures in general is weakened by international competition and those who advocate it. For example, in 1968 funds for space ventures were reduced only when another variety of international competition, war, received higher congressional priority.

The Competitive Ethic

The competitive ethic is the belief that our monopoly-dominated political economy not only works to the benefit of the competitors but at the same time provides optimal social welfare. Although economists might tend to dismiss the ritual of the competitive ethic as an overly simplistic bit of political rhetoric, it is an altogether obvious fact that political rhetoric is a formidable factor in public policy making and that voters and consumers thrive on such simplifications. Moreover, the cabalistic appeal to the competitive ethic may dissuade dissenters and activists by proselytizing the virtue of "working within the system." The decline in the pervasiveness of this ceremonial belief – that the invisible hand of the monopoly-dominated market and the visible claw of the welfare-warfare state will resolve most problems – partly explains the increase in the demand for many kinds of information. The incipient repudiation of the competitive ethic, as mentioned earlier, underlies much of today's information revolution.

Let us consider how the competitive ethic relates to the much-heralded disruptive cultural dangers of technological change. Some have called for a cultural early-warning system that would divine the impact of new technology [8, 6, 21]. To the extent that information-disseminating processes function

---

29. For instance, the noted entomologist E. H. Smith says, "It is a striking fact that knowledge of the mode of action has rarely preceded the use of any insecticide" [12].

smoothly, such a system already exists.[30] To the extent that these processes are suppressed by a resurgence of the competitive ethic, we should be alarmed. The resolution of fancied cultural emergency may rest more squarely on improving extant information-disseminating mechanisms rather than on erecting new technocratic commissions to prophesy the future.

As a mundane example, suppose that pollution-free products suddenly become fashionable. Oligopolists will accommodate the market pressure for ostensible "technological advance." If recent history is our guide, after a few genuine improvements a stream of increasingly trivial and perhaps odious innovations and advertising will ensue.[31] Will consumers then lose their sense of environmental citizenship and reduce their demand for environmental information? Will we easily become anesthetized by this process, view today's public indignation over the ecological crisis as a quaint hysterical aberration, and warm up to the competitive ethic? I think not. The deluge of environmental concern is more than a temporary retreat from mindless acceptance of the competitive ethic; it is a continuing elevation of the consumer and voter to a new level of awareness and informedness. In short, it is not technological innovativeness or even the market mechanism that are, as some believe, innately "evil." The problems lie in a ceremonial attitude – the competitive ethic.

The Technologist – Old and New

Consider next the traditional role of the technologist. He is typically neither a Schumpeterian hero nor a docile technocrat; he traditionally exhibits neither tenacity nor defiance beyond his calling to "do a good job." As indicated above, risks and costs to society of this ennui are problematic. They consist of both the risks of the technologist transcending the prevailing

---

30. Most scientific concern centers on a fear of allowing technology to "impose" severe cultural stress. For example, the new technology of fallout shelters was used to alleviate the externality stemming from nuclear rivalry and would seem to have promised considerable degenerative effects on our life styles. Nuclear limitations may have been impeded by the competitive ethic's tendency to suppress criticism of this solution and, moreover, by its tendency to suppress criticism of any form of rivalry – even chauvinism. As an extreme example, the new technology of universal antidotes to counter the virulent externality stemming from competition in the development of tools for chemical and biological warfare would have posed a particularly grotesque secondary threat to the community life style unless ethical injunctions against suppressing this form of rivalry were not overcome.

31. For example, consider the effect of allocating resources to affect the appearance of technological change. American oligopoly capitalism must foster the appropriate "progressive" image. Consequently, the public is treated to the "secret ingredient" ploy as well as to the new, improved product ploy. Yet orthodox economic analysis maintains that oligopolists, unless influenced by a well-informed public, suppress products that might reduce certain externalities because they are costly – that is, they result in retooling expenses and risky competition when adopted by rivals. The result is an endless stream of insipid product variations.

technique ("doing a better job") and the costs of engaging in banal product variation programs or unsafe mining and manufacturing process innovations.[32] Yet the traditional technologist, even though he was in a position to know better, in professional fervor typically has disregarded these risks and costs, although, *qua homo*, he may later deeply regret the effects of his professionalism. The traditional (Augustinian) dichotomy between science and ethics has prevailed. The retrospective plea of the twentieth century technologist, time after time, has been that "he was only taking orders."

Critical technologists who are concerned with the ultimate effects of their efforts have often been moral victors but economic failures. For example U.S. Army Captain Howard Levy was imprisoned for refusing to use his training as a tool of war. Although a moral professionalism and economic imperative permitted few Captain Levys among the corps of traditional technologists, it is becoming increasingly apparent to a critical minority of technologists that a sense of public commitment today need not require immense economic sacrifice.

The traditional technologist may be on the retreat. As pointed out earlier, the new technologist has the information that minority groups in ecology, product safety, and so on demand. As a responsible source of valuable information, a growing minority of technologists are thus becoming socially responsive and (although not as readily as our skilled lawyer crusaders) are induced to enter the public forum. This is reflected in the growing disaffection of applied scientists with the persistence of laissez-faire attitudes toward the allocation of technological resources. Unlike the solitary and largely retrospective acts of older technologists, the new breed anticipates a new morality rather than regrets an old amorality. There is a growing number of technologists who are disassociating themselves from morally repugnant research in order to redirect scientific effort away from military problems. Applied scientists increasingly recoil from the consequence of modern technology bridled to the whims of those who possess market power. They ask why our enormous technological wealth, unlike many other resources, must be shackled to nineteenth century ideology.

This trend in the scientific community may herald a waning of the traditional dichotomy between science and ethics, as well as a closing of the chasm between science–technology and the voter-consumer. If this is true, the new technologist employed in pollution abatement may be more likely to strike, protest, quit, organize, and seek legal safeguards in order that he may speak his mind on the activities of his employer (for example, as a polluter or as an ineffective pollution abater). Moreover, in his valuable professional-ethical

---

32. Without the appropriate public policy, the technology of production will always outrace the technology of worker, consumer, and environmental safety. Repeated industrial disasters, industrial disease rates, and devastated countryside in Appalachia are testimony to the monopoly power–informational aspects of this problem. In many states in Appalachia workman's compensation rates are abominably low, and not a penny of severance taxes was ever paid.

commitment to the community, he may be expected to inform them of damaging secondary side effects of technological change [19] (for example, of the rush to abate pollution or to "appear" to abate pollution). The dissent of applied scientists may at last awaken many to a prominent development in contemporary society (discussed earlier) – the growing repudiation of the competitive ethic (and all its psychological trappings) as the highest expression of morality.

Coping with Technological Innovativeness

Some scientists are alarmed at the rapid diffusion of new technology and view it as a degenerative threat to the human condition [2, 4]. Nonetheless, the information revolution simultaneously increases our ability to learn to cope with the stresses of technological change as man adopts new ways of satisfying his basic need for privacy, participation, relaxation, and so on. The competitive ethic is a constraint on this learning process. As a cultural ceremony that fosters complacency, it contrasts sharply with applied science and technology, forms of inquiry, and manifestations of man's faith in himself.[33] Public policy that helps to disseminate information, as I discussed earlier, acclimates cognitive man and facilitates his adaptive responses to the stresses of technological change. The balanced integration of technological change into the social motif depends largely on public policy in the information market. Technological innovativeness can come to be viewed as an exciting prospect rather than as a threat to survival.

References

1. Ayres, R. U., and Kneese, Allen V. "Production, Consumption, and Externalities." *American Economic Review*, July 1969.
2. Ayres, R. U. "The Range of Policy Alternatives for Maintaining Environmental Quality." Paper prepared for the American Association for the Advancement of Science Meetings, Chicago, Illinois, December 28, 1970.

---

33. When, in conjunction with the information revolution, the fervor for scientific questioning and criticism is transmitted to increasing numbers of students, the possibility of the young and hitherto disenfranchised completely abandoning the competitive ethic poses a threat to individuals whose power, sense of identity and government subsidy is tied to this moralism. As a result, in a whirlwind of political tirade against "permissiveness" (as well as the demise of cold-war and space-race hysteria), support for higher education has partially evaporated. Yet our political economy will be paralyzed without growth in science and technology. Sooner or later the inherent inconsistency of reducing the funding of universities will become apparent. Perhaps a new missile, space, talent, or economic growth crisis will be the catalyst. (Already the percentage of foreigners enrolled in our graduate programs is significantly higher.) The crucial question is: On what terms will applied science accommodate the next wave of international rivalry?

3. Bauer, R. *Second-Order Consequences*. Cambridge, Mass.: M.I.T. Press, 1969.
4. Boulding, K. "No Second Chance for Man." *The Progressive*, April 1970.
5. Carter, L. "Galveston Bay: Test Case of an Estuary Crisis." *Science*, February 20, 1970, pp. 1102–8.
6. Dubos, R. "The Crisis of Man in His Environment." In *Proceedings on Symposium on Human Ecology*. Public Health Service, 1968.
7. Galbraith, J. K. *The New Industrial State*. Boston: Houghton Mifflin Co., 1967.
8. George, H. *Progress and Poverty*. New York: Robert Schalkenbach Foundation, 1955.
9. Gilmour, R. S. "Private Interests and Public Lands." *Current History*, July 1970.
10. Katona, G. *The Mass Consumption Society*. New York: McGraw-Hill Book Co., 1964.
11. Kneese, A. V. "Environmental Pollution." Paper presented before the American Economic Association Meetings, December 28, 1970.
12. Kramer, J. "Pesticide Research: Industry, USDA Pursue Different Paths." *Science*, December 12, 1969, pp. 1383–86.
13. Lancaster, K. *Mathematical Economics*. New York: Macmillan Co., 1969.
14. Linden, F., ed. *Market Profiles of Consumer Products*. New York: National Industrial Conference Board, 1967.
15. Nader, R. "The Profits in Pollution." *The Progressive*, April 1970.
16. Noll, R. G. *Institutions and Techniques for Managing Environmental Quality*. Paper prepared for the California Institute of Technology Conference on Technological Change and the Human Environment, October 19–21, 1970.
17. "Pollution: Puffery or Progress." *Newsweek*, December 28, 1970.
18. Ridgeway, J. *The Politics of Ecology*. New York: E. P. Dutton & Co., 1970.
19. "Rise of Anti-Ecology." *Time*, August 17, 1970.
20. U.S., Congress, Senate, Committee on Interior and Insular Affairs, and House, Committee on Science and Astronautics. *Congressional White Paper on National Policy for the Environment*. 90th Cong., 2d sess., serial T, October 1968.
21. U.S., Congress, House, Committee on Science and Astronautics. *Environmental Pollution a Challenge to Science and Technology*. 89th Cong., 2d sess., serial S, rev. August 1968.
22. U.S., Congress. *Economic Analysis and the Efficiency of Government*. 1969.
23. Veblen, T. B. *The Engineers and the Price System*. New York: Viking, 1947.
24. Vickrey, W. "Theoretical and Practical Possibilities and Limitations of a Market Mechanism Approach to Air Pollution Control." Paper presented at the annual meeting of the Air Pollution Control Association, June 11, 1967.
25. Wolozin, H., ed. *The Economics of Air Pollution*. New York: W. W. Norton & Co., 1966.

16

A. Allan Schmid:
The Role of Grants, Exchange, and
Property Rights in Environmental
Policy

The growth of the grants economy or unilateral transfers is in part a response to demands for a different performance by the market economy; grants are a device to supplement the performance of the market. But it is my judgment that the essentially marginal adjustments now possible within either the grants economy or the market economy given present property rights, will not result in substantially different treatment of the environment. It is difficult to imagine that reliance on public spending alone or even land-use zoning, which has largely failed to direct the use of developing areas, will produce extensive environmental improvement.

Both bilateral and unilateral exchange depend on underlying property rights, which make exchange possible and which shape the subsequent exchanges and transfers. If we are to achieve nonmarginal improvement in the environment, we will have to make a nonmarginal change in institutions, and that means adjusting property rights. We will need to be more aggressive in such directions as capturing the land value gains due to public actions and defining more explicitly public ownership of natural resources.

A Grants-Exchange Taxonomy
Related to Environment

Before this argument can be developed, it is necessary to set out the relevant conceptual taxonomy. Some choose to categorize any nonmarket decision as an element of the grants economy, but whatever name is used for this broad category of transactions, it is useful to distinguish several sub-categories. One class is *collective purchase*, in which the government acts as agent for a group and collects taxes to purchase some good or service. This is the situation when the federal government makes a "grant" to a municipality for a sewage treatment plant, for purchase of a scenic easement, or for tax forgiveness on pollution-control equipment. All of these transactions involve

Presented at the Symposium on the Grants Economy held between the Association for the Study of the Grants Economy and the American Association for the Advancement of Science, Chicago, Illinois, December, 1970. Reprinted by permission of the author, who is in the departments of agricultural economics and resource development, Michigan State University.

the exchange of exchangeables. The exchange is not wholly organized by the market, but it has a *quid pro quo* characteristic involving market-valued opportunity costs on both sides. Money is paid to obtain the tangible product of a cleaner stream or an unobstructed view; it commands a reallocation of the use of market-valued resources (steel, concrete, land, and so on) in return for money that has been obtained collectively outside the market.

Another subcategory is *one-way transfer* of an exchangeable (money), in which case nothing tangible is received in return. My preference is to restrict the term *grant* to this kind of transaction. Most grants economists have in mind the transfer of wealth involved in private charity or public welfare payments. The party receiving the grant need do nothing in return, although the giver may be transformed and may gain utility in the process. In national income accounting these are termed *transfer payments*. Is anything in the environmental field analogous? It is possible to observe private firms that could legally detract from the environment more than they do but who choose to forbear because of an affinity with those affected. This seems to fit the definition of a one-way transfer of a market-valued good where nothing of similar character is returned. Does the obverse occur? Does the government ever fail to exercise its rights and essentially transfer its resources without obtaining anything in return? Perhaps this is what is meant by the popular phrase describing some government policy as a "giveaway." When the government gives away television and radio airwaves rather than selling them, there is a grant from the public to specific individuals. Because the government asks little in return, this is a one-way transfer, with predictable impact on the environment of television programming.

The use of the air waves is at least licensed, but in the case of many natural resources, the right of use is merely appropriated. In effect the public legitimates use of resources to whomever can make physical use. Many states are moving away from this policy to declare public ownership and then grant permits to use water for withdrawal or waste disposal, with accompanying conditions that retain some aspects of the resources for public use. Still, the essential feature of the grant remains. Only the new proposals for effluent charges, such as those introduced by Senator William Proxmire, which require payment for waste disposal, are a departure from the usual pattern of the grants economy of resource use.

As noted at the outset of the paper, the grants economy is often seen as a corrective to the exchange economy. In the natural resource field we may have to institute the exchange economy in some areas to obtain a different performance than that of the grants system.

Another subcategory of public action that has grants implications is the use of public spending for goods and services to affect income distribution. The collective purchase of goods and services seldom involves taxes in proportion to benefits received. Some groups receive a larger share of benefits than they pay in taxes. Public purchase then frequently also involves a grant in kind.[1] Some goods go to the bottom end of the wealth scale, but much goes to the top as well. Many natural resource development projects enhance property values of large landowners much more than they enhance the welfare of the poor. In addition to personal redistributions, geographical transfers of income are also involved in public natural resource spending, which will be explored below.

Before leaving the discussion of taxonomy, I should add the category of *rule making and prohibitions* and explore its implications for the grants economy. Government can affect economic performance by collective purchase, grants, rule making, or outright commands. These rules affect the use of resources like spending and transfers;[2] a rule change can affect a grant without the existence of a public treasury payment.[3] Reference has already been made to licensing that reserves certain use rights for the public, and we are seeing more outright prohibitions and "thou shalt nots" in environmental policy. These often redistribute and transfer rights to resources without any tangible return to their former users. Zoning, which prohibits some uses, is of this variety. Often this rations the remaining allowable sites, to their great price enhancement. Zoning giveth and taketh away without *quid pro quo*.

The Failure of Both Exchange and Grants

Critics of the performance of the market exchange economy in the environmental field are numerous. The voluminous literature of market failure need not be repeated here; it is sufficient for the argument of this paper to note only that the correctives seem to be of two main types: collective purchase and prohibitions.

Because the private market fails to produce the environment that some people want, citizens have turned increasingly to public spending financed by general taxation. The effect is that the cost of environmental improvement is spread on the general taxpayer rather than increasing the cost to the consumer of goods whose production detracts from the environment. For example, if we are offended by the visual pollution of billboards on the highways, we turn to public purchase of scenic easements or payment to tear down the billboards. This points out the base upon which all exchange

---

1. Robert Lampman calls this distributive allocation or transfer-in-kind in his article "Transfer Approaches to Distribution Policy," *American Economic Review*, May 1970, p. 270.

2. A. A. Schmid, "Effective Public Policy and the Government Budget: A Uniform Treatment of Public Expenditures and Public Rules," in *The Analysis and Evaluation of Public Expenditures: The PPB System* (Washington, D.C.: Joint Economic Committee, U.S. Congress, 1969), pp. 579–91.

3. Rules affect the distribution of factor incomes out of which subsequent grants can be made. The role of government rules on preredistribution incomes is noted by Michael Taussig in his discussion of Lampman's "Transfer Approaches."

rests, whether bilateral or unilateral. The basic right to construct the billboards in the first place is not challenged by public-spending efforts to modify the environment. Collective purchase just makes a type of exchange work; it facilitates Pareto-better trades, which make at least one party better off than he was before, with initial rights specification and distribution as a given. In this sense the institution of public spending is a marginal modification of environmental performance. In some instances this will satisfy, but some people are clamoring for more basic and thorough changes, and to them my message is to look elsewhere.

There are many instances in which public spending places the cost of improvement on the total population. State and federal "grants" for municipal treatment plants are paid for by all taxpayers, including those in sparsely settled areas. Those who specifically created the congestion effects are not required to make any special contribution. Their rights of waste disposal are unaffected by such public spending.

The institution of an effluent charge is a different case, however. It would be a nonmarginal change because it affects the basic underlying property rights that are antecedent to subsequent marginal exchanges and transfers. If the public exacts a charge (collects a rent), the ownership right is implied in the government and not in the private user, who might physically appropriate it.[4] This situation could be expected to produce a much greater change in environment. Instead of all taxpayers paying for the change, the specific users of products requiring high-resource inputs for waste disposal would pay more.

Although there is talk of spending much more public money for environmental improvement, I believe that the talk will never go very far. There are such heavy demands on the public purse now that a significantly greater proportion for buying the rights of polluters or cleaning up after the exercise of polluters' present rights does not seem likely. Pareto-better exchange will not move us very far, whether we are talking of agricultural land reform in Latin America or environmental land reform in the United States.

Public spending is an attempt to redirect resources essentially by facilitating bilateral exchange. If it is subject to the limitations of the underlying property rights, shall we then turn more to rule making? A popular institution is that of zoning. In a sense it is a redefinition of property rights. It says for a specified site that the "owner" does not have the right of certain specified uses, which appears at first glance to be along the lines that I am suggesting if people want to change the environment in major ways. Yet zoning has largely been a failure in shaping land and water use in developing areas. Although it looks good in theory, it fails in administration and practice.

---

4. Government can of course tax a privately owned input, but a tax usually is only a portion of total value, whereas a rental value can approach the whole value. Any tax approaching total value is regarded as confiscatory and would not stand constitutionally unless public ownership is legitimated. A regulatory tax is relatively marginal in its effect compared to the greater latitude of rental charges.

Grand public plans are made, but after a series of exceptions and new spot zoning changes, little is left. This is because zoning leaves another basic property right unaffected.

Zoning is a variety of grant. It transfers use rights from the specific "owner" to the general public, or, in effect, to another specific owner. In one respect it removes the right of a certain use; it transfers the right from site owner to the public. At the same time, the value of the remaining sites, where the specified use is allowed, may be enhanced. If high-rise apartments are prohibited by zoning in one area, the remaining zones where high-rise apartments are allowed may become more valuable. This is a transfer or grant of wealth from one private owner to another private owner, although there is also a gain in public welfare in the resulting pattern of land use. Zoning is now a grant to a lucky few of a right that is directly translated into an exchangeable with market value. The public that directs the grant gets nothing in exchange from the new "owner," although it hopes in the process to obtain a total performance of land use more to its liking. Incidentally, the "old owner," who is denied access to future land value increases, is not paid for his loss but suffers a negative grant. This transfer is not looked upon with disinterest by private owners. They will try to break the public land-use plan in order to redistribute and to capture some of the potential grant of value. The numerous cases where they succeed make a mockery of zoning. One can always urge better administration, but the fact is that zoning grants are the victim of the thrust of the underlying property rights in land value changes. This type of grant will fail to achieve the implementation of public plans and the intended change in environment. The failure to conceive of zoning as part of the grants economy has meant that we have not recognized the one-way transfers that it engenders and the barrier that these present to realization of desired patterns of population settlement and resource use. Unless we change the basic thrust of present law and deny some of the publicly created value to the owner who did nothing in exchange for it,[5] the marginal grants institution of zoning will never guide us to substantial changes in our environment.

A final point relating to zoning is relevant. If we cannot redirect major patterns of population settlement and land use, it is going to be very expensive to correct the result by public spending which will essentially be of a cosmetic character at that point. We are going to have to redirect where and how people settle in the first place, environmental correction after this becomes a given and will be prohibitively expensive. This makes it even more imperative to solve the problem created by competition over land value increase distribution. If zoning has failed when instituted on a local government basis, it is doomed as a device to institute a national policy on population settlement.

---

5. Except perhaps to bribe a zoning official.

Court Action as Related to
Exchange and Grants

People have seen various private users gain use rights in resources by a slow process of attrition and appropriation. They may have felt that implicitly the public really held these rights, but there were problems of administering them and getting the public's agents to properly guard them. This has lead to a growing interest in court action to protect the public rights even when administrative agencies have failed to do so. To put this in terms of the grants economy, people may be saying that there have been some unintended grants from the public domain, or what was earlier termed giveaways.

Michigan has just passed a law allowing citizens to sue polluters or state agencies that violate the public trust in natural resources.[6] This is probably a laudable law, but it begs the real question of where the property rights lie. The new law does not clarify what constitutes the public right in resources in the first place. The law and the subsequent court action seem to facilitate decisions on grants – in this case to prevent unwanted grants. However, it adds nothing to defining whether the public has any right to reserve grants or whether the rights have already been vested in others.

The court in general is an institution that facilitates exchange and grants by clarifying disputed rights at the margin. However, it is not well suited for large changes in the definition of those rights, although cases can be found in which the courts have made nonmarginal, substantive changes in ownership rights. There is not space here to fully explore the relative merits of judicial or legislative definition of new rights but only to express the judgment that the courts will move very slowly in this regard and will require clear indication from the public of support for nonmarginal changes, which seems to be lacking in present legislative actions. Also, because I have a basic preference for democracy, I would prefer to see legislative declaration of new public rights in natural resources.

Court action could both declare and define the public right in various natural resources as well as prevent unwanted grants and transfer of use rights to these resources. However, even if this were done, this process does not institute the exchange of these resources where such trades are in order. Earlier it was pointed out that government spending to solve the public goods problem, which often frustrates potentially Pareto-better exchange, is a marginal change and thus could not be expected to produce major environmental change. If we push use prohibitions and flat public use reservation too far, we may block some potentially favorable trades where the public might prefer to sell some of the waste assimilating capacity of a stream in exchange for money to build a new school or hospital. To summarize, even if courts

---

6. Act 127, P.A. 1970. Hearings have also been held in 1970 on a similar bill S.3575 in the United States Senate.

are able to define new public rights and then to prevent unwanted grants, it is a much more complex job to create agencies and to institute rules for exchange of public rights.

Grants for System Maintenance

An argument has been presented that many of our present environmental policies are marginal in character and do not change the underlying property rights and should not be expected to produce big environmental changes. It should be recognized that some people like it that way and will try to maintain the system as it is. For example, a polluter may make a big show of making a grant and forbearing his use in a certain area while he appropriates like crazy in another area out of public view. The grant is made so that no one will begin to question the polluter's power in general.

Still another technique of system maintenance is for polluters and their consumers to volunteer to tax themselves if others will. This collective purchase of a different environment leaves unchanged the rights of initiative to use resources and cleverly shifts the costs of improvement to the public at large rather than to those who consume products that pollute. This willingness of polluters to participate along with others has a hollow ring to it. It is a "grant" that deserves little respect from the public.

Grants for System Change

Turning now from system maintenance to system change, we need first to ask whether a governmentally declared new property right and redefinition can be regarded as the result of a grant, an exchange, or a separate category of transaction. There is a peculiar thrust to American property law as regards the extension of rights to newly valuable aspects of resources. This thrust runs in favor of uses that involve a physical taking, such as irrigation or waste disposal, and against public goods use, such as fishing or scenic enjoyment, even when the latter constitute prior uses. Public use has been a residual category rather than a firm declaration of public right, which would require explicit exchange or grant for title to shift. Now we find ourselves in the peculiar position of trying to get some of these rights back again for public use. In a sense we frequently have an open-ended system of rights vesture in which resource use by breathers of air and fishermen proceeds until some physical appropriator, such as a waste discharger, comes along and then the use shifts. Can this be called a redistribution? A one-way "exchange" of use is made, albeit involuntarily. Usually, involuntary one-way exchange is called theft, but in this case it has the sanction of law in regard to some natural resources in some jurisdictions simply because the public use had never been made an explicit property right. Physical taking for waste disposal only requires the acquiescence of law, whereas public goods consumption for scenic use or fishing requires law to actively protect that use against others.

If the act of pollution sets in motion the above situation, some people might term it redistributive. However, if the "polluter" always owned the use right, there is no redistribution. The owner merely begins to use what was always his and there is no transfer of *right*, although there may be of actual *use*.

Is a new publicly declared property right a grant from the former user or from the public as prior owner? It depends on whether the former user simply used the resource or whether he also had the *right* of use. The above distinctions are the delight and sustenance of lawyers. But political and economic factors underlie actual change in property rights. Whether the polluter had the right or not, if he is to support new public rights, he will want something for his vote as a citizen, and he has an economic motivation to try to maintain his income based on the actual past use.

Suppose a polluter supports a new law to define public interests in small trout streams that might result in the reservation of this resource for fishing rather than industry. These former users may regard their support for this law as an exchange for retention of other rights or the creation of new ones in other resources. In other words, are property rights the product of exchange as well as the basis for further exchange?

The political process certainly can be studied with exchange models. Perhaps it is of a different variety than Kenneth Boulding's definition of exchange as the trade of exchangeables with market values. Here it is perhaps the two-way exchange of nonexchangeables, which sounds like a contradiction in terms, but perhaps it points up the similarities of political and market exchange. It appears that the basis for property rights can be pushed back to some fundamental human covenant in which there is an exchange of respect and recognition as a person rather than as an object. I am not sure it helps to regard this as an exchange relationship. The only reason the question is raised is to contrast it with opportunities for gaining assent to new property rights definitions and distributions, which seem to involve grants.

Nonmarginal change is rare, and one reason is that although the total long-run effect of the change may be thought of as creating a better world, some of the parties seem to be asked to bear a disproportionate share of the costs of getting there. This is why the question of the use of grants to achieve property system change is raised. A basic thrust in present property law lets losses and gains fall where they may regardless of the cause. This extends to gains and losses created by public action. We have already examined the consequences of letting land value gains accrue willy nilly. Often when we institute new public rules and ownership it destroys the assets of some while enhancing others. A dramatic example would be a public rule banning the sale of cigarettes. What is one to do with a specialized cigarette-making machine or a tobacco farm? The public has been remarkably cavalier about the questions and tends to regard the necessary readjustment as similar to any other loss due to bad business judgment. This attitude engenders a fight to the death response from those affected and explains a large part of the failure to make large changes in our environment even when we recognize great public danger.

I suggest that the public should adopt an expanded program of explicit purchase of assets whose value is substantially destroyed by public policies where there is no duplicity on the part of their owners.[7] If we destroy the value of outdoor advertising firms by prohibiting billboards, we may have to make a grant to these firms to cover some of their fixed asset losses. Otherwise their concentrated opposition, which means greater lobbying power, will prevent change in the property rights.

This brings the argument back to where this paper began, when it was observed that public purchase of acknowledged use rights could only produce marginal change in environment. Is this an inescapable conundrum? I think not, but the answer is only tentative. There is surely an instrumental value in stable property rights. No long-run investment is possible if one cannot expect prediction based on stable rights. This is a problem seen around the world with unstable governments. Yet this does not require complete ossification. In other words, the price of outright purchase of a property right (going business) in the market is in some instances not the same as indemnification for fixed asset losses. The latter may be enough to preserve investor interest in the long-term commitment of capital. This is an empirical question that should be open to test to determine how much property right change with limited losses will result in failure to invest.

Second, a grant program to limit loss due to public policy change would not have to pay for the economic rent value of destroyed assets. This would not remove the lobbying effort by those affected, but it would reduce their ability to extract public sympathy – or would it?

Third, such a program could substitute creation of new rights for those destroyed. For example, to get support, or at least relative acquiescence, for a property right change that would expand the public's use of a trout stream may require that those harmed would be granted the rights to storage of surplus water for subsequent market sale, a right now very uncertain in a state like Michigan.

Is this then a grant or an exchange? There is a movement of a right with market value or outright cash payment in return for support for new laws. Perhaps the development of a tight taxonomy can wait. The point is that we should look for ways to broaden the currencies for transactions, or what Boulding once called the widening of the agenda, which may make it possible to move off the contract (or conflict) line.

One hypothesis of this paper is that if we want to substantially alter the performance of the economy with respect to the environment for man, we

---

7. And where there is a shift in the transferable resources to new uses. The problem with farm subsidies is that they have not tied payment to actual new employment of mobile resources, and this has resulted in losses to the economy.

shall have to look beyond the usual forms of exchange or grants to modification of property rights. And as one inquires as to how this can be done, some of the concepts of grants and exchange come back into play at another level.

Conclusion

If people wish to make only small changes in their environment they can continue to try to expand some of the present public programs and policies, such as public spending for scenic easements or sewage treatment plants and land-use zoning. If they want to implement a much different way of life than that which now prevails, the institutional analyst must prescribe additional and more fundamental institutional changes, which might properly be called environmental land reform and some of which will be non–Pareto-better. Examples of such changes would be public capture of some of the publicly created land value increases and declaration of new public rights in some natural resources. Hopefully, this latter can be done with provision for exchange if there are opportunities for profitable trades. If public ownership were clarified, it would be possible to utilize the market exchange process to a greater extent by renting limited use for waste disposal and relying less on flat police power prohibition.

It is easy to call for reformation of property rights in natural resources, but difficult to institute peacefully and without destroying confidence in long-term investments. Indeed, this is an ingredient of many problems elsewhere in the world. Reformations seem to become dammed up until they explode in revolutions, which often do as much harm as good. Those who study the grants economy must not only measure the results of existing grants and exchanges but must also create new forms for directing these transactions in new directions without destroying the social system itself or condemning us all to the environment that exists.

17

George Daly and Fred Giertz
Pollution Abatement, Pareto
Optimality, and the Market
Mechanism

Introduction

In the economists' frame of reference environmental pollution is labeled an "external diseconomy." Thus it may not be coincidental that the decade of the 1960s witnessed a rapid expansion of both the public awareness of such pollution and the academic literature dealing with externalities. However, it is disturbing, if not surprising, to note that the analysis and prescriptions of the latter seem to have little relationship to and/or influence on the former.

For example, the general thrust of this "new" or "post-Pigovian" externalities literature has been that there exists a substantial range of problems involving the generation of external costs and/or benefits in which optimality can be achieved through voluntary exchange relationships between the relevant parties.[1] In terms of policy recommendations the general thrust of this literature has been to suggest minimizing the role of direct government intervention and instead allowing "markets in externalities" to develop. Yet in contemporary America we find increased concern with the "pollution problem" and the apparent public political realization that this problem is likely to result in increased government intervention in the economy.

Similarly, both the orthodox Pigovian analysis and the new literature have prescribed that the optimal solution to a problem involving the generation of external costs will find, if the externalities are relevant, a direct reduction in the externality generating activity. However, in the real world we find that many of the proposed solutions to pollution problems do not directly concern the volume of the primary activity, but rather concern an abatement process that is designed to allow the primary activity to continue at or near normal levels. Real-world approaches to automobile air pollution are a clear example.

Presented at the Symposium on the Grants Economy held between the Association for the Study of the Grants Economy and the American Association for the Advancement of Science, Chicago, Illinois, December, 1970. Reprinted by permission of the authors, who are members of the economics department, Miami University, Oxford, Ohio.

1. See especially R. Coase, "The Problem of Social Cost," *Journal of Law and Economics*, October 1960; O. Davis and A. Whinston, "Externalities Welfare and the Theory of Games," *Journal of Political Economy*, June 1962; J. Buchanan and W. Stubblebine, "Externality," *Economica*, November 1962; and R. Turvey, "On Divergences between Social Cost and Private Cost," *Economica*, August 1963.

In this paper we construct a simplified model in which the act of pollution is viewed as imposing on external cost, which is shared equally by all members of some group. The purpose of this paper is to analyze the general nature of pollution abatement in such a model and, more specifically, the role and relevance of market processes in its optimal provision.

The Model

The world we analyze consists of $i = 1, 2 \ldots, n$ individuals and two commodities, X_1 and X_2. X_1^i and X_2^i are, respectively, the units of X_1 and X_2 consumed by the *ith* individual. X_1^i generates no external effects. However, the consumption of X_2^i generates an external diseconomy (pollution), the quantity of which is measured as Z^i. Further, it is assumed that Z^i is collectively consumed, meaning that each individual consumes not only his own pollution but that created by all other individuals as well. Thus, each individual has a utility function of the form:

$$U^i = U^i \left(X_1^i, X_2^i, \sum_{j=1}^{n} Z^j \right) \text{ where} \tag{1}$$

$$\frac{\partial U^i}{\partial X_2^i} > 0, \frac{\partial U^i}{\partial X_2^i} > 0, \frac{\partial U^i}{\partial Z^j} < 0 \; i = 1, 2, \ldots, n; j = 1, 2, \ldots, n.$$

Note that the Z term of equation (1) is preceded by a summation sign, thus reflecting that everyone's consumption of X_2 and not that of the *i*th individual alone influences the *i*th individual's utility. This means that pollution generated anywhere in this world will be consumed in full strength by all of its members. Although such a formulation ignores the spatial element of many types of real-world pollution, it allows us to isolate and analyze the essential "publicness" of many types of pollution. For this reason our analysis is of primary relevance to those types of pollution that can be considered "public bads" in a Samuelsonian sense.[2]

Finally, we assume the existence of a technique by which the external effect of the consumption of X_2 can be abated. Letting the quantity of abatement activity engaged in by the *i*th individual be represented by A^i, the technological relationship between consumption, pollution abatement, and pollution can be described by:

$$Z^i = Z^i (X_2^i, A^i) \text{ where}$$

$$\frac{\partial Z^i}{\partial X_2^i} > 0, \frac{\partial Z^i}{\partial A^i} < 0. \tag{2}$$

---

2. P. Samuelson, "The Pure Theory of Public Expenditure," *Review of Economics and Statistics*, November 1954.

It is assumed that abatement, like the two other commodities, is available to individuals at a constant price. A^i, because its consumption reduces Z^i, may be considered a public good because any reduction of pollution benefits all individuals.

Independent Behavior and Abatement

In this section we examine the behavior of the ith individual as he attempts to maximize his utility on a strictly private basis. We specifically assume that the individual does not concern himself with the effects his consumption has on others and that neither he nor any other individual attempts to influence the behavior of any other party. As a real-world analogy one might consider automobile travel and its subsequent pollution when there are no controls, taxes, subsidies, or possible negotiations that might reflect the efforts of others, individually or collectively, to influence quantity of pollution (or pollution abatement) generated by any individual.

The problem so framed is one of maximizing equation (1) [as modified by equation (2)] above, subject to the constraints imposed by prices and money incomes. The general mathematical solution to this problem is shown in the appendix to this paper. Here, however, we wish simply to illustrate those factors relevant to the isolated individual's choice of his privately optimal quantity of abatement, and for such a purpose a simple geometrical exposition will suffice.

The individual's preferences can be in part described by a system of indifference curves which illustrate his tastes between units of X_1 and A.[3] To avoid income effect complications we will assume that the marginal utility of X_1 is constant. The slope of any one of these indifference curves will measure the evaluation the individual places on an additional unit of one of these commodities in terms of the other. Such an analytical device is, of course, a Hicksian marginal evaluation curve. In figure 1 below we measure units of A on the horizontal axis and units of X_1 on the vertical. The schedule MB_A measures the marginal benefit (evaluation) the individual feels he will obtain from one additional unit of abatement, as measured by the amount of X_1 he would be willing to give up to attain it. Such a schedule slopes downward from left to right, reflecting the fact that the individual's preferences exhibit the usual diminishing marginal rate of substitution. Because the

---

3. It should be noted that the individual must simultaneously make a decision concerning the amount of X_2 to consume, which also relates to the amount of pollution generated. This is discussed more fully in the mathematical appendix.

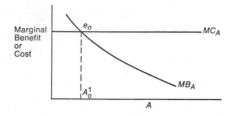

Figure 1.

individual faces a fixed price for abatement, the marginal cost of abatement is represented by the horizontal schedule MC_A.

The individual achieves his private optimum at point e_o, where his marginal private costs and benefits of abatement are equated. In our example, this leads him to consume A_o^1 units of abatement. It should be noted that in a many-person world in which the isolated individual is but one of many generators of collectively consumed pollution, his private marginal benefit may be very small. For example, whether or not a resident of Los Angeles has a car that emits pollution is virtually unrelated to the amount of pollutants he consumes. In terms of figure 1 this might well mean that the MB_A schedule would lie below the MC_A schedule at all levels of A and hence that the individual would optimize privately by purchasing no abatement.

Pareto Optimality

In the context of our model we can easily discuss the properties of Pareto optima and compare these properties with those that result from the strictly private behavior discussed in the last section. This means, of course, that we must consider the effects the individual's actions have on all other members of the society, effects we specifically excluded from consideration in the last section. A general treatment of this subject requires mathematics and is included in the concluding appendix. As before, however, the aspects of this case that are critical to the purposes of this paper require only geometry.

It must be remembered that the model specifies that pollution generated anywhere in the economy will be consumed in full strength by all individuals, thus making pollution a public "bad." For this reason the provision of abatement by any individual necessarily reduces everyone's pollution—that is, abatement is a public good. In terms of figure 1 this means that the MB_A schedule understates the marginal social benefit of pollution abatement because that schedule ignores the benefits others derive from this action.

In figure 2 we include this factor.[4] Let the individual providing the abatement be the first of the n individuals in the society and his marginal benefit and abatement be labeled MB_A^1 and A^1 respectively. As before, the MB_A^1 schedule measures the benefits individual 1 privately experiences from his own pollution abatement. The schedule $\sum_{i=2}^{n} MB_A^i$ measures the marginal benefits his abatement extends to all other individuals. Finally, the schedule $\sum_{i=1}^{n} MB_A^i$ measures the marginal benefit 1's pollution abatement extends to all members of the society including himself. As such, this last schedule is simply a vertical summation of the first two. It measures the social or public benefits of 1's abatement activities. If we take the utility levels of the other $n-1$ individuals as given, the point of Pareto optimality is indicated as e_p, where the public benefits schedule crosses the marginal cost schedule. Thus, the Pareto optimal level of pollution abatement by 1 is A_p^1. This quantity exceeds the privately optimal quantity and always will if abatement exerts net public benefits. Viewing the same problem from an alternative perspective, it could be said that the marginal private cost of pollution abatement over-states the cost to society of such actions.

Pollution Abatement and the Market Mechanism

We have seen that in a model of the type discussed above, voluntary, independent action will, according to the Pareto criteria, produce relatively too little abatement and, consequently, relatively too much pollution. It is important to note, however, that this does not imply that government action is necessary to secure the Pareto optimal quantity of abatement. It is quite possible that through private negotiations the other members of the society could persuade the individual to supply that Pareto optimal quantity. For example, in terms of figure 2 it can be shown that the externally affected parties would be willing to bribe individual 1 an amount sufficient to ensure his provision of A_p^1 of abatement. The thought of bribes being paid to prevent socially harmful acts may not seem very appealing, but it must be remembered that the Pareto criteria apply to allocative efficiency and not to distributive ethics.

This conclusion – that voluntary behavior may achieve Pareto optimality even when external effects are present through the formation of a "market in

---

4. It is important to note that the Pareto optimal solution depicted in figure 2 is but one of an infinity of such optima, each of which is associated with a particular income distribution. A social welfare function is required if a choice is to be made from among such optima.

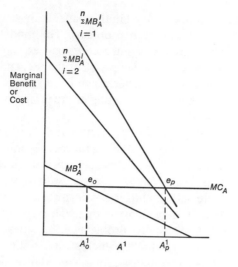

Figure 2.

externalities" – is, of course, the central proposition of the "new externalities" literature referred to earlier. In an article that summarizes and amplifies this new literature Ralph Turvey writes: "The first [main conclusion of this literature] is that if the party imposing external diseconomies and the party suffering them are *able and willing to negotiate* to their mutual advantage, state intervention is unnecessary to secure optimum resource allocation."[5] The critical issue, then, is whether or not and when negotiations can take place to internalize the social costs of his actions in the decision calculus of the polluter.

It has been argued that the vital determinants of whether or not an activity should be publicly supplied are the divisibility of the activity (that is, its "publicness") and the number of parties affected by it.[6] In terms of our model – with pollution as a public "bad" and its abatement as a public good – this issue is thus critically tied to the number of parties affected by the relevant external effects. This is for two distinct yet related reasons. First, in a world of transactions costs, the economic expense of achieving agreement through voluntary negotiations rapidly increases as the size of the group grows. Second, even if transactions costs were zero, as the interacting group becomes larger, each individual will have less incentive to reduce his pollution because such an act will have an insignificant effect on his own welfare. That is, pollution abatement as a public good has significant "free-rider" effects.

---

5. Turvey, "Divergence between Social Cost and Private Cost," p. 309.

6. See J. M. Buchanan, *The Supply and Demand of Public Goods* (New York: Random House, 1968).

It is our belief that the model offered in this paper is an accurate depiction of many types of real-world pollution problems. The model, in attaching critical significance to the number of interacting parties, suggests that the socially optimal solution to a particular problem will depend on the particular type of pollution and the characteristics of the society in which it is done. It also suggests that when the interacting group is large there are strong reasons for suspecting "market failure."[7]

We do not mean to suggest that the authors of the "new" literature cited earlier have been ignorant of this issue. Indeed, several have explicitly noted the difficulties encountered by the market when the interacting group involved in an externality relationship is large. Rather, we feel that this literature and much of the scholarship it has inspired have suffered from a misplaced emphasis. Once it is recognized that voluntary negotiations *can* lead to optimal solutions to externality problems, it becomes truly critical to analyze the proximate conditions under which such a result can be reasonably expected to follow. It is our conclusion that, viewed from this perspective, the policy recommendations of this literature are limited in the area of environmental pollution.

Abatement Techniques

As we noted at the outset, the policy prescriptions of both the "new" and the "old" externalities literature have been framed in the context of achieving Pareto optimality through a direct reduction in the primary activity (production or consumption) that produces the relevant externality. On the other hand, the major techniques of reducing many types of real-world pollution emphasize changes in the conditions of the "joint supply" of a good and a bad (for example, the use of a filter) that characterizes pollution problems. We feel that the literature of applied welfare economics could benefit from the explicit inclusion of this factor, perhaps along the lines suggested in this paper. That is, the direct reduction of the primary activity should be thought of as one of perhaps many possible techniques of pollution abatement. After all, if two or more techniques exist for reducing a relevant external diseconomy the selection of the most efficient one becomes a necessary condition for Pareto optimality. Perhaps even more important, economists should investigate the most appropriate government techniques (for example, taxes, subsidies, class action law suits, sales of pollution rights, and so on) for the provision of abatement.

---

7. Needless to say, although it shows circumstances under which private behavior will not lead to optimality, it does not show that collective action will achieve optimality. Clearly, government intervention may harm more than it helps. In this regard see: J. M. Buchanan, "Politics, Policy, and Pigovian Margins," *Economica*, February 1962.

Mathematical Appendix

Equations (1) and (2) specify the utility and abatement functions respectively:

$$U^i = U^i(X_1^i, X_2^i, \sum_{i=1}^{n} Z^j) \tag{1}$$

$$Z^i = Z^i(X_2^i, A^i) \quad i = 1, 2, \ldots, n; \quad j = 1, 2, \ldots, n. \tag{2}$$

The partial derivatives of these equations are given above.

Utility Maximization on a Strictly Private Basis

The ith individual faces the constraints imposed by his fixed money income, M^i, and by the parametric prices of the three goods: P_1, P_2, and P_A. Private utility maximization thus implies the maximization of (1) subject to his budget constraint. To solve for the appropriate values of his choice, variables X_1^i, X_2^i, and A^i, we form the Lagrangian function:

$$L = U^i + \lambda (P_1 X_1^i + P_2 X_2^i + P_A A^i - M^i). \tag{3}$$

By differentiating (3) with respect to X_1^i, X_2^i, and A^i and by rearranging the equations, we obtain the marginal conditions of equations (4) and (5) below:

$$\frac{\dfrac{\partial U^i}{\partial X_2^i} + \dfrac{\partial U^i}{\partial Z^i}\dfrac{\partial Z^i}{\partial X_2^i}}{\dfrac{\partial U^i}{\partial X_1^i}} = \frac{P_2}{P_1} \tag{4}$$

$$\frac{\dfrac{\partial U^i}{\partial Z^i}\dfrac{\partial Z^i}{\partial A^i}}{\dfrac{\partial U^i}{\partial X_1^i}} = \frac{P_A}{P_1} \tag{5}$$

Equation (4) says that in order to maximize his utility, the individual will consume commodity X_2 until his marginal rate of substitution (MRS) between it and X_1 is equal to the market price ratio of the two commodities. Equation (5) says the same thing with respect to his purchase of abatement, A^i. Notice that the MRS of equation (4) includes the effect that the individual's own consumption of X_2 has on pollution (Z^i) and hence on his level of utility. As the number of individuals becomes large it is likely that the effects of an individual's own pollution, and hence of his own abatement on his private utility, will become negligible. As this happens, the numerator of equation (5), which shows the individual's marginal utility of abatement, will approach zero and he will purchase no abatement.

Pareto Optimality

In the context of the above model we can obtain the necessary conditions for the achievement of Pareto optimality by maximizing the level of individual 1's utility subject to the constraints (a) that individual's 2, . . . , n's utilities are held constant at some predetermined level and (b) imposed by the production possibility function for X_1, X_2, and A. To do this we form the Lagrangian expression:

$$L = U^1 + \sum_{i=2}^{n} \lambda^i (U^i - C^i) + \alpha F (X_1, X_2, A) \tag{6}$$

Differentiating (6) with respect to X_1, X_2, and A and rearranging, we derive the following equations:

$$\frac{\dfrac{\partial U^1}{\partial X_2^1} + \dfrac{\partial U^1}{\partial Z^1}\dfrac{\partial Z^1}{\partial X_2^1}}{\dfrac{\partial U^1}{\partial X_1^1}} + \sum_{i=2}^{n} \frac{\dfrac{\partial U^i}{\partial Z^1}\dfrac{\partial Z^1}{\partial X_2^1}}{\dfrac{\partial U^i}{\partial X_1^i}} = \frac{\dfrac{\partial F}{\partial X_2^1}}{\dfrac{\partial F}{\partial X_1^1}} \tag{7}$$

and

$$\frac{\dfrac{\partial U^1}{\partial Z^1}\dfrac{\partial Z^1}{\partial A^1}}{\dfrac{\partial U^1}{\partial X_1^1}} + \sum_{i=2}^{n} \frac{\dfrac{\partial U^i}{\partial Z^1}\dfrac{\partial Z^1}{\partial A^1}}{\dfrac{\partial U^i}{\partial X_1^i}} = \frac{\dfrac{\partial F}{\partial A^1}}{\dfrac{\partial F}{\partial X_1^1}} \tag{8}$$

Equations (7) and (8) are the conditions necessary for Pareto optimality concerning person 1 and the rest of society. The MRS between X_1 and X_2 includes not only the effect that person 1's polluting activity has on his own utility but also the effect that this activity has on the rest of society as well. Likewise, the MRS for Pareto optimality between X_1 and A shown in equation (8) includes not only the benefit derived by person 1 from his own abatement activity, but also the benefit that the rest of society derives from this activity. Thus, expressions (7) and (8) are the standard "marginal rate of substitution equal to the marginal rate of transformation" conditions. They differ from the strictly private case only in that, due to the externality present, they are summed over all individuals.

18

Robert H. Strotz and Colin Wright
Externalities, Welfare Economics,
and Environmental Problems

During recent years substantial literature has arisen on the subject of externalities.[1] It appears as a clarification and critique of what may be called the classic position of Pigou[2] elaborated by Meade.[3] The classic argument is, in essence, that if there is a divergence between social and private marginal costs or benefits, a tax or subsidy should be introduced to make private marginal cost or benefit equal to the social. In this recent literature several issues and claims have been made:

1. To equate private and social marginal cost should not be the policy criterion for maximum economic welfare. Thus, "When an economist is comparing alternative social arrangements, the proper procedure is to compare the total social product yielded by these different arrangements. The comparison of private and social products is neither here nor there."[4]

2. Merger is a solution to the externality problem.

3. In principle, private bribes are as good a solution as the classic tax solution (Coase, Buchanan, and Stubblebine).

4. The classic tax solution is unsatisfactory because it does not lead to a Pareto equilibrium (Buchanan and Stubblebine).

5. The feasibility of the classic solution depends on whether or not externalities are separable (Davis and Whinston).

We shall comment on these propositions by examining an externality

Presented at the Symposium on the Grants Economy held between the Association for the Study of the Grants Economy and the American Association for the Advancement of Science, Chicago, Illinois, December, 1970. Reprinted by permission of the authors. Dr. Strotz is president of Northwestern University and professor of economics; Dr. Wright is assistant professor of economics at Northwestern. The work in this paper was supported by a grant from Resources for the Future.

1. R. H. Coase, "The Problem of Social Cost," *Journal of Law & Economics* 3 (October 1960): 1–44; O. A. Davis and A. Whinston, "Externalities, Welfare, and the Theory of Games," *Journal of Political Economy* 70, no. 3 (June 1962): 241–62; J. M. Buchanan and W. C. Stubblebine, "Externality," *Economica* 29, no. 116 (November 1962): 371–84; R. Turvey, "On Divergences between Social Cost and Private Cost," *Economica* 30, no. 119 (August 1963): 309–13; S. Wellisz, "On External Diseconomies and the Government-Assisted Invisible Hand," *Economica* 31, no. 124 (November 1964): 345–62; O. A. Davis and A. B. Whinston, "On Externalities, Information and the Government-Assisted Invisible Hand," *Economica* 33, no. 131 (August 1966): 303–18.

2. A. C. Pigou, *The Economics of Welfare*, 4th ed. (London: Macmillan & Co., 1932).

3. J. E. Meade, "External Economies and Diseconomies in a Competitive Situation," *Economic Journal* 62, no. 245 (March 1952): 45–67.

4. Coase, "Problem of Social Cost," p. 34.

occurring in the form of air pollution – although our analysis is applicable to a wide spectrum of externalities. We shall first obtain directly the conditions for a Pareto optimum and then try to find such market constraints and parameters that individuals, in maximizing their own utilities subject to these constraints, will establish a Pareto optimum.

Consider first a community of two individuals, A and B, in necessarily fixed locations, where A produces steel (x) and B produces flowers (y). Each individual will be considered as both a consumer and a firm. Suppose, in addition, that in the process of producing steel A emits pollutants that are encountered by B, the consequence of which adversely affects the production of flowers. If both A and B receive utility from steel and flowers and if there is a fixed aggregate quantity, R, of a homogeneous productive service per unit time to produce steel, R_x, to produce flowers, R_y, and to reduce pollution, R_p, the necessary conditions for a Pareto optimum are obtained by finding a critical value of the Lagrangean expression:

$$U^A(x^A, y^A) + w^B [U^B (x^B, y^B) - C^B] + \lambda_1 [x^A + x^B - f(R_x)]$$
$$+ \lambda^2 [y^A + y^B - g(R_y, R_x, R_p)] + \mu [R - R_x - R_y - R_p], \tag{1}$$

where the superscript A or B indicates individual consumption, where $f(R_x)$ is the production function for steel and $g(R_y, R_x, R_p)$ is the production function for flowers.

The deleterious effect of pollutants on flower production is reflected by having R_x and R_p appear as arguments in the production function for flowers:

$$y^A + y^B = g(R_y, R_x, R_p).$$

The marginal products, g_x and g_p, are respectively negative and positive. The marginal product of R in producing steel and flowers directly, f_x and g_y, are assumed positive and diminishing in the relevant range. We shall assume g_x to increase with increases in R_x and g_p to decrease with increases in R_p, reflecting the assumption of increasing marginal damage from air pollution and decreasing marginal effectiveness of abatement devices.

Differentiating equation (1) partially with respect to the x^A, x^B, y^A, y^B, R_x, R_y, R_p, the variables under the control of the community, we obtain:

    a. $u_x^A + \lambda_1 = 0$,

    b. $u_y^A + \lambda_2 = 0$,

    c. $w^B u_x^B + \lambda_1 = 0$,

    d. $w^B u_y^B + \lambda_2 = 0$,   (2)

    e. $-\lambda_1 f_x - \lambda_2 g_x - \mu = 0$,

    f. $-\lambda_2 g_y - \mu = 0$,

    g. $-\lambda_2 g_p - \mu = 0$.

Eliminating w^B, λ_1, λ_2, and μ by using equations (2a, b, c, g), we may express the conditions for a Pareto optimum as:

$$\text{d.}\quad \frac{u_x^A}{u_y^A} = \frac{u_x^B}{u_y^B},$$

$$\text{e.}\quad u_x^A f_x + u_y^A (g_x - g_p) = 0, \tag{3}$$

$$\text{f.}\quad g_y - g_p = 0.$$

Because both A and B are consumers and producers of goods, each maximizes his utility subject to a budget constraint that reflects not only his income from owning a portion of R but also profits he receives from his entrepreneurial activity. Moreover, although we have assumed that each individual accounts for the total output of a single commodity, we shall assume that he behaves competitively, which is in effect to regard each "firm" as an aggregate of a number of competitive firms producing the same product and each individual consumer as facing fixed prices.

It is well known that when two individuals maximize their utilities subject to the same prices, their marginal rates of substitution between pairs of goods (e.g., u_x^A/u_y^A) are the same. Hence, if we confront A with the budget constraint:

$$p_x x^A + p_y y^A = \pi_x + R^A + S^A, \tag{4}$$

where π_x is his profit from steel, R^A is his endowment per unit time of productive services, and S^A is any subsidy he may receive (a tax if negative), and B with:

$$p_x x^B + p_y y^B = \pi_y + R^B + S^B, \quad (R^A + R^B = R) \tag{5}$$

with the notation a natural extension of the foregoing, we know that the following relationship holds:

$$\frac{u_x^A}{u_y^A} = \frac{u_u^B}{u_y^B} = \frac{p_x}{p_y}, \tag{6}$$

so that (3d) is satisfied.

The remaining task is to determine the optimal values for p_x and p_y while reconciling (3e, f) with individual optimal conditions. This is accomplished by investigating the profit-maximizing behavior of both individuals acting as firms. Initially we shall assume that the legal framework within the community allows a tax to be imposed upon A for pollution damages, and we shall assume that the proceeds of the tax, however distributed, are regarded by A and B to be parametric (not affected by their decisions). The profit function for A in producing steel is then:

$$\pi_x = p_x(x^A + x^B) - R_x - R_p - T, \tag{7}$$

where:

$$T = T(R_x, R_p) \tag{8}$$

and denotes the annual tax imposed upon A for polluting B, the size of which is a function of the amount of R used in the production of steel and the amount of the resource he uses in pollution abatement. Substituting (8) into (7) and $f(R_x)$ for $(x^A + x^B)$, we obtain:

$$\pi_x = p_x f(R_x) - R_x - R_p - T(R_x, R_p). \tag{9}$$

Differentiating (9) partially with respect to R_x and R_p, the variables under the control of firm A, we obtain:

$$
\begin{aligned}
\text{a.} \quad & p_x f_x - T_x - 1 = 0, \\
\text{b.} \quad & \qquad - T_p - 1 = 0,
\end{aligned}
\tag{10}
$$

which are the necessary conditions for maximum profit. The profit function in flower production is:

$$\pi_y = p_y\, g(R_y, R_x, R_p) - R_y, \tag{11}$$

and the necessary condition for maximum profit is:

$$p_y g_y = 1. \tag{12}$$

Given the values of variables and derivatives that satisfy a Pareto optimum (3), suppose we establish the following prices and tax function:

$$
\begin{aligned}
\text{g.} \quad & p_y = \frac{1}{g_y}, \\
\text{b.} \quad & p_x = \left(1 - \frac{g_x}{g_y}\right)\frac{1}{f_x}, \\
\text{c.} \quad & T(R_x, R_p) = -p_y(g_x R_x + g_p R_p) + k,
\end{aligned}
\tag{13}
$$

where k is an arbitrary constant. Because we have already reconciled individual utility maximization with condition (3d) for a Pareto optimum, we need only to reconcile profit maximization with conditions (3e, f). The profit maximization conditions (10a, b) and (12) can now be written, using (13), as:

$$
\begin{aligned}
\text{a.} \quad & p_x f_x + p_y g_x - 1 = 0, \\
\text{b.} \quad & p_y g_p - 1 = 0, \\
\text{c.} \quad & p_y g_y - 1 = 0.
\end{aligned}
\tag{14}
$$

Using (6) the optimality conditions (3e) may be written:

$$p_x f_x + p_y g_x - p_y g_p = 0, \tag{3'e}$$

which can be obtained from (14a and b); it is thus satisfied. The remaining optimality condition (3f) can be obtained directly from (14b and 14c) and is thus also satisfied.

The values of k, S^A, and S^B may be determined arbitrarily, provided only that the following constraint is satisfied:

$$T = S^A + S^B. \tag{15}$$

This constraint is obtained by adding the budget constraints of A and B as individuals and of A and B as firms – namely, equations (4), (5), (7), and (11). By appropriate choice of these variables (k could in any case be set equal to zero), lump-sum income transfers may be effected between A and B to select a particular Pareto optimum. The choice of c^B (or w^B if it is to be regarded as a welfare weight rather than a Lagrange multiplier) implies the appropriate selection of S^A and S^B to satisfy (15). Having displayed a set of prices and a tax function that reconcile individual utility and profit maximization with a Pareto optimum, we interpret these prices and the tax function.

Because we have normalized on the aggregate resource R, thereby making its unit price, or wage, one dollar, $1/g_y$ is the marginal cost of producing flowers. The function $T(R_x, R_p)$ is the annual tax imposed upon the producer of steel and is related to the use of resources in steel production and pollution abatement. In particular, the change in the annual tax as a result of using an additional unit of R_x, denoted as T_x, is $-g_x/g_y$, which, recalling the definition of the price of flowers, is the product of the price of flowers and the marginal "disproduct" of R_x in flower production. Using this relationship we may express the price of steel as $(1 + T_x)/f_x$. In the absence of such a tax the price of steel would be $1/f_x$.

Employing commonly used terms, we may interpret $1/g_y$ and $1/f_x$ as the marginal private cost of producing flowers and steel respectively and $(1 + T_x)/f_x$ as the marginal social cost of producing steel. The latter follows from the difference between the private and social cost of using resources in steel production – namely, T_x, the external cost of using R_x.

The change in the tax function resulting from the incremental use of resources in pollution abatement, denoted as T_p, is $-p_y g_p$, the negative of the value of the marginal product of R_p in flower production. Because g_p is by assumption positive, T_p is negative and thus indicates the rate at which the annual tax is reduced as the use of R_p is increased. Equation (10b) serves to restrict the use of R_p such that its contribution to flower production is equal in value to its opportunity cost of one dollar.

We shall now comment on the issues raised in the recent literature on externalities, especially in the light of the air pollution problem:

1. That equating private and social marginal cost should not be a policy desideratum. This objection we can put aside because our derivation of the classic solution did not emerge from such an approach (although we did provide a verbal interpretation of the results in these terms). We proceeded in a direct way to find the conditions for a Pareto optimum and the market arrangements that would yield one, in a general equilibrium context. At no point did we have to contend with social versus private marginal costs, with consumer surpluses, with any assumptions of constant marginal utility of income, or with graphic two-dimensional arguments. We are persuaded that we have tackled the problem in a straightforward way.

2. Appropriate merger, as is well known, can internalize the externalities that give rise to the problem. But merger as a general or important solution to the problem of the external diseconomies of air pollution is preposterous.

3. Are private bribes as good a solution, from the standpoint of Pareto welfare economics, as the classic tax solution?

With reference to the problem just analyzed, suppose that A were not taxed. In such a situation (13b) becomes:

$$p_x = \frac{1}{f_x}. \qquad (16)$$

This implies that the price of steel is set equal to its private marginal cost, and hence the Pareto optimum conditions are not satisfied.[5] Suppose now that firm B considers "bribing" firm A to decrease its pollution emissions (by a "bribe" we mean that B pays A to reduce its pollution). Firm A may decrease pollution by using either less R_x or more R_p. Because T_x ($= -p_y g_x$) measures the marginal dollar loss to B of A using a given quantity of R_x, it also denotes the maximum per unit amount B is willing to pay to induce A to use less R_x. In using one unit less of R_x, A loses in revenue $p_x f_x$ but gains in decreased costs \$1. Therefore, as long as:

$$-p_y g_x > p_x f_x - 1, \qquad (17)$$

B can advantageously and effectively bribe A to decrease his use of R_x. He will cease to do so when:

$$-p_y g_x = p_x f_x - 1. \qquad (18)$$

---

5. This follows directly from our proof that $p_x = \dfrac{(1+T_x)}{f_x}$ did satisfy the Pareto optimum conditions.

A similar argument applies to the use of R_p. B can advantageously and effectively bribe A as long as:

$$p_y g_p > \$1, \tag{19}$$

that is, as long as B is willing to pay more than a unit of R_p costs. It will no longer be possible for B to bribe A advantageously once:

$$+ p_y g_p = 1. \tag{20}$$

To derive (18) and (20) analytically, suppose that before a bribe is proposed, firm A is using R_x^o units of R_x and R_p^o units of R_p. Consider a bribe function $h_x(\beta_x)$, which indicates a scheduled amount of $R_x (\leq R_x^o$ for $\beta_x \leq 0)$ that firm A offers to use as a function of a bribe receipt in the amount β_x. This function will be of negative slope and will have an inverse $\beta_x = h_x^{-1} (R_x)$. Let $h_p(\beta_p)$ be a similar function, in an obvious notation, though of positive slope and with inverse $\beta_p = h_p^{-1} (R_p)$.

Firm B maximizes its profit function:

$$\pi_y = p_y g \left[h_x(\beta_x), R_y, h_p(\beta_p) \right] - R_y - \beta_x - \beta_p \tag{21}$$

by establishing the conditions:

$$
\begin{array}{ll}
\text{a.} & p_y g_y - 1 = 0, \\
\text{b.} & p_y g_x h_x' - 1 = 0, \\
\text{c.} & p_y g_p h_p' - 1 = 0,
\end{array}
\tag{22}
$$

the prime indicating a derivative. So in the neighborhood of the initial (prebribe) equilibrium, $h_x' = 1/p_y g_x$. There h_x' is maximal (minimal in absolute value) because of the assumed negative second derivative of $g(R_x, R_y, R_p)$ with respect to R_x. Therefore, in absolute value $h_x^{-1'}$ is greatest at this initial equilibrium, and it is equal to $p_y g_x$. Therefore, the maximum bribe that B will offer for a unit reduction in R_x is $- p_y g_x$. Similarly, the maximum bribe it will offer for a unit increase in R_p is $p_y g_p$. A similar analysis can be used to find that the minimum bribe firm A will accept for a unit reduction in R_x is $p_x f_x - 1$ and for a unit increase in R_p, \$1.

Equations (18) and (20) must hold as equilibrium conditions when bribery is possible. These conditions, however, are identical to (14a) and (14b), which hold for a Pareto optimum in the classic solution. We have therefore shown that allowing B to bribe A, when no tax exists, results in a Pareto optimum and is equivalent to the classic tax solution. By "equivalent" to the classic solution we do not mean that the two solutions are identical, because they would entail different distributions of income between A and B as consumers. They could, of course, be made identical by the appropriate lump-sum transfer. They are equivalent, however, in that they are both Pareto optimal, each satisfies the same optimality conditions.

Reversing the inequalities in the preceding paragraphs results in conditions that are necessary for A to be able to bribe B into accepting a given amount of pollution, as might occur if A were legally forbidden to pollute without B's consent. Bribing ceases when the inequalities become equalities, and consequently the Pareto optimum conditions once again are satisfied.

The tax case and the two bribery solutions are analytically the same. In the tax case A pays a tax of:

$$T = -p_y g_x R_x - p_y g_p R_p + k. \tag{23}$$

This receipt, if positive, may be paid to B as a subsidy S^B or even refunded to A as a subsidy S^A. In either case the payment is in the form of a lump sum regarded as parametric – that is, neither A nor B recognizes that its subsidy receipt is in fact determined by production decisions. If S^B is negative and k is negative, T may be negative, although reduced in absolute value by either an increase in R_x or a reduction in R_p. In short, T, *which can be positive or negative*, can be defined as the bribe paid by B to A; as a subsidy to firm A paid by the state on a sliding scale, decreasing with pollution reduction; or as a bribe paid by firm A to B to obtain B's consent to the pollution.

4. Is the classic tax solution unsatisfactory? The argument that it is unsatisfactory rests on the contention that it does not lead to a Pareto equilibrium. This is to say, under the classic solution there remain private incentives to depart from it – the incentives to offer and accept a bribe.

Suppose that the classic tax solution has been imposed; moreover, that the tax receipts are distributed as subsidies in such a way that the recipients regard these subsidies as parametric (i.e., the recipients are unaware that anything they might do could alter the amounts received). Then if $h_x(\beta_x)$ is the bribe function that A will accept, as before, B maximizes (20) as before. The maximal bribe he will offer for a unit reduction in R_x is $-p_y g_x$, as before,[6] and the maximal bribe he will offer for a unit increase in R_p is $p_y g_p$.

For firm A, let $H_x(\beta_x)$ be the amount of R_x he must limit himself to in order to collect a bribe β_x from B, and let $H_p(\beta_p)$ be the amount of R_p he must use to receive a bribe of β_p from firm B. $H_x^{-1}(\beta_x)$ and $H_p^{-1}(\beta_p)$ are B's bribe-offer functions. A, subject also to the classic externalities tax, wishes to maximize:

$$\pi_x = p_x f[H_x(\beta_x)] - H_x(\beta_x) - H_p(\beta_p) - T[H_x(\beta_x), H_p(\beta_p)] + \beta_x + \beta_p \tag{24}$$

---

6. It should be noted that $-p_x g_x$ is not a fixed quantity but depends on the existing allocation of resources. The maximal bribe, $-p_y g_x$, is a function of that allocation. For any given allocation $-p_y g_x$ is the greatest amount that B will offer for a reduction of one unit of R_x. In the neighborhood of a Pareto equilibrium $-p_y g_x$ will differ from its value in the neighborhood of the unregulated situation where externalities go uncontrolled.

with respect to β_x and β_p. A maximum requires:

$$\text{(a)} \quad p_x f_x H'_x - H'_x - T_x H'_x + 1 = 0,$$
$$\text{(b)} \quad - H'_p - T_p H'_p + 1 = 0,$$

(25)

or

$$\text{(a)} \quad H'_x = \frac{-1}{p_x f_x - 1 - T_x},$$

$$\text{(b)} \quad H'_p = \frac{1}{1 + T_p}.$$

(26)

If R^*_x and R^*_p are the amounts of R_x and R_p used at the Pareto optimum, firm A will be willing to reduce these amounts until (26a, b) are satisfied. As H'_x and H'_p diminish algebraically (H'_x negative and H'_p positive), A has an incentive to accept B's bribes until the bribe for a unit reduction in R_x has fallen to $p_x f_x - 1 - T_x$ and the bribe for a unit increase in R_p has fallen to $1 + T_p$ (remember, $T_p < 0$).

Bribe offer and acceptance schedules meet when

$$\text{(a)} \quad - p_y g_x = p_x f_x - 1 - T_x,$$
$$\text{(b)} \quad p_y g_p = 1 + T_p.$$

(27)

These conditions are inconsistent with the Pareto-optimality conditions precisely because of the presence of the terms T_x and T_p. It is clear that in principle either the classic tax solution or a private bribe solution can lead to a Pareto optimum. But if either device is in effect, it is inappropriate to superimpose the other one as well; that overcorrects.

If it is feasible for A and B to agree upon a bribe (of the right amount), there is no need for the tax solution. To impose the tax solution would be harmful because it would not eliminate the incentive for the bribe because of its parametric nature. To impose such a tax solution in a case where a private bribe is feasible and is paid simply takes the economy away from a Pareto optimum.

The situation in which this is a concern, however, is created by an analytical asymmetry. It is assumed that there are only two firms, one polluting only the other, and that the polluted firm has the polluting firm well identified. It is under these conditions that a bribe may be agreed upon. If, however, a tax were imposed on firm A and the proceeds paid as a subsidy (in effect, an indemnity) to firm B, it is not realistic to assume that B would treat its subsidy as parametric. If it did not, conditions (27) would be

$$\text{(a)} \quad - p_y g_x - T_x = p_x f_x - 1 - T_x,$$
$$\text{(b)} \quad p_y g_p + T_p = 1 + T_p,$$

(28)

conditions already satisfied at the Pareto optimum, and so no bribe would be paid. The Pareto optimum achieved by the classic tax-subsidy solution would be what Buchanan and Stubblebine call a Pareto equilibrium.

To summarize, we shall distinguish (although not identify in detail) two different situations:

a. The non parametric case, in which damaged and damaging parties are well aware of each other. In this case, the state can impose a pollution tax on A and pay the proceeds to B as an indemnity; A can bribe B for the privilege of polluting; the state can impose a flat tax on B, effect a transfer payment to A, and then impose a pollution tax on A and pay the proceeds to B as an indemnity; or B can bribe A. Any of the four solutions can take us to a Pareto optimum, and either tax solution will eliminate any incentive for a private bribe. Analytically all four solutions are equivalent.

b. The parametric case, in which B does not identify A or, in the realistic extension of our model, there are many firms A and many firms B, and private bribes are strategically and informationally unachievable. Here the only available solution is the classic tax solution, and it does not matter whether the proceeds are paid to the injured firms as indemnities or not; in fact, they could be refunded to the damaging firms, provided the refunds are regarded by them as parametric. Certainly in the case of air pollution (and, for that matter, for most externalities we can think of), the parametric case is generally the more relevant one. This judgment leaves the classic analysis quite intact.

5. Davis and Whinston have found it purposeful to distinguish between the cases where externalities are separable and where they are not. In our example, externalities are separable if $g(R_x, R_y, R_p)$ can be written as $g^1(R_y) + g^2(R_x, R_p)$. This means that the *marginal* productivity of R_y in producing flowers is independent of R_x and R_p, although total productivity is not. If it pays B to produce any flowers at all, the profit-maximizing amount will be independent of R_x and R_p. Davis and Whinston accept the classic tax-subsidy solution for the case of separable externalities. Wellisz, however, argues that this case is trivial because no tax or subsidy is needed. This seems evident to him because no tax or subsidy could affect the output decisions of firms because these are determined by price and marginal cost. Hence the allocation of resources would be independent of any tax-subsidy structure, and he assumed that meant it would be optimal in the first place. However, his analysis is erroneous, as Davis and Whinston have subsequently shown (*Economica*, August 1966). What must be noticed is that, although altering the amount of R_x or R_p does not affect either the marginal cost or marginal productivity of firm B, nevertheless, a unit tax on A does affect the marginal cost of firm A and can therefore reduce its output, reduce the price ratio p_y/p_x, yet raise p_y in terms of the numeraire, and increase the output of firm B. Firm B's total output was not optimal before the tax and can be altered by a change in its price, even though its marginal cost remains the same.

It is not worth the bother of a separate mathematical demonstration of the above. Our previous analysis [equations (1) through (15)] suffices. Seperability simply requires in that context that the cross-partial derivatives

$\partial^2 g/\partial R_x \partial R_y$ and $\partial^2 g/\partial R_p \partial R_y$ are identically zero. At no point in the previous analysis did we need to assume the contrary; nor would we have needed to assume the contrary to establish the second order conditions for an optimum. Perhaps the case that Wellisz had in mind was one in which $g^2(R_x, R_p)$ was a negative constant for any positive value of R_x. Then, unless a Pareto optimum required that absolutely no steel be produced whatever, it could be obtained without any tax being imposed because g_x and g_p would both have been zero [see equation (13c)].

Davis and Whinston contend that in the nonseparable case the classic tax-subsidy solution will not work. In part their argument rests on the difficulty for the state in determining quantitatively what tax-subsidy structure to impose. This difficulty arises, of course, even in the separable case, as has been obvious to everybody. In the nonseparable case, however, there is the further complication that an injured firm's marginal cost function depends on the output of the damaging firm. This really introduces nothing very extraordinary in the theory of, or in the environment of the firm so long as the injured firm can regard the output of the other firm as parametric. If the externalities are mutual, however, and are not parametric, then the two (or more) firms are caught in a strategic situation in which each must take account of the effect of its behavior on that of the other firm. Davis and Whinston then proceed to a game-theoretic analysis of this situation, and, as in duopoly theory generally, there may not be a single dominant pair of strategies for the participants that determines a unique solution (the game being non–zero sum). If bribery is considered (a cooperative game) all the issues in bargaining theory arise. The state, of course, can intervene. Its problem, which is the same in the parametric and the nonparametric cases, is to compute the solution point for a Pareto optimum and to impose the appropriate tax-subsidy structure. But this must be done even in the separable case, so that nothing new is introduced into the classical analysis by non-separability. The Davis-Whinston analysis is best viewed as a critique of bribery solutions for the nonparametric and nonseparable case. Although the production externalities of air pollution are generally nonseparable (at least in the long run, when plant size may be regarded as variable), the non-parametric case is not generally applicable, and hence the bribery solution is not to be expected in any case.

We conclude this section on externalities with the following observations:

1. Neither merger nor a system of private bribes is a practical solution to the air pollution problem; government intervention is the only recourse if the problem is to be significantly mitigated.

2. The question may be raised: Is it better to tax firms or individuals who pollute or to subsidize the installation of pollution abatement devices? The answer is that there is no analytical distinction from the standpoint of resource allocation between taxing someone for doing something or subsidizing him not to do it. The only difference has to do with lump-sum income transfers.

Thus, suppose that there is an objectionable activity α subject to quantitative variation and that it pays an economic decision maker to use this activity to the level α^o. Suppose then that a tax τ is imposed on each unit of α. Tax receipts will be given by the function

$$T = \tau\alpha. \tag{29}$$

Subject to this tax, the decision maker will find it in his interest to use the activity at, say, the level α^*, $\alpha^* < \alpha^o$, and tax receipts will be $T^* = \tau\alpha^*$. If instead a subsidy were paid of σ dollars per unit reduction of α beneath α^o, the subsidy payment would be given by the function

$$S = \sigma(\alpha^o - \alpha), \tag{30}$$

and by choosing $\sigma = \tau$, the firm will come to the maximum profit level α^*.
   In the first case

$$T^* = \tau\alpha^*; \tag{31}$$

in the second case

$$S^* = \tau\alpha^o - \tau\alpha^*. \tag{32}$$

But a flat tax, say, in the amount k, could also be levied on the firm along with the subsidy arrangement, or a flat subsidy, say, in the amount $-k$, could be awarded along with the pollution tax arrangement. If k is set at $\tau\alpha^o$, the total tax or subsidy would be financially the same in either case.
   3. A further question that may be asked is whether it matters if the tax (or subsidy) is based exclusively on the use of R_x (the amount of pollution-creating production) or on the use (or nonuse) of R_p (the amount spent on pollution-control equipment). The answer, according to our model, is that it does make a difference.

   Reviewing the optimizing tax formula (13c):

$$T(R_x, R_p) = -p_y(g_x R_x + g_p R_p) + k, \tag{13c}$$

and assuming $g_x < 0$, $g_p > 0$, we see that a tax varying only with R_x or only with R_p is unsatisfactory, as it is necessary both to discourage the production of steel to some degree and to encourage the installation of pollution-control equipment to some degree. This is a bit illusory, however. If the production function for flowers had been written as:

$$y^A + y^B = G(R_y, P), \tag{33}$$

where P is pollution experienced $(G_p < 0)$, and if we had introduced a pollution production function:

$$P = P(R_x, R_p),\tag{34}$$

then the production function for flowers would have been:

$$y^A + y^B = G[R_y, P(R_x, R_p)] \equiv g(R_x, R_y, R_p).\tag{35}$$

Then g_x would have been $G_p P_x$, in obvious notation, and g_p would have been $G_p P_p$.

A tax directly on pollution of:

$$T(P) = -p_y G_p P + k\tag{36}$$

would have solved the problem, with $-p_y G_p$ being evaluated at a Pareto optimum and being presented to firm A as a tax parameter. The firm would translate this tax imposed directly on the pollution it emits into a tax on its use of R_x and R_p. At the margin – that is, for small increments – the firm could assume:

$$P = P_x R_x + P_p R_p,\tag{37}$$

and the tax function would become:

$$T(R_x, R_p) = -p_y(G_p P_x R_x + G_p P_p R_p),\tag{38}$$

which is identically:

$$T(R_x, R_p) = -p_y(g_x R_x + g_p R_p),\tag{39}$$

as originally obtained [equation (13c)], apart from any flat tax k.

The point of this, however, is that in principle one ought not to tax or to subsidize only the production that yields pollution or only the nonuse or use of pollution-abatement equipment. Instead, both should be taxed or subsidized at appropriate rates, or alternatively, the tax should be imposed on the quantity of pollution emitted. The latter has the obvious advantage of allowing the firm to determine how to respond to the tax, whether to reduce output or to install more pollution-control equipment. Although this is not an advantage in principle, it may well be in practice because of the difficulty in computing the optimal tax precisely. If the state can estimate only G_p, firm A could itself (better than the state) estimate P_x and P_p.

4. A final comment concerns the practical application of the classic tax-subsidy solution. This is nothing to be sanguine about. The optimizing tax formula requires knowledge of the derivatives of production functions (or

in the case where a consumer creates or experiences the externality, of marginal rates of substitution) as well as knowledge of Pareto-optimal prices, for a vast multiplicity of firms and households. In short, the information requirements for the application of the classic theory are excessive from the practical point of view, especially in so complex a network of externalities as that presented by the pollution problem. One can hope that by trial and error the classic solution could be approximated, but other devices may be more suitable both informationally and administratively, especially the use of legally fixed standards for pollution control and the use of zoning. Perhaps the main value of the classic analysis is that it illuminates the policy norms of the resource allocation problem as the welfare economist sees them.

A further caveat is that the conditions for a Pareto optimum are established in the context of a general model embracing all economic activities that are interrelated and require that *all* the optimality conditions be satisfied. If any one condition is not satisfied (for example, because of a monopoly somewhere in the economy), it is not established that a particular violation of any remaining condition is harmful to economic welfare. It is something of an "act of faith" that an external diseconomy ought to be corrected when other imperfections are widespread in the economy. Yet in their policy recommendations many economists seem motivated by this "act of faith." The presumption must be that reducing the number of optimality conditions that are violated will in general produce a change in the right direction, or that although correcting the violation of an optimality condition even in the presence of other violations may be off-target, it will likely be a move in the proper direction.

This cannot be assured short of empirical information. Imposing pollution taxes (or other restrictions) may be expected to reduce the output of heavily polluting industries or of acts of consumption that yield pollution. The present levels of these activities may, however, be too small or too great for reason of other imperfections, and a reduction in their levels caused by a pollution tax may incrementally be in either the wrong or the right direction.

In the case of pollution caused by the automobile, we need to know whether in our cities we are at present – and apart from the pollution problem – using cars too little or too much. We need to judge whether gasoline taxes that yield revenues exceeding road maintenance and interest costs, thereby discouraging the use of the automobile excessively, more or less offset the externalities of congestion that result from a free (nontoll) road system, which encourages the use of the automobile excessively. Moreover, we need to know whether monopoly-type restraints in the production of the automobile (and its component parts) and in the production of gasoline are peculiarly strong or weak compared to similar restraints in other sectors of the economy. We do not believe that a reasonable judgment on this matter can be based on the existing literature of economics, but it is probably not out of the reach of the economist, with further research, to come to an informed opinion on the matter.

Similar remarks might apply to a heavy industry that contributes significantly to pollution. Is the industry, because of other violations of optimality conditions, producing too much or too little? If the latter, a pollution tax could do more harm than good. Under these circumstances it would seem reasonable to concentrate more on subsidizing the use of pollution-abatement devices than to tax the industry's product. These are all empirical questions about which some judgment might be derived. To do so, however, is beyond the scope of the present work.

Nothing has been said about the distribution of income from the standpoint of social attitudes about inequality. This is characteristic of Pareto welfare economics. It is assumed that if a Pareto optimum is achieved and the consequent distribution of income is unsatisfactory, a system of transfer payments[7] can be introduced to move the economy to a different Pareto optimum, one for which the distribution of income is judged acceptable.

We may adopt either of two positions. We might feign indifference to the distribution of income, regarding any distribution as being as acceptable as any other, so that the effect of pollution-control measures on the distribution of income can be ignored. Alternatively, we might simply assume that the state at all times does whatever is necessary to establish a distribution of income judged proper by social agreement. We then need not worry about the distribution effects of pollution-control measures because, if adverse, they will be remedied in other ways.

If the problem is not to be ducked in either of these ways, however, it may be of comfort to egalitarians to know that pollution-control measures probably work more to the benefit of the poor, who live and work under polluted conditions, than of the rich, who are better able to avoid pollution, for example, by living in suburbs and by working in air conditioned surroundings. Pollution, aggravating a problem of urban blight, may foster a second round of externalities by encouraging a concentration of the poor in the polluted enclaves of society, where they spin off further external diseconomies on each other.

---

7. Neutral from the standpoint of resource allocation.

6

Conclusion

The reader who has come this far does not have to be told that these papers exhibit a great diversity, both of method and of subject matter. Nevertheless, they do have a common thread in the impact of the whole complex system of redistributions of income, especially through the public grants economy, on urban poverty and deterioration. The conclusion is almost inescapable: the grants economy is not functioning well in the United States, although no doubt we would be worse off without it. As a corrective to the defects of the exchange economy, however, it still leaves much to be desired.

The papers do not indicate clearly what ought to be done, for the good reason that we do not know. A great deal more thought, study, and empirical research must go into this problem before we can propose a clear and consistent program for reform. What this volume does suggest is that we now have the beginnings of a conceptual framework and a set of techniques that may eventually lead us into very far-reaching improvement of the whole grants economy. One of the great problems in the past is that we were not aware of the grants economy as a total system, integrated with the rest of the total social system. Consequently public policies in this regard have been a hopeless hodgepodge of unrelated efforts, many of which have undone with the right hand any good that the left hand may have been doing.

One notable omission from this volume is a section on crime, partly because the volume is overly long already, but mainly because this is an area that has received inadequate attention, especially from economists. Indeed, we are only now beginning to look on crime as a segment of the economy rather than as an example of personal psychopathology. The redistributive effects of crime are almost completely unknown; nor do we know how far it pays to try to reduce it or to what extent the cost of trying to reduce crime would exceed the social costs of crime itself. This is clearly a subject in which the concepts and methods of grants economics are highly applicable. Much crime is illegitimate redistribution, and it thus falls squarely within the framework of the grants economy. Its irregularity of incidence, however, and to some extent the very organizations that are set up to combat it, easily create deteriorating situations. The role crime plays in the deterioration of central cities and in the perpetuation of poverty cultures is something that social scientists seem to have been almost unwilling to investigate up to now. This is clearly a subject for a subsequent volume.

If this volume has a single message, it is that in the field of one-way transfers we are still a very long way from having a complete and continuous information system. A number of the studies of this volume are of particular localities – Delaware, Syracuse, Washington, D.C., and so on. We really have little in the way of systematic cross-sectional, cross-cultural, and comparative studies, even of cities, and we seem to be still further away from that continuous collection of time series of social indicators, which is perhaps the only way in which longitudinal studies ever really take place. Longitudinal studies are notoriously hard to finance and to staff, mainly because the span of attention of foundations, granting agencies, and social scientists themselves rarely extends beyond three or five years. Hence, many of the crucial mechanisms by which the deteriorating cultures, especially of central cities, develop over time are apt to be missed by studies that are merely cross-sectional or of a very short time duration. We would like to see studies of the impact of the grants input for single persons from birth through maturity and even into old age. One suspects that they would reveal what is also revealed in this volume – that deficiencies in the structure of one-way transfers, especially in the case of the growing child, where they are absolutely necessary, have a great deal to do with the perpetuation of poverty cultures and the development of deteriorating cultures. But this again must be the subject of later volumes.

Another neglected field in this area is that of comparative studies, especially across national boundaries. The differences in the dynamic processes of cities like Stockholm in contrast with Chicago, or even more dramatically, Calcutta would be of enormous interest and would throw a great deal of light on the possible diversity of pattern. This again will have to be the subject of future studies. What we can say now is that we have made a beginning in what will probably be a large field.

Grants Economics Series

The Economy of Love and Fear:
A Preface to Grants Economics

Kenneth E. Boulding

Contents

The Grants Economy

Martin Pfaff

Redistribution to the Rich and the Poor
The Grants Economics of Income Distribution

Edited by Kenneth E. Boulding and
Martin Pfaff

Contents